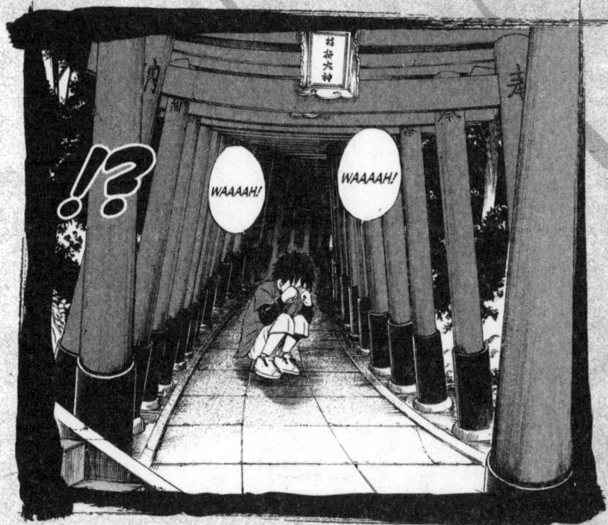
WAAAAH!
WAAAAH!
!?

IN THE NEXT VOLUME...

TORII LABRYINTH

The Nura clan and their allies encounter a forest of Torii Gates on their way to find Hidemoto's lost seals. There, Rikuo and the others find themselves at the mercy of a yokai capable of using the thousand Torii Gates to form a massive, deadly labyrinth. Awashima falls prey to the labyrinth and is transported to another dimension, diminishing their numbers. Awashima will have to battle a mysterious and powerful yokai before attempting an escape.

AVAILABLE OCTOBER 2012!

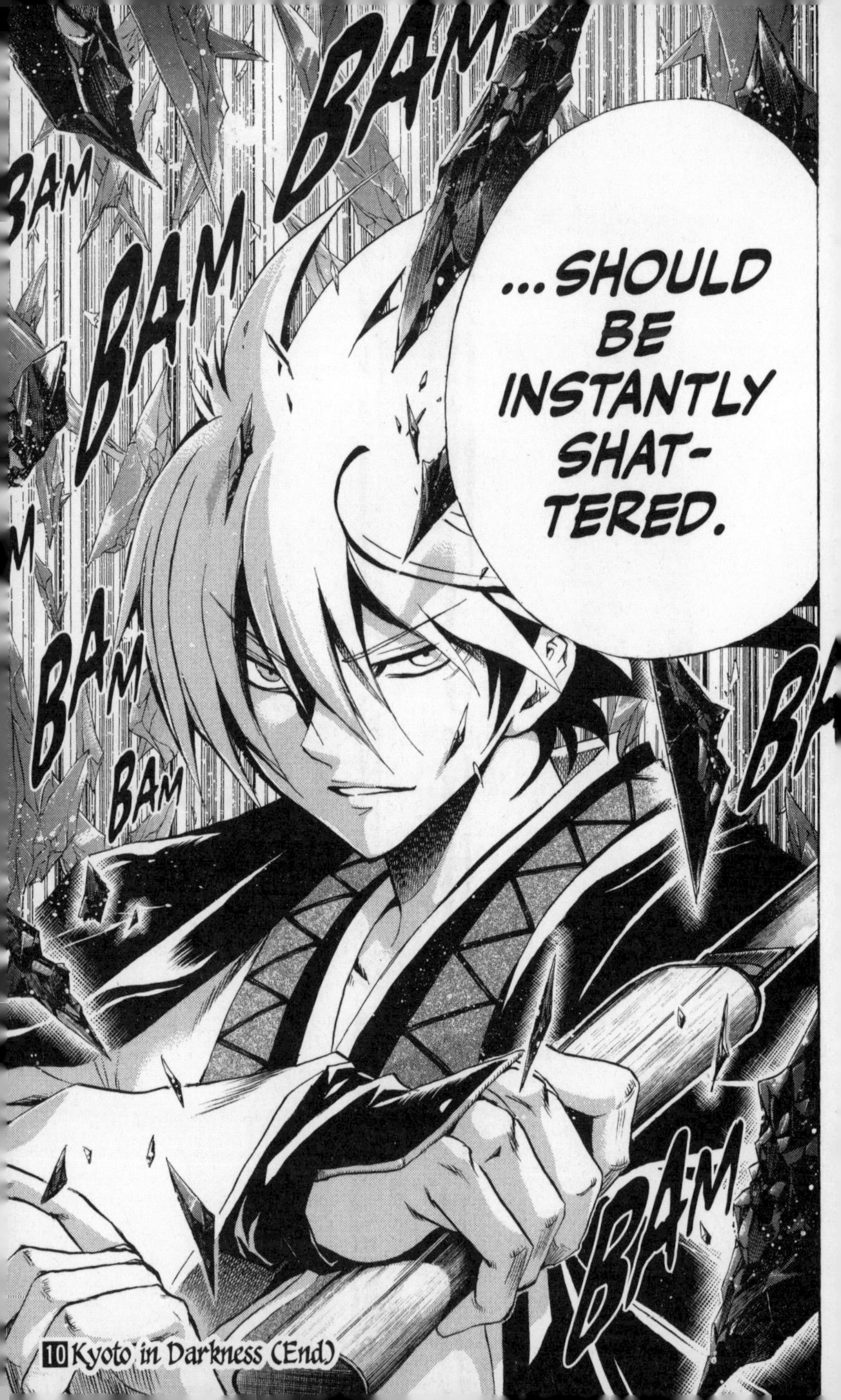
...SHOULD BE INSTANTLY SHAT-TERED.
BAM BAM BAM
BAM BAM
BAM
BAM BAM
BAM
BAM

10 Kyoto in Darkness (End)

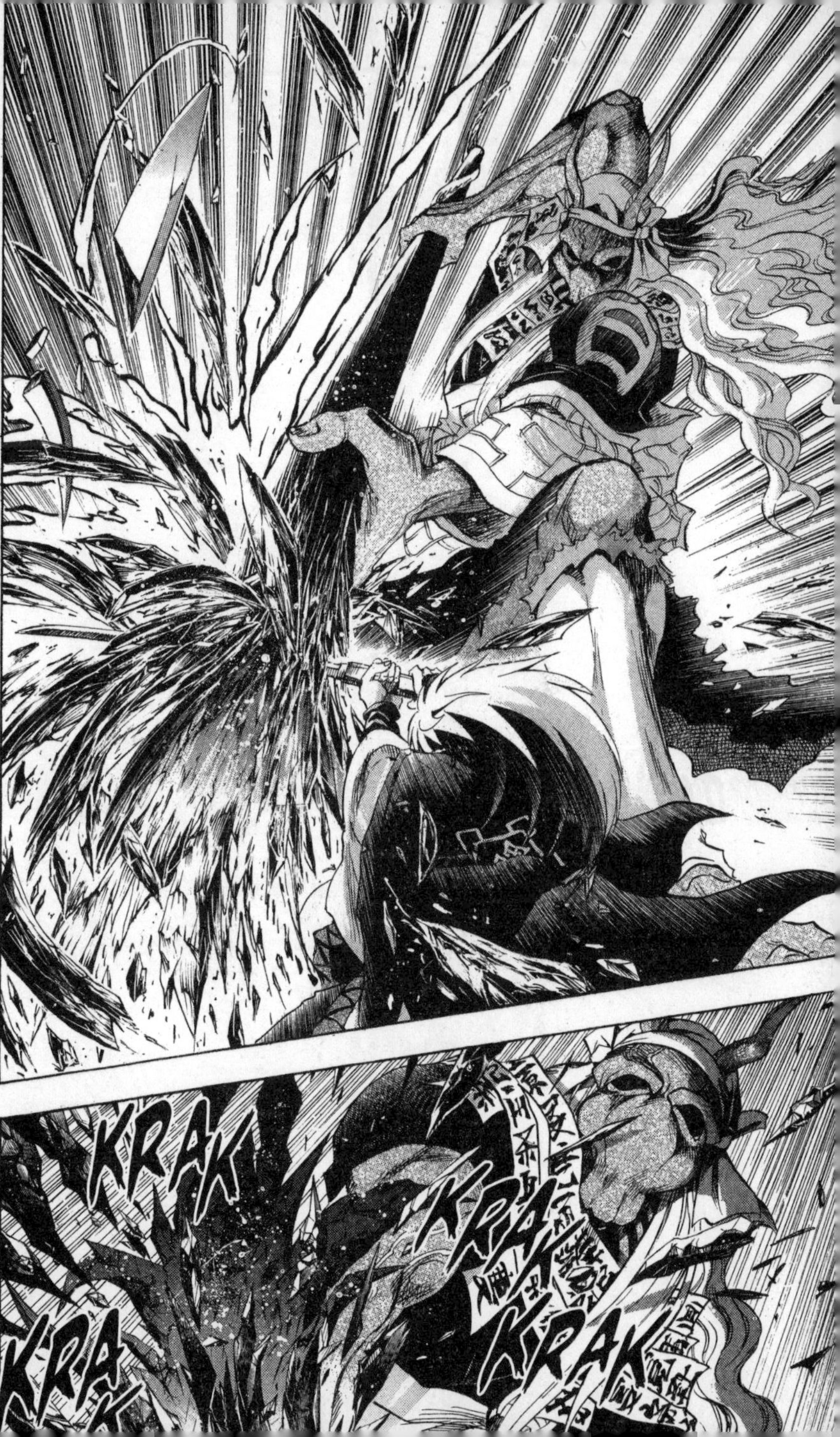
KRAK
KRAK
KRAK
KRA

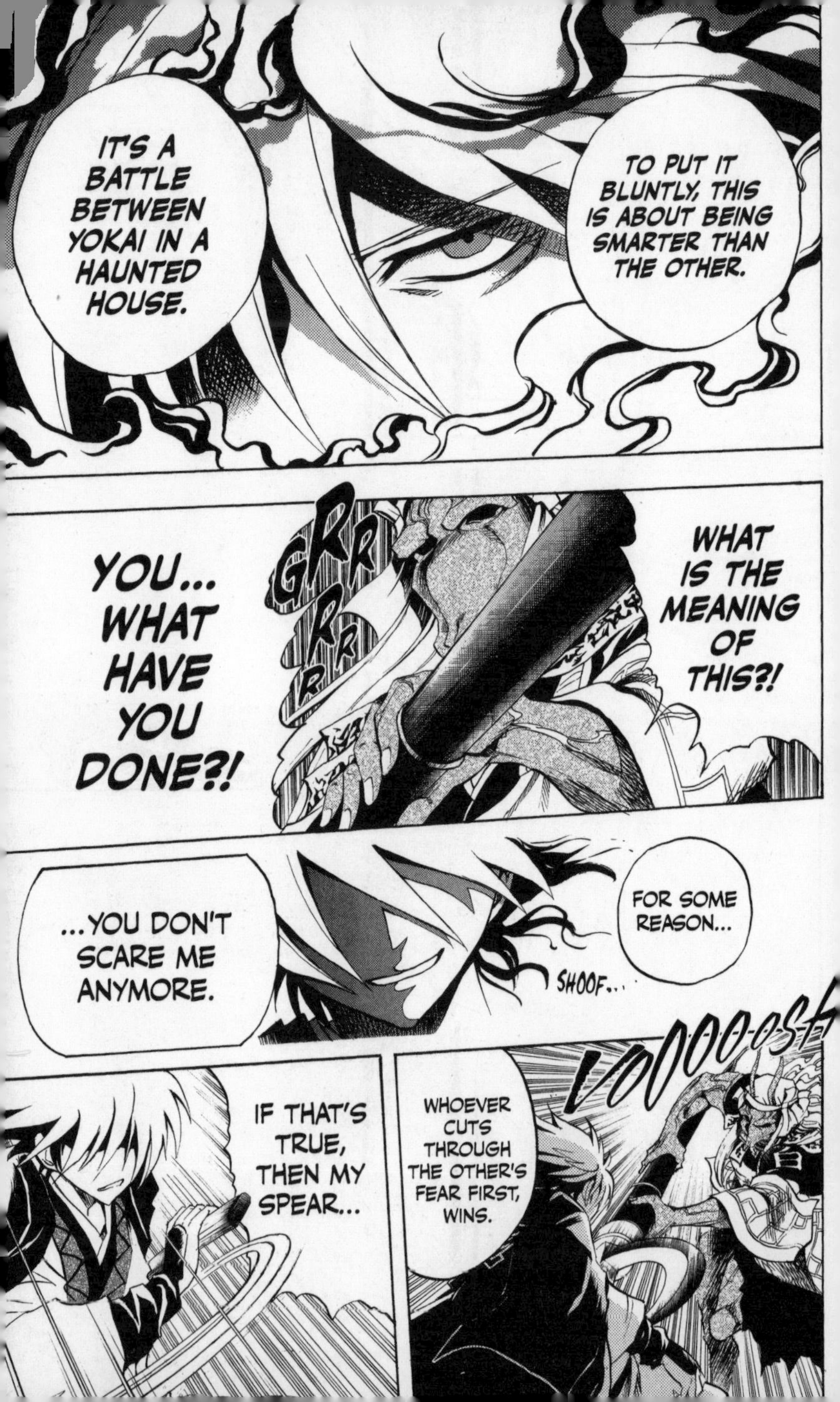
TO PUT IT BLUNTLY, THIS IS ABOUT BEING SMARTER THAN THE OTHER.
IT'S A BATTLE BETWEEN YOKAI IN A HAUNTED HOUSE.
WHAT IS THE MEANING OF THIS?!
GRRR
YOU... WHAT HAVE YOU DONE?!
FOR SOME REASON...
SHOOF...
...YOU DON'T SCARE ME ANYMORE.
VOOOO-O-OSH
WHOEVER CUTS THROUGH THE OTHER'S FEAR FIRST, WINS.
IF THAT'S TRUE, THEN MY SPEAR...

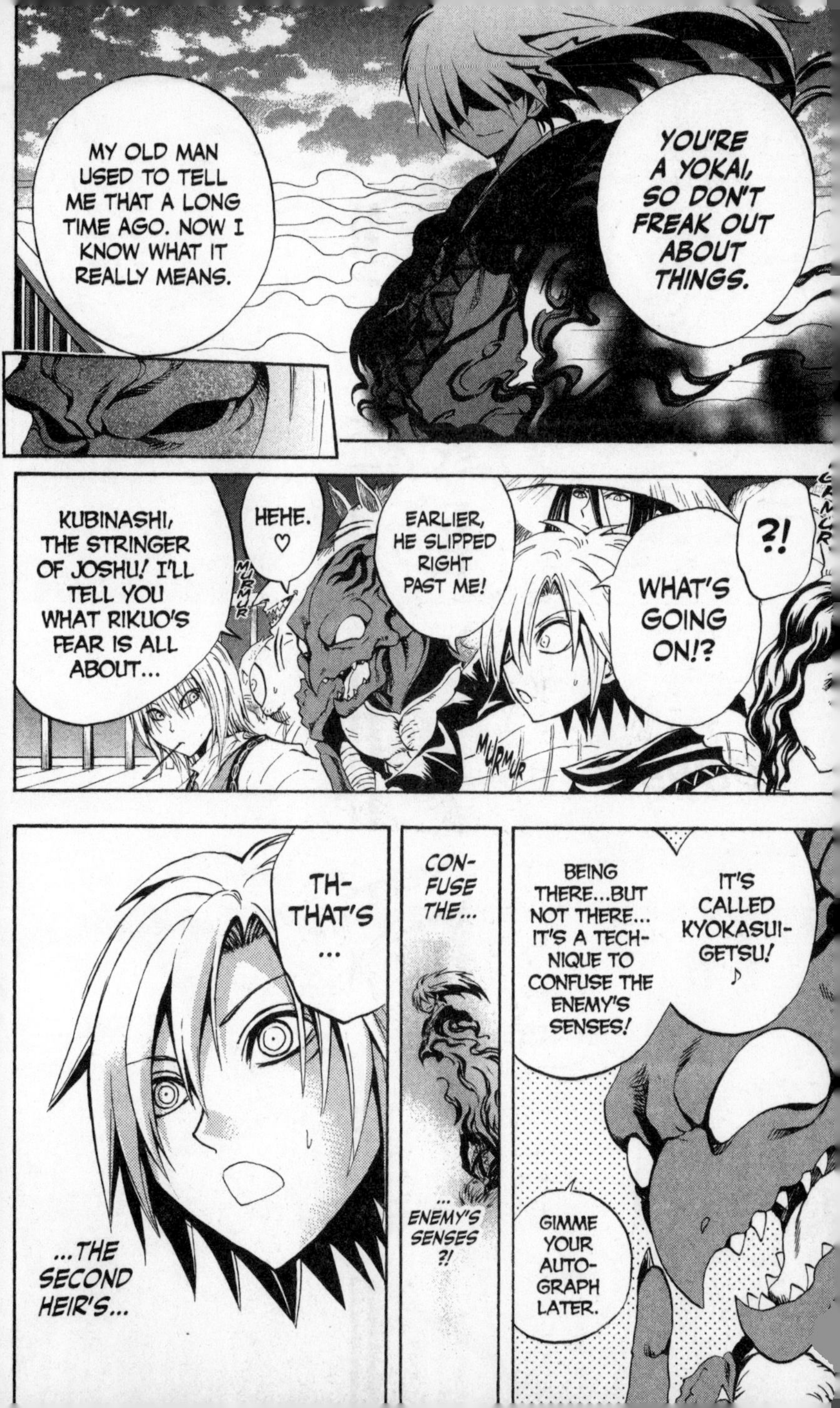
YOU'RE A YOKAI, SO DON'T FREAK OUT ABOUT THINGS.
MY OLD MAN USED TO TELL ME THAT A LONG TIME AGO. NOW I KNOW WHAT IT REALLY MEANS.
?!
WHAT'S GOING ON!?
EARLIER, HE SLIPPED RIGHT PAST ME!
HEHE. ♡
MURMUR
KUBINASHI, THE STRINGER OF JOSHU! I'LL TELL YOU WHAT RIKUO'S FEAR IS ALL ABOUT...
MURMUR
IT'S CALLED KYOKASUIGETSU! ♪
BEING THERE...BUT NOT THERE... IT'S A TECHNIQUE TO CONFUSE THE ENEMY'S SENSES!
GIMME YOUR AUTOGRAPH LATER.
CONFUSE THE...
...ENEMY'S SENSES ?!
TH-THAT'S ...
...THE SECOND HEIR'S...

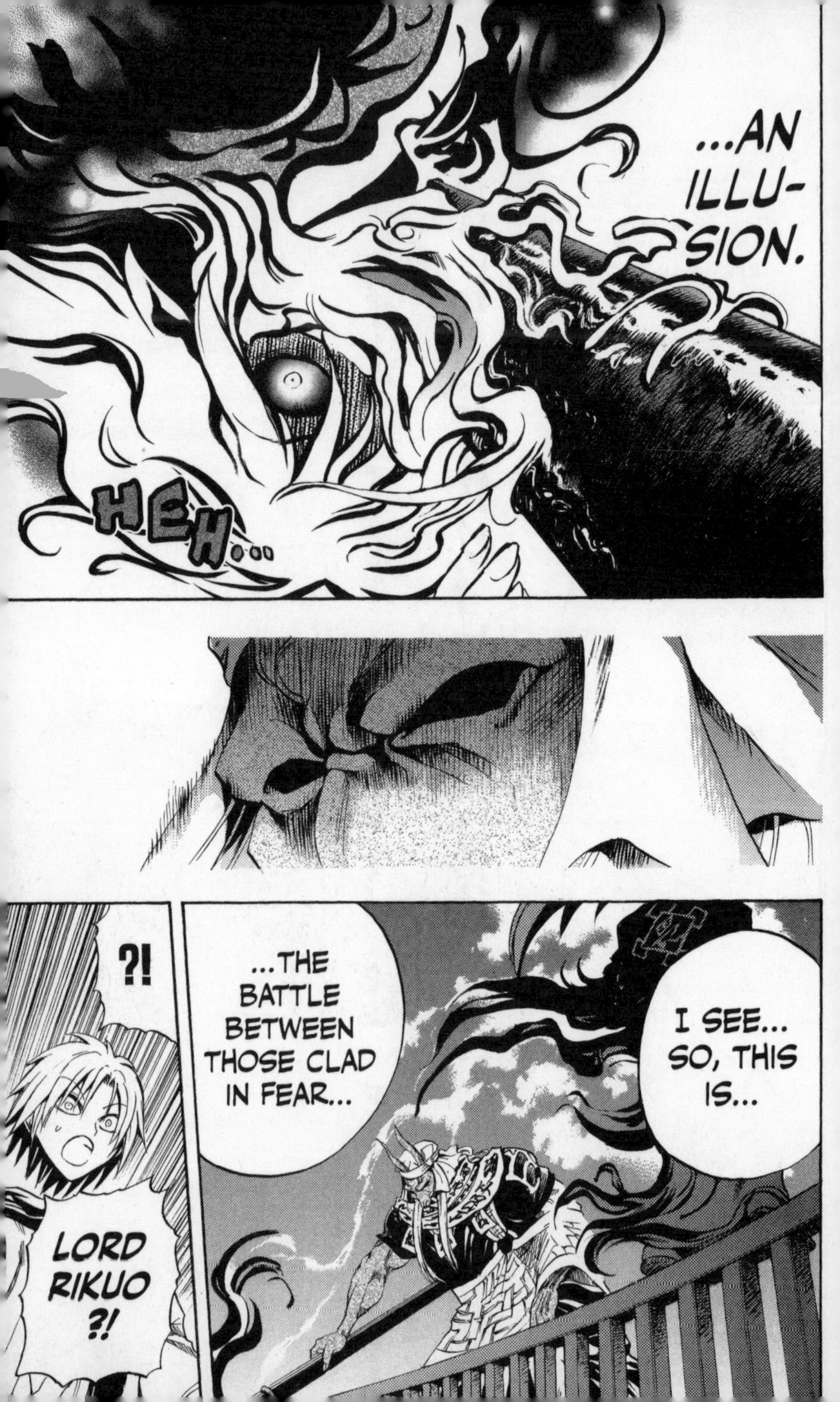
...AN ILLUSION.
HEH...
I SEE... SO, THIS IS...
...THE BATTLE BETWEEN THOSE CLAD IN FEAR...
?!
LORD RIKUO ?!

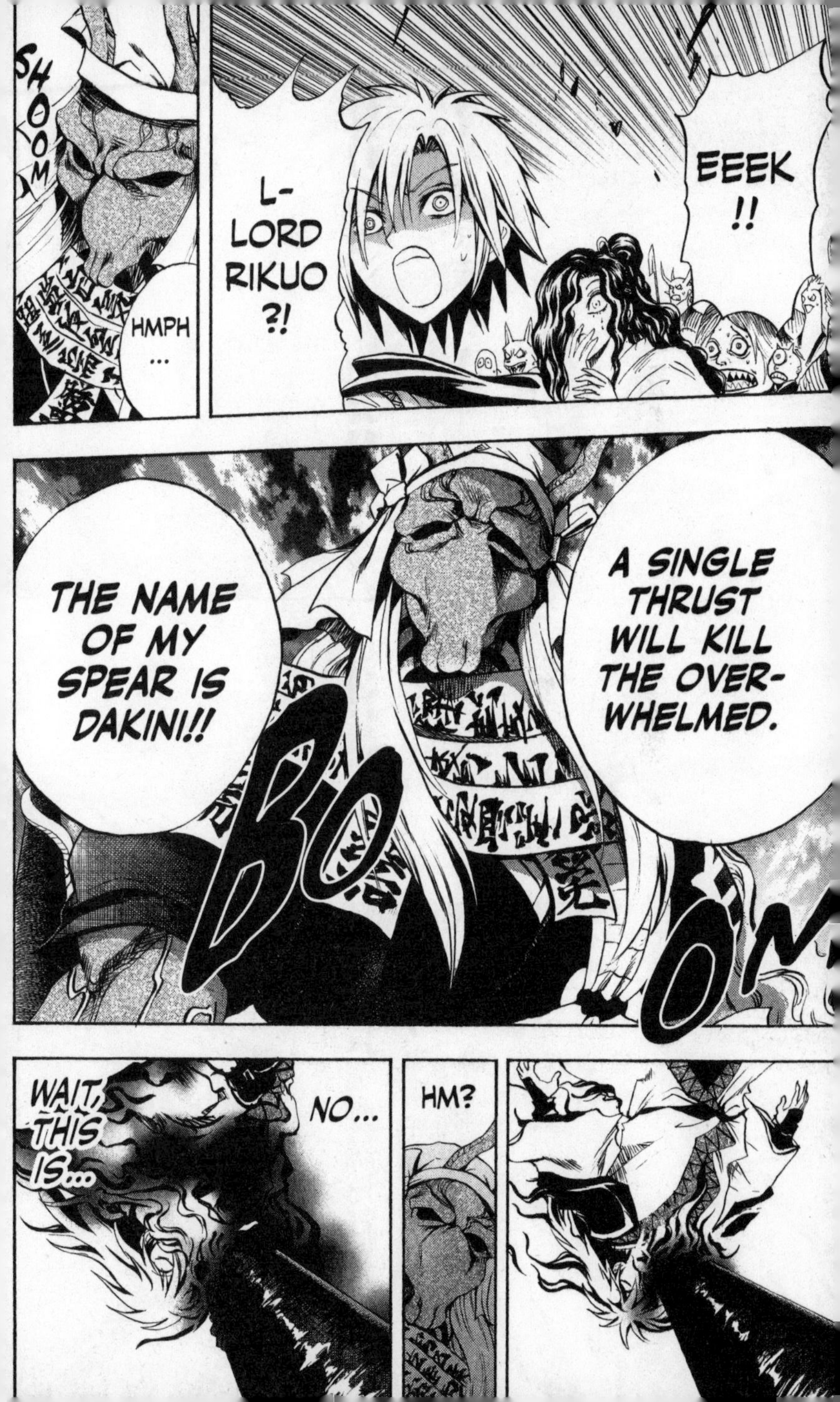
EEEK !!
L-LORD RIKUO ?!
SHOOOM
HMPH ...
A SINGLE THRUST WILL KILL THE OVER-WHELMED.
THE NAME OF MY SPEAR IS DAKINI!!
BOOM
HM?
NO...
WAIT, THIS IS...

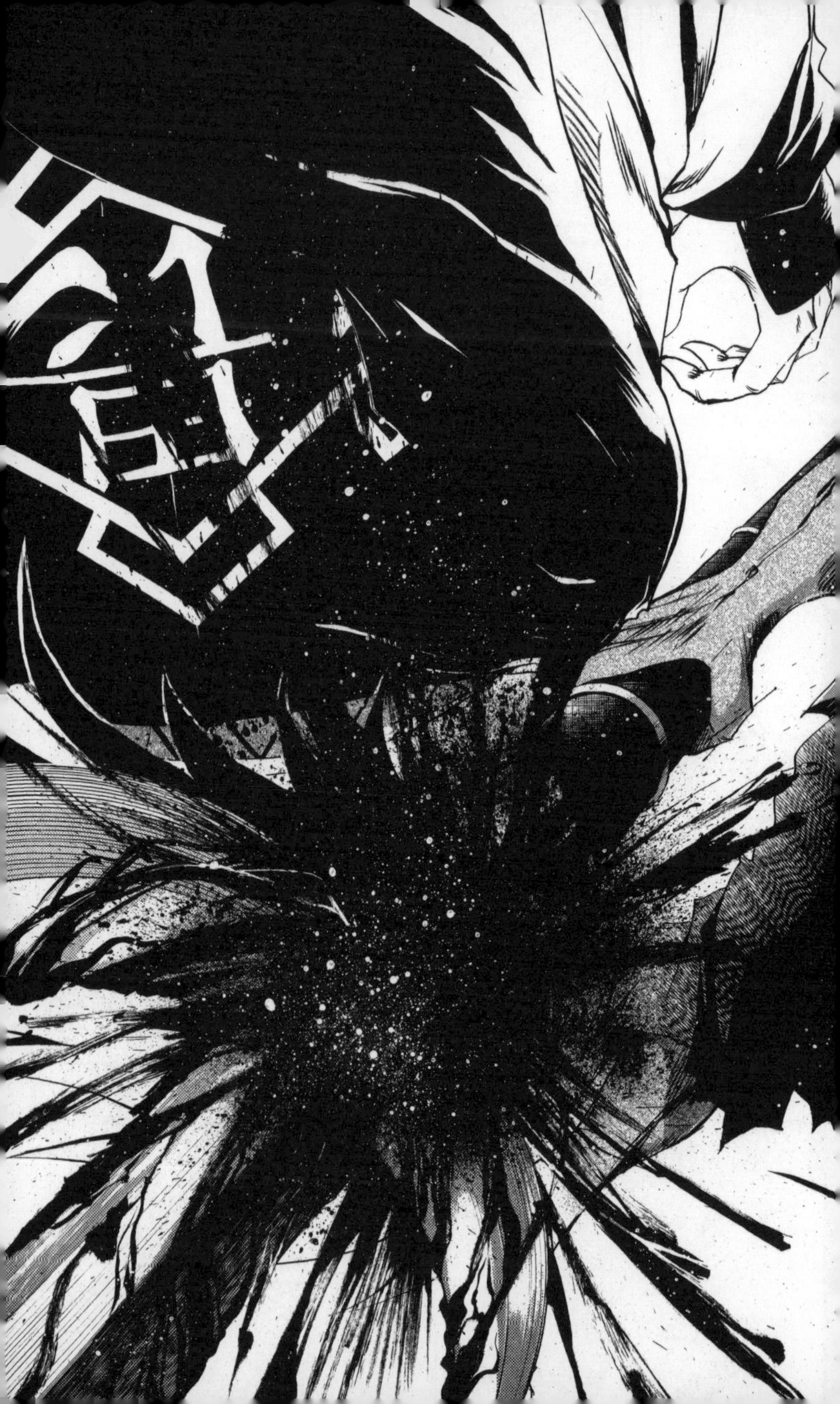

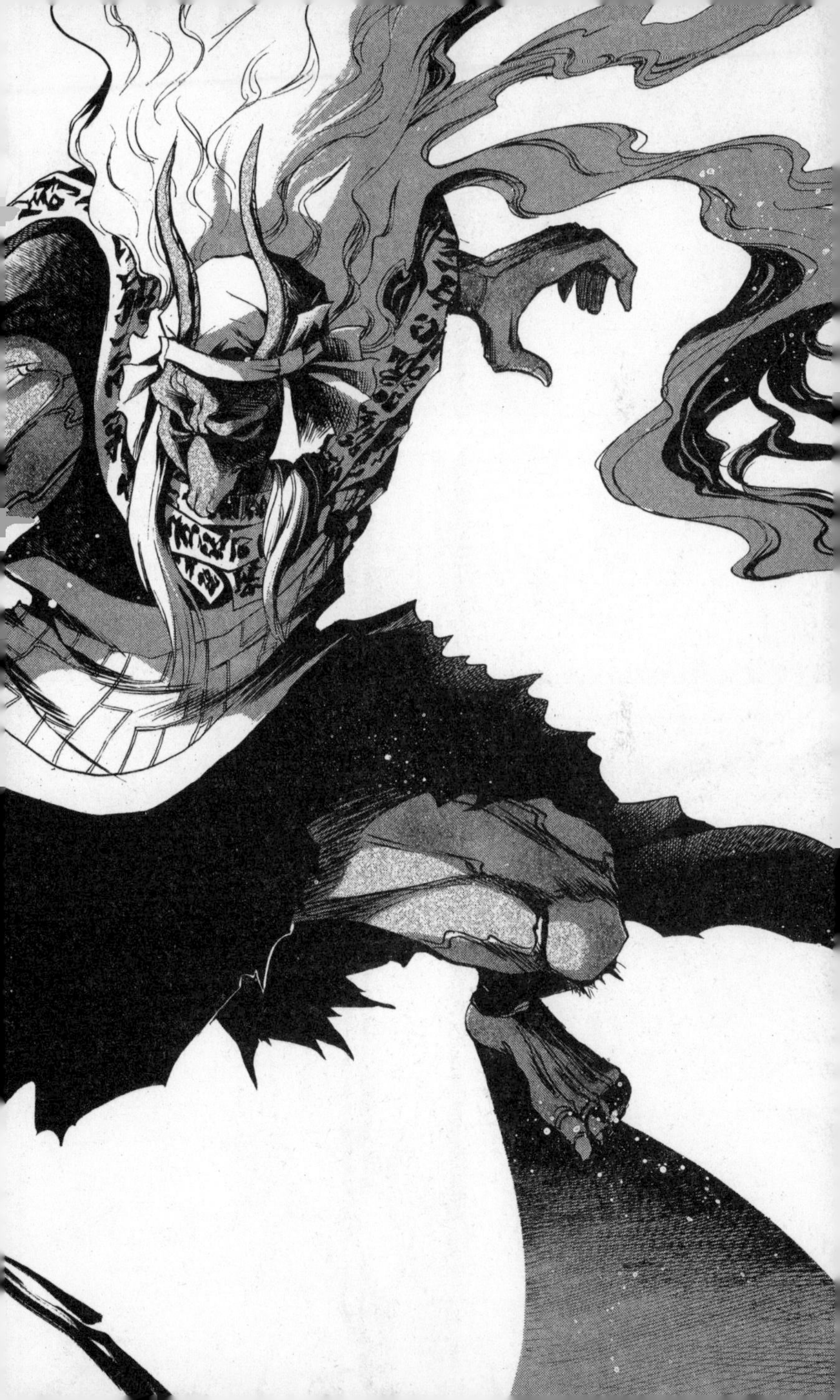

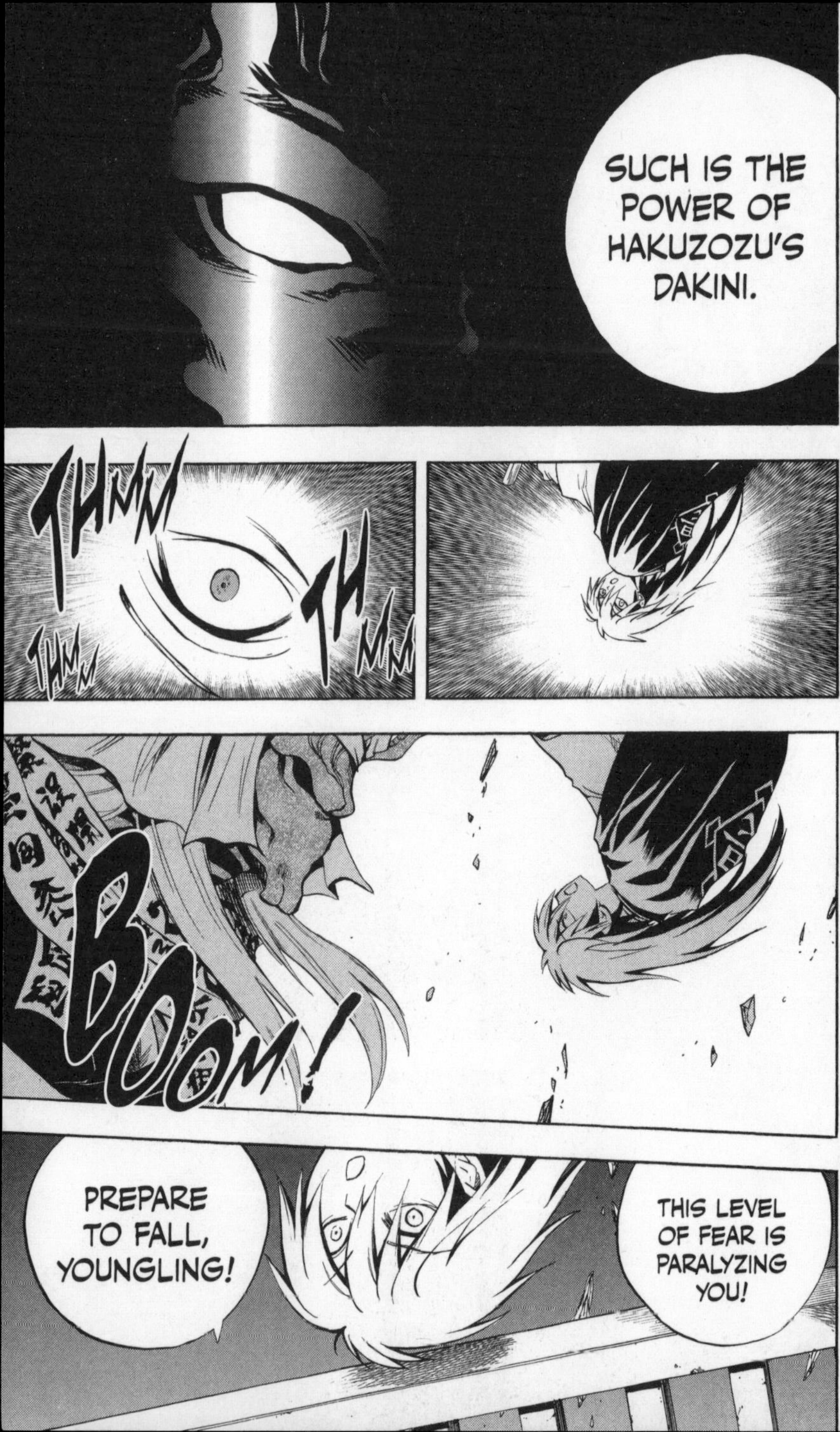
SUCH IS THE POWER OF HAKUZOZU'S DAKINI.
THMM
THMMM
THMM
BOOM!
THIS LEVEL OF FEAR IS PARALYZING YOU!
PREPARE TO FALL, YOUNGLING!

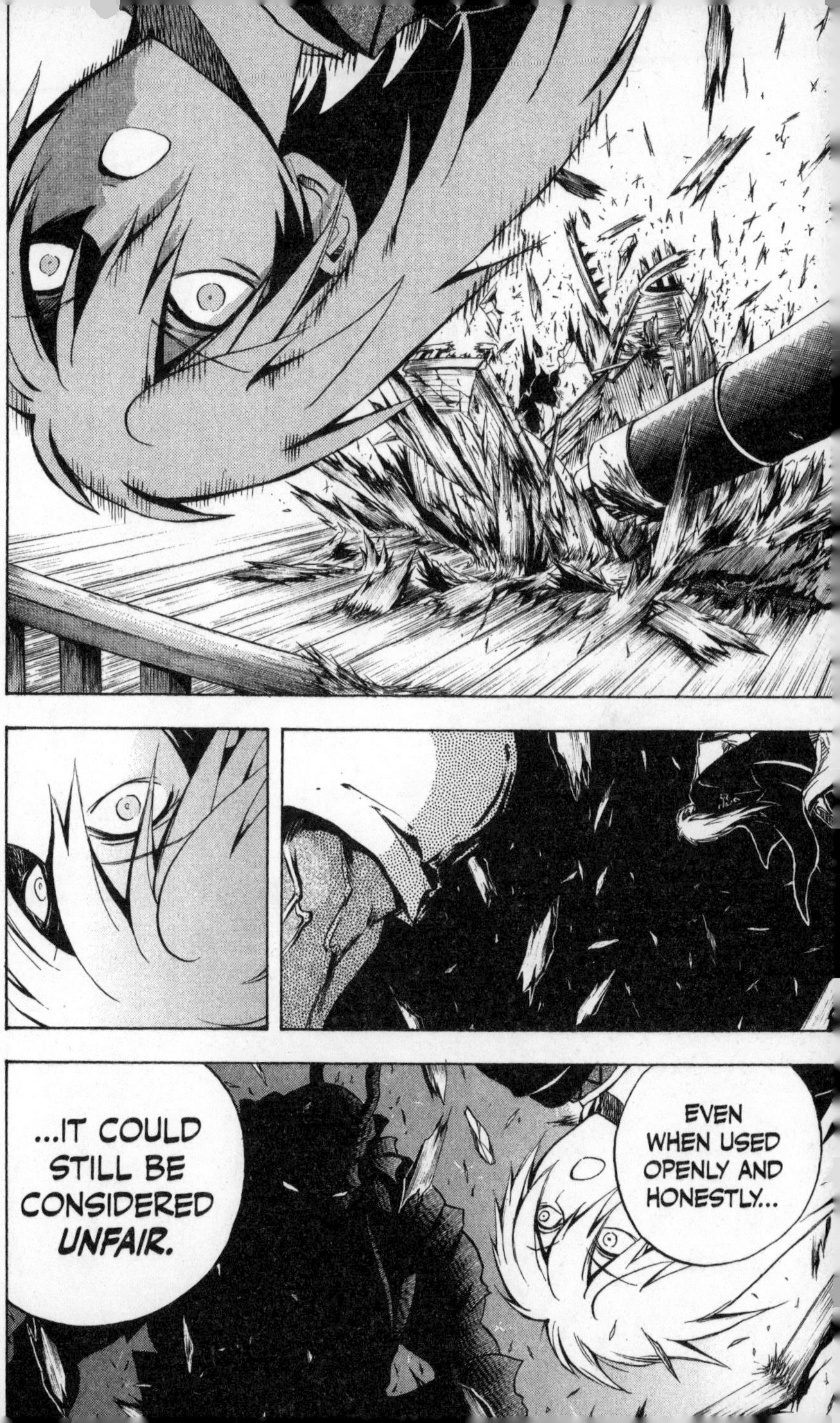
EVEN WHEN USED OPENLY AND HONESTLY...
...IT COULD STILL BE CONSIDERED *UNFAIR.*

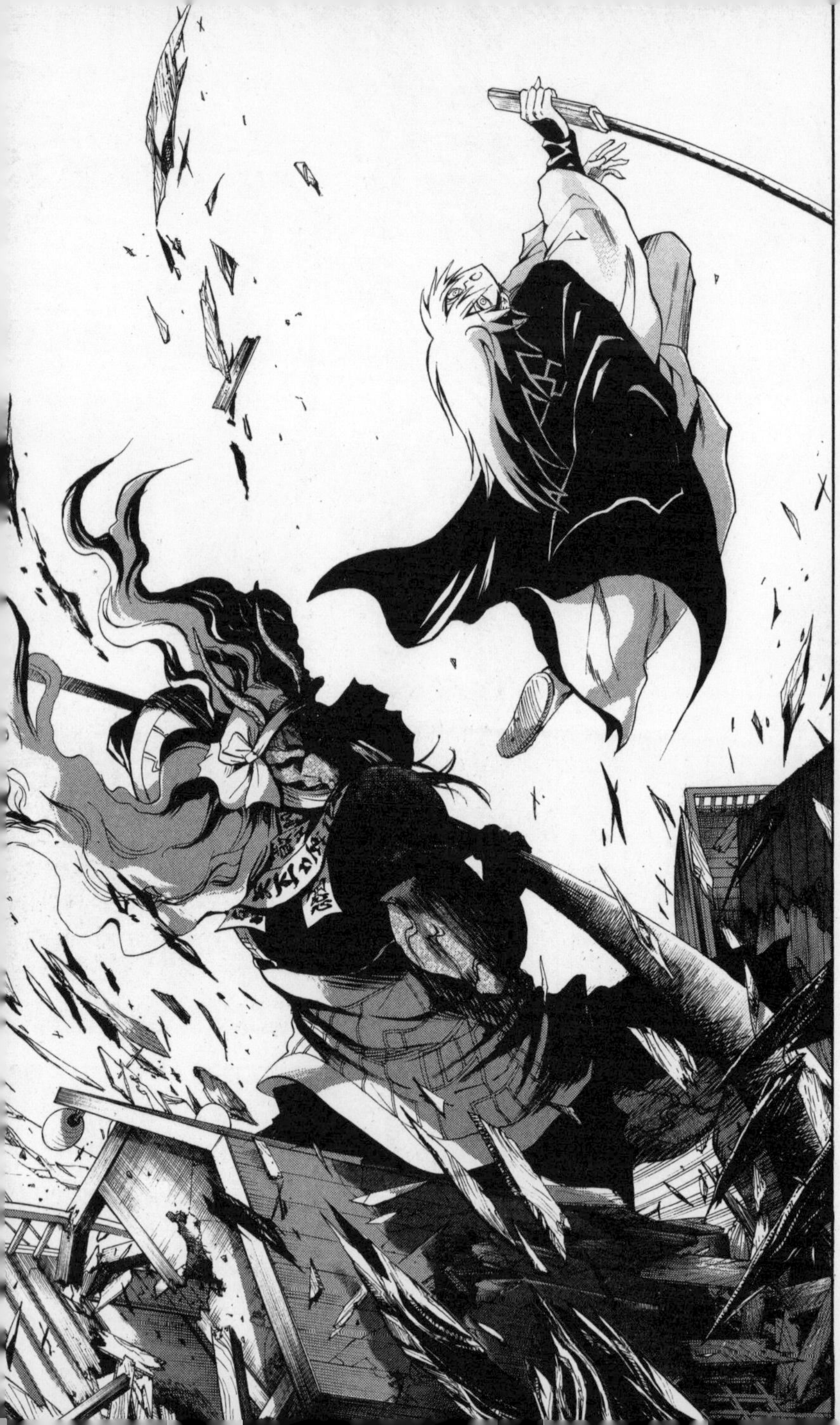

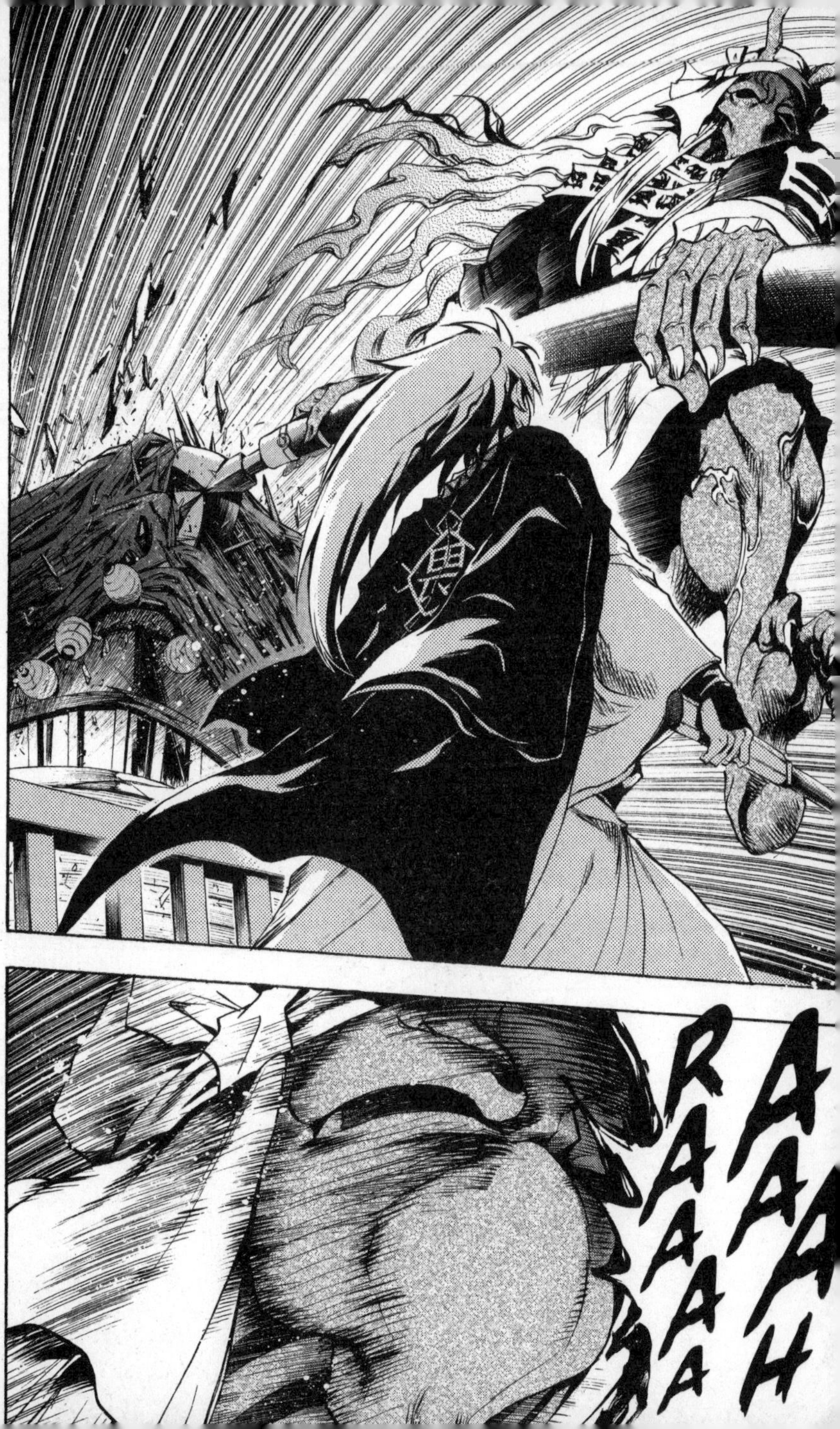
RAAAA
AAAAH

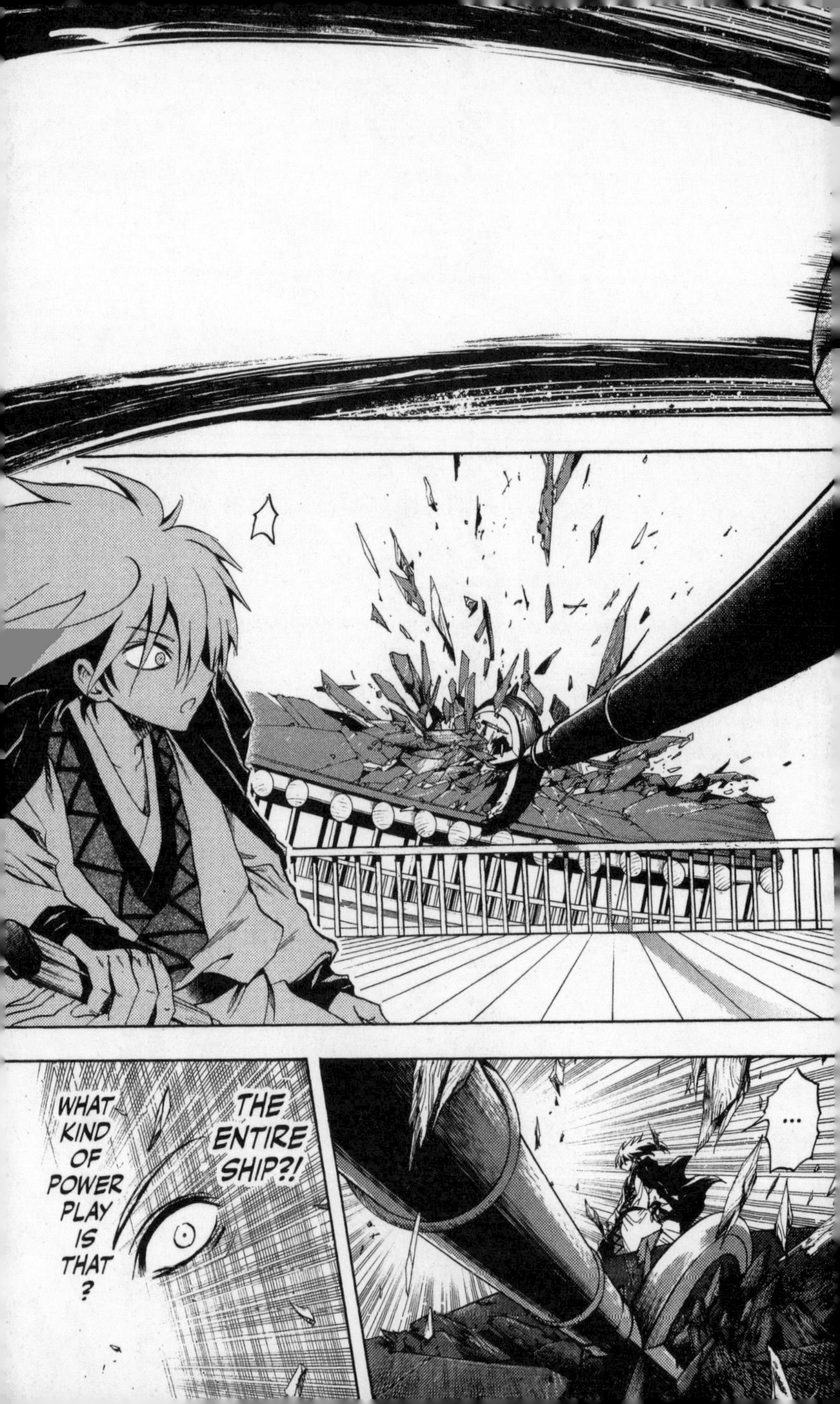
...
THE ENTIRE SHIP?!
WHAT KIND OF POWER PLAY IS THAT?

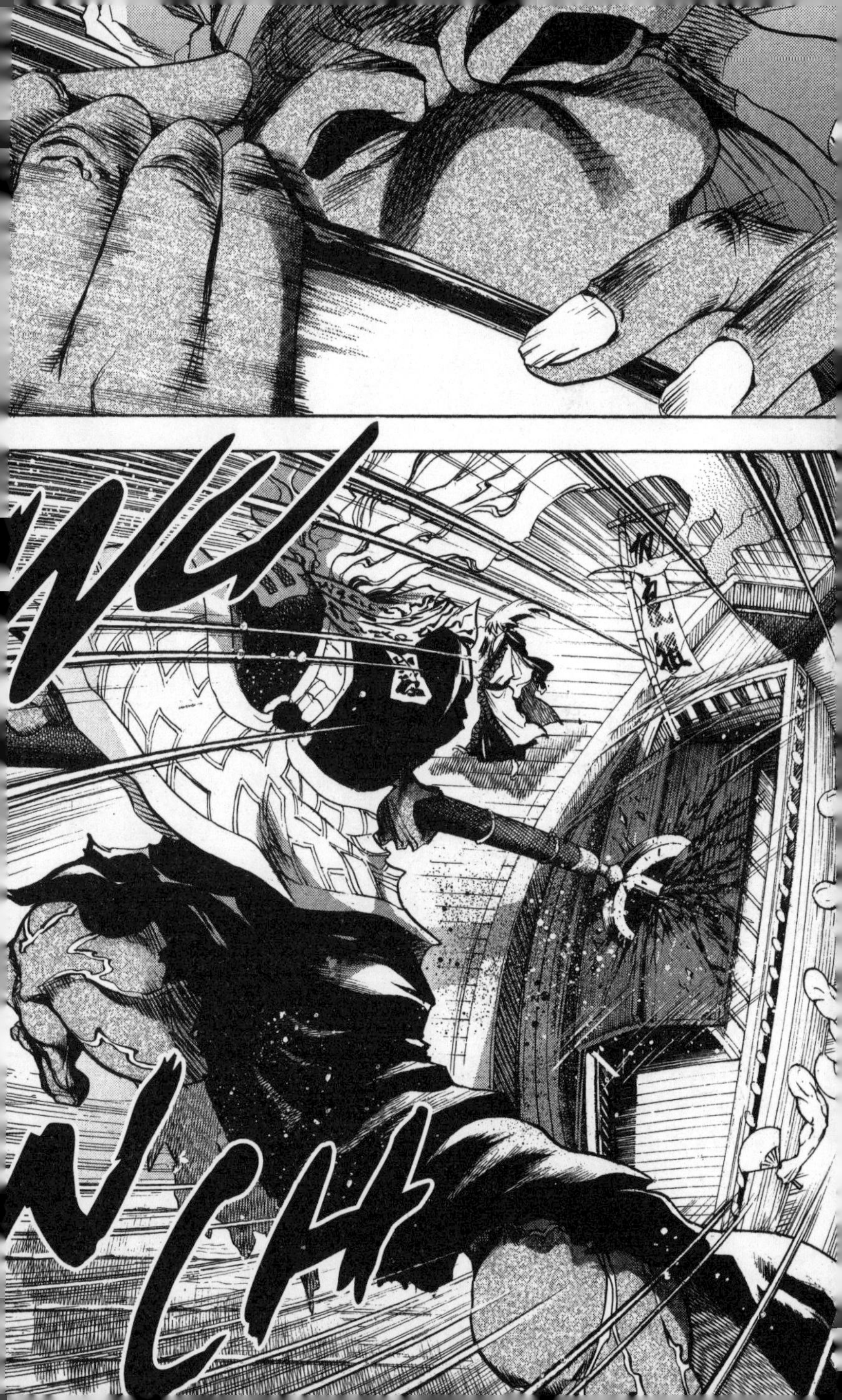
WU
NCH

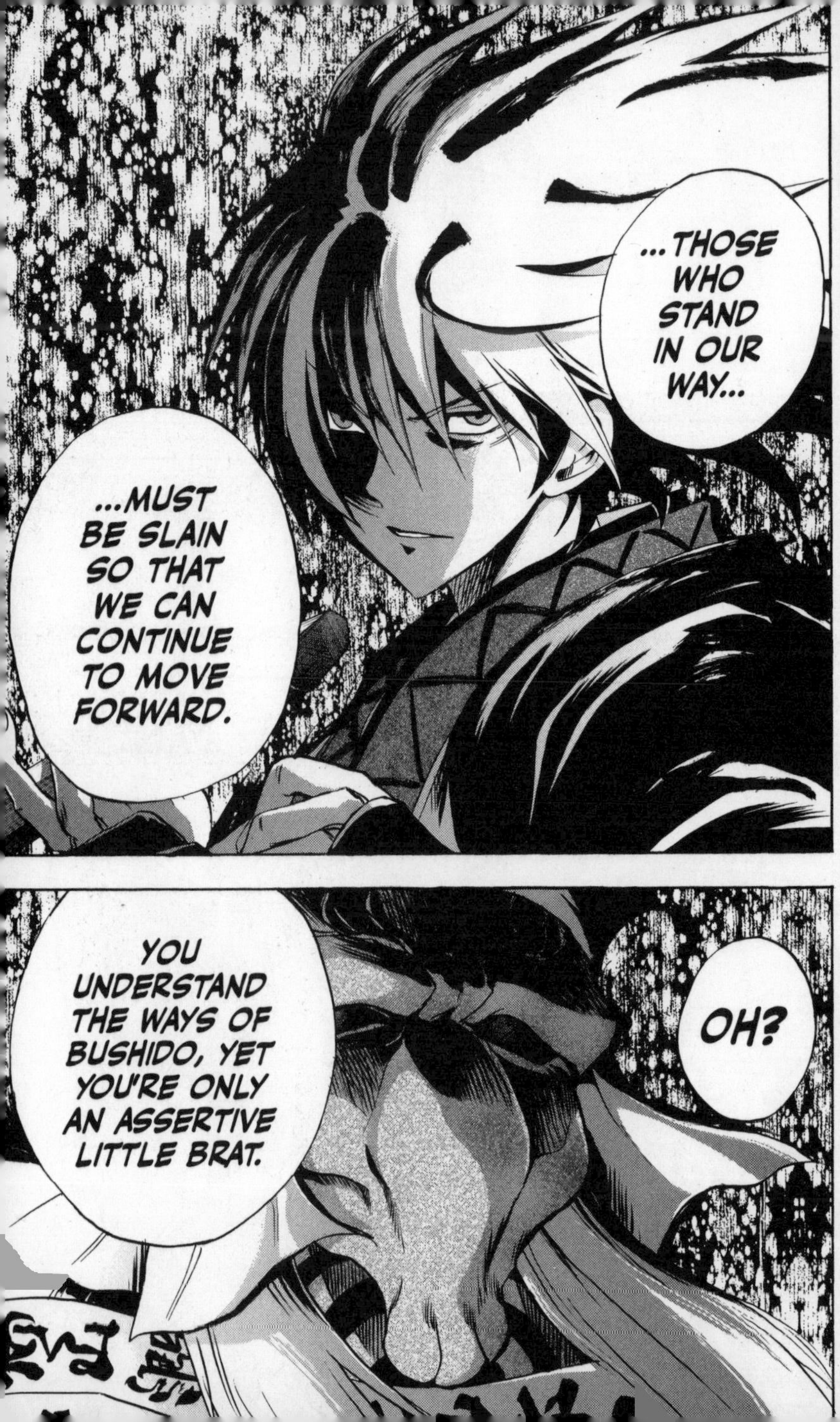
...THOSE WHO STAND IN OUR WAY...
...MUST BE SLAIN SO THAT WE CAN CONTINUE TO MOVE FORWARD.
OH?
YOU UNDERSTAND THE WAYS OF BUSHIDO, YET YOU'RE ONLY AN ASSERTIVE LITTLE BRAT.

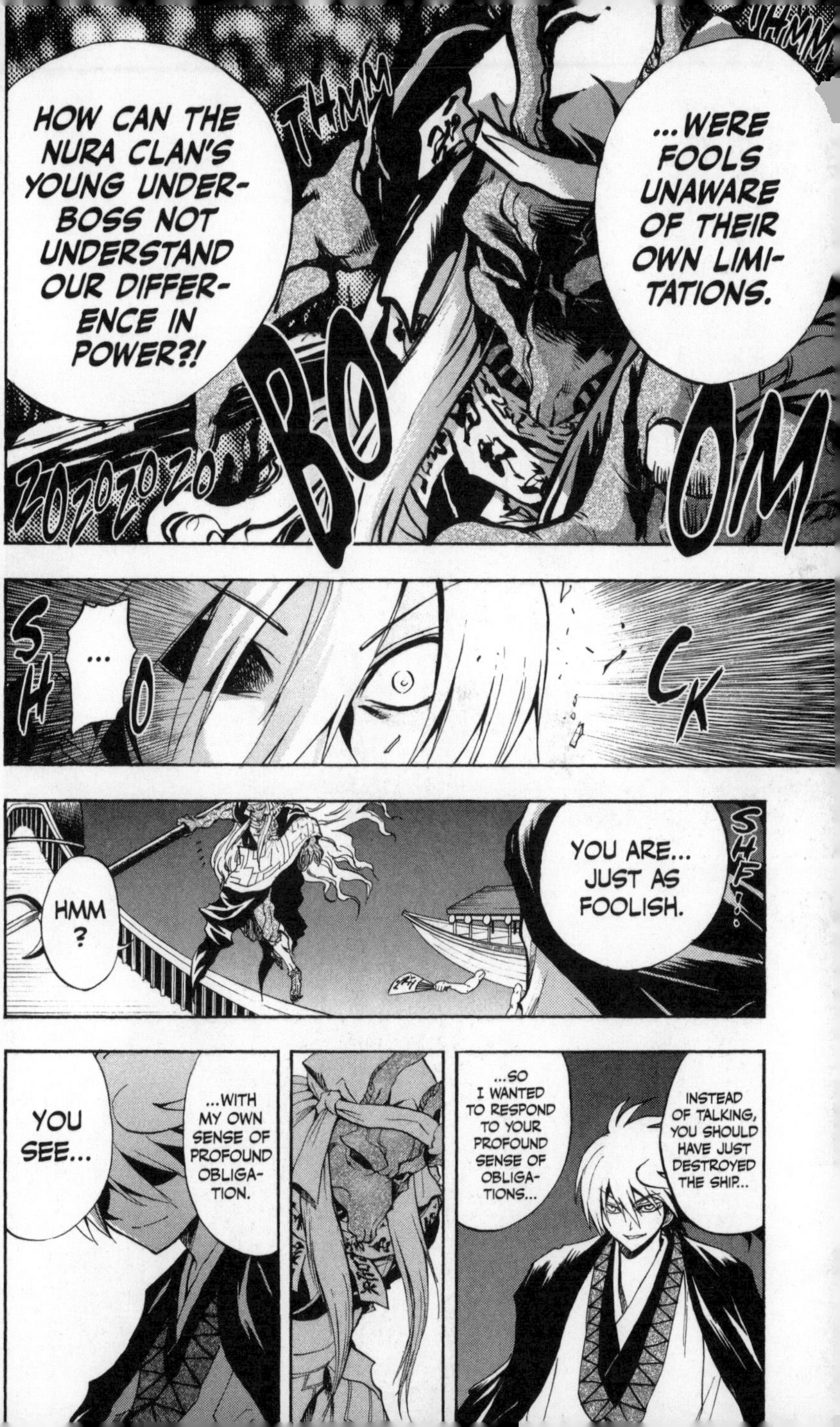
THMM
...WERE FOOLS UNAWARE OF THEIR OWN LIMITATIONS.
THMM
HOW CAN THE NURA CLAN'S YOUNG UNDER-BOSS NOT UNDERSTAND OUR DIFFER-ENCE IN POWER?!
BOOM
ZOZOZOZOZO
SHOCK
...
SHF!
YOU ARE... JUST AS FOOLISH.
HMM?
INSTEAD OF TALKING, YOU SHOULD HAVE JUST DESTROYED THE SHIP...
...SO I WANTED TO RESPOND TO YOUR PROFOUND SENSE OF OBLIGA-TIONS...
...WITH MY OWN SENSE OF PROFOUND OBLIGA-TION.
YOU SEE...

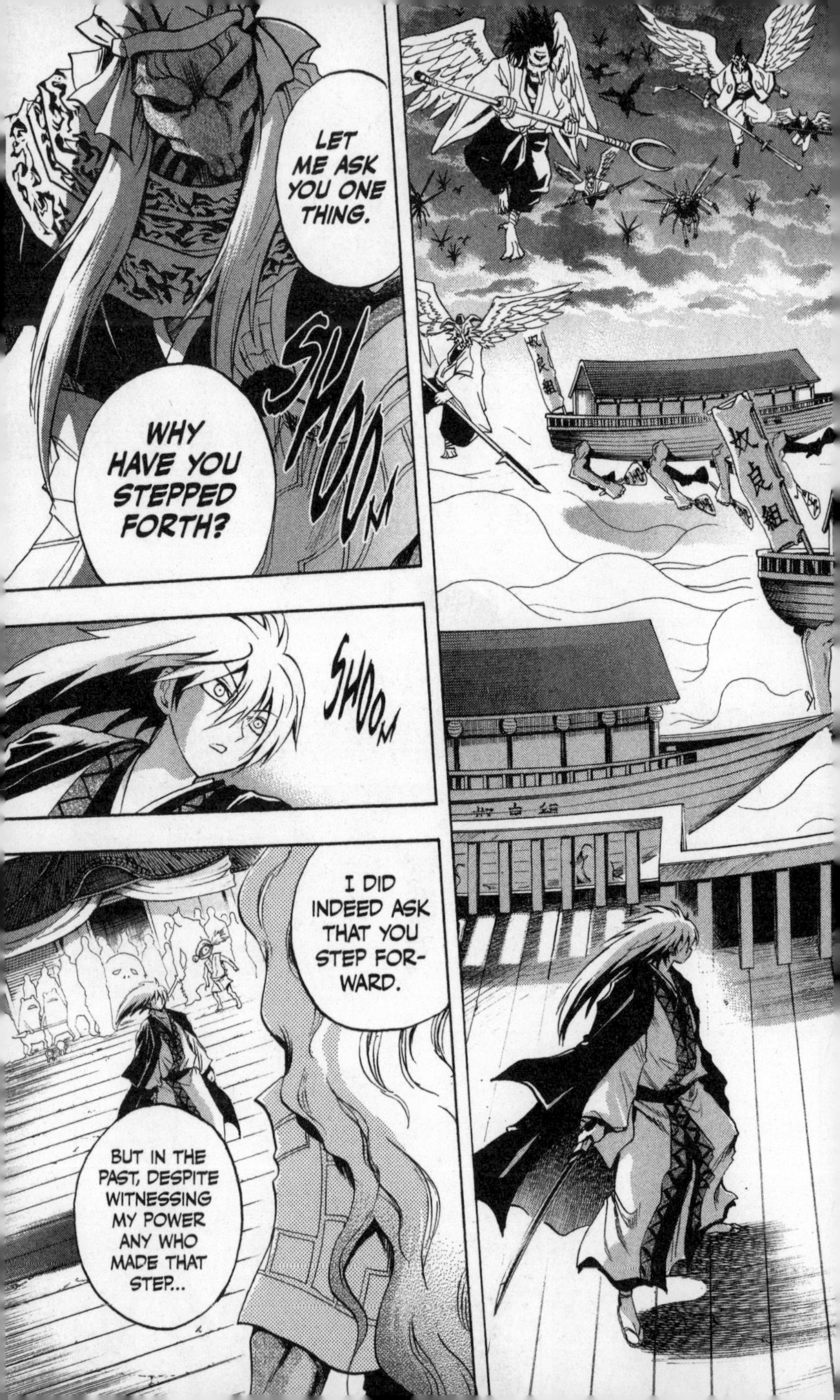
LET ME ASK YOU ONE THING.
WHY HAVE YOU STEPPED FORTH?
SHOOM
SHOOM
I DID INDEED ASK THAT YOU STEP FOR-WARD.
BUT IN THE PAST, DESPITE WITNESSING MY POWER ANY WHO MADE THAT STEP...

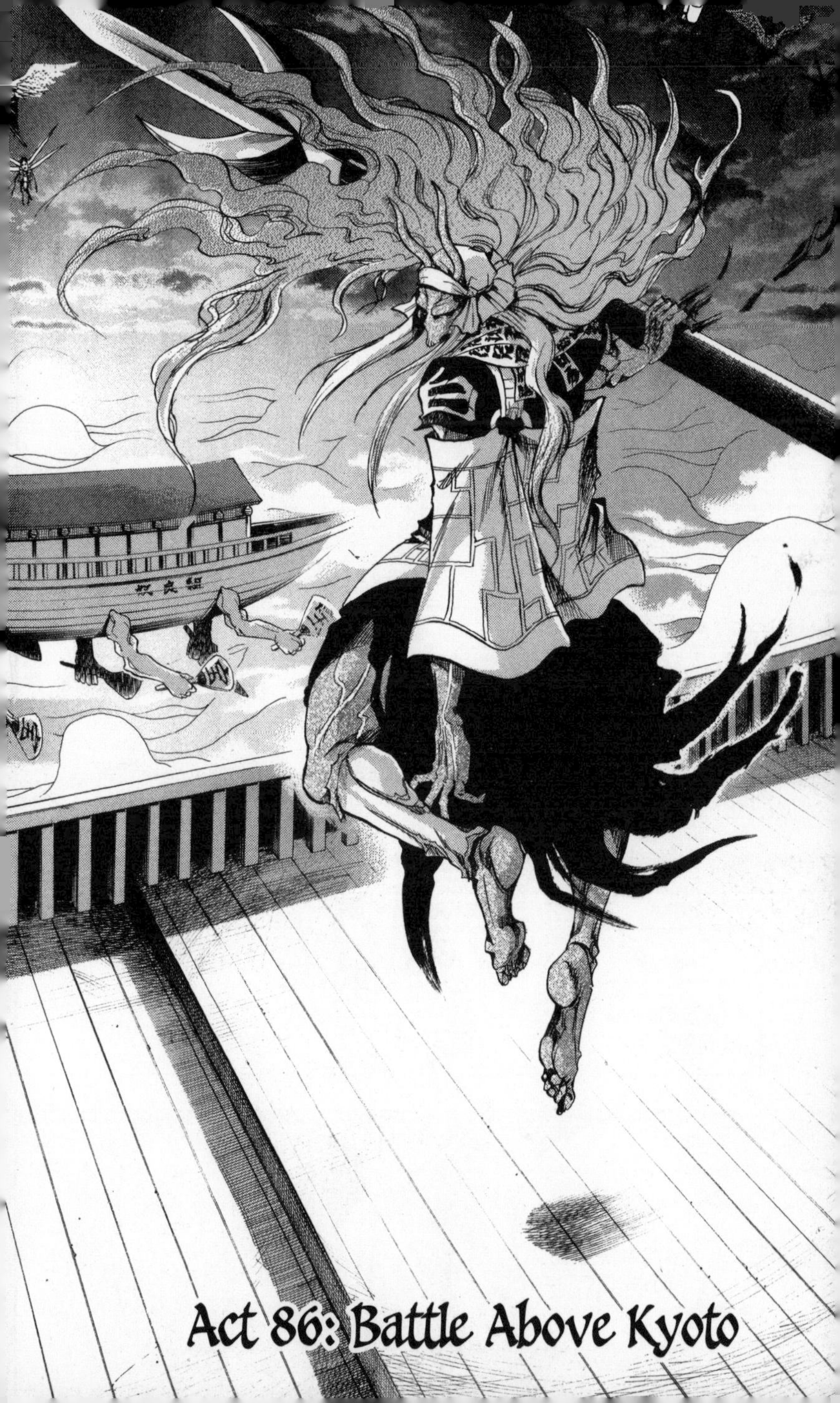

Act 86: Battle Above Kyoto

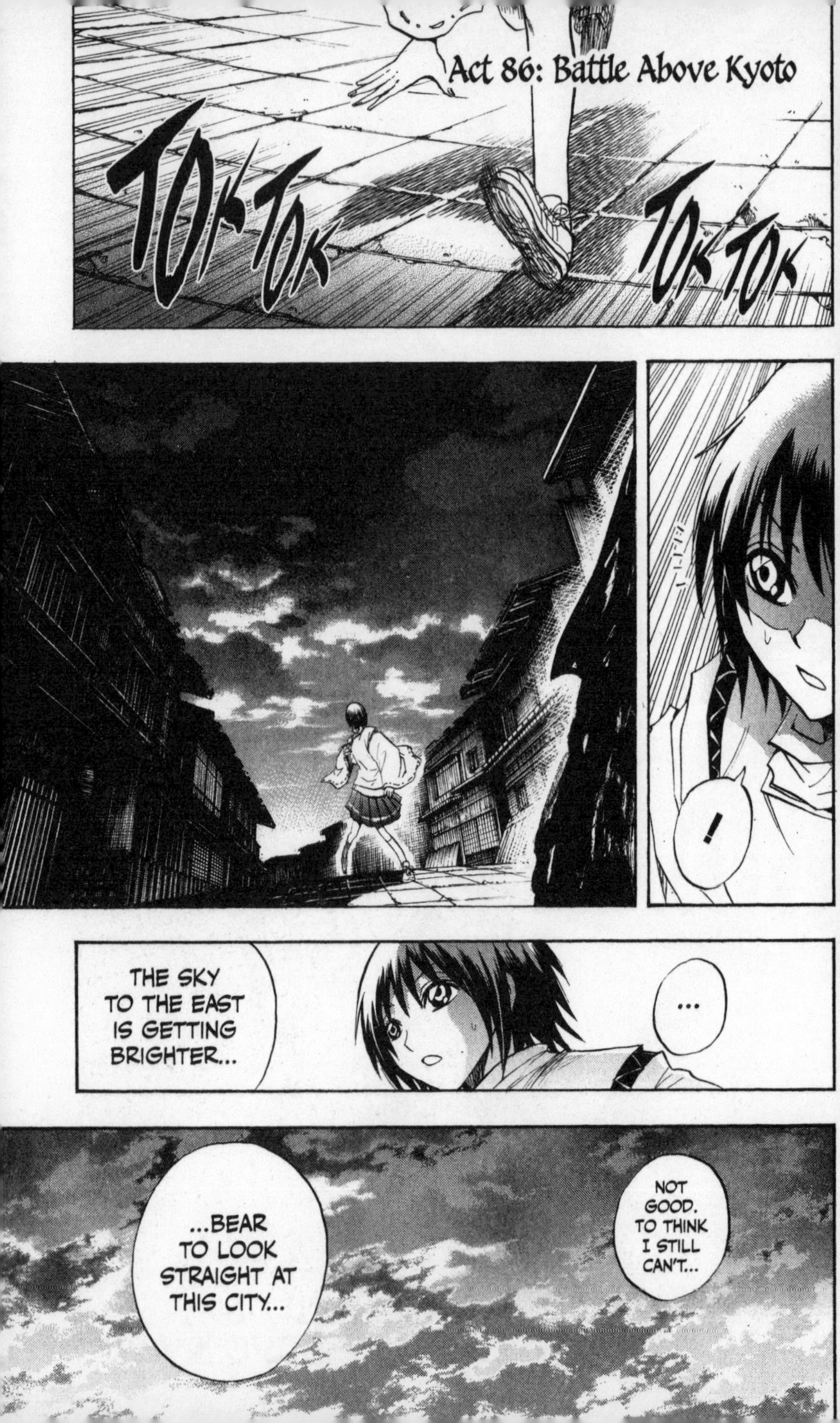
Act 86: Battle Above Kyoto
TOK TOK
TOK TOK
!
...
THE SKY TO THE EAST IS GETTING BRIGHTER...
NOT GOOD. TO THINK I STILL CAN'T...
...BEAR TO LOOK STRAIGHT AT THIS CITY...

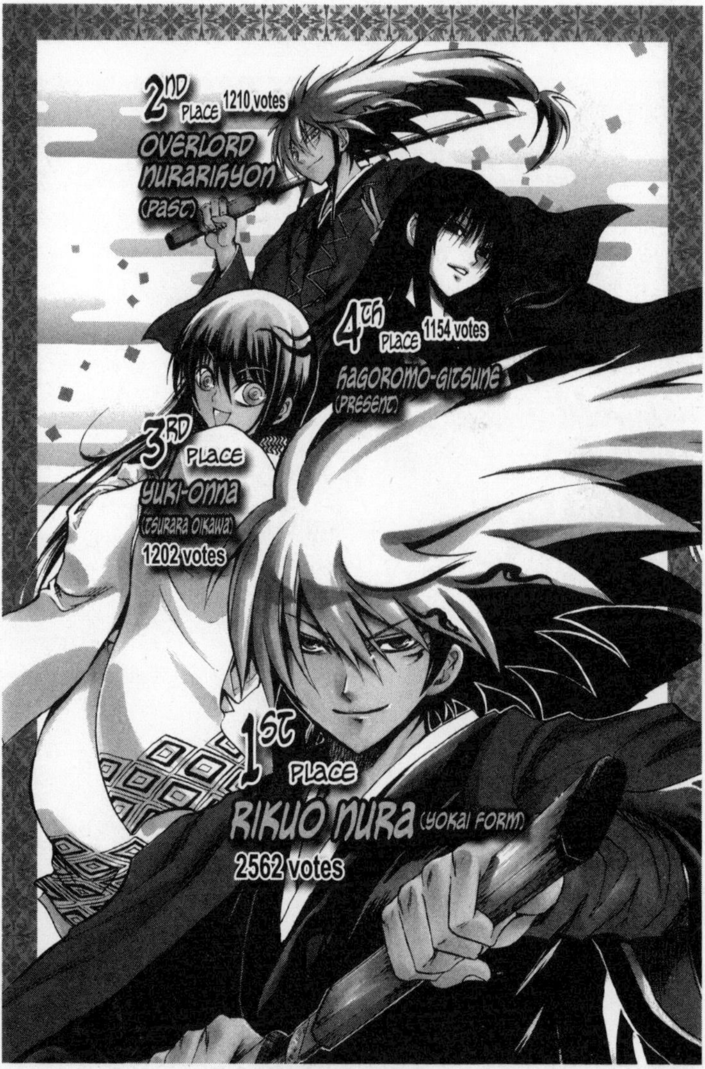
2ND PLACE 1210 votes
OVERLORD NURARIHYON (PAST)
4TH PLACE 1154 votes
HAGOROMO-GITSUNE (PRESENT)
3RD PLACE
YUKI-ONNA
(TSURARA OIKAWA)
1202 votes
1ST PLACE
RIKUO NURA (YOKAI FORM)
2562 votes

Illustration from Weekly Shonen Jump, Vol. 53, 2009

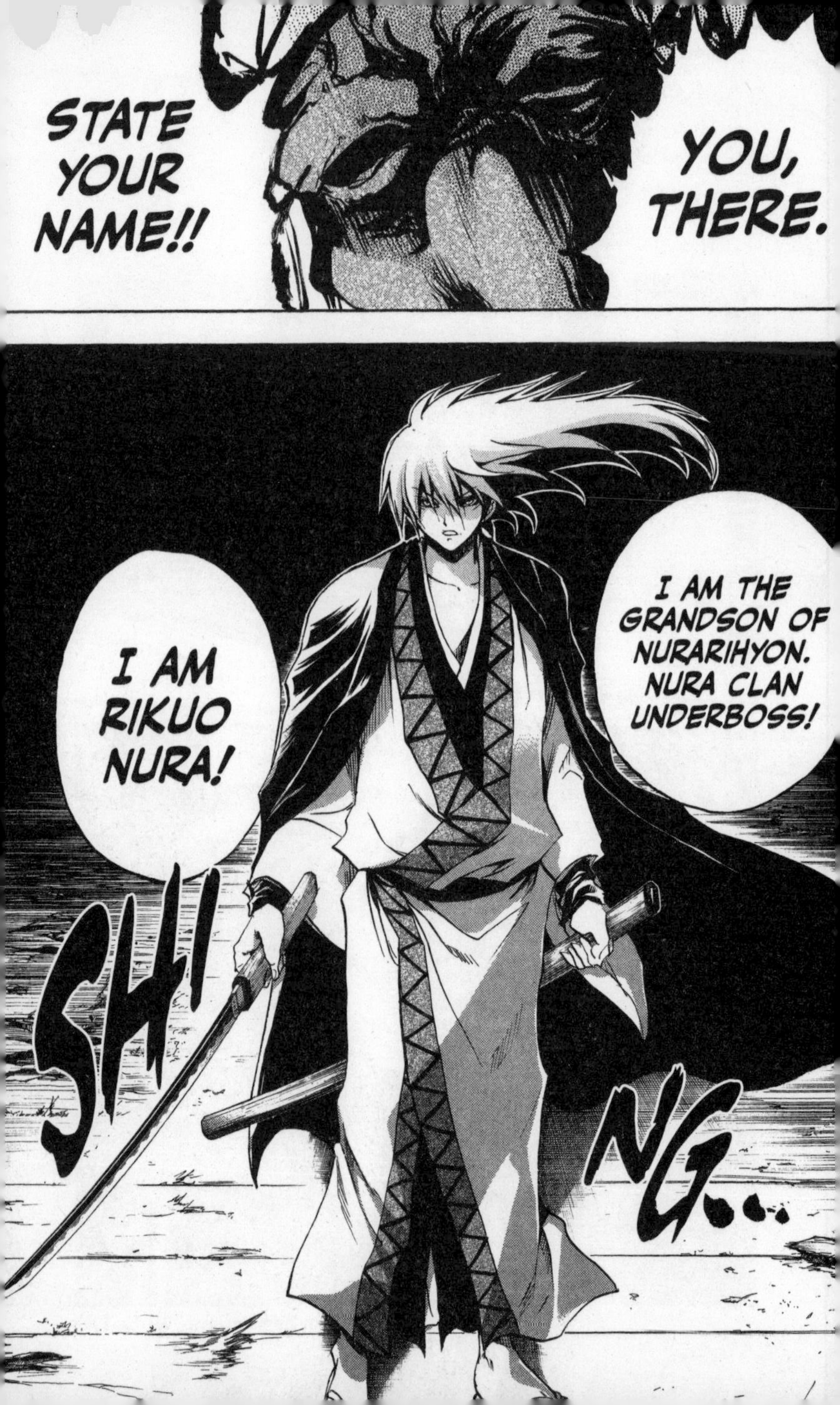
YOU, THERE.
STATE YOUR NAME!!
I AM THE GRANDSON OF NURARIHYON. NURA CLAN UNDERBOSS!
I AM RIKUO NURA!
SH
NG...

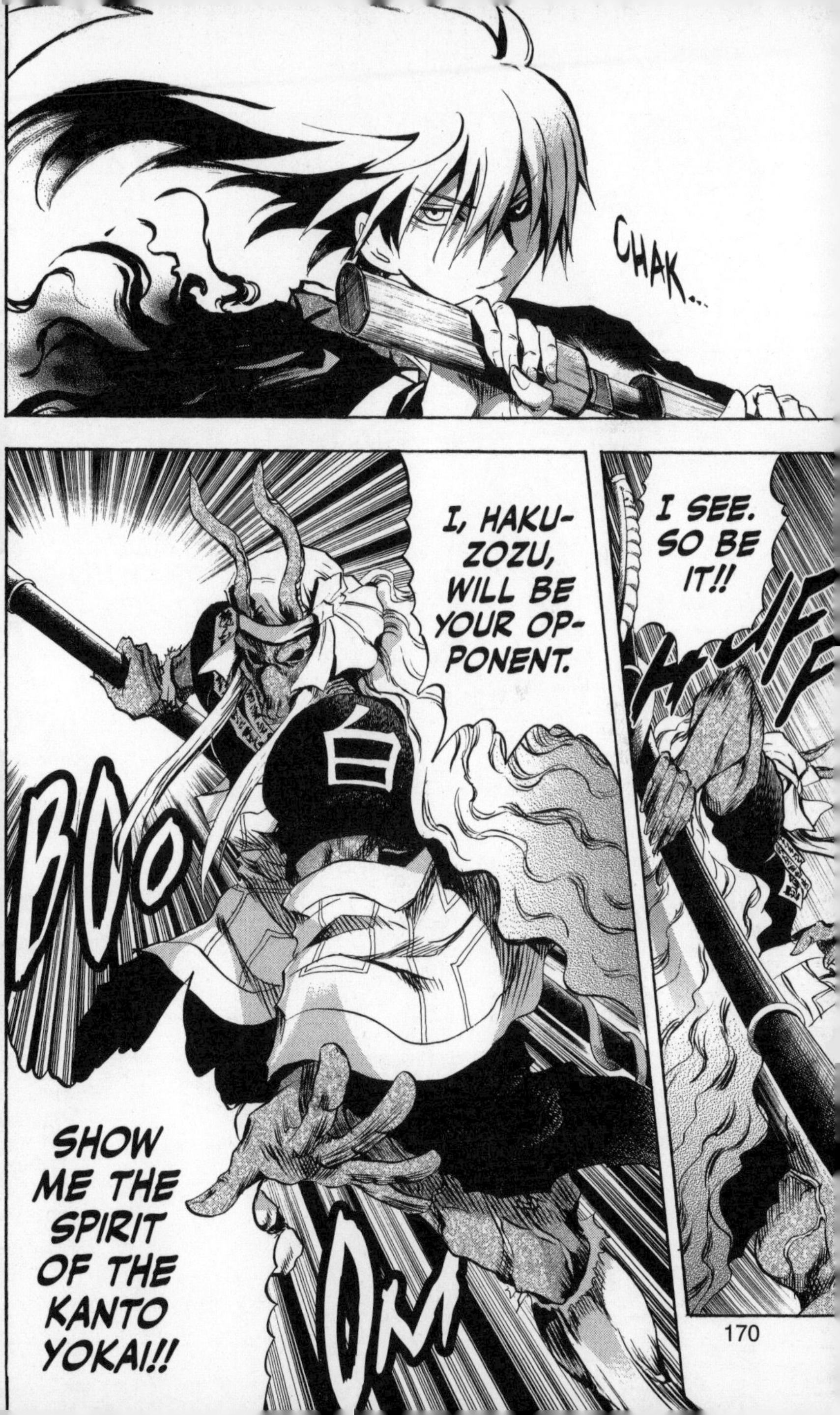
CHAK...
I SEE. SO BE IT!!
I, HAKU-ZOZU, WILL BE YOUR OP-PONENT.
BOOOM
SHOW ME THE SPIRIT OF THE KANTO YOKAI!!

READ THIS WAY

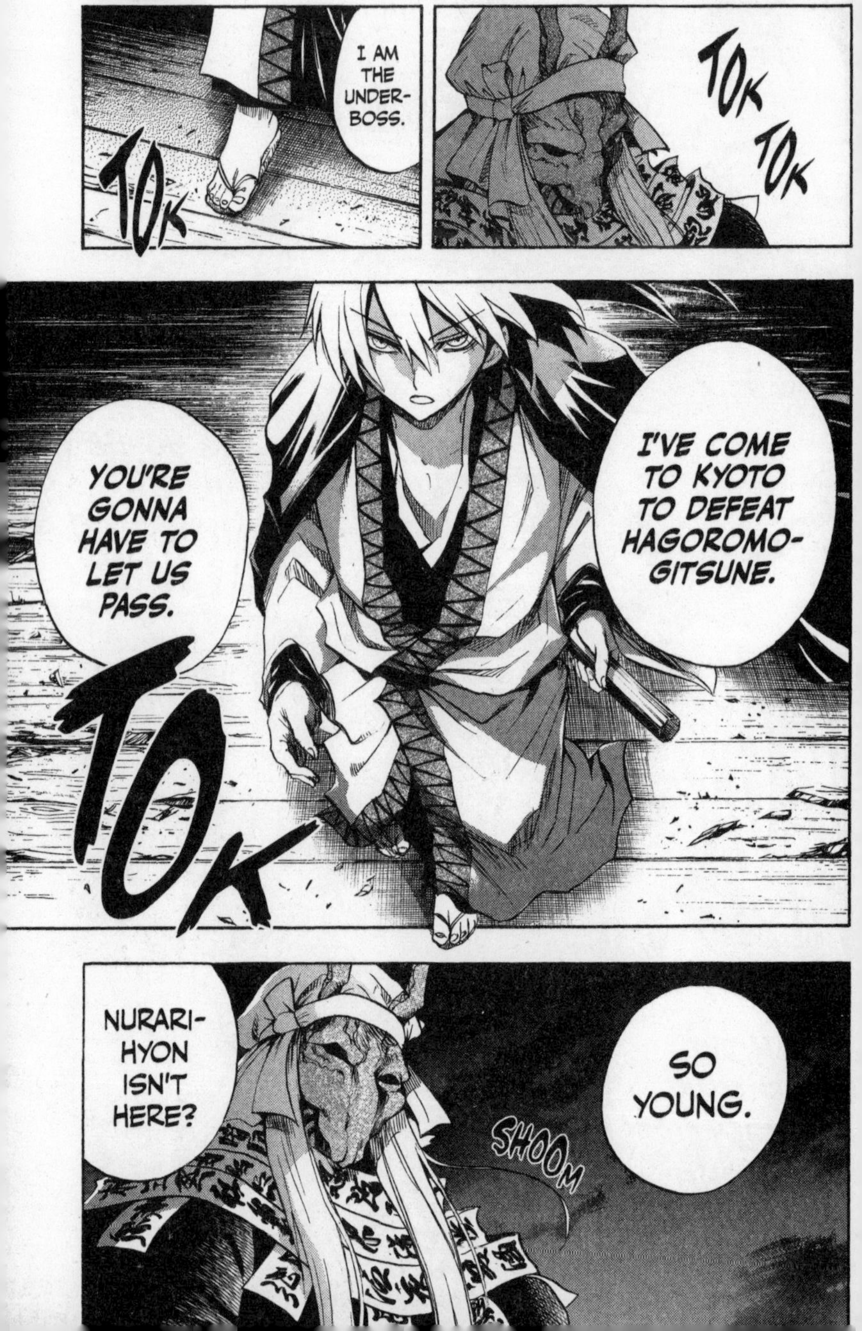
TOK
TOK
I AM THE UNDER-BOSS.
TOK
I'VE COME TO KYOTO TO DEFEAT HAGOROMO-GITSUNE.
YOU'RE GONNA HAVE TO LET US PASS.
TOK
SO YOUNG.
SHOOM
NURARI-HYON ISN'T HERE?

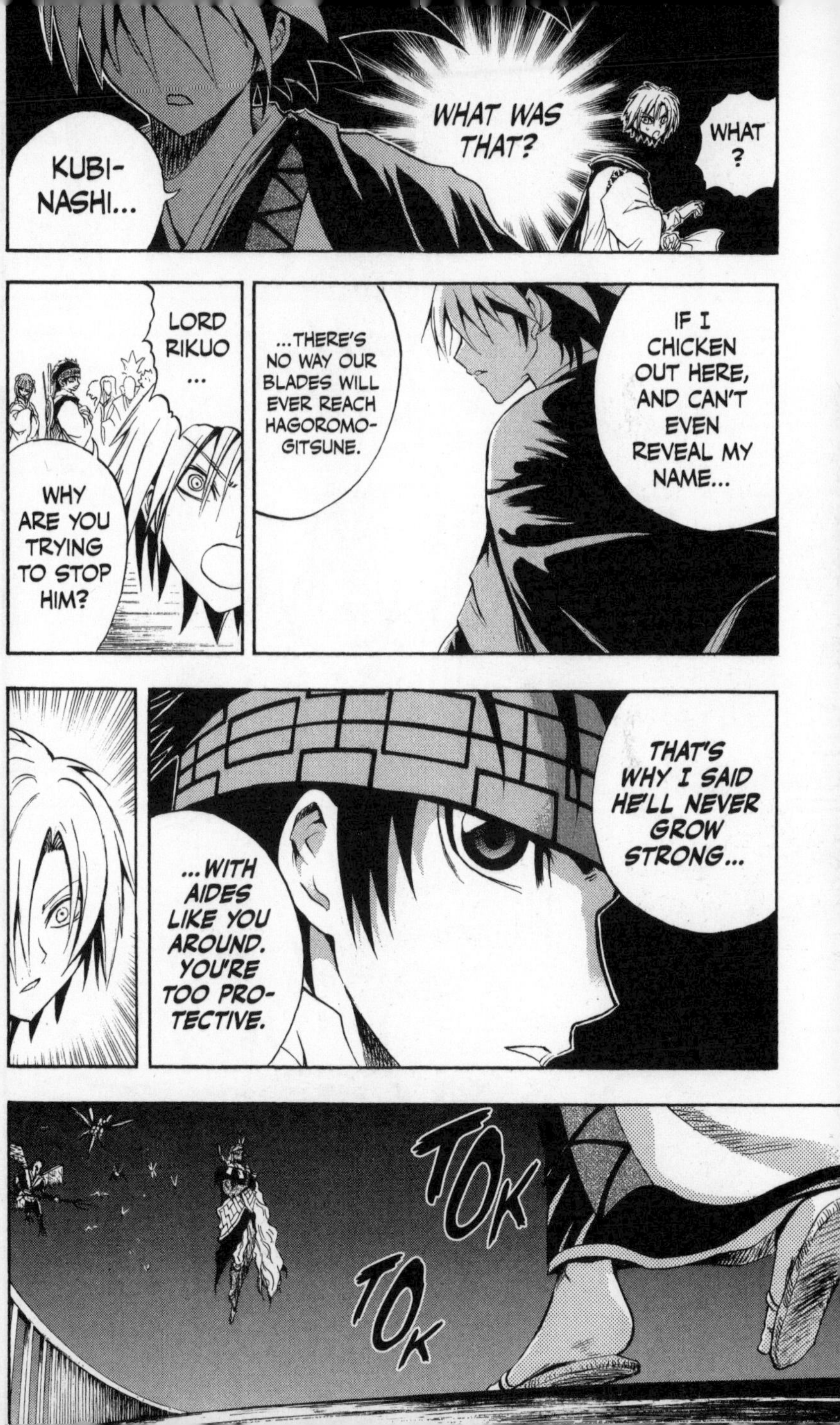
WHAT ?
WHAT WAS THAT?
KUBI-NASHI...
IF I CHICKEN OUT HERE, AND CAN'T EVEN REVEAL MY NAME...
...THERE'S NO WAY OUR BLADES WILL EVER REACH HAGOROMO-GITSUNE.
LORD RIKUO ...
WHY ARE YOU TRYING TO STOP HIM?
THAT'S WHY I SAID HE'LL NEVER GROW STRONG...
...WITH AIDES LIKE YOU AROUND. YOU'RE TOO PROTECTIVE.
TOK
TOK

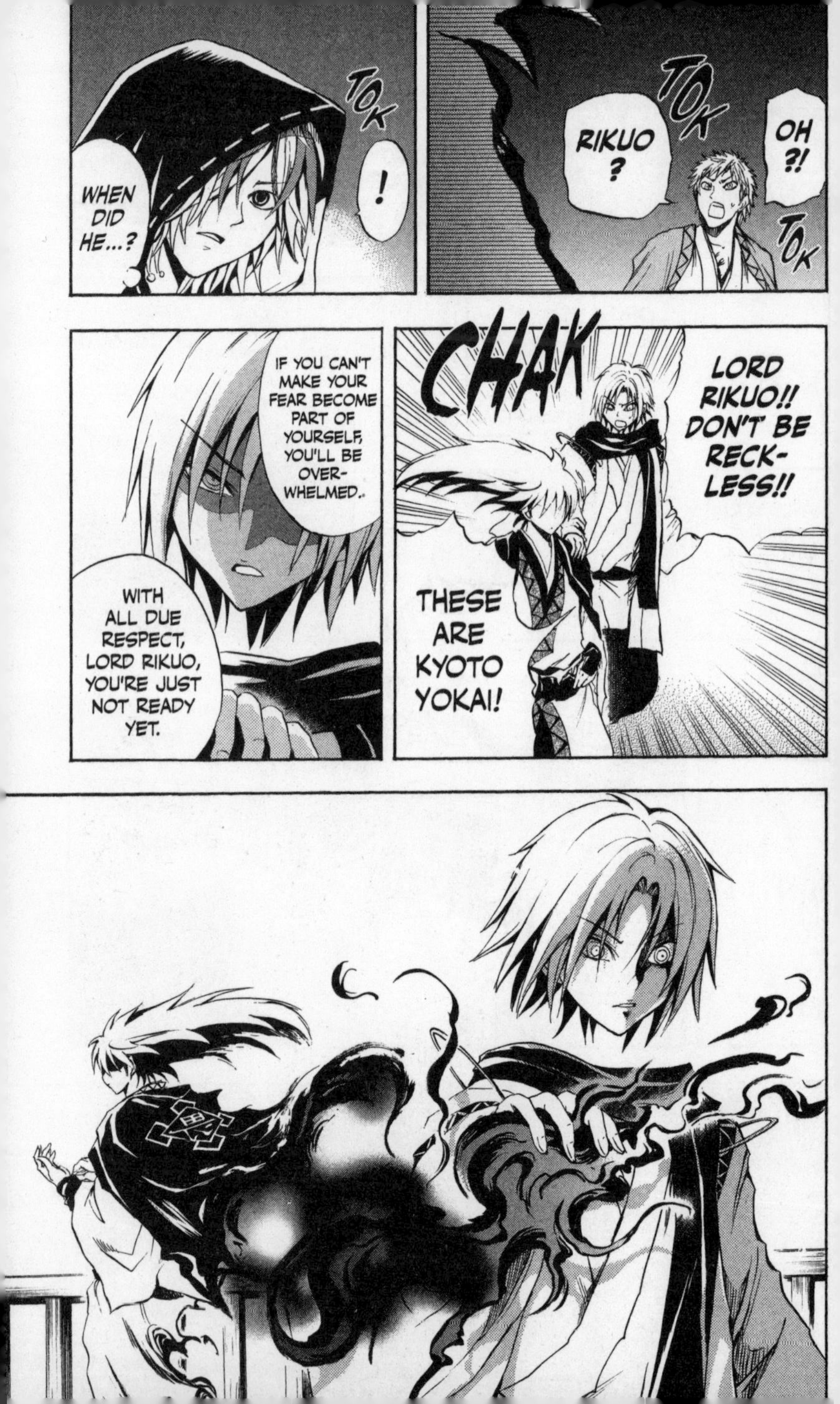
OH ?!
TOK
RIKUO ?
TOK
TOK
!
WHEN DID HE...?
CHAK
LORD RIKUO!! DON'T BE RECK-LESS!!
THESE ARE KYOTO YOKAI!
IF YOU CAN'T MAKE YOUR FEAR BECOME PART OF YOURSELF, YOU'LL BE OVER-WHELMED..
WITH ALL DUE RESPECT, LORD RIKUO, YOU'RE JUST NOT READY YET.

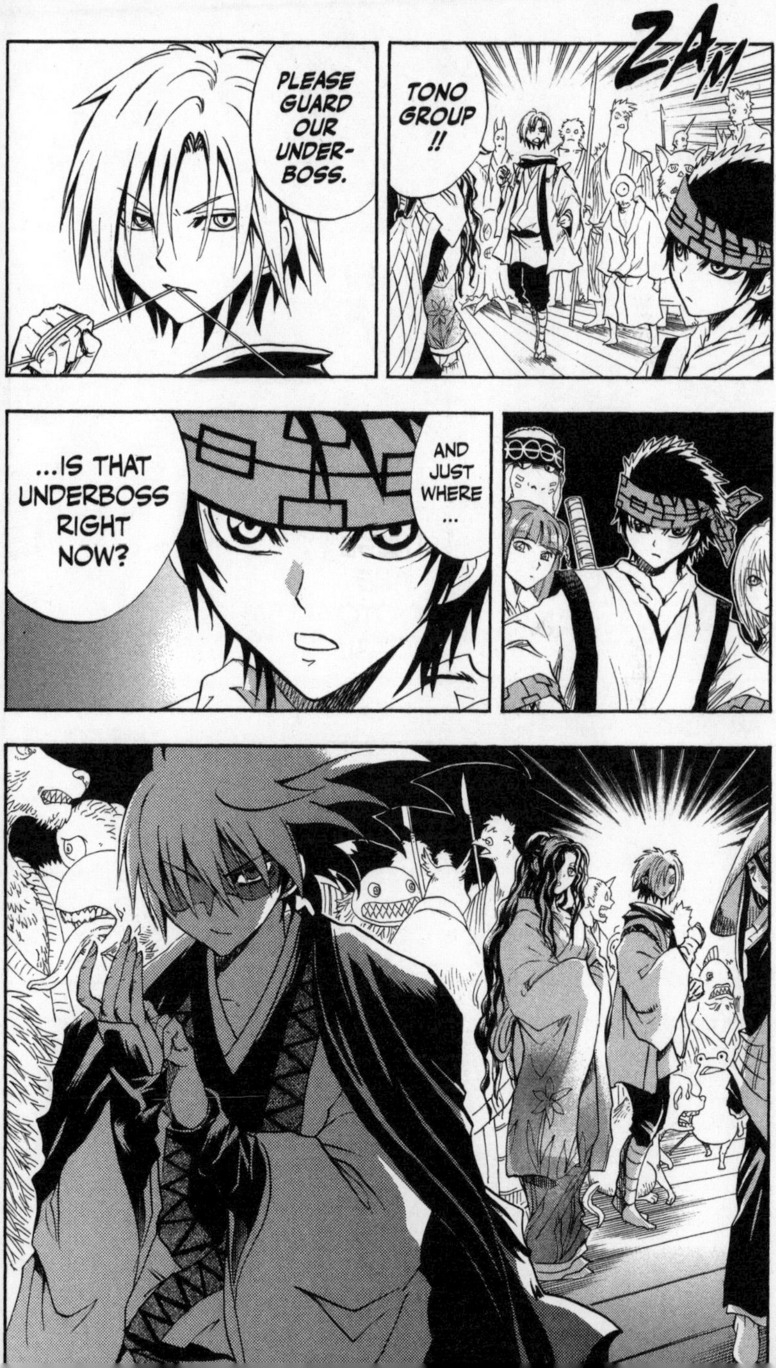
ZAM
TONO GROUP !!
PLEASE GUARD OUR UNDER-BOSS.
AND JUST WHERE ...
...IS THAT UNDERBOSS RIGHT NOW?

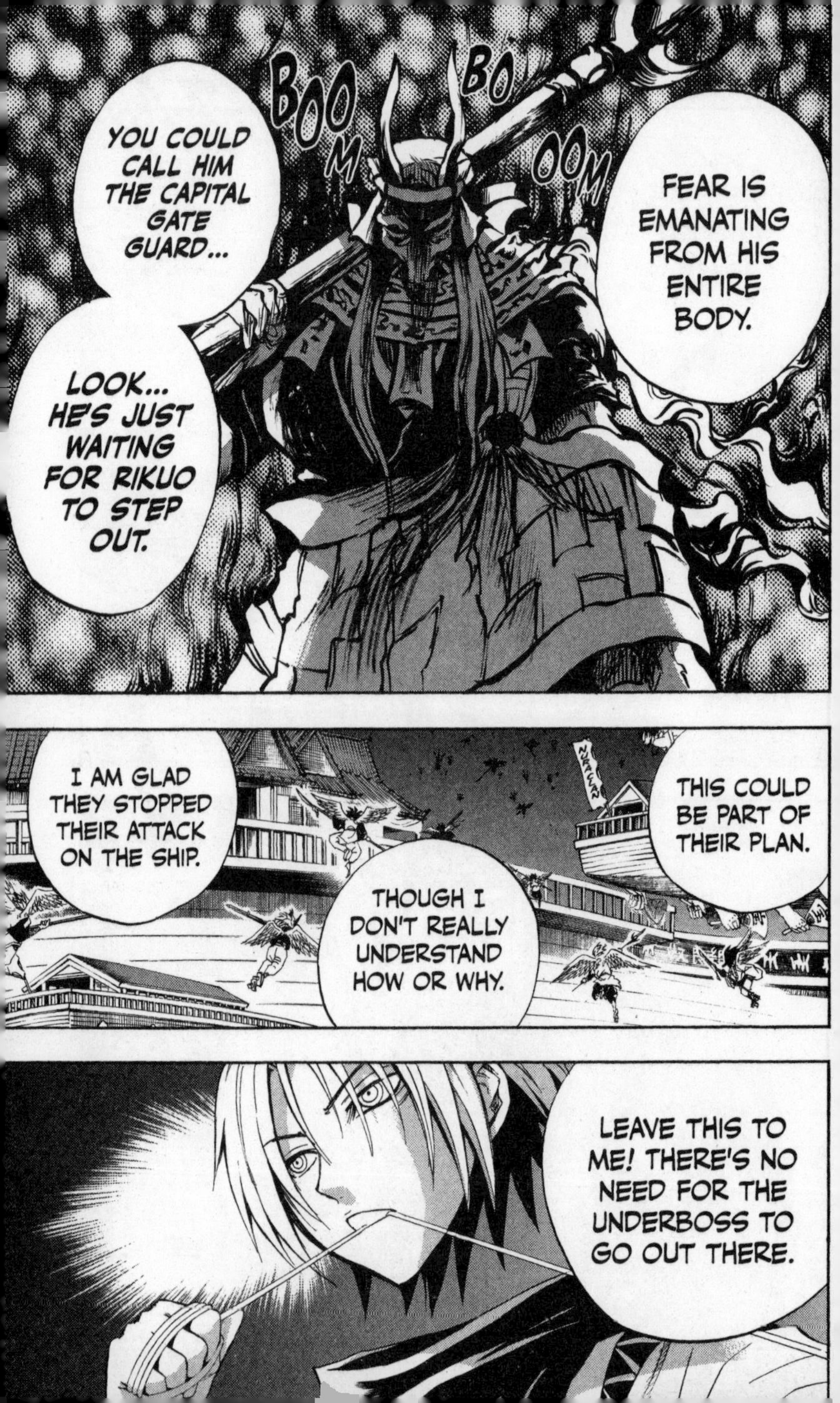
BOOOM
BOOOM
FEAR IS EMANATING FROM HIS ENTIRE BODY.
YOU COULD CALL HIM THE CAPITAL GATE GUARD...
LOOK... HE'S JUST WAITING FOR RIKUO TO STEP OUT.
THIS COULD BE PART OF THEIR PLAN.
I AM GLAD THEY STOPPED THEIR ATTACK ON THE SHIP.
THOUGH I DON'T REALLY UNDERSTAND HOW OR WHY.
LEAVE THIS TO ME! THERE'S NO NEED FOR THE UNDERBOSS TO GO OUT THERE.

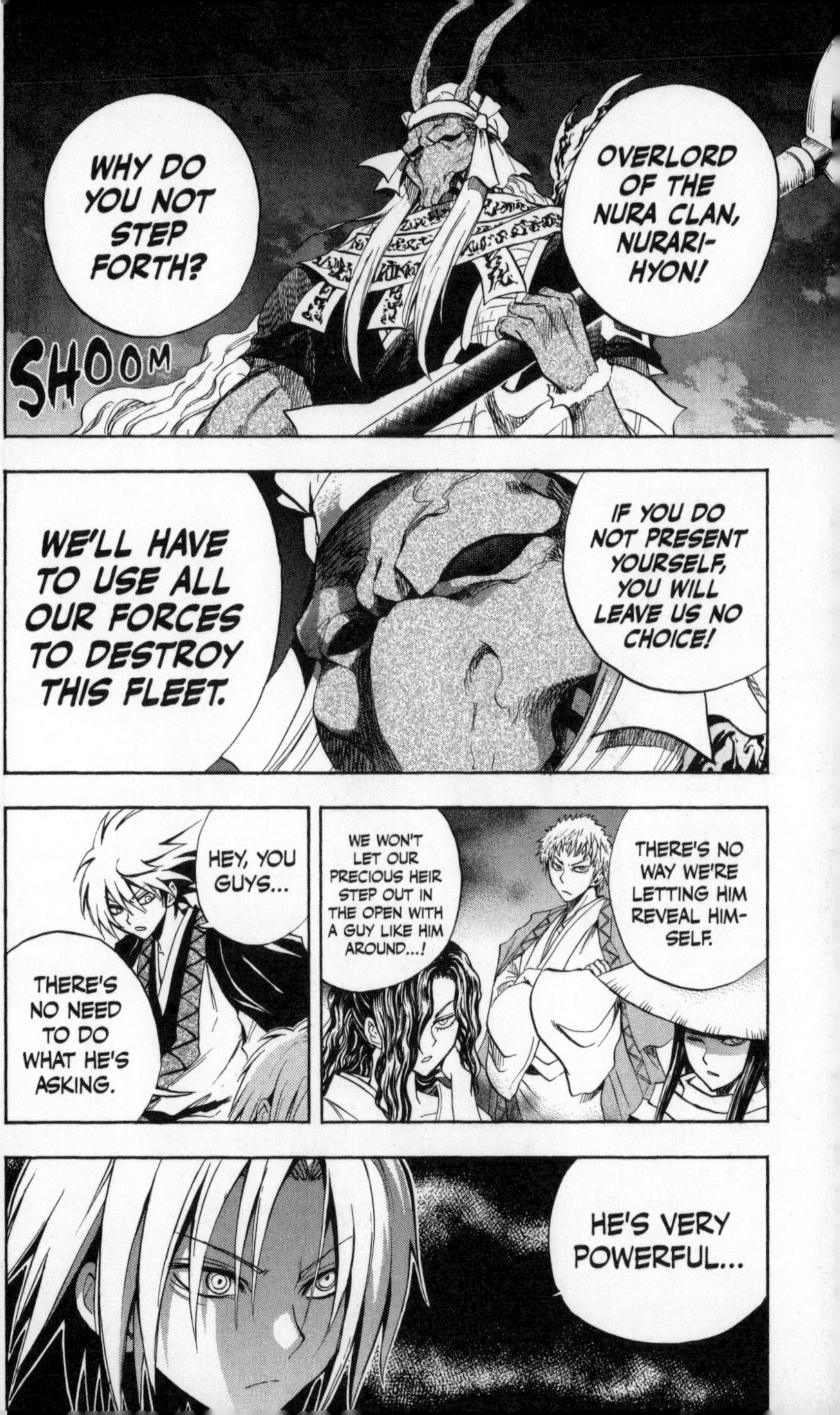
OVERLORD OF THE NURA CLAN, NURARI-HYON!
WHY DO YOU NOT STEP FORTH?
SHOOM
IF YOU DO NOT PRESENT YOURSELF, YOU WILL LEAVE US NO CHOICE!
WE'LL HAVE TO USE ALL OUR FORCES TO DESTROY THIS FLEET.
THERE'S NO WAY WE'RE LETTING HIM REVEAL HIM-SELF.
WE WON'T LET OUR PRECIOUS HEIR STEP OUT IN THE OPEN WITH A GUY LIKE HIM AROUND...!
HEY, YOU GUYS...
THERE'S NO NEED TO DO WHAT HE'S ASKING.
HE'S VERY POWERFUL...

READ THIS WAY

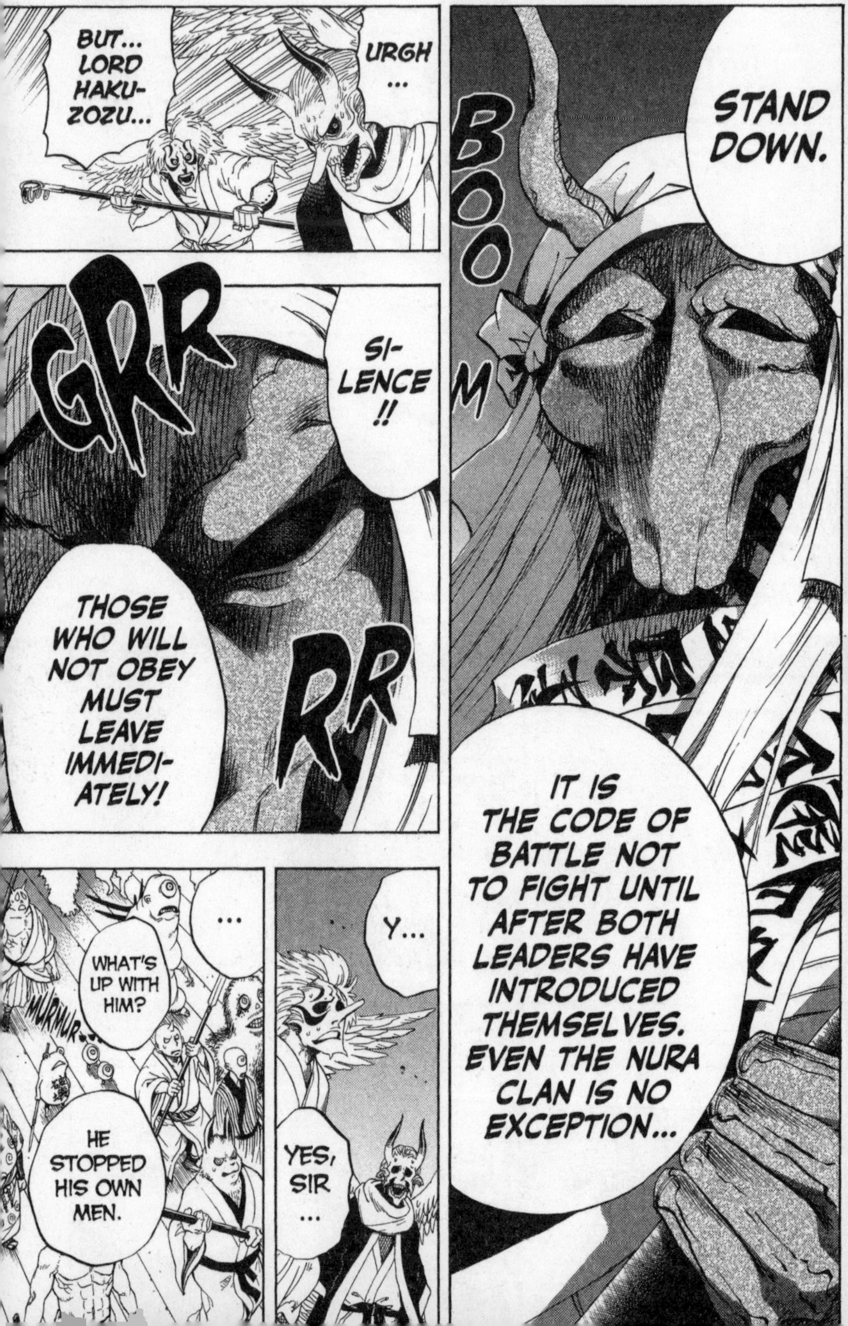

STAND DOWN.
BOOOM
IT IS THE CODE OF BATTLE NOT TO FIGHT UNTIL AFTER BOTH LEADERS HAVE INTRODUCED THEMSELVES. EVEN THE NURA CLAN IS NO EXCEPTION...
URGH...
BUT... LORD HAKU-ZOZU...
SI-LENCE!!
GRR
RR
THOSE WHO WILL NOT OBEY MUST LEAVE IMMEDI-ATELY!
Y...
YES, SIR...
...
WHAT'S UP WITH HIM?
MURMUR...
HE STOPPED HIS OWN MEN.

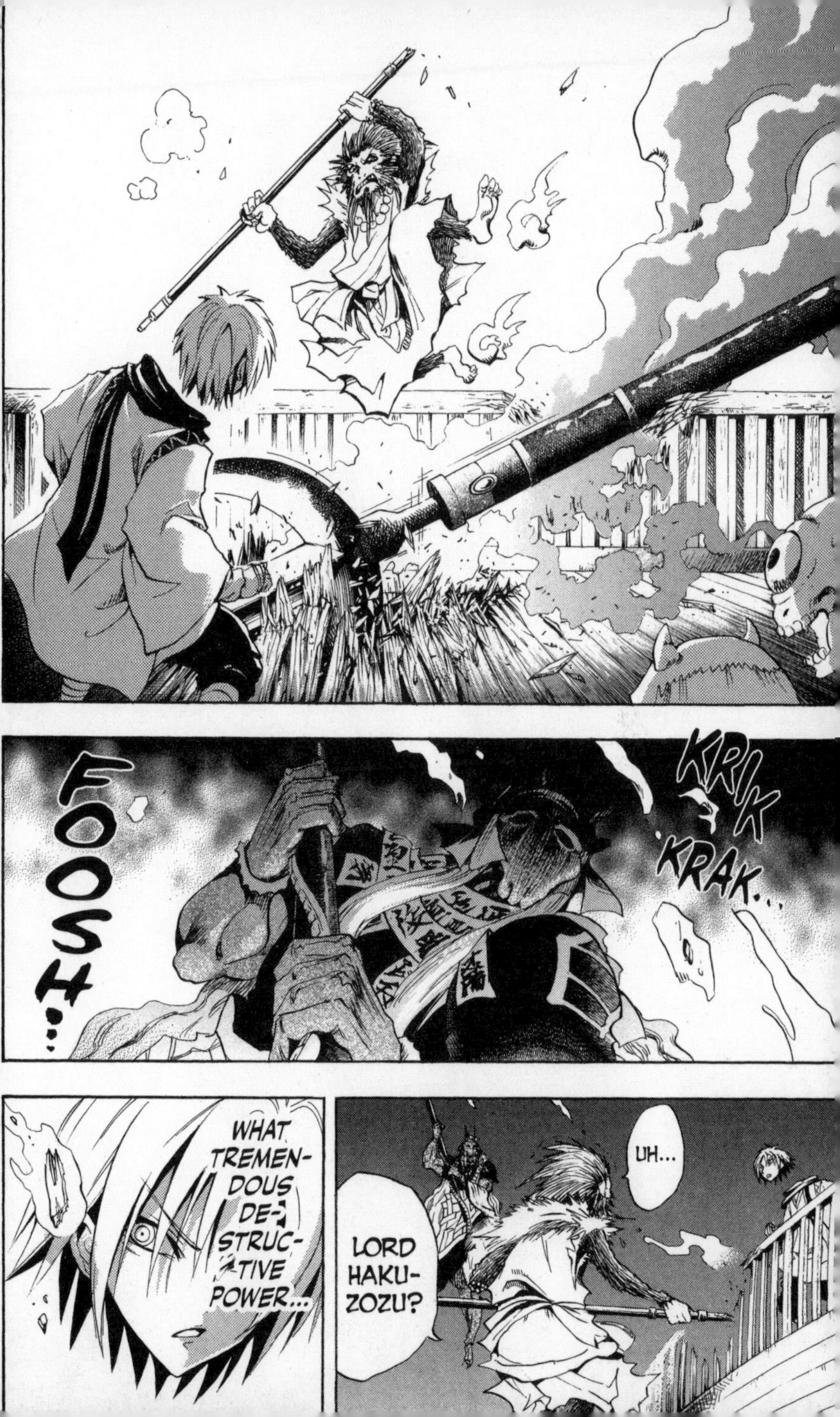
KRIK KRAK...
FOOSH...
UH...
LORD HAKUZOZU?
WHAT TREMENDOUS DESTRUCTIVE POWER...

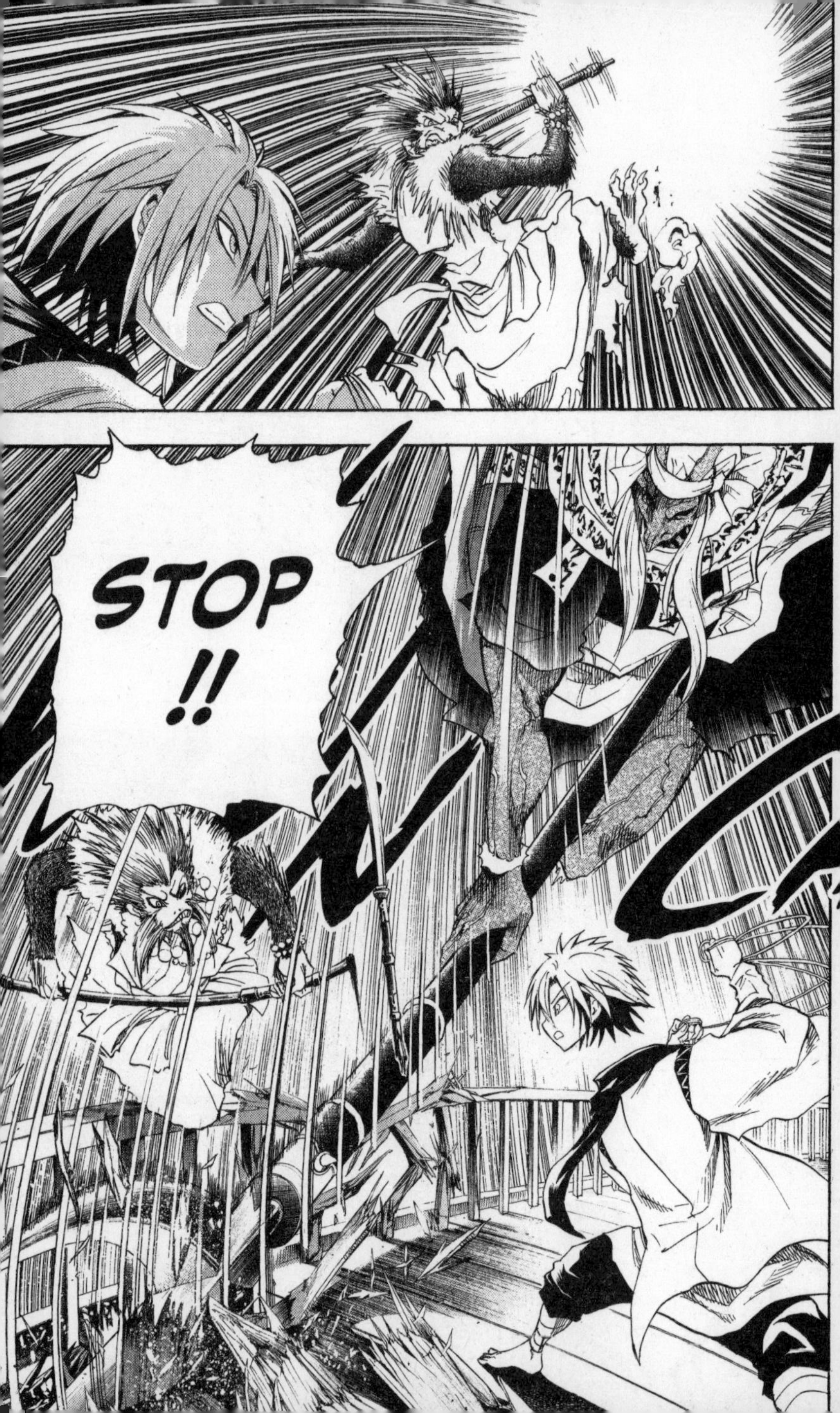
STOP !!

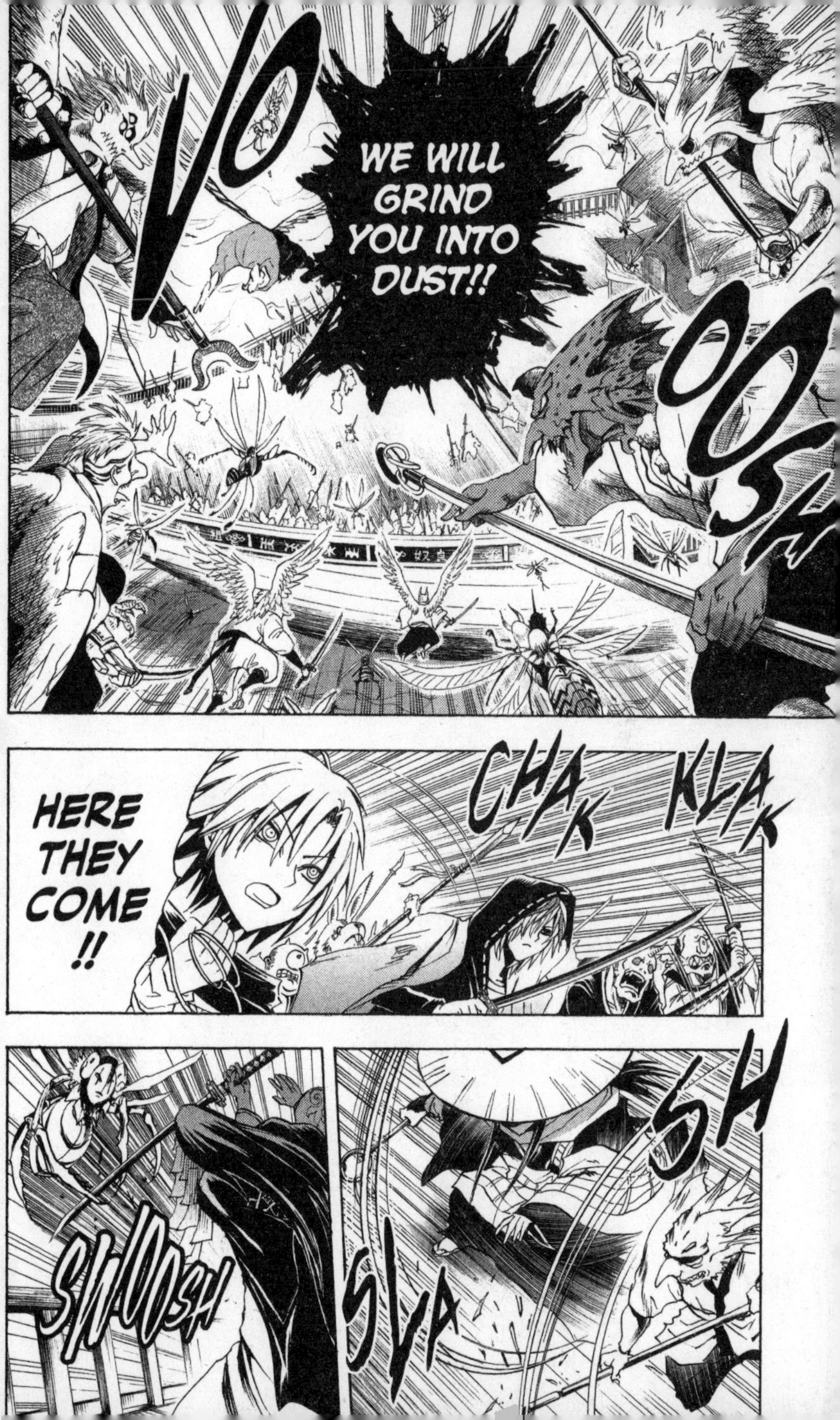
VO
WE WILL GRIND YOU INTO DUST!!
OOSH
CHAK KLAK
HERE THEY COME!!
SH
SHOOSH

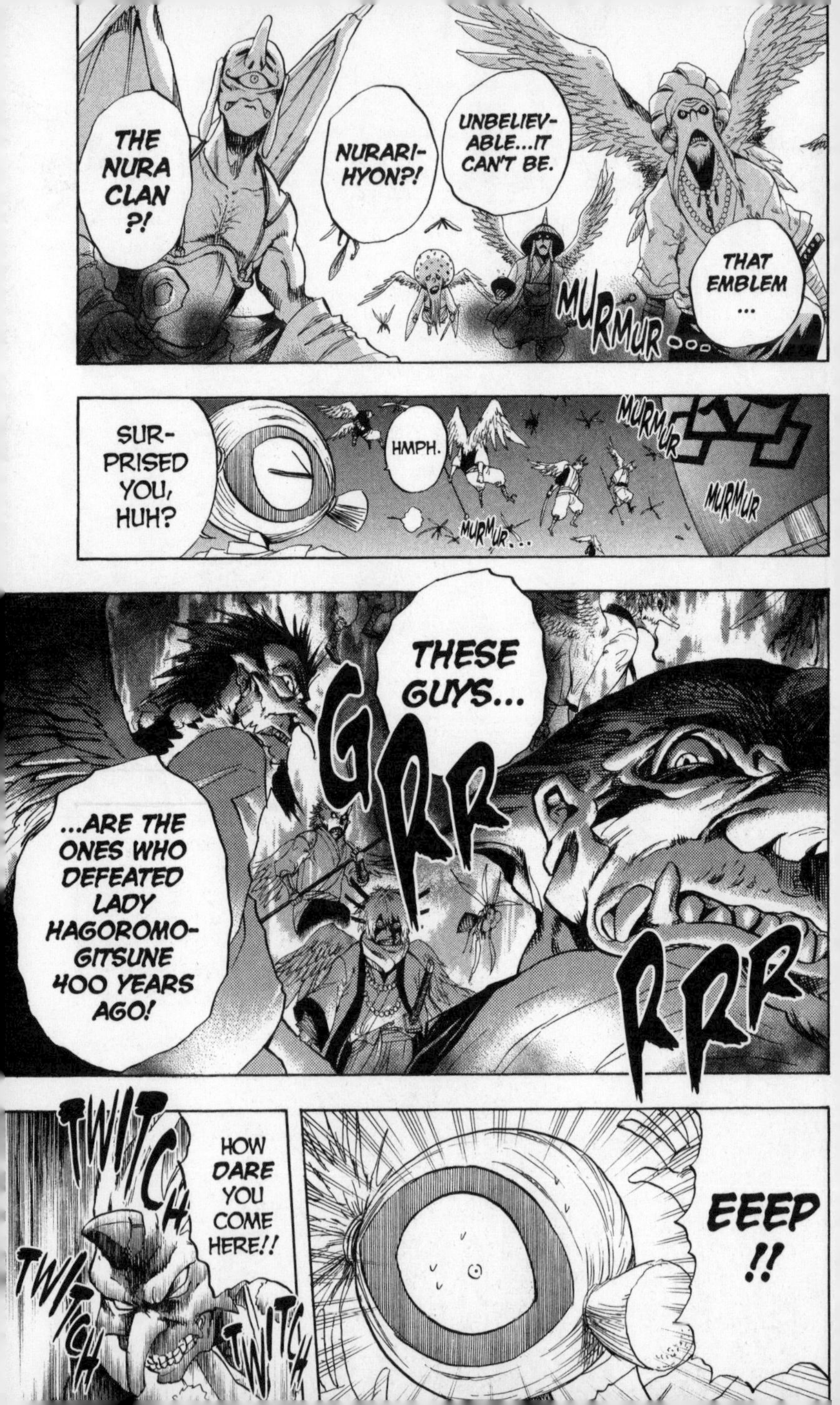
THAT EMBLEM...
UNBELIEVABLE...IT CAN'T BE.
NURARIHYON?!
THE NURA CLAN?!
MURMUR...
MURMUR
MURMUR
HMPH.
MURMUR...
SURPRISED YOU, HUH?
THESE GUYS...
GRRR
RRR
...ARE THE ONES WHO DEFEATED LADY HAGOROMO-GITSUNE 400 YEARS AGO!
EEEP!!
HOW DARE YOU COME HERE!!
TWITCH
TWITCH
TWITCH

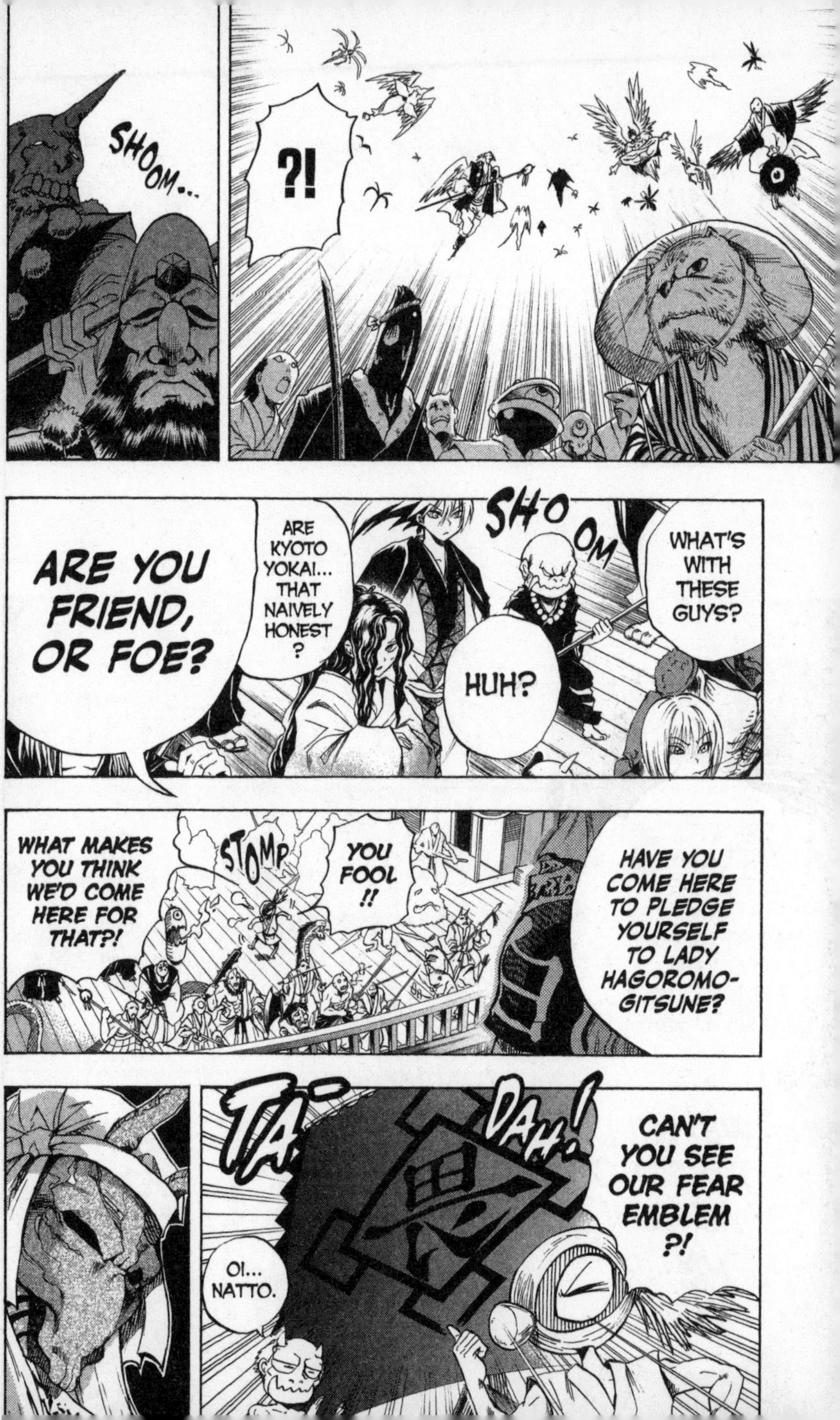
?!
SHOOM...
WHAT'S WITH THESE GUYS?
SHOOM
ARE KYOTO YOKAI... THAT NAIVELY HONEST ?
HUH?
ARE YOU FRIEND, OR FOE?
HAVE YOU COME HERE TO PLEDGE YOURSELF TO LADY HAGOROMO-GITSUNE?
YOU FOOL !!
STOMP
WHAT MAKES YOU THINK WE'D COME HERE FOR THAT?!
TA-DAH!
CAN'T YOU SEE OUR FEAR EMBLEM ?!
OI... NATTO.

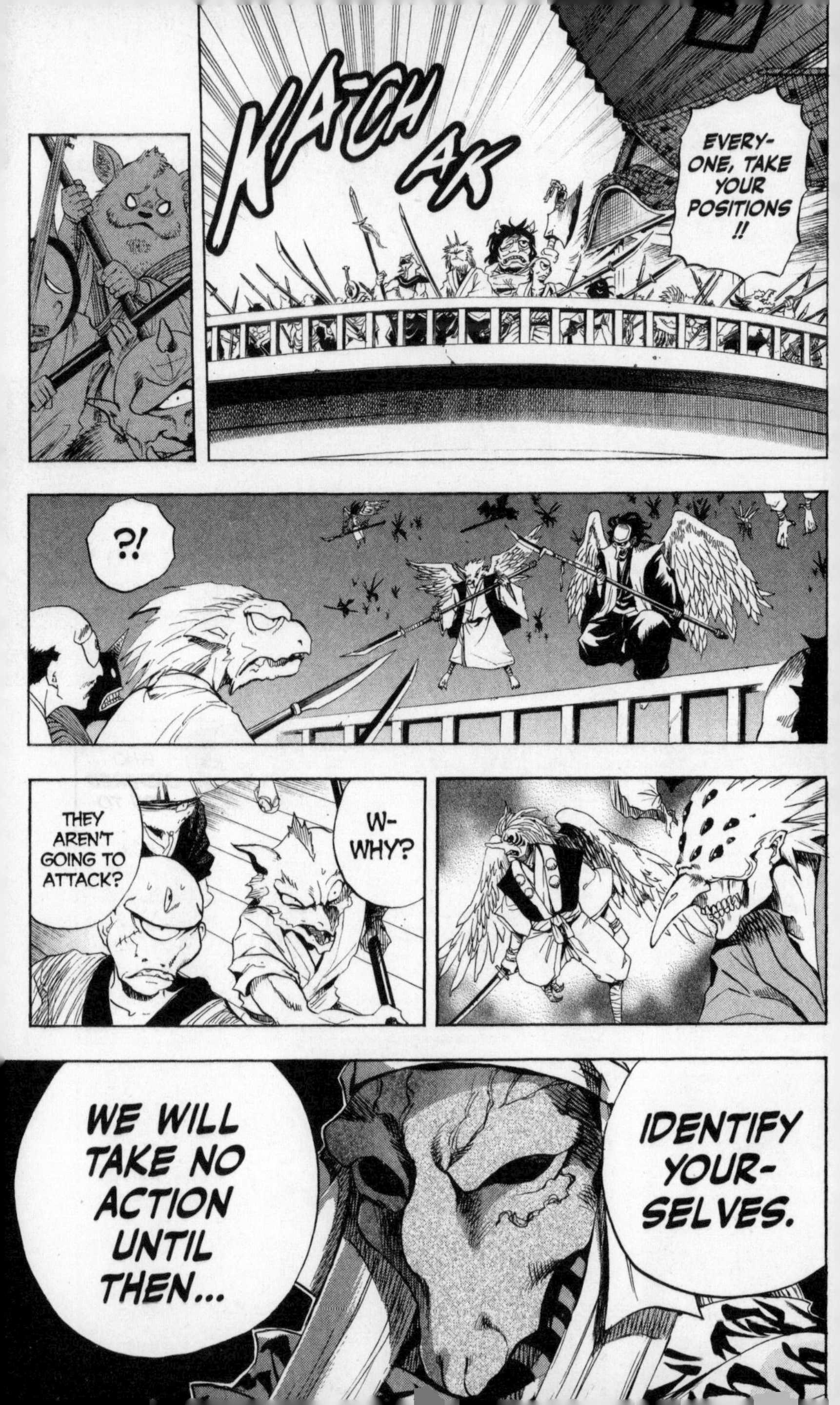
EVERY-ONE, TAKE YOUR POSITIONS!!
KA-CHAK
?!
W-WHY?
THEY AREN'T GOING TO ATTACK?
IDENTIFY YOUR-SELVES.
WE WILL TAKE NO ACTION UNTIL THEN...

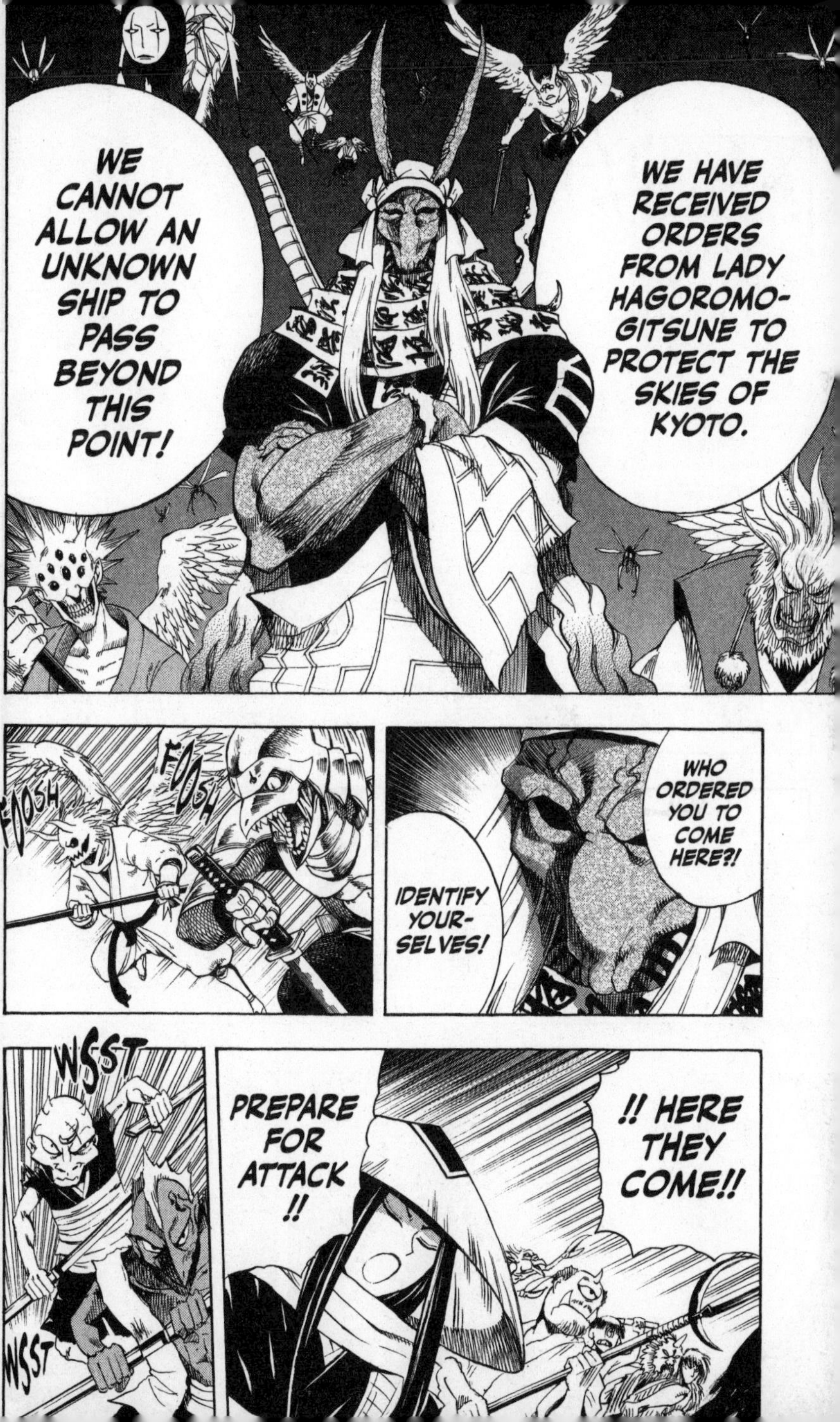
WE HAVE RECEIVED ORDERS FROM LADY HAGOROMO-GITSUNE TO PROTECT THE SKIES OF KYOTO.
WE CANNOT ALLOW AN UNKNOWN SHIP TO PASS BEYOND THIS POINT!
WHO ORDERED YOU TO COME HERE?!
IDENTIFY YOUR-SELVES!
FOOSH
FOOSH
!! HERE THEY COME!!
PREPARE FOR ATTACK !!
WSST
WSST

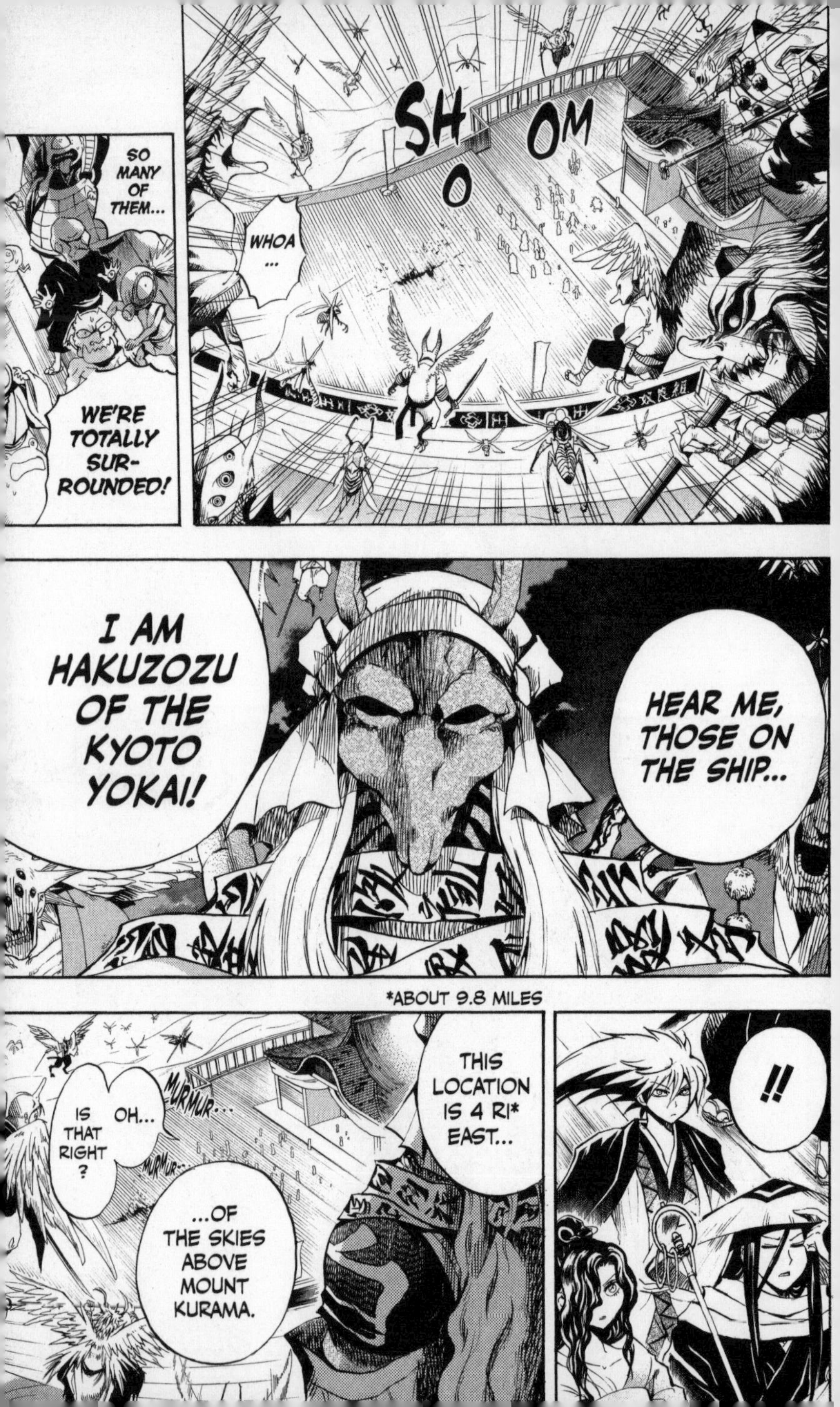
SHOOM
WHOA ...
SO MANY OF THEM...
WE'RE TOTALLY SUR-ROUNDED!
HEAR ME, THOSE ON THE SHIP...
I AM HAKUZOZU OF THE KYOTO YOKAI!
!!
THIS LOCATION IS 4 RI* EAST...
...OF THE SKIES ABOVE MOUNT KURAMA.
OH...
IS THAT RIGHT?
MURMUR...
MURMUR...
*ABOUT 9.8 MILES

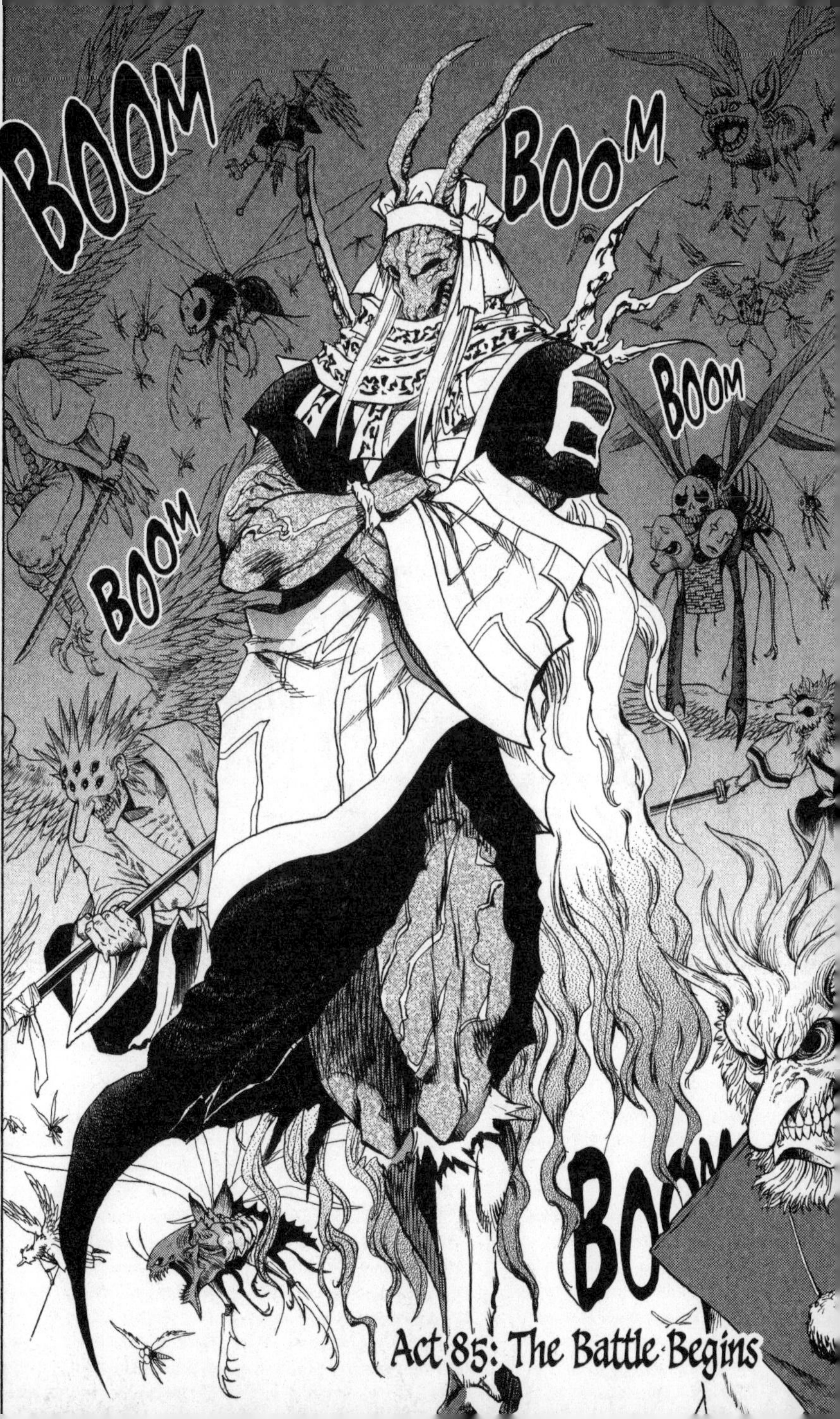
BOOM
BOOM
BOOM
BOOM
BOOM
BOOM

Act 85: The Battle Begins

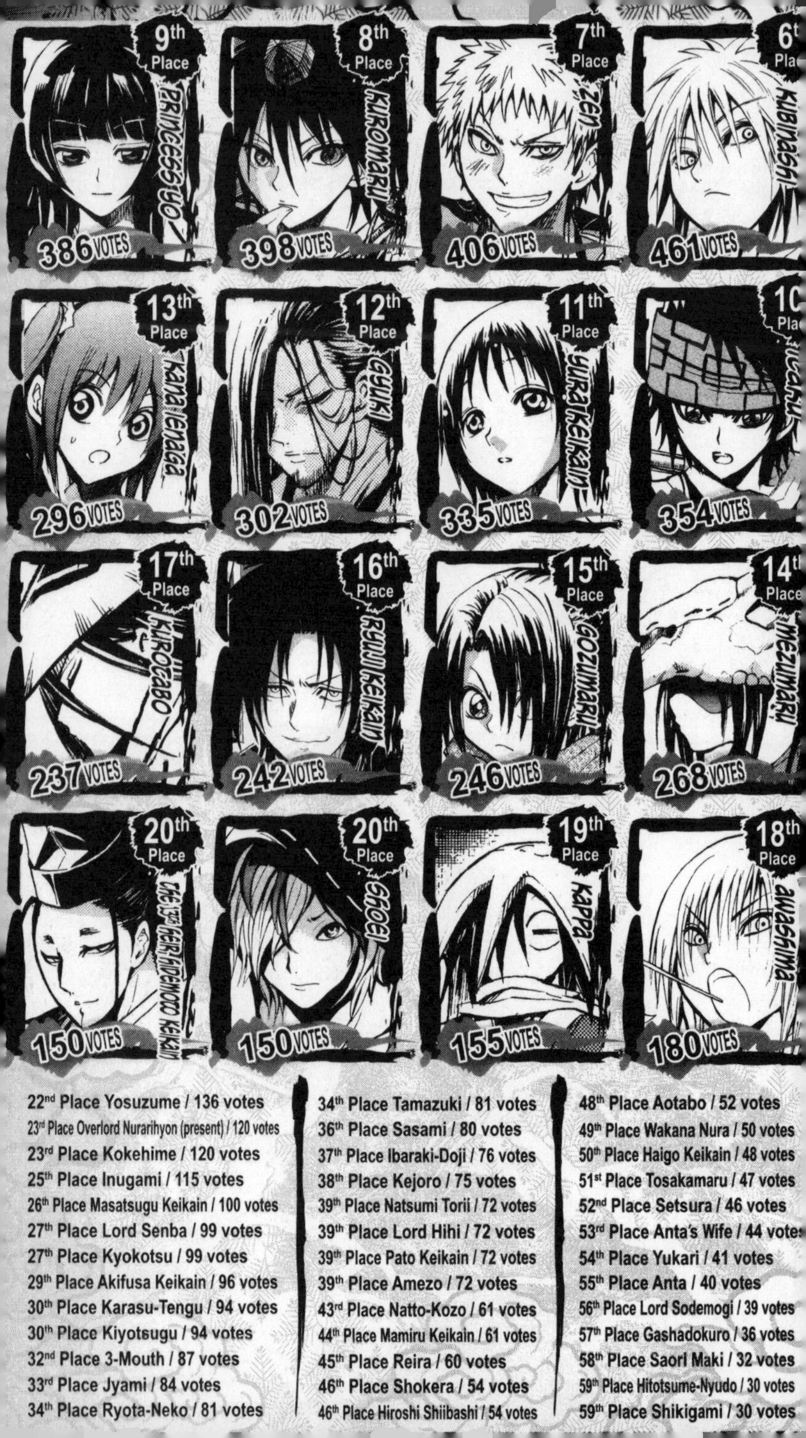
6t
Pla
Kubinashi
461 VOTES
7th
Place
Zen
406 VOTES
8th
Place
Kuromaru
398 VOTES
9th
Place
Princess Yo
386 VOTES
1C
Pla
354 VOTES
11th
Place
Yura Keikain
335 VOTES
12th
Place
Gyuki
302 VOTES
13th
Place
Kana Ienaga
296 VOTES
14t
Place
Mezumaru
268 VOTES
15th
Place
Gozumaru
246 VOTES
16th
Place
Ryuji Keikain
242 VOTES
17th
Place
Kurotabo
237 VOTES
18th
Place
Awashima
180 VOTES
19th
Place
Kappa
155 VOTES
20th
Place
Shoei
150 VOTES
20th
Place
The 13th Heir Hidemoto Keikain
150 VOTES

22nd Place Yosuzume / 136 votes
23rd Place Overlord Nurarihyon (present) / 120 votes
23rd Place Kokehime / 120 votes
25th Place Inugami / 115 votes
26th Place Masatsugu Keikain / 100 votes
27th Place Lord Senba / 99 votes
27th Place Kyokotsu / 99 votes
29th Place Akifusa Keikain / 96 votes
30th Place Karasu-Tengu / 94 votes
30th Place Kiyotsugu / 94 votes
32nd Place 3-Mouth / 87 votes
33rd Place Jyami / 84 votes
34th Place Ryota-Neko / 81 votes

34th Place Tamazuki / 81 votes
36th Place Sasami / 80 votes
37th Place Ibaraki-Doji / 76 votes
38th Place Kejoro / 75 votes
39th Place Natsumi Torii / 72 votes
39th Place Lord Hihi / 72 votes
39th Place Pato Keikain / 72 votes
39th Place Amezo / 72 votes
43rd Place Natto-Kozo / 61 votes
44th Place Mamiru Keikain / 61 votes
45th Place Reira / 60 votes
46th Place Shokera / 54 votes
46th Place Hiroshi Shiibashi / 54 votes

48th Place Aotabo / 52 votes
49th Place Wakana Nura / 50 votes
50th Place Haigo Keikain / 48 votes
51st Place Tosakamaru / 47 votes
52nd Place Setsura / 46 votes
53rd Place Anta's Wife / 44 vote
54th Place Yukari / 41 votes
55th Place Anta / 40 votes
56th Place Lord Sodemogi / 39 votes
57th Place Gashadokuro / 36 votes
58th Place Saori Maki / 32 votes
59th Place Hitotsume-Nyudo / 30 votes
59th Place Shikigami / 30 votes

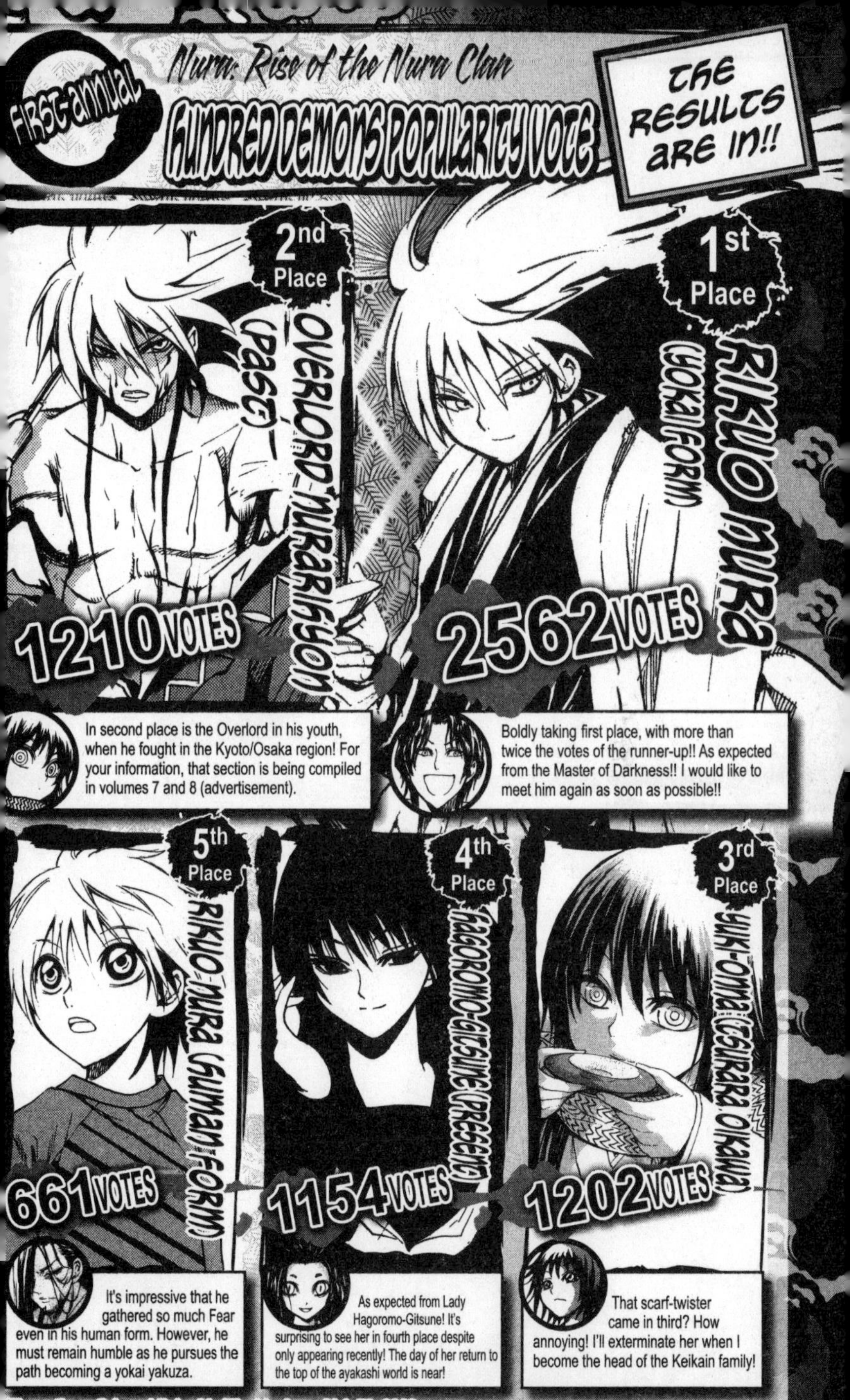

FIRST ANNUAL
Nura: Rise of the Nura Clan
HUNDRED DEMONS POPULARITY VOTE
THE RESULTS ARE IN!!
1st Place
RIKUO NURA (YOKAI FORM)
2562 VOTES
Boldly taking first place, with more than twice the votes of the runner-up!! As expected from the Master of Darkness!! I would like to meet him again as soon as possible!!
2nd Place
OVERLORD NURARIHYON (PAST)
1210 VOTES
In second place is the Overlord in his youth, when he fought in the Kyoto/Osaka region! For your information, that section is being compiled in volumes 7 and 8 (advertisement).
3rd Place
YUKI-ONNA (TSURARA OIKAWA)
1202 VOTES
That scarf-twister came in third? How annoying! I'll exterminate her when I become the head of the Keikain family!
4th Place
HAGOROMO-GITSUNE (PRESENT)
1154 VOTES
As expected from Lady Hagoromo-Gitsune! It's surprising to see her in fourth place despite only appearing recently! The day of her return to the top of the ayakashi world is near!
5th Place
RIKUO NURA (HUMAN FORM)
661 VOTES
It's impressive that he gathered so much Fear even in his human form. However, he must remain humble as he pursues the path becoming a yokai yakuza.

*From the article published in Weekly Jump Vol. 53, 2009.

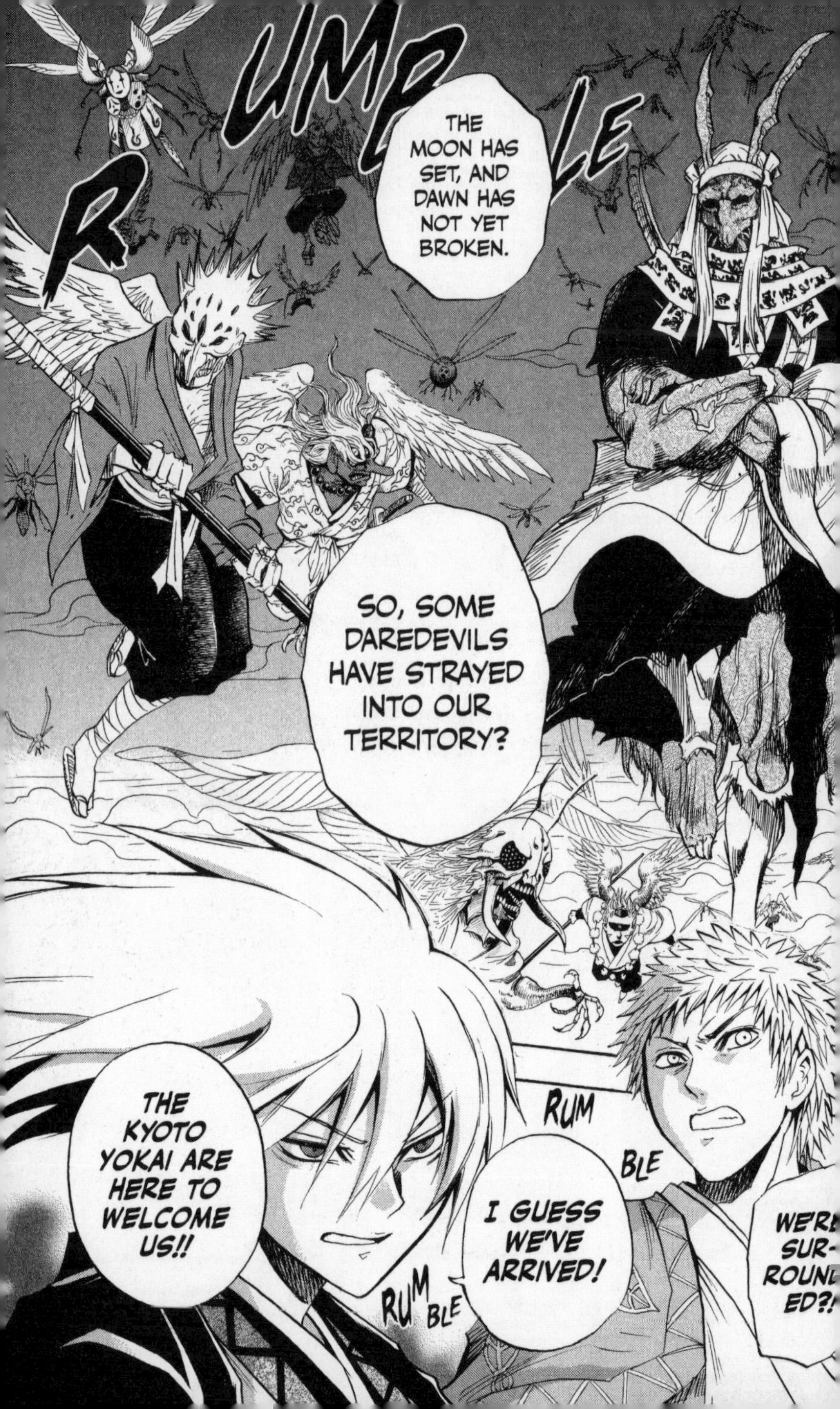
RUMBLE
THE MOON HAS SET, AND DAWN HAS NOT YET BROKEN.
SO, SOME DAREDEVILS HAVE STRAYED INTO OUR TERRITORY?
WE'RE SUR-ROUNDED?!
RUMBLE
I GUESS WE'VE ARRIVED!
RUMBLE
THE KYOTO YOKAI ARE HERE TO WELCOME US!!

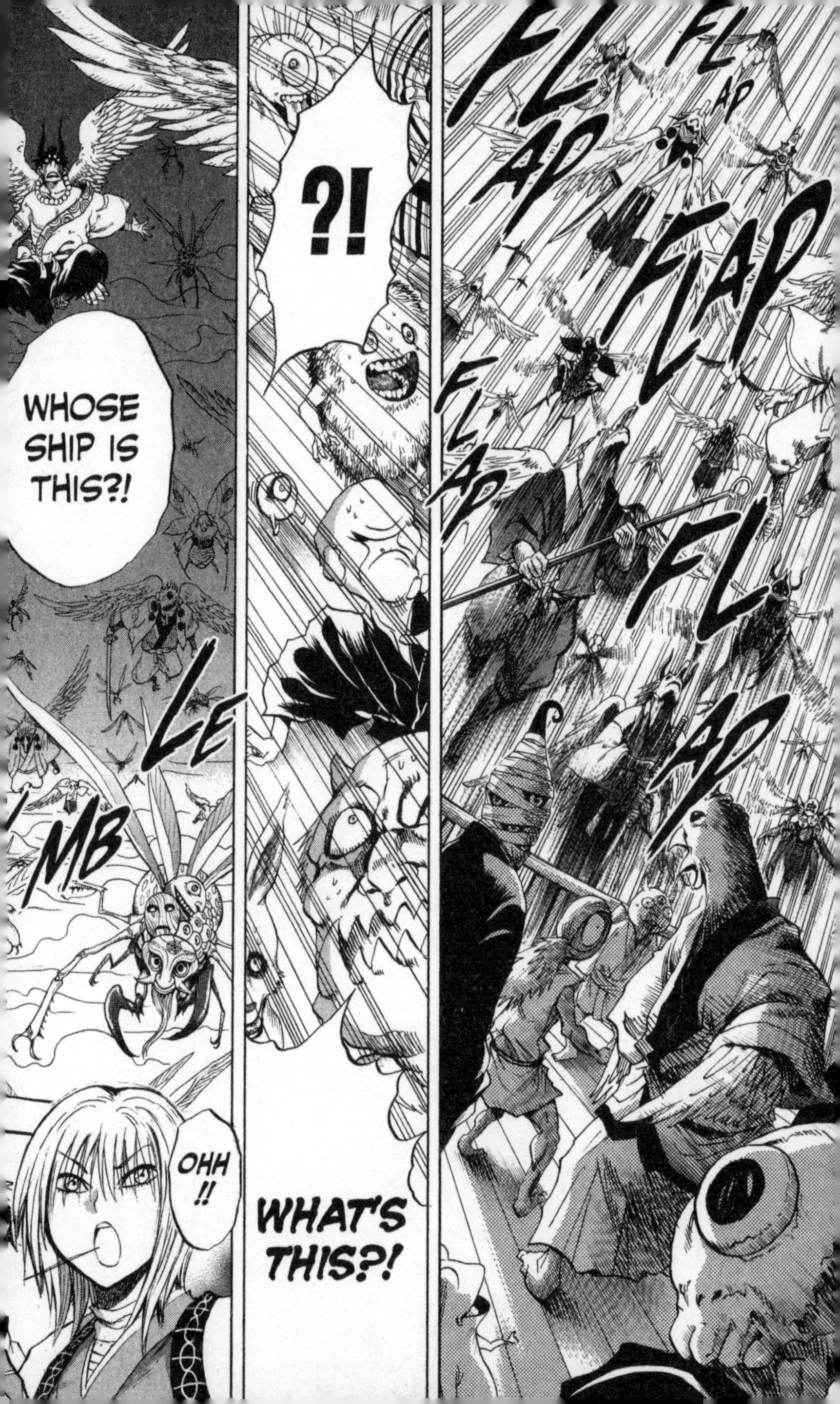

FLAP
FLAP
FLAP
FLAP
FLAP
FLAP
?!
WHAT'S THIS?!
WHOSE SHIP IS THIS?!
LE
MB
OHH!!

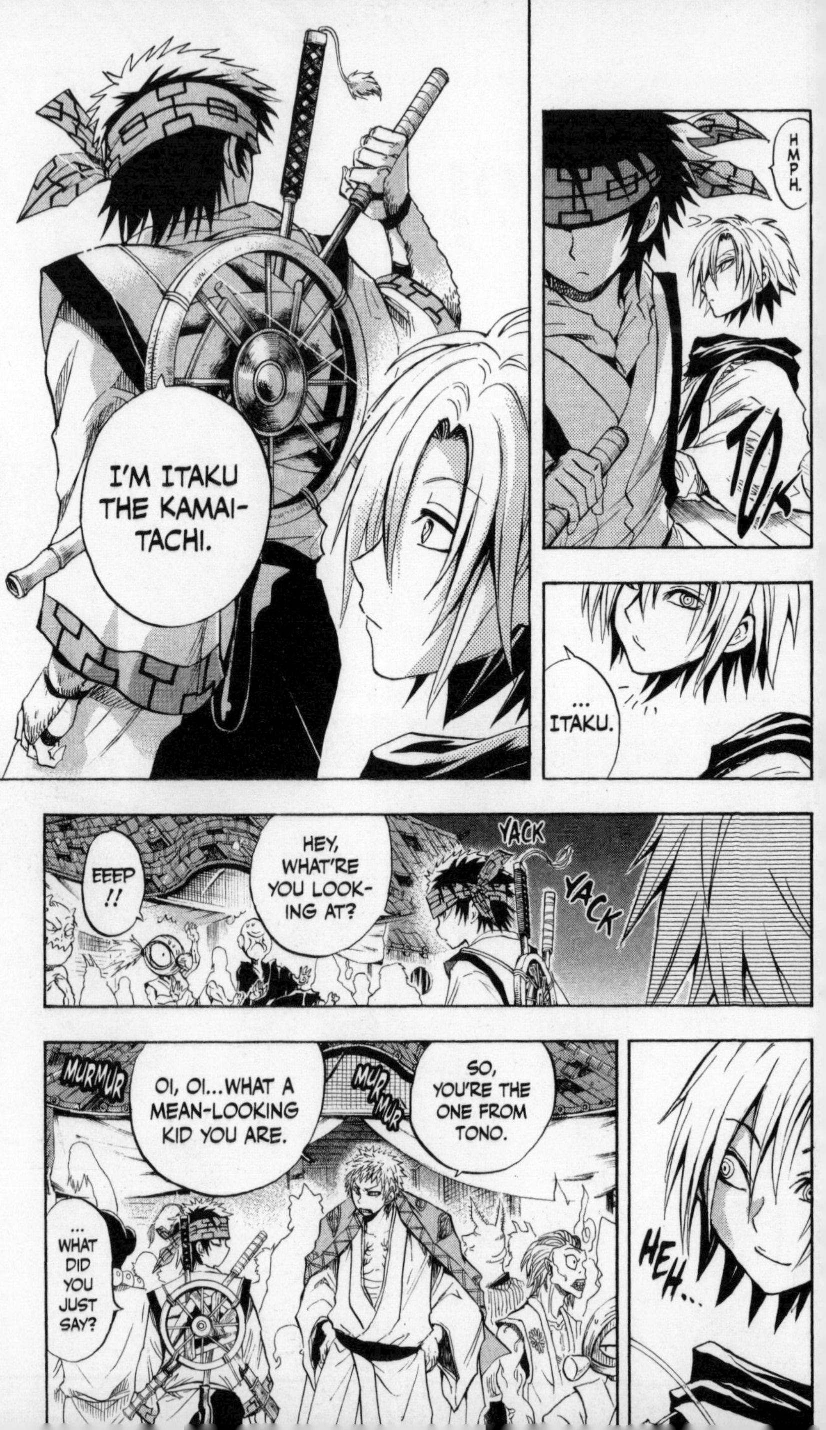
HMPH.
TOK
...ITAKU.
I'M ITAKU THE KAMAI-TACHI.
YACK
YACK
HEY, WHAT'RE YOU LOOK-ING AT?
EEEP!!
HEH...
SO, YOU'RE THE ONE FROM TONO.
MURMUR
OI, OI...WHAT A MEAN-LOOKING KID YOU ARE.
MURMUR
...WHAT DID YOU JUST SAY?

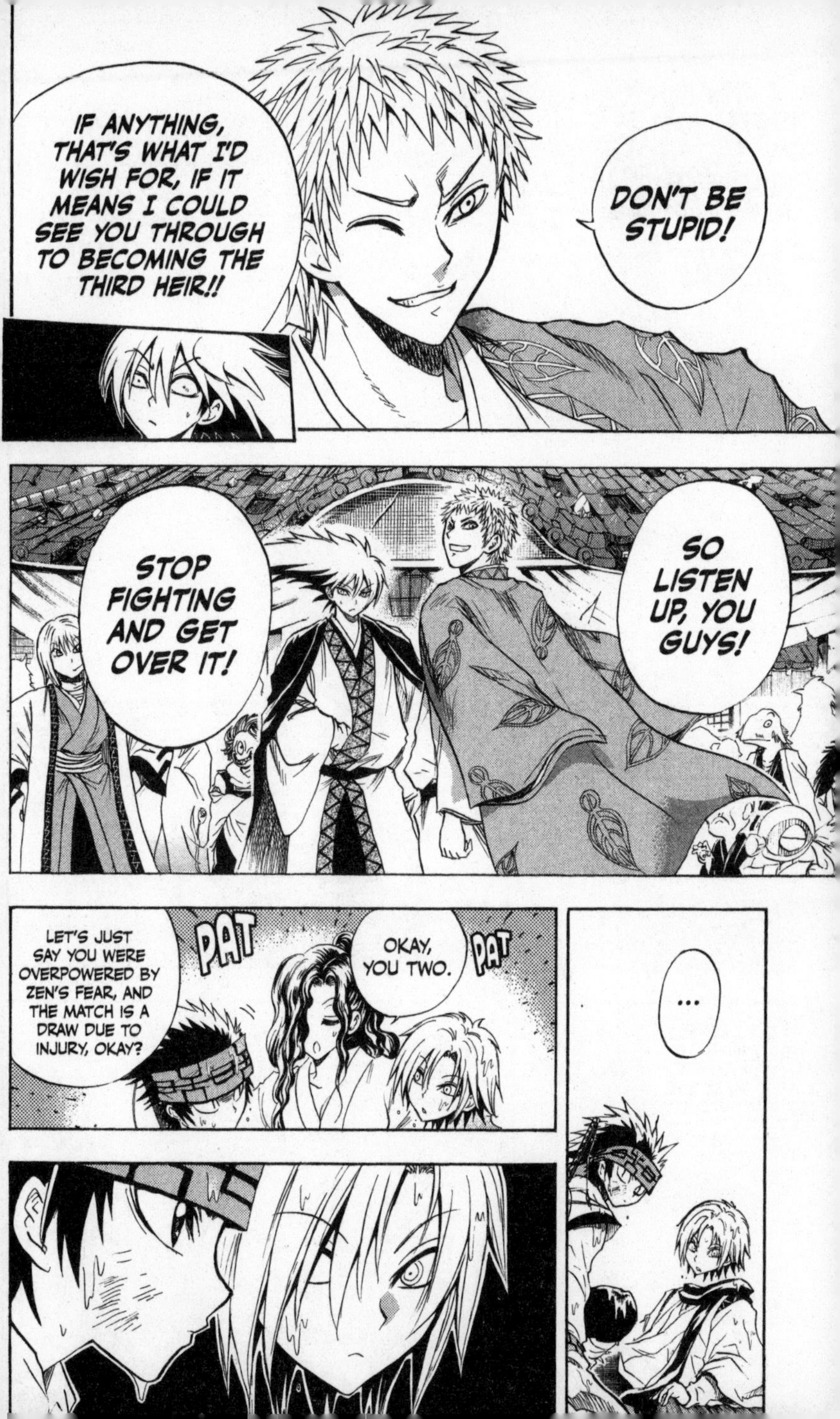
DON'T BE STUPID!
IF ANYTHING, THAT'S WHAT I'D WISH FOR, IF IT MEANS I COULD SEE YOU THROUGH TO BECOMING THE THIRD HEIR!!
SO LISTEN UP, YOU GUYS!
STOP FIGHTING AND GET OVER IT!
...
PAT
OKAY, YOU TWO.
PAT
LET'S JUST SAY YOU WERE OVERPOWERED BY ZEN'S FEAR, AND THE MATCH IS A DRAW DUE TO INJURY, OKAY?

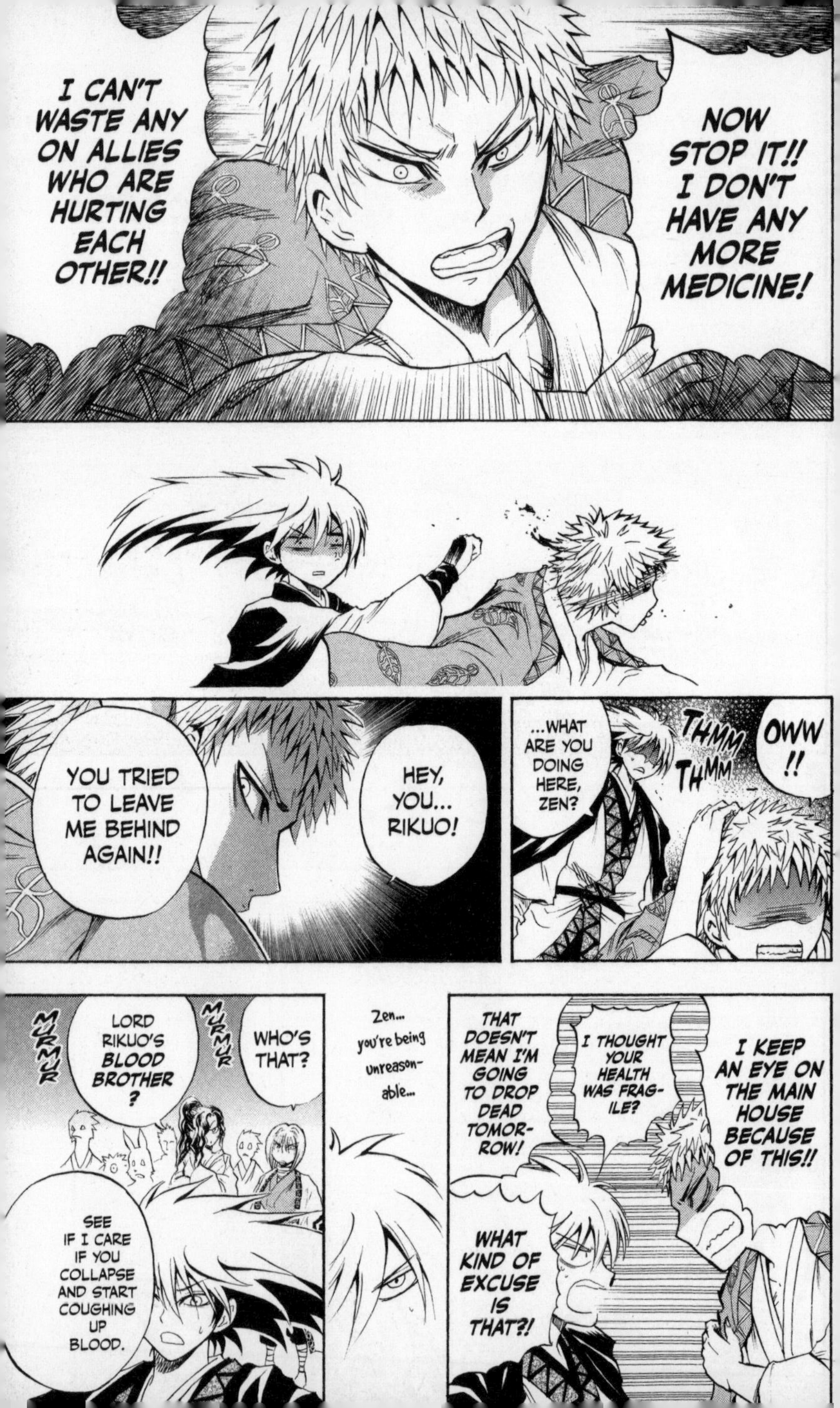
NOW STOP IT!! I DON'T HAVE ANY MORE MEDICINE!
I CAN'T WASTE ANY ON ALLIES WHO ARE HURTING EACH OTHER!!
OWW!!
THMM THMM
...WHAT ARE YOU DOING HERE, ZEN?
HEY, YOU... RIKUO!
YOU TRIED TO LEAVE ME BEHIND AGAIN!!
I KEEP AN EYE ON THE MAIN HOUSE BECAUSE OF THIS!!
I THOUGHT YOUR HEALTH WAS FRAGILE?
THAT DOESN'T MEAN I'M GOING TO DROP DEAD TOMORROW!
WHAT KIND OF EXCUSE IS THAT?!
Zen... you're being unreasonable...
WHO'S THAT?
MURMUR
LORD RIKUO'S BLOOD BROTHER?
MURMUR
SEE IF I CARE IF YOU COLLAPSE AND START COUGHING UP BLOOD.

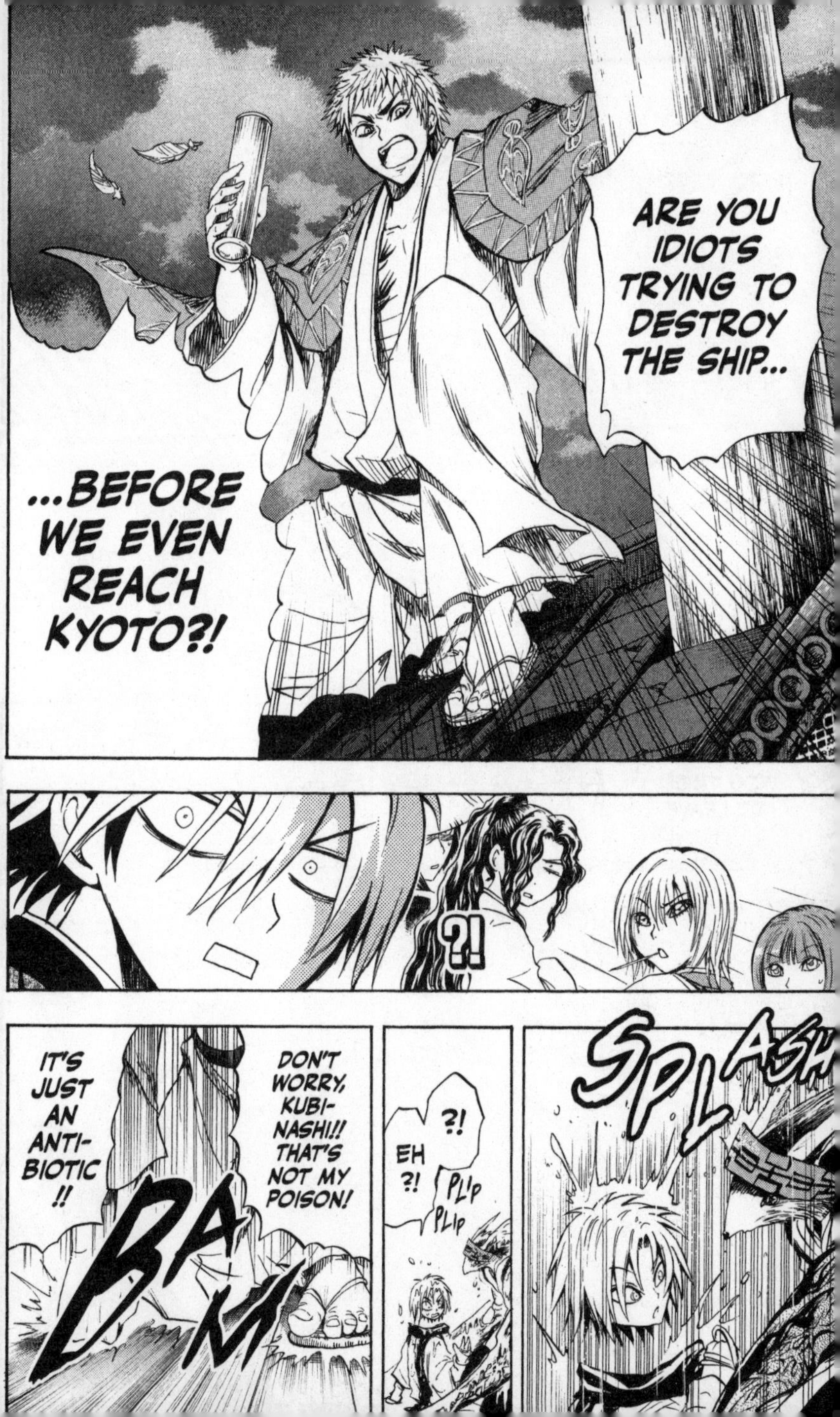
ARE YOU IDIOTS TRYING TO DESTROY THE SHIP...
...BEFORE WE EVEN REACH KYOTO?!
?!
SPLASH
?!
EH ?!
PLIP PLIP
DON'T WORRY, KUBI-NASHI!! THAT'S NOT MY POISON!
IT'S JUST AN ANTI-BIOTIC !!
BAM

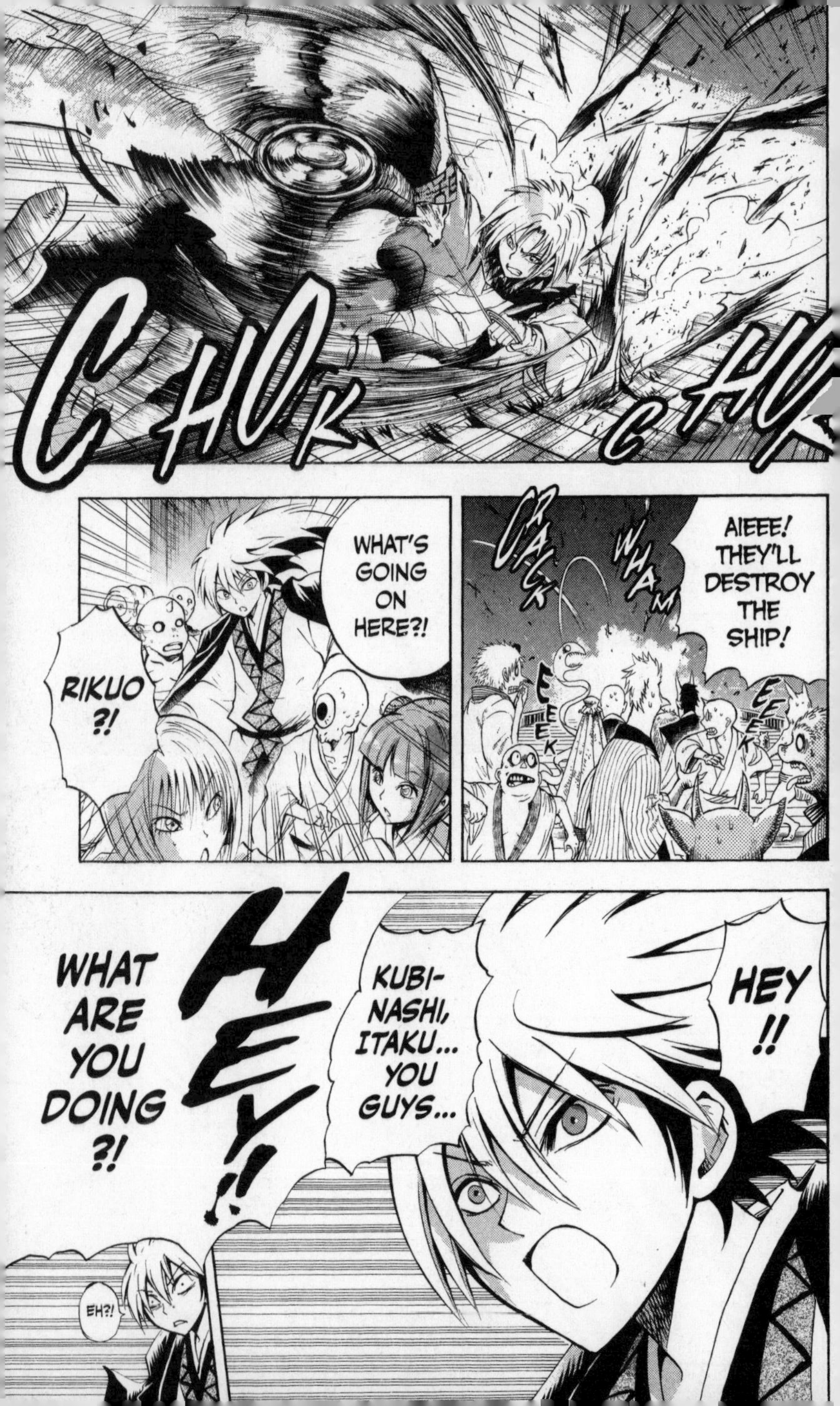
CHOK
CHUK
AIEEE! THEY'LL DESTROY THE SHIP!
WHAM
CRACK
EEEK
EEEK
WHAT'S GOING ON HERE?!
RIKUO ?!
HEY !!
KUBI-NASHI, ITAKU... YOU GUYS...
HEY!!
WHAT ARE YOU DOING ?!
EH?!

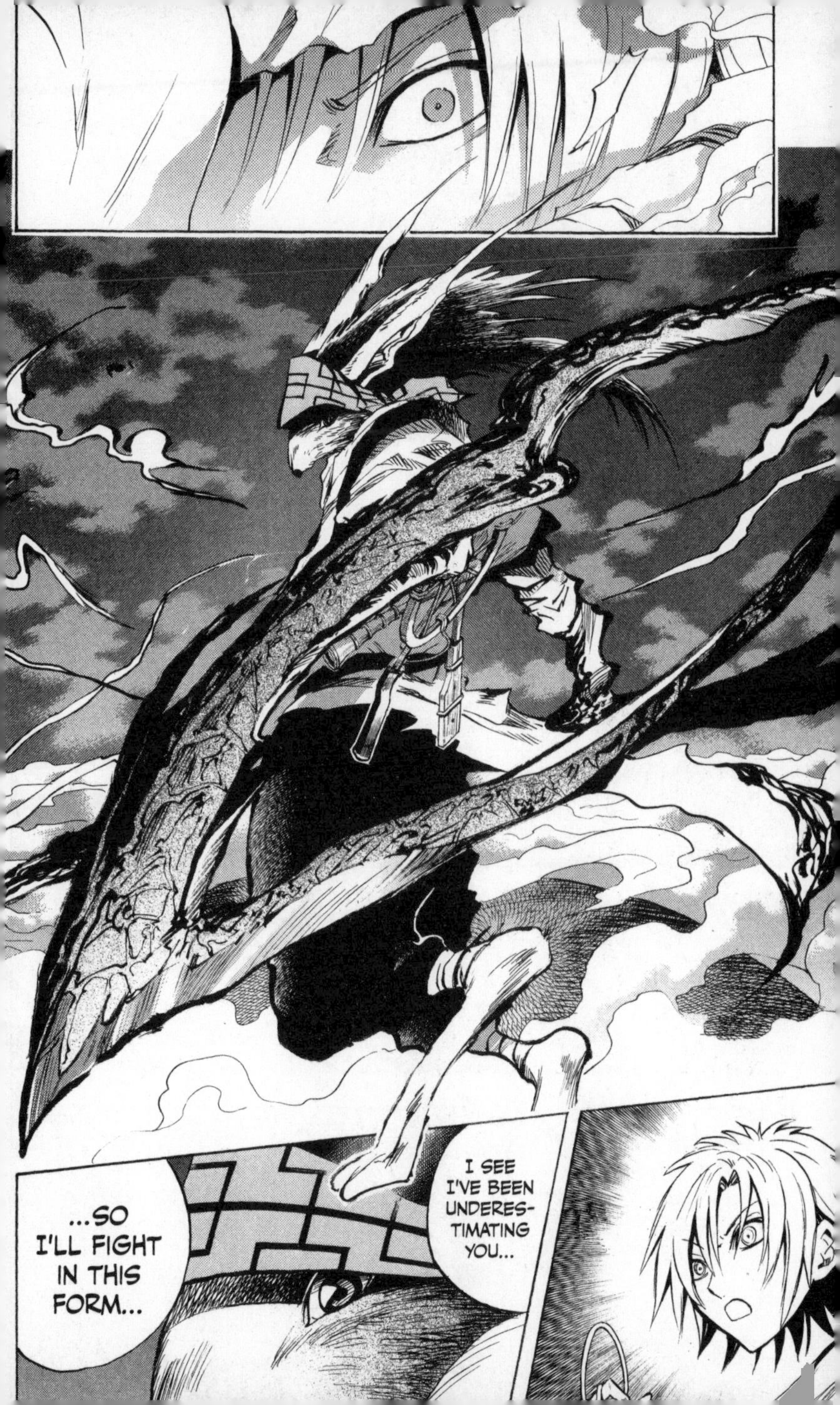
I SEE I'VE BEEN UNDERES-TIMATING YOU...
...SO I'LL FIGHT IN THIS FORM...

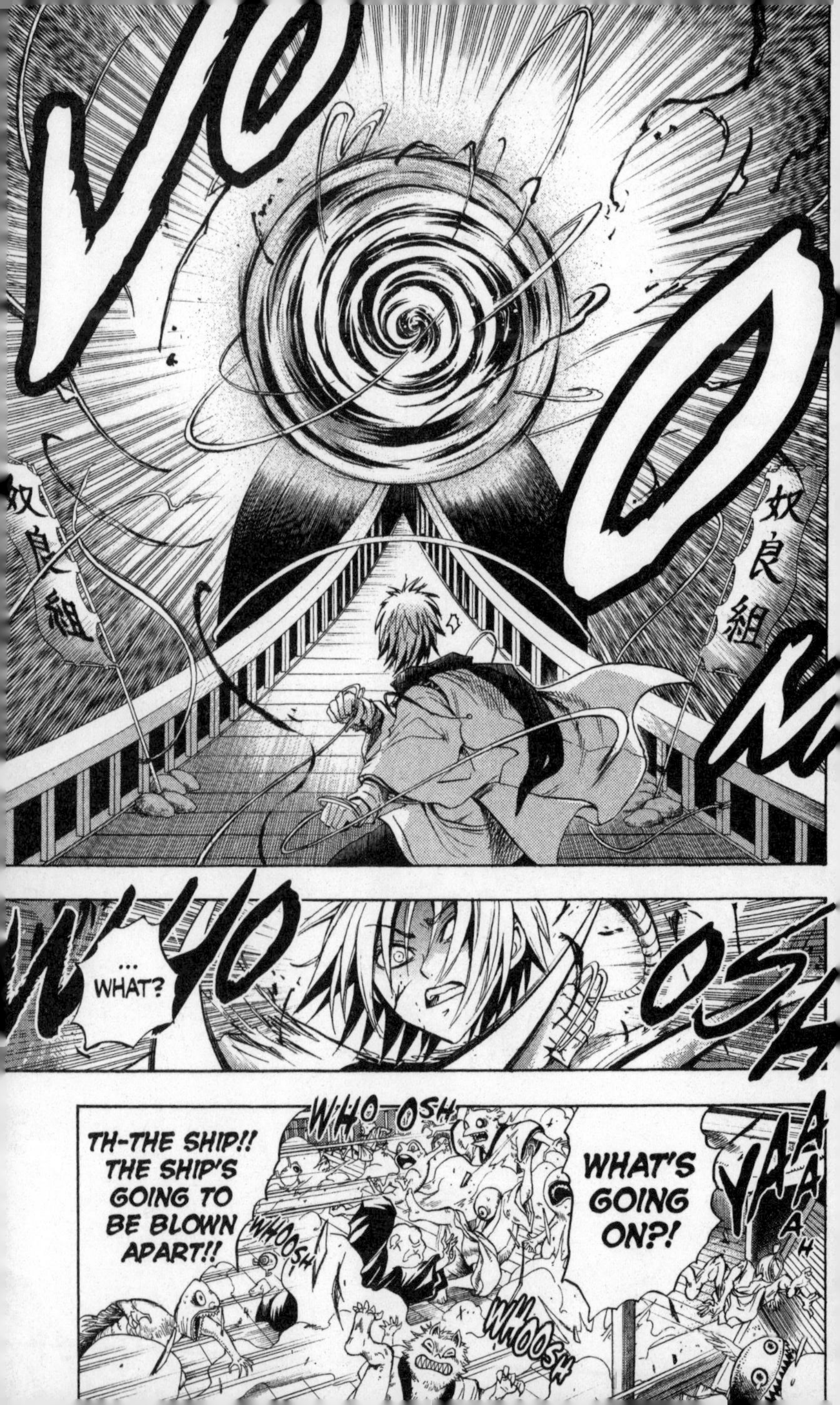
奴良組
奴良組
WHOOSH
... WHAT?
YAAAAAH
WHAT'S GOING ON?!
WHOOSH
TH-THE SHIP!! THE SHIP'S GOING TO BE BLOWN APART!!
WHOOSH
WHOOSH

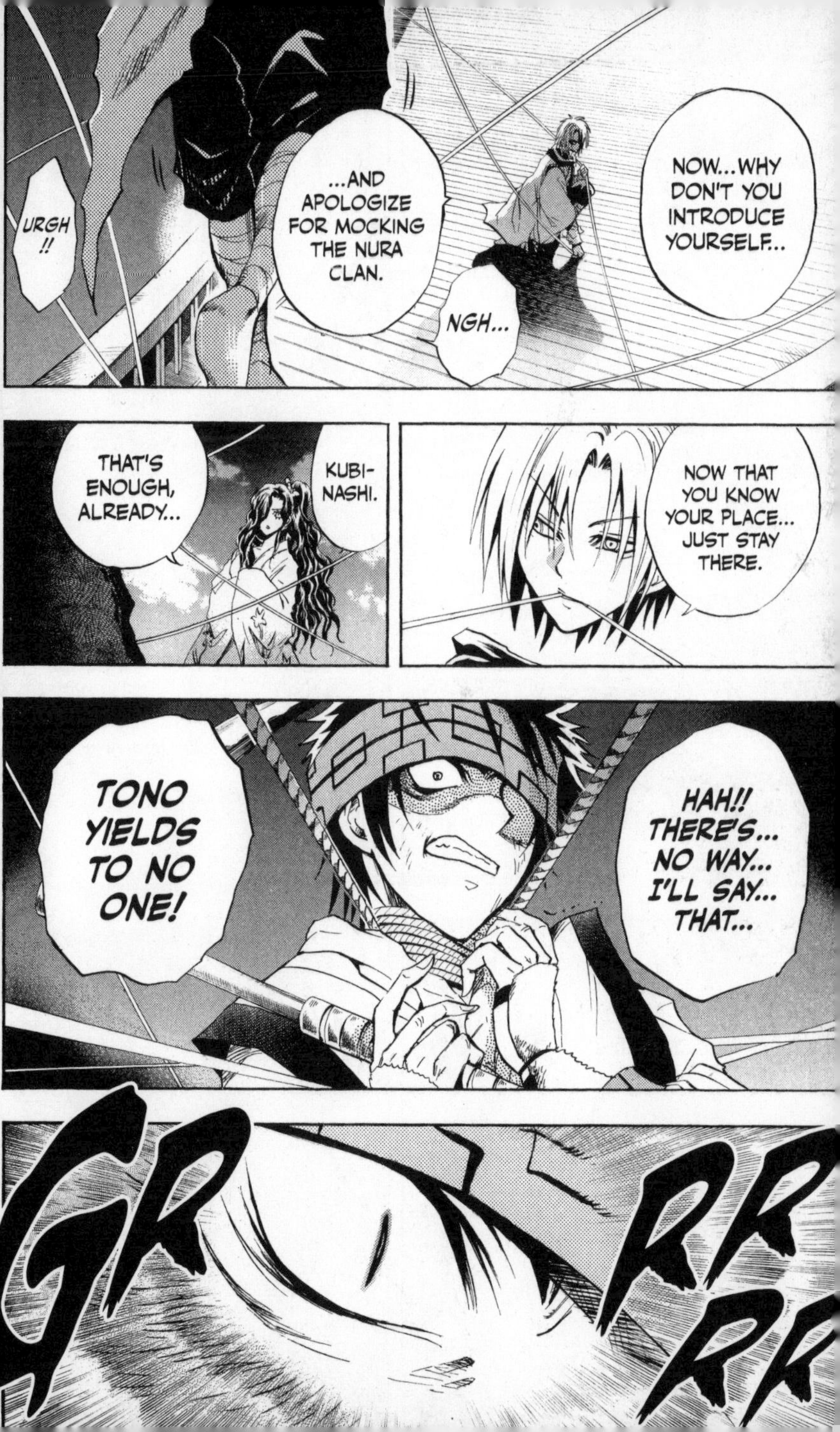
NOW...WHY DON'T YOU INTRODUCE YOURSELF...
NGH...
...AND APOLOGIZE FOR MOCKING THE NURA CLAN.
URGH !!
NOW THAT YOU KNOW YOUR PLACE... JUST STAY THERE.
KUBI-NASHI.
THAT'S ENOUGH, ALREADY...
HAH!! THERE'S... NO WAY... I'LL SAY... THAT...
TONO YIELDS TO NO ONE!
GRRRRR

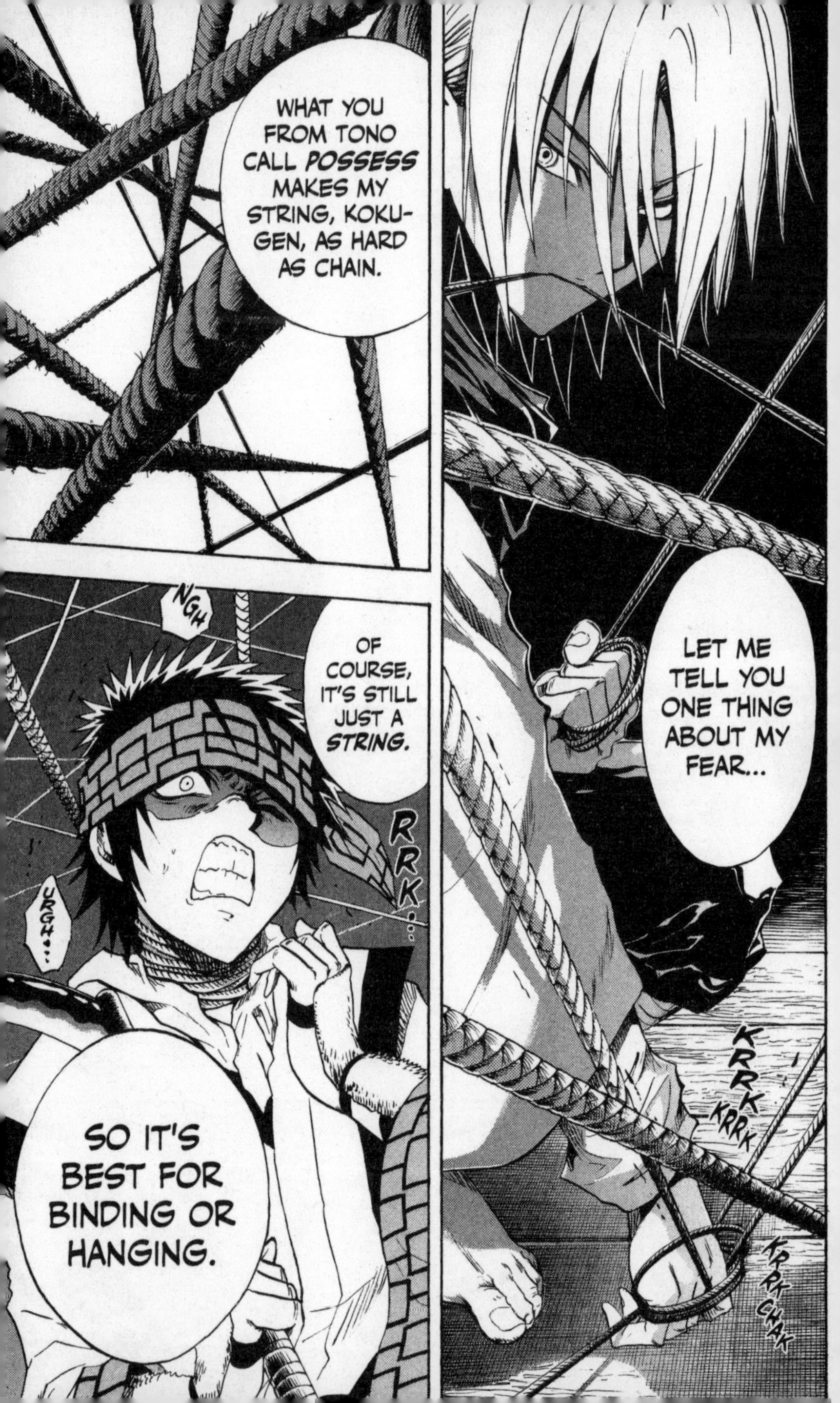
LET ME TELL YOU ONE THING ABOUT MY FEAR...
KRRK KRRK
KRRK CHAK
WHAT YOU FROM TONO CALL *POSSESS* MAKES MY STRING, KOKU-GEN, AS HARD AS CHAIN.
NGH
OF COURSE, IT'S STILL JUST A *STRING.*
RRRK...
URGH...
SO IT'S BEST FOR BINDING OR HANGING.

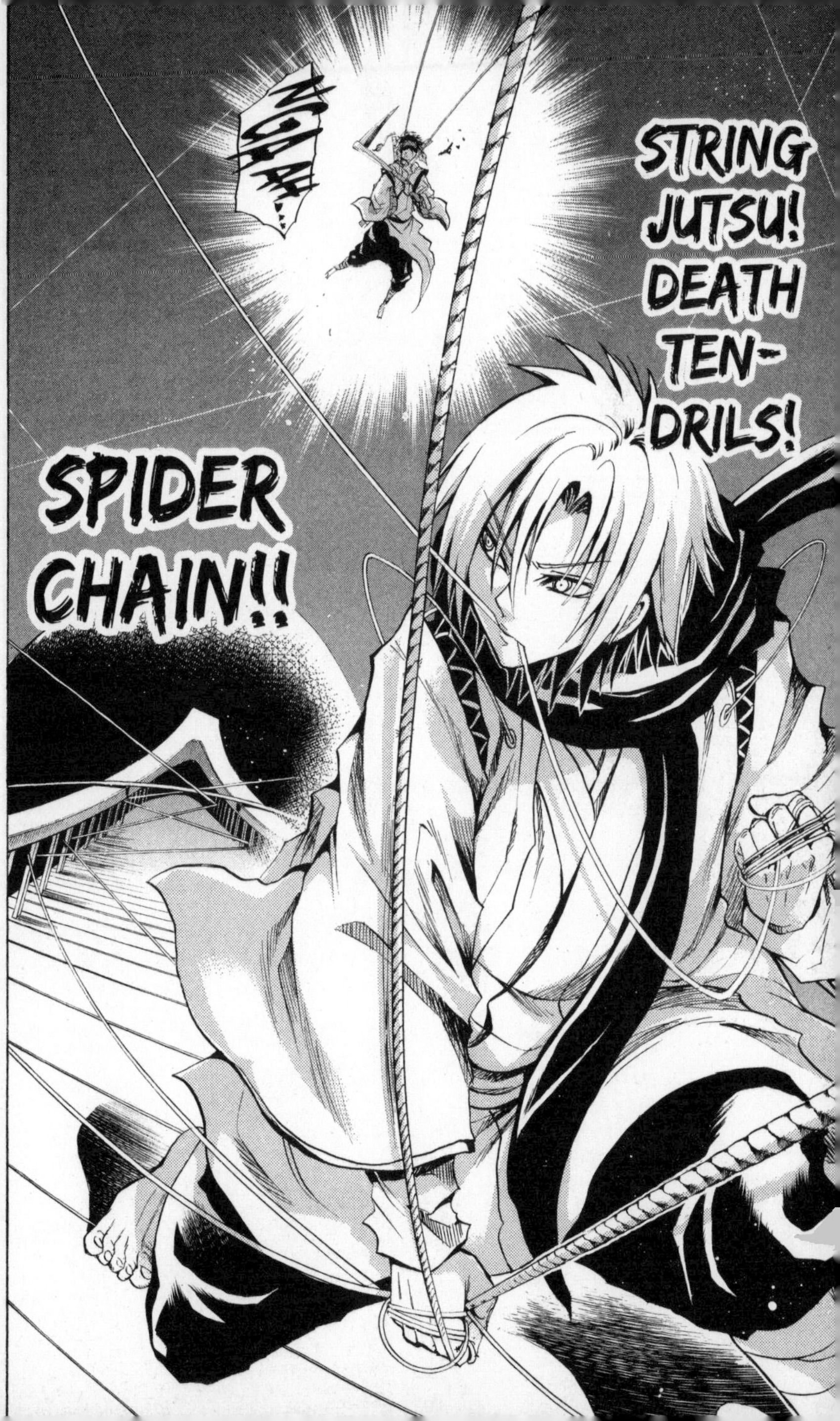
STRING JUTSU! DEATH TEN-DRILS!
NGAAH...
SPIDER CHAIN!!

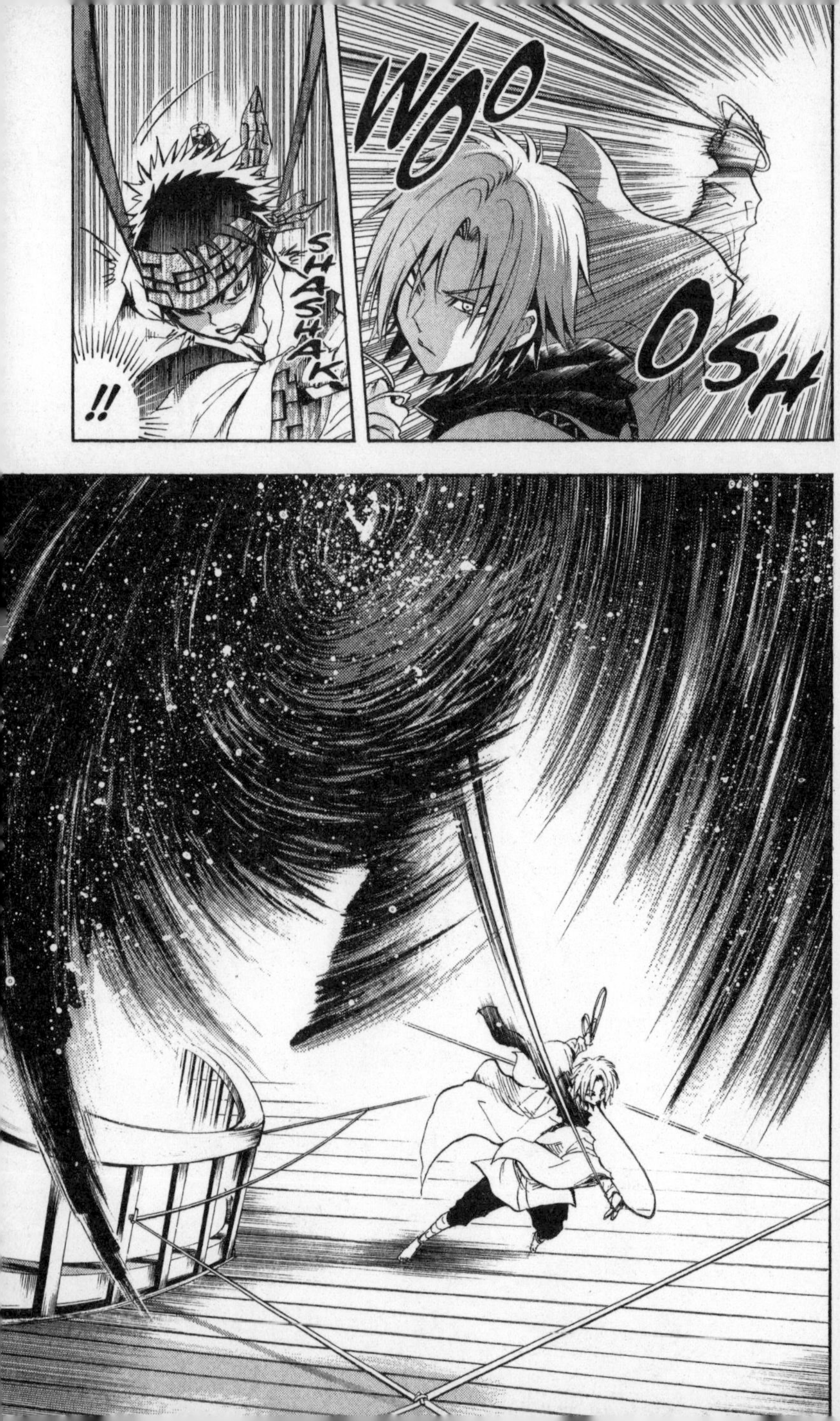
WOO
OSH
SHASHAK
!!

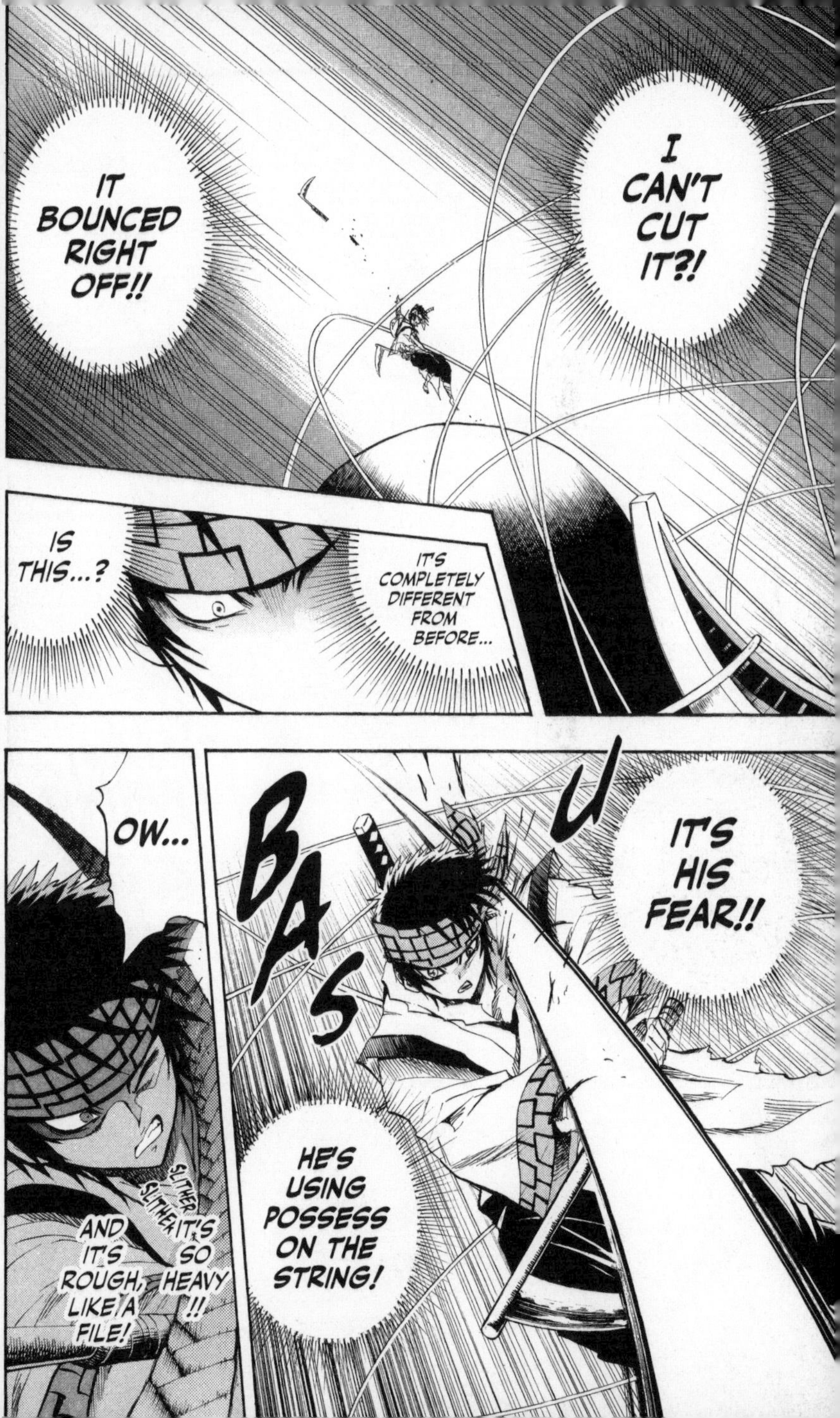
I CAN'T CUT IT?!
IT BOUNCED RIGHT OFF!!
IT'S COMPLETELY DIFFERENT FROM BEFORE...
IS THIS...?
BASU
IT'S HIS FEAR!!
HE'S USING POSSESS ON THE STRING!
OW...
SLITHER SLITHER
IT'S SO HEAVY!!
AND IT'S ROUGH, LIKE A FILE!

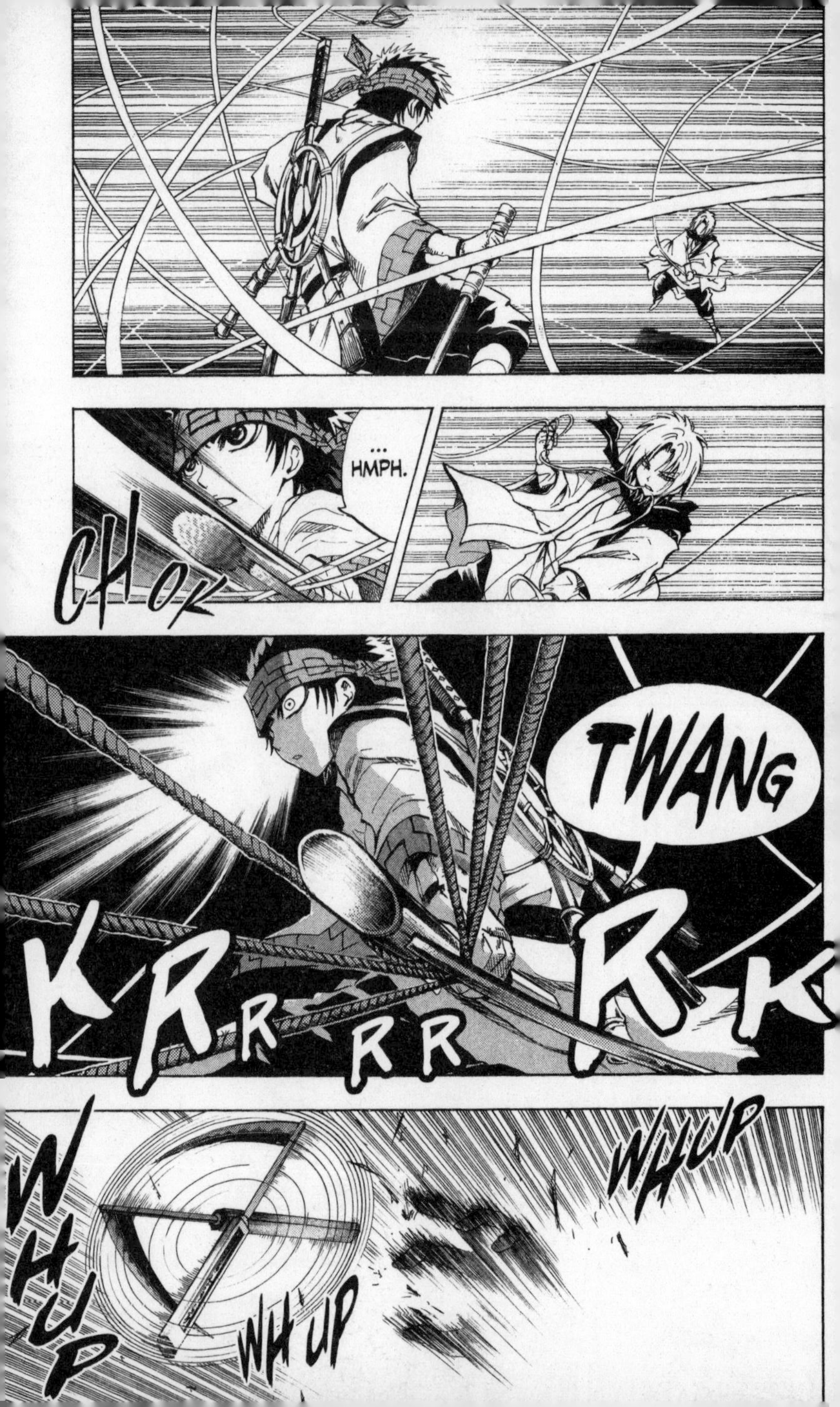

... HMPH.
CHOK
TWANG
KRRRRRRK
WHUP
WHUP
WHUP

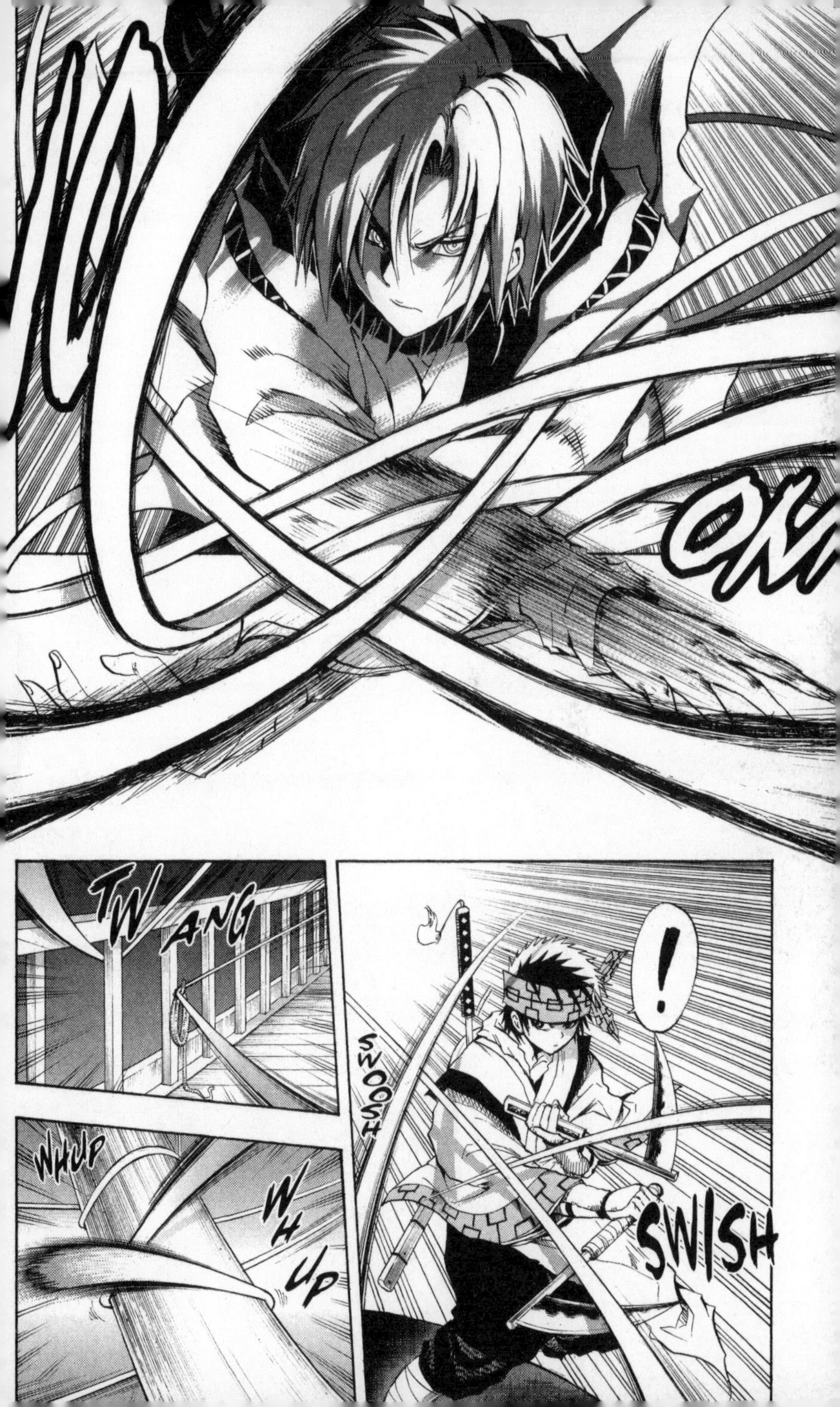
!
SWOOSH
SWISH
TWANG
WHUP
WHUP

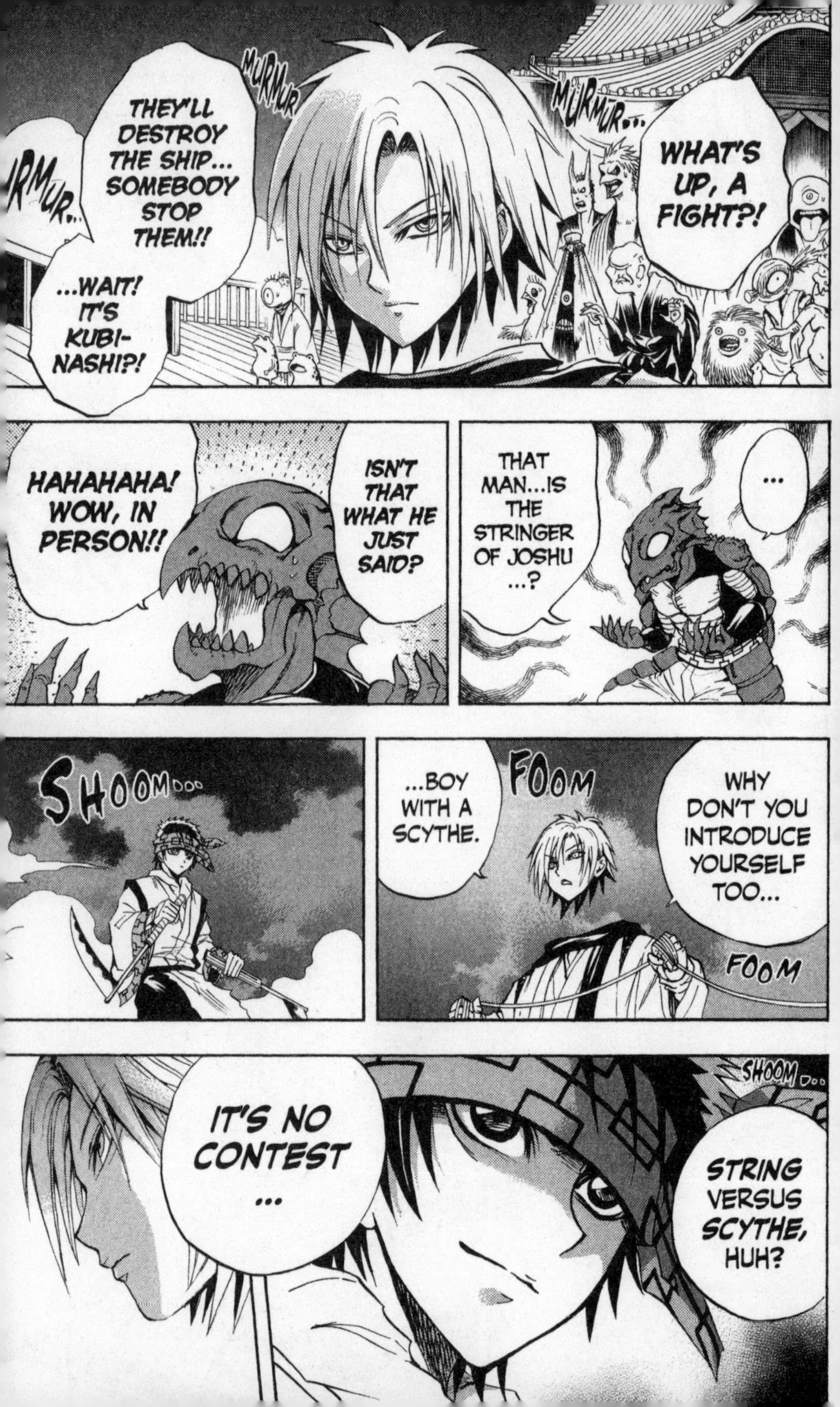

WHAT'S UP, A FIGHT?!
MURMUR...
MURMUR
THEY'LL DESTROY THE SHIP... SOMEBODY STOP THEM!!
RMUR...
...WAIT! IT'S KUBI-NASHI?!
...
THAT MAN...IS THE STRINGER OF JOSHU ...?
ISN'T THAT WHAT HE JUST SAID?
HAHAHAHA! WOW, IN PERSON!!
WHY DON'T YOU INTRODUCE YOURSELF TOO...
FOOM
...BOY WITH A SCYTHE.
FOOM
SHOOM...
SHOOM...
STRING VERSUS SCYTHE, HUH?
IT'S NO CONTEST ...

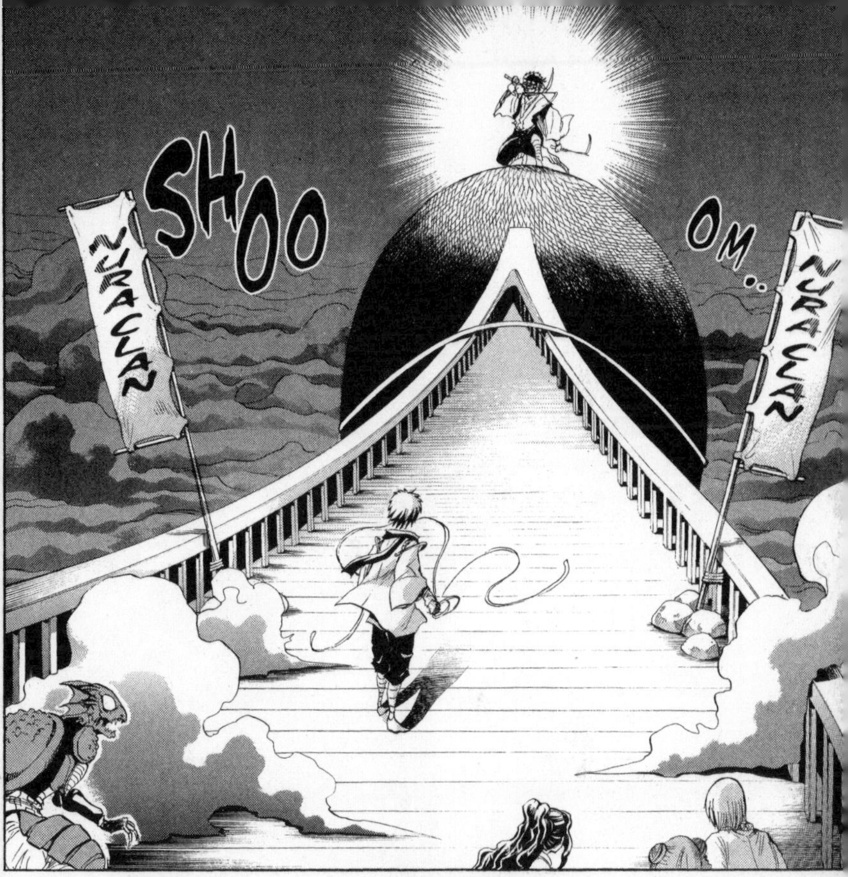
SHOO
OM..
NURA CLAN
NURA CLAN
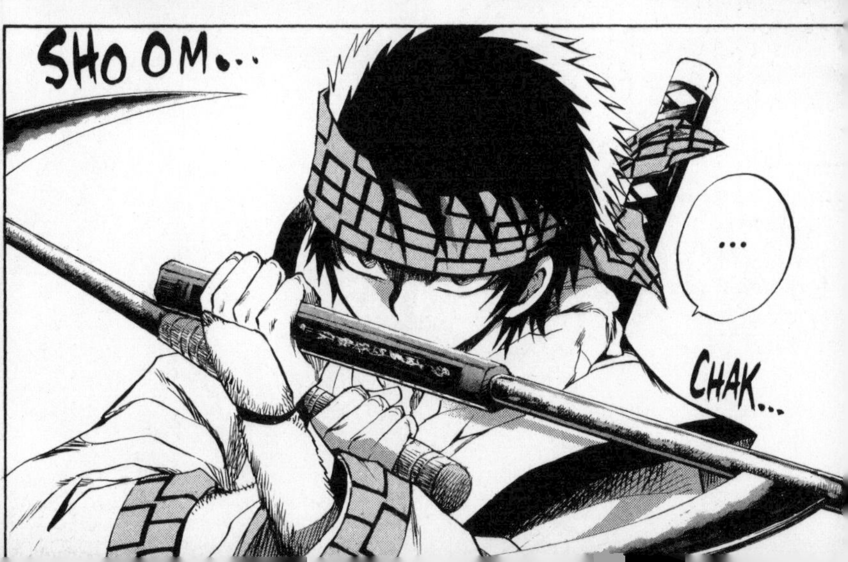
SHOOM...
...
CHAK...

Act 84: Scythe and Cat's Cradle

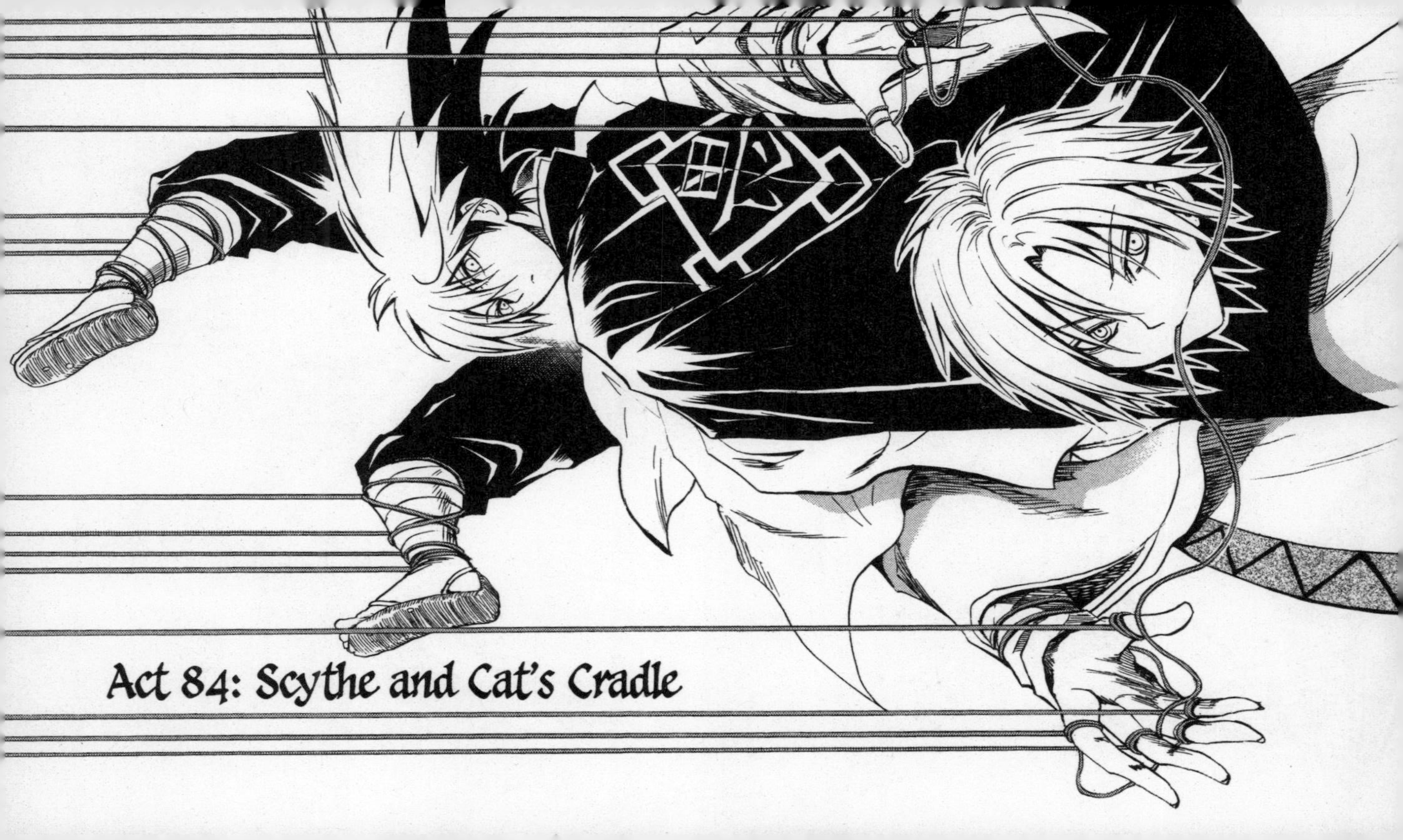

Kyoto Yokai Design Assistance by Yuji Samukawa

Monkey type
Rides on a flying ayakashi
3/8/2009
Paper wasp
Subordinate-looking
↓Hornet
Stretches out long
7/24/2009

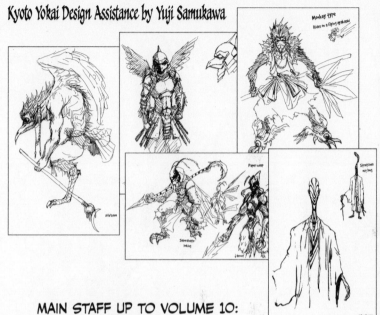

MAIN STAFF UP TO VOLUME 10:

HIDEAKI NAKASHIMA
HIROYUKI SENDA
KENTARO HIDANO
HAJIME YOSHIMURA
MIORI NISHIKUBO

EDITOR:
SEIJIRO NAKAMICHI

Special Thanks!!

NURA: RISE OF THE YOKAI CLAN

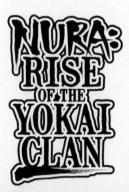

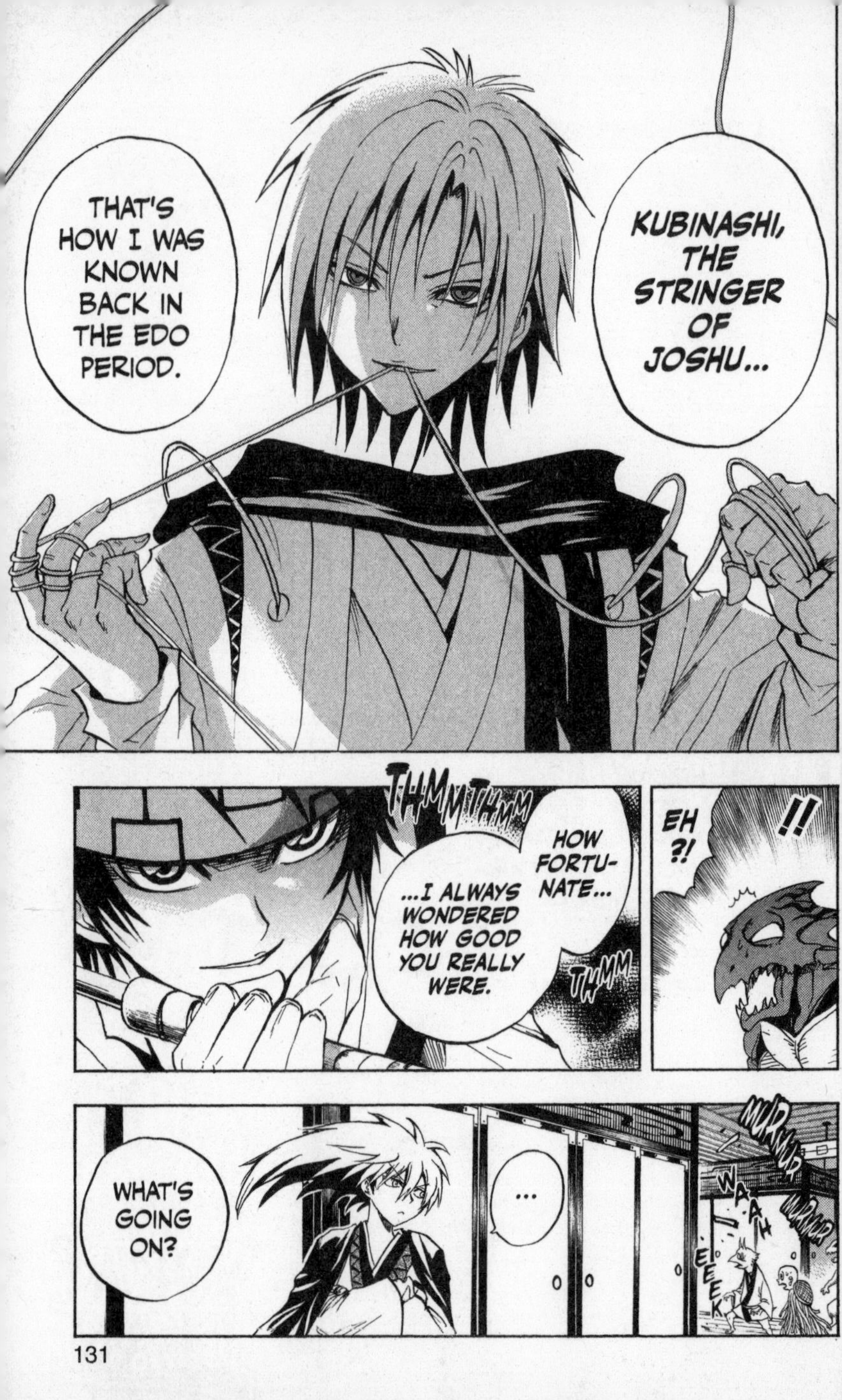
KUBINASHI, THE STRINGER OF JOSHU...
THAT'S HOW I WAS KNOWN BACK IN THE EDO PERIOD.
EH ?!
!!
THMMTHMM
HOW FORTU-NATE...
...I ALWAYS WONDERED HOW GOOD YOU REALLY WERE.
THMM
MURMUR
WAAAH
MURMUR
EEEEK
...
WHAT'S GOING ON?

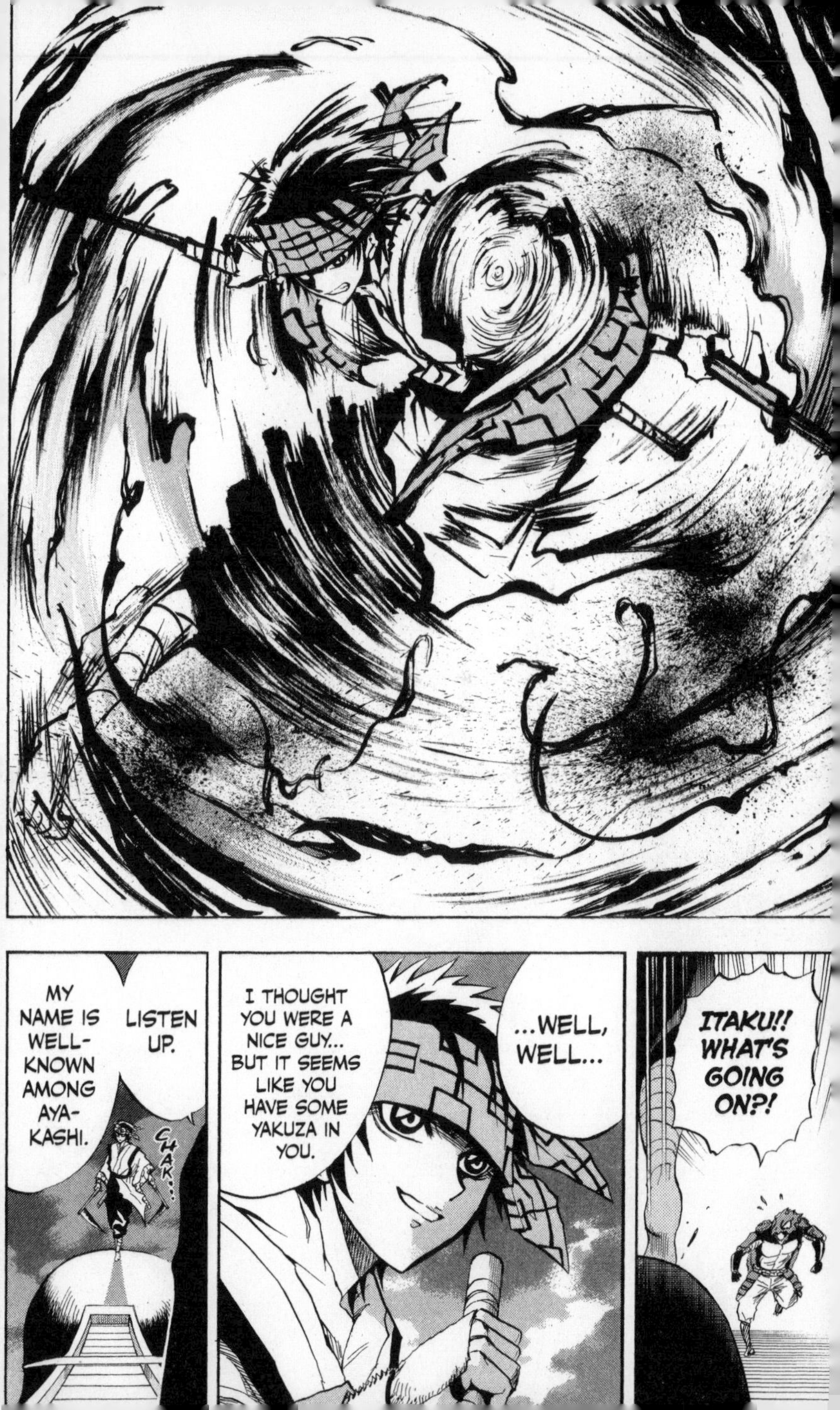
ITAKU!! WHAT'S GOING ON?!
...WELL, WELL...
I THOUGHT YOU WERE A NICE GUY... BUT IT SEEMS LIKE YOU HAVE SOME YAKUZA IN YOU.
LISTEN UP.
MY NAME IS WELL-KNOWN AMONG AYA-KASHI.
CHAK...

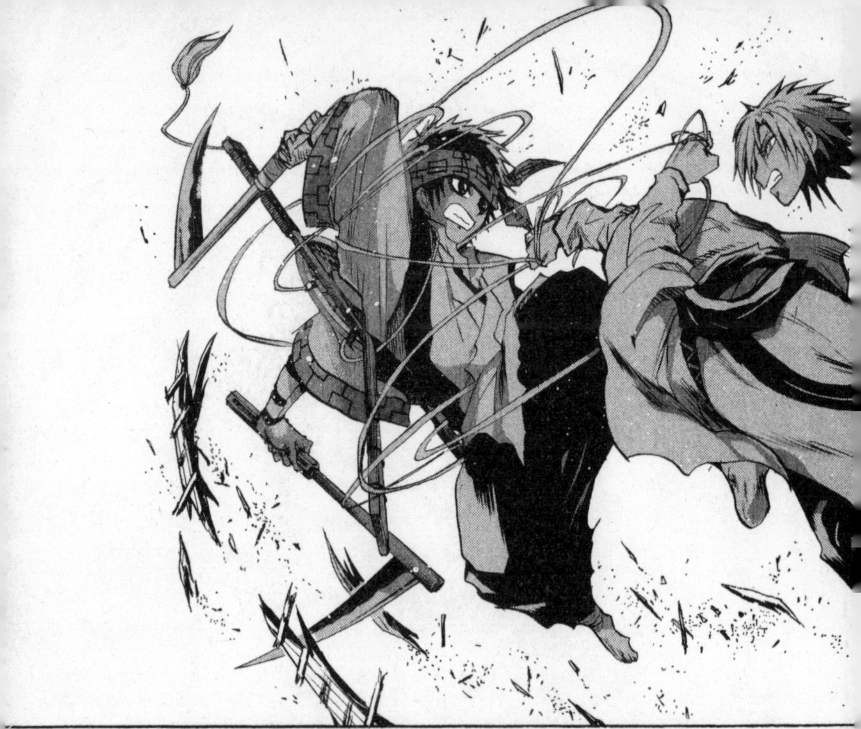
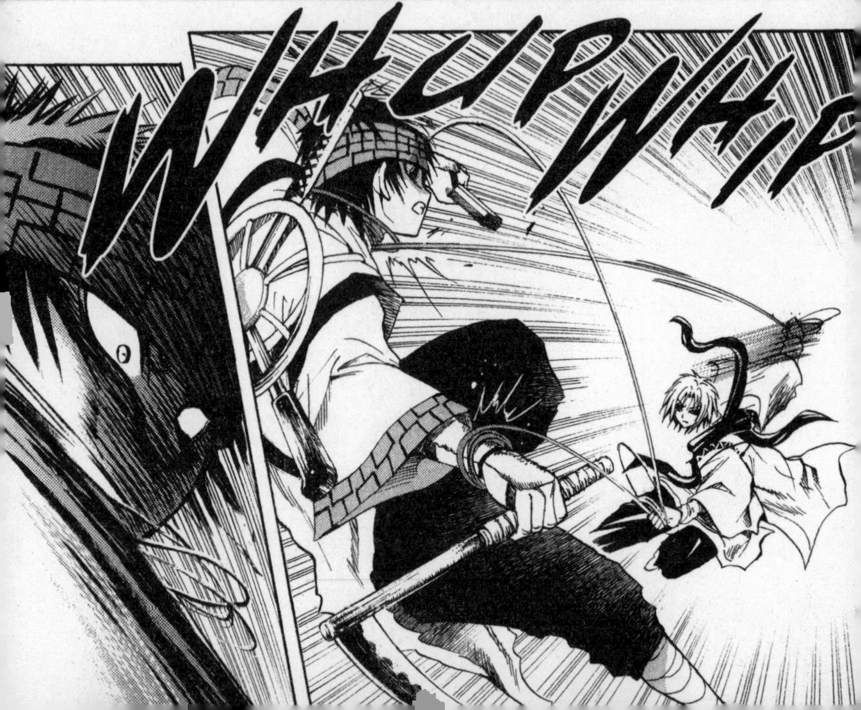
WHIPWHIP

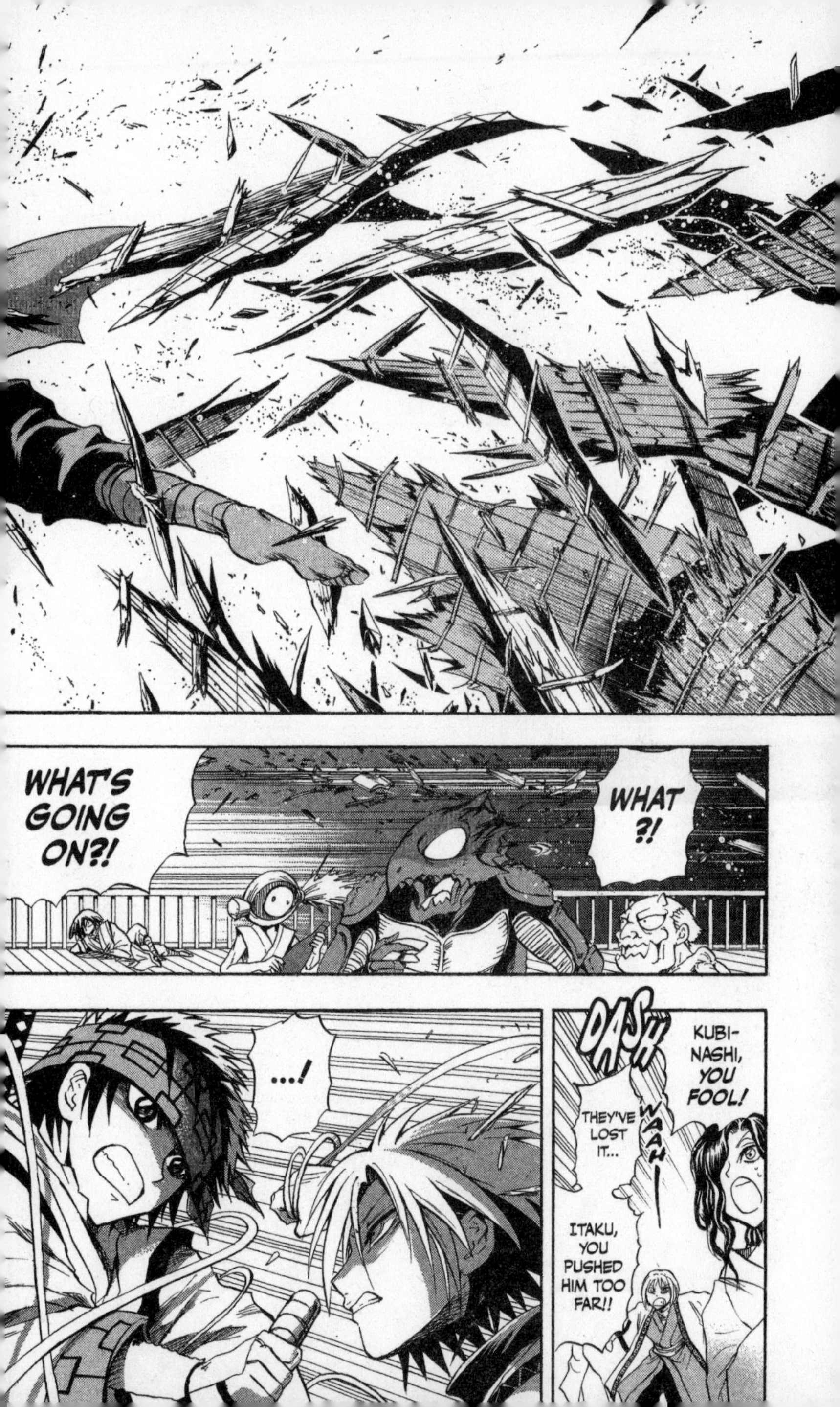
WHAT ?!
WHAT'S GOING ON?!
DASH
KUBI-NASHI, YOU FOOL!
WAAH
THEY'VE LOST IT...
ITAKU, YOU PUSHED HIM TOO FAR!!
...!

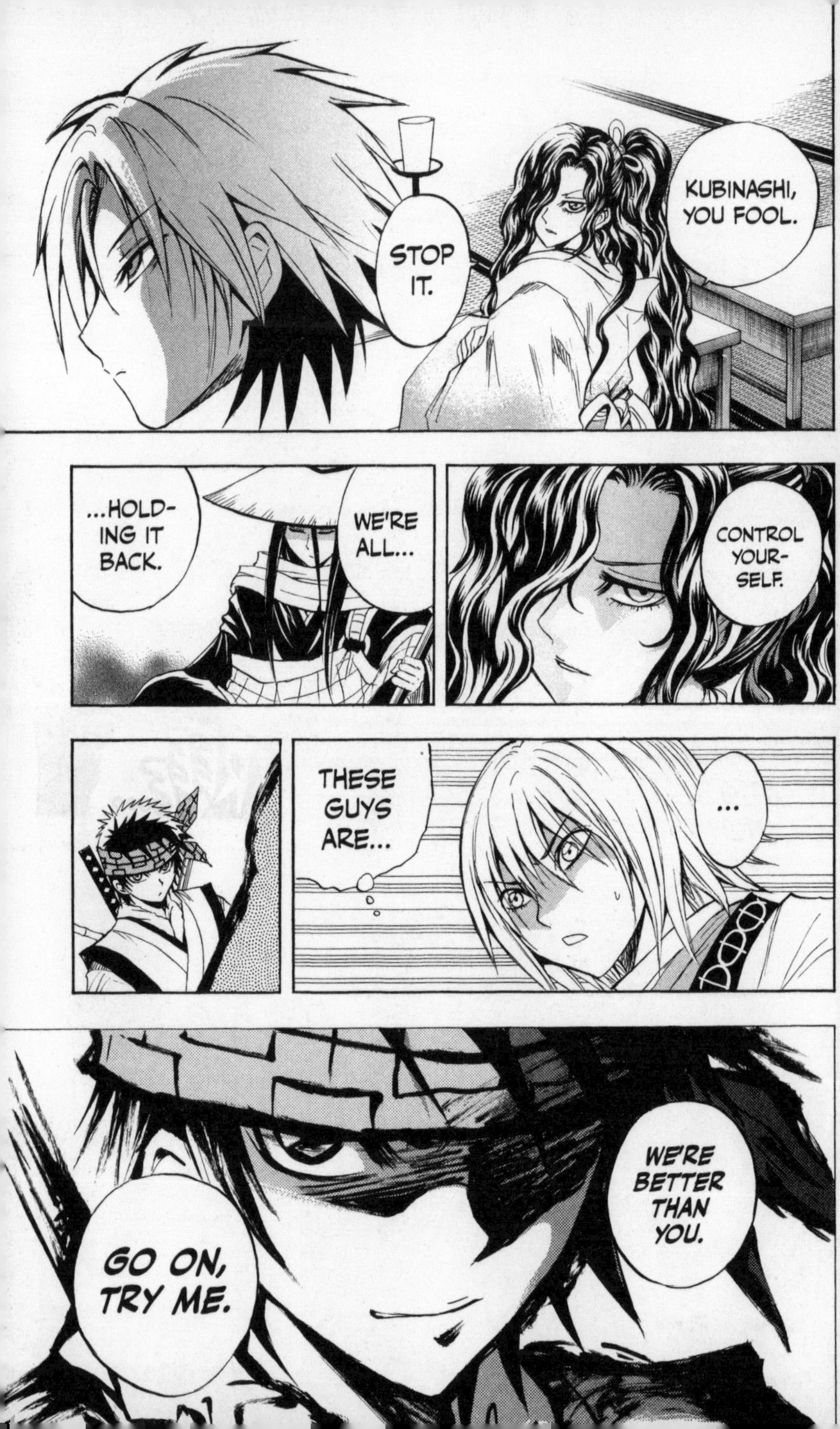
KUBINASHI, YOU FOOL.
STOP IT.
CONTROL YOUR-SELF.
WE'RE ALL...
...HOLD-ING IT BACK.
...
THESE GUYS ARE...
WE'RE BETTER THAN YOU.
GO ON, TRY ME.

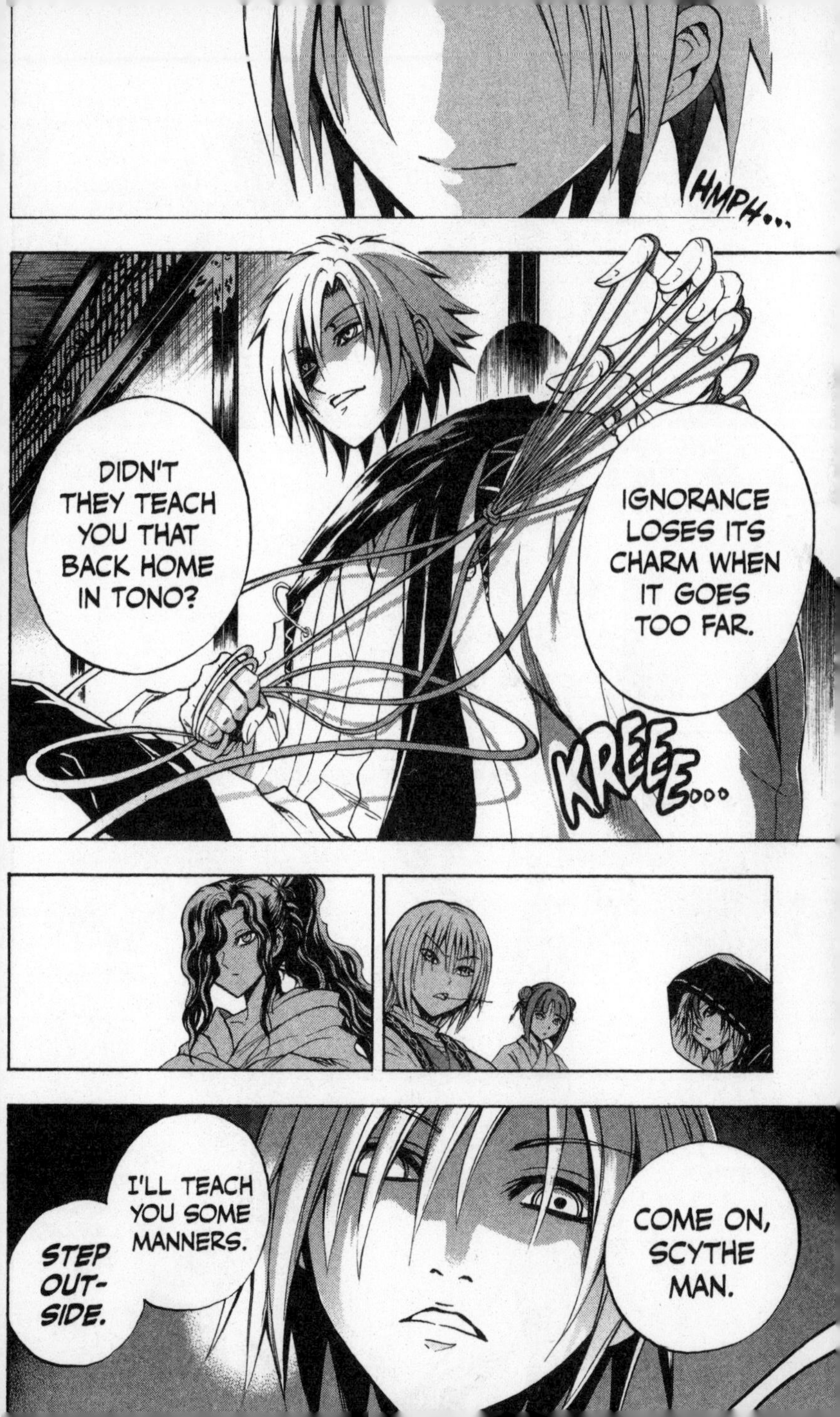
HMPH...
IGNORANCE LOSES ITS CHARM WHEN IT GOES TOO FAR.
DIDN'T THEY TEACH YOU THAT BACK HOME IN TONO?
KREEEE...
COME ON, SCYTHE MAN.
I'LL TEACH YOU SOME MANNERS.
STEP OUT-SIDE.

READ THIS WAY

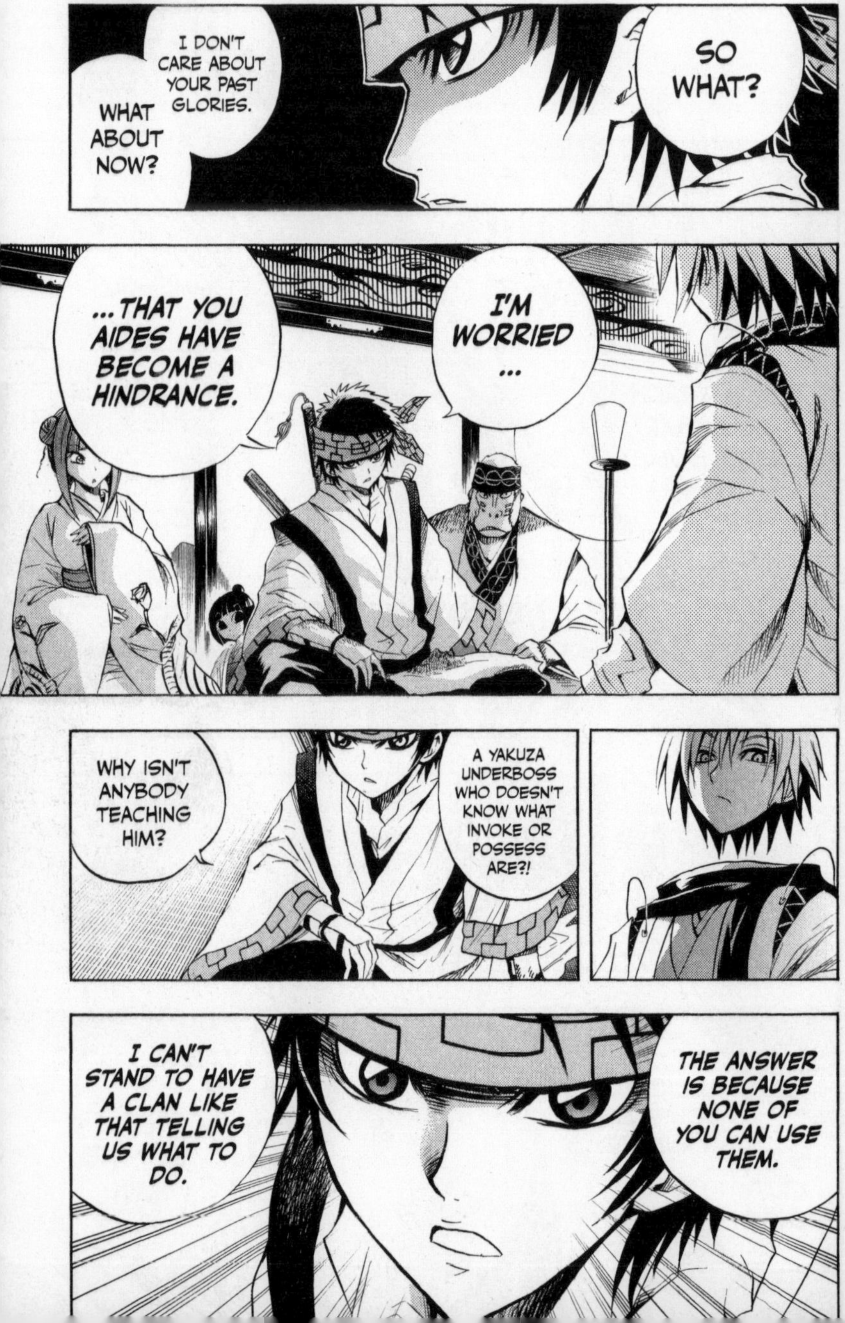
SO WHAT?
I DON'T CARE ABOUT YOUR PAST GLORIES.
WHAT ABOUT NOW?
I'M WORRIED ...
...THAT YOU AIDES HAVE BECOME A HINDRANCE.
A YAKUZA UNDERBOSS WHO DOESN'T KNOW WHAT INVOKE OR POSSESS ARE?!
WHY ISN'T ANYBODY TEACHING HIM?
THE ANSWER IS BECAUSE NONE OF YOU CAN USE THEM.
I CAN'T STAND TO HAVE A CLAN LIKE THAT TELLING US WHAT TO DO.

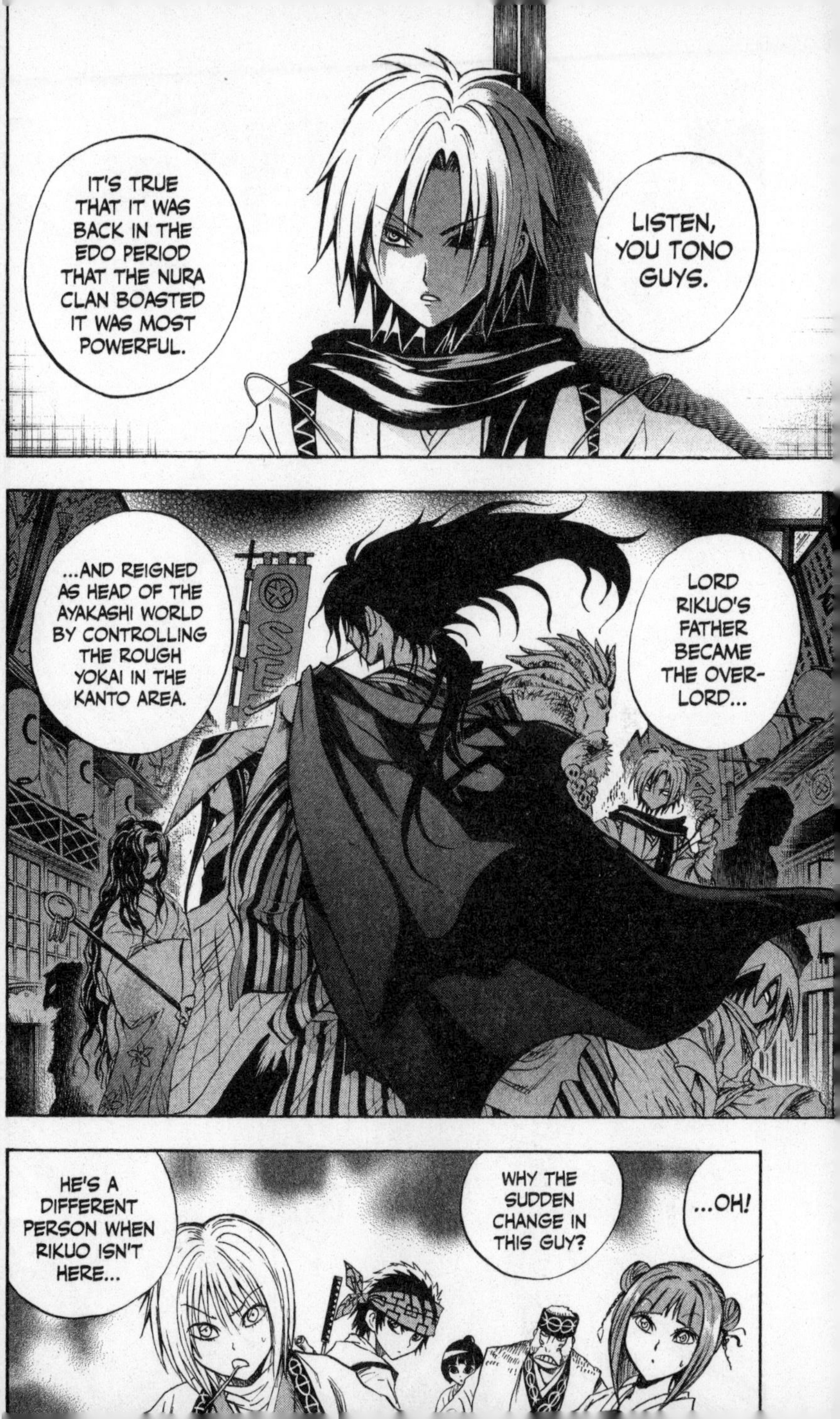
LISTEN, YOU TONO GUYS.
IT'S TRUE THAT IT WAS BACK IN THE EDO PERIOD THAT THE NURA CLAN BOASTED IT WAS MOST POWERFUL.
LORD RIKUO'S FATHER BECAME THE OVER-LORD...
...AND REIGNED AS HEAD OF THE AYAKASHI WORLD BY CONTROLLING THE ROUGH YOKAI IN THE KANTO AREA.
...OH!
WHY THE SUDDEN CHANGE IN THIS GUY?
HE'S A DIFFERENT PERSON WHEN RIKUO ISN'T HERE...

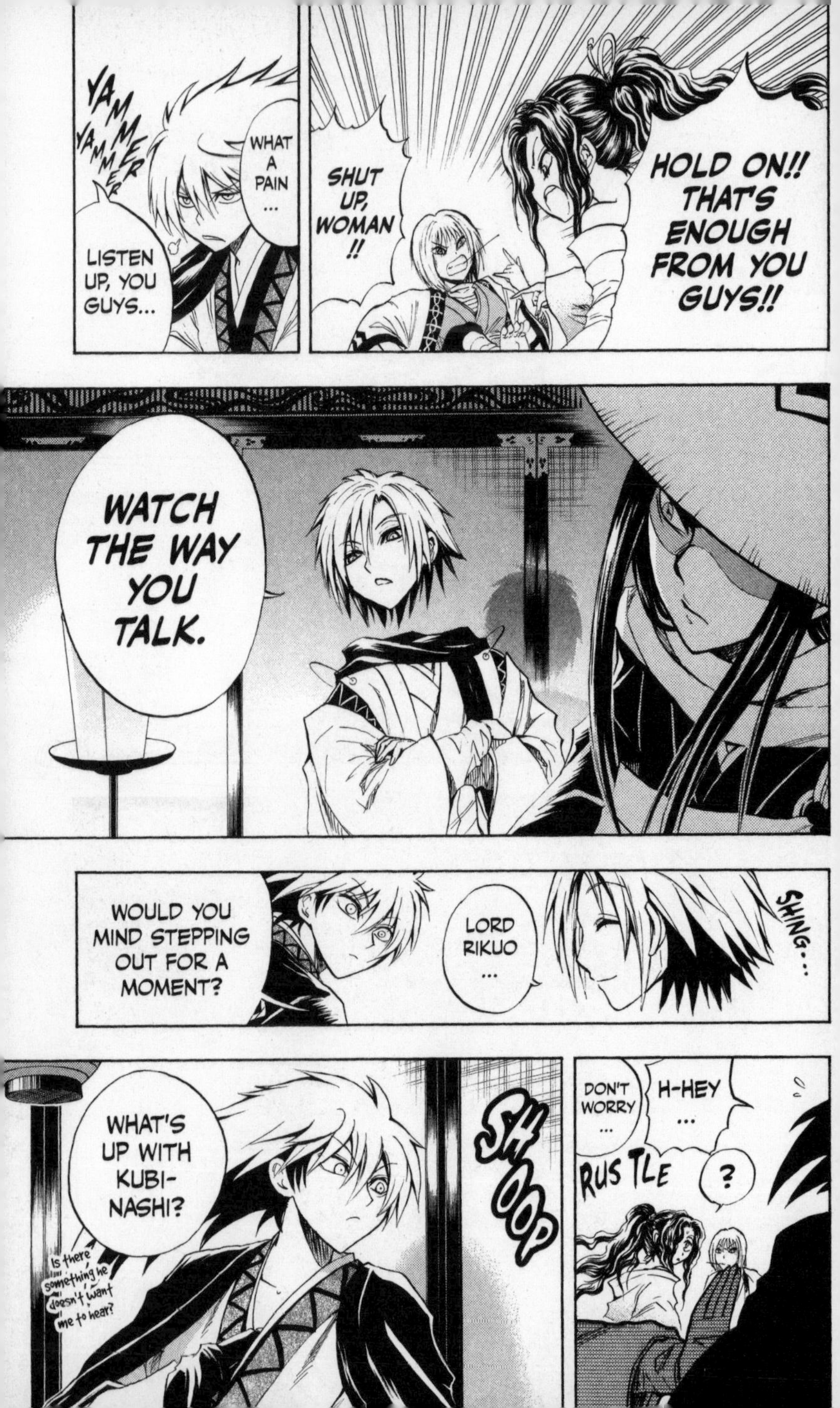
HOLD ON!! THAT'S ENOUGH FROM YOU GUYS!!
SHUT UP, WOMAN!!
WHAT A PAIN...
YAMMER YAMMER
LISTEN UP, YOU GUYS...
WATCH THE WAY YOU TALK.
SHING...
LORD RIKUO...
WOULD YOU MIND STEPPING OUT FOR A MOMENT?
H-HEY...
DON'T WORRY...
?
RUSTLE
SHOOP
WHAT'S UP WITH KUBI-NASHI?
Is there something he doesn't want me to hear?

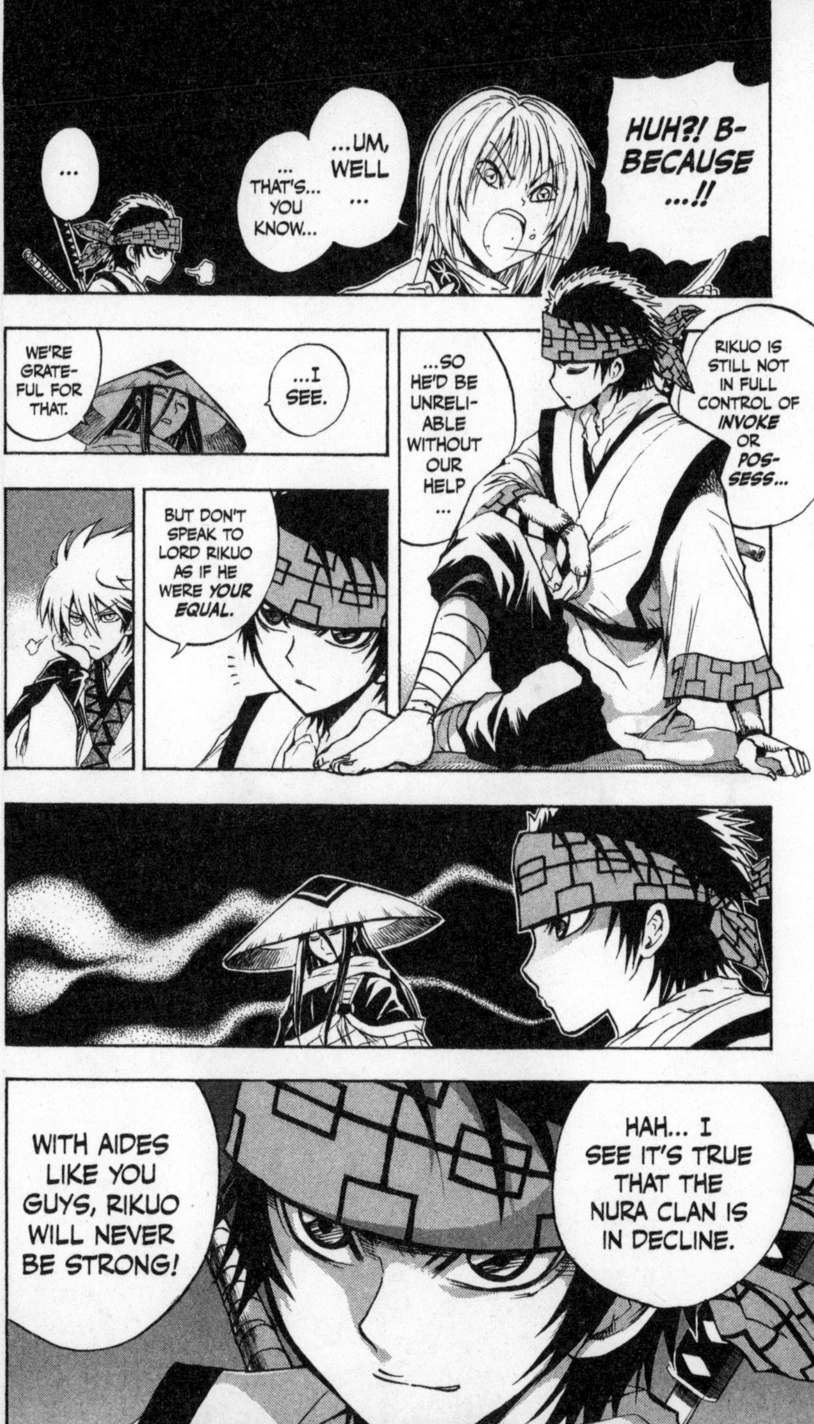
HUH?! B-BECAUSE ...!!
...UM, WELL ...
... THAT'S... YOU KNOW...
...
RIKUO IS STILL NOT IN FULL CONTROL OF INVOKE OR POSSESS...
...SO HE'D BE UNRELIABLE WITHOUT OUR HELP ...
...I SEE.
WE'RE GRATEFUL FOR THAT.
BUT DON'T SPEAK TO LORD RIKUO AS IF HE WERE YOUR EQUAL.
HAH... I SEE IT'S TRUE THAT THE NURA CLAN IS IN DECLINE.
WITH AIDES LIKE YOU GUYS, RIKUO WILL NEVER BE STRONG!

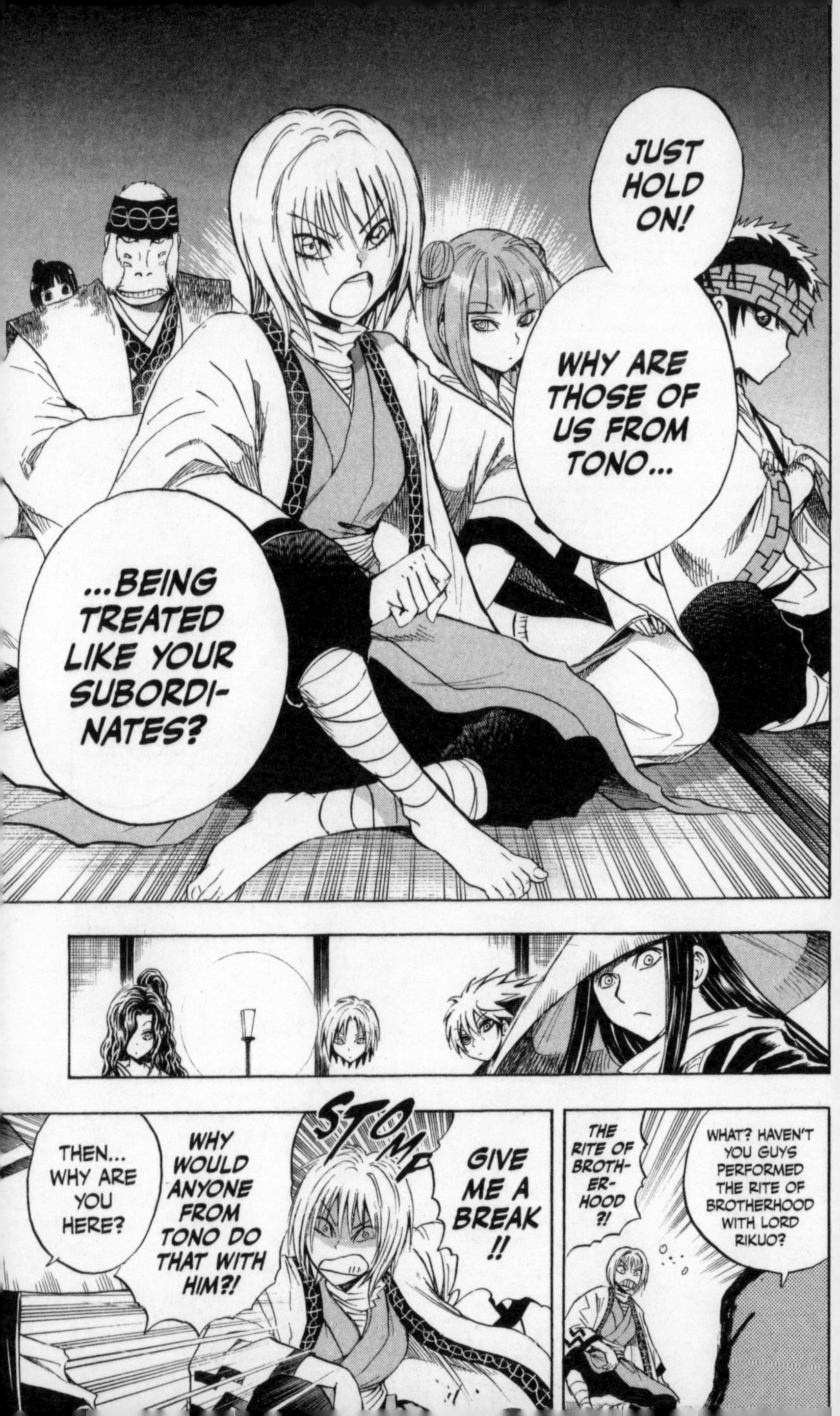
JUST HOLD ON!
WHY ARE THOSE OF US FROM TONO...
...BEING TREATED LIKE YOUR SUBORDI-NATES?
WHAT? HAVEN'T YOU GUYS PERFORMED THE RITE OF BROTHERHOOD WITH LORD RIKUO?
THE RITE OF BROTH-ER-HOOD ?!
GIVE ME A BREAK !!
STOMP
WHY WOULD ANYONE FROM TONO DO THAT WITH HIM?!
THEN... WHY ARE YOU HERE?

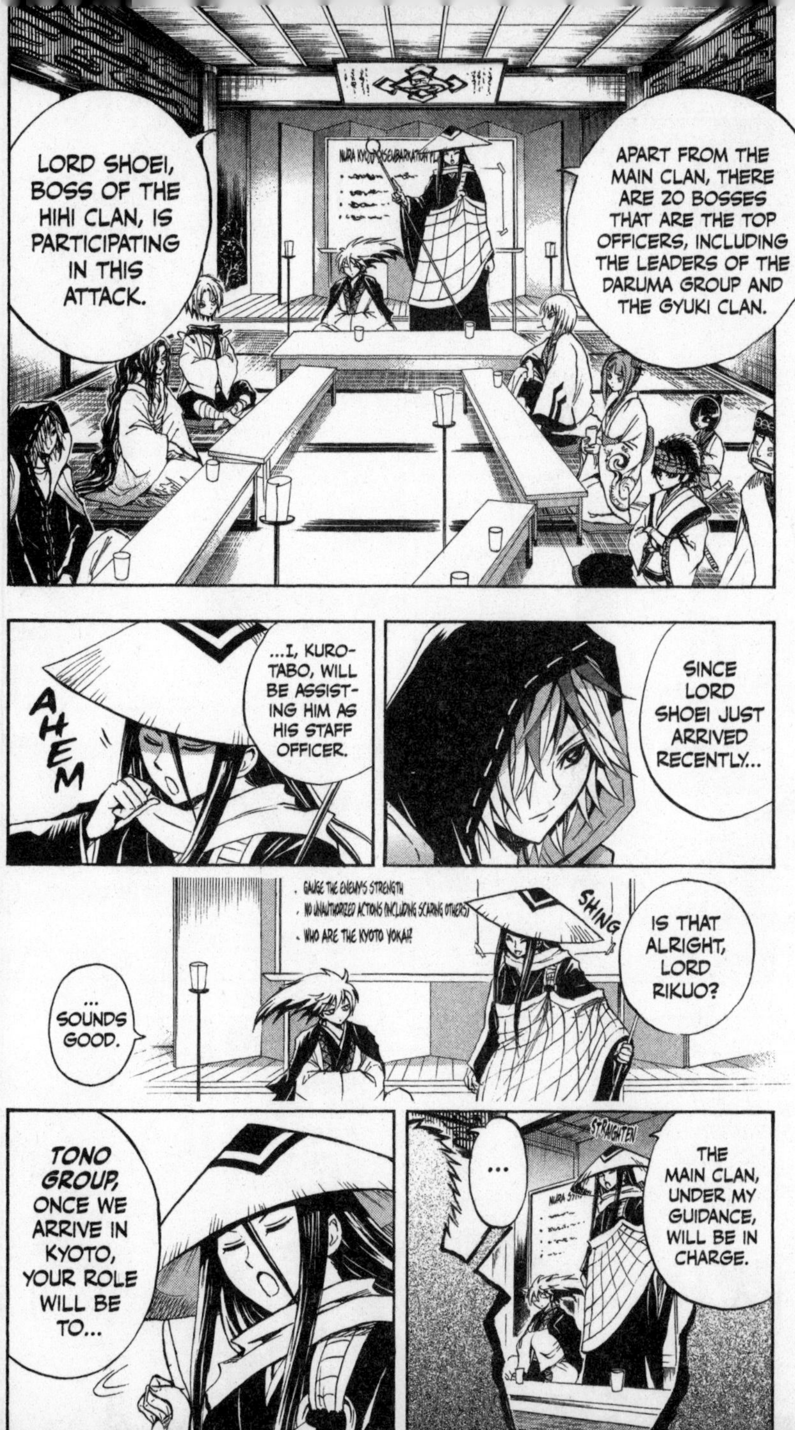
APART FROM THE MAIN CLAN, THERE ARE 20 BOSSES THAT ARE THE TOP OFFICERS, INCLUDING THE LEADERS OF THE DARUMA GROUP AND THE GYUKI CLAN.
LORD SHOEI, BOSS OF THE HIHI CLAN, IS PARTICIPATING IN THIS ATTACK.
SINCE LORD SHOEI JUST ARRIVED RECENTLY...
...I, KURO-TABO, WILL BE ASSISTING HIM AS HIS STAFF OFFICER.
AHEM
SHING
IS THAT ALRIGHT, LORD RIKUO?
· GAUGE THE ENEMY'S STRENGTH
· NO UNAUTHORIZED ACTIONS (INCLUDING SCARING OTHERS)
· WHO ARE THE KYOTO YOKAI?
... SOUNDS GOOD.
STRAIGHTEN
THE MAIN CLAN, UNDER MY GUIDANCE, WILL BE IN CHARGE.
...
TONO GROUP, ONCE WE ARRIVE IN KYOTO, YOUR ROLE WILL BE TO...

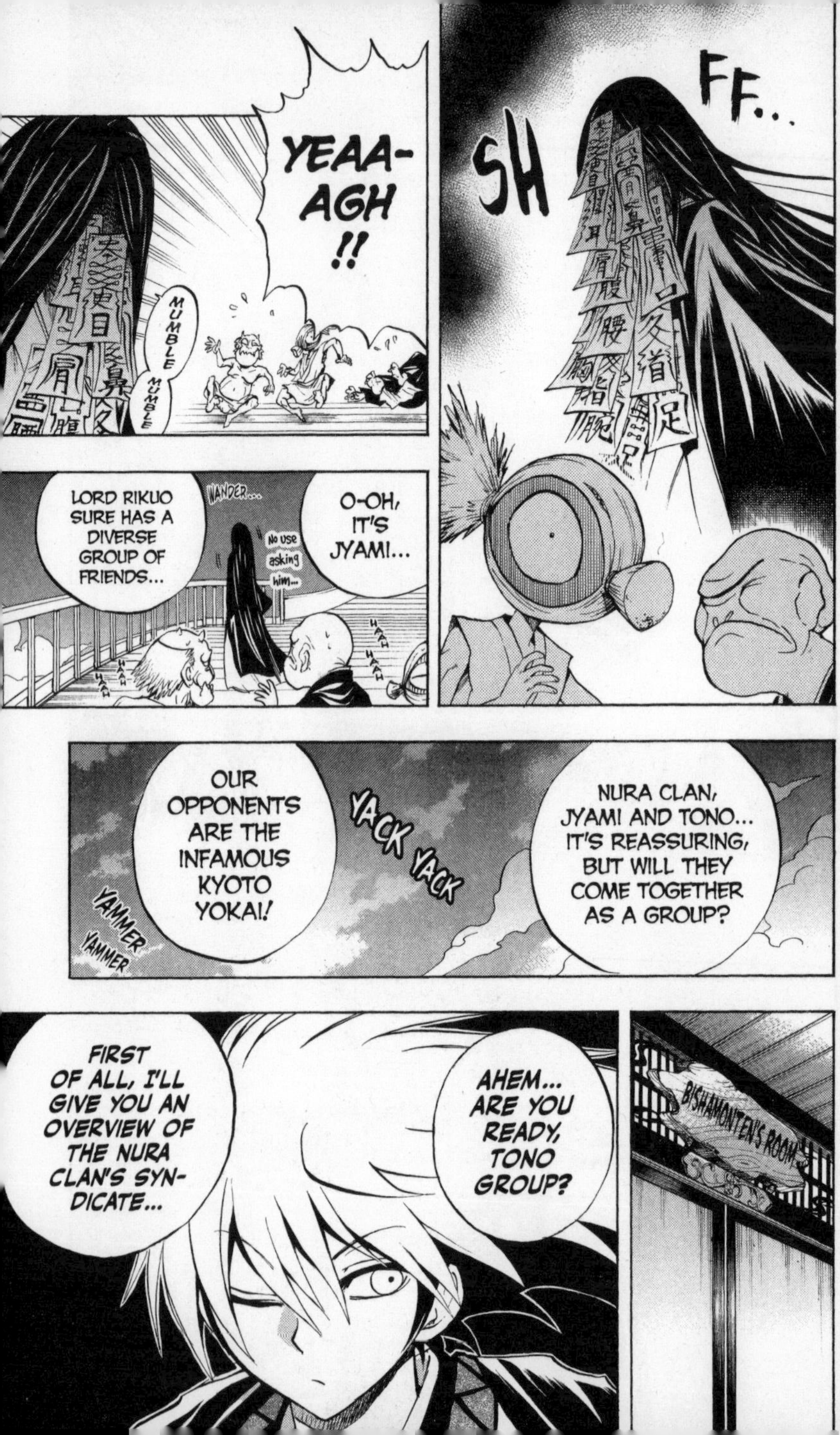
SH
FF...
YEAA-AGH!!
MUMBLE MUMBLE
O-OH, IT'S JYAMI...
No use asking him...
WANDER...
LORD RIKUO SURE HAS A DIVERSE GROUP OF FRIENDS...
HAAH HAAH
HAAH HAAH
NURA CLAN, JYAMI AND TONO... IT'S REASSURING, BUT WILL THEY COME TOGETHER AS A GROUP?
YACK YACK
OUR OPPONENTS ARE THE INFAMOUS KYOTO YOKAI!
YAMMER YAMMER
BISHAMONTEN'S ROOM
AHEM... ARE YOU READY, TONO GROUP?
FIRST OF ALL, I'LL GIVE YOU AN OVERVIEW OF THE NURA CLAN'S SYN-DICATE...

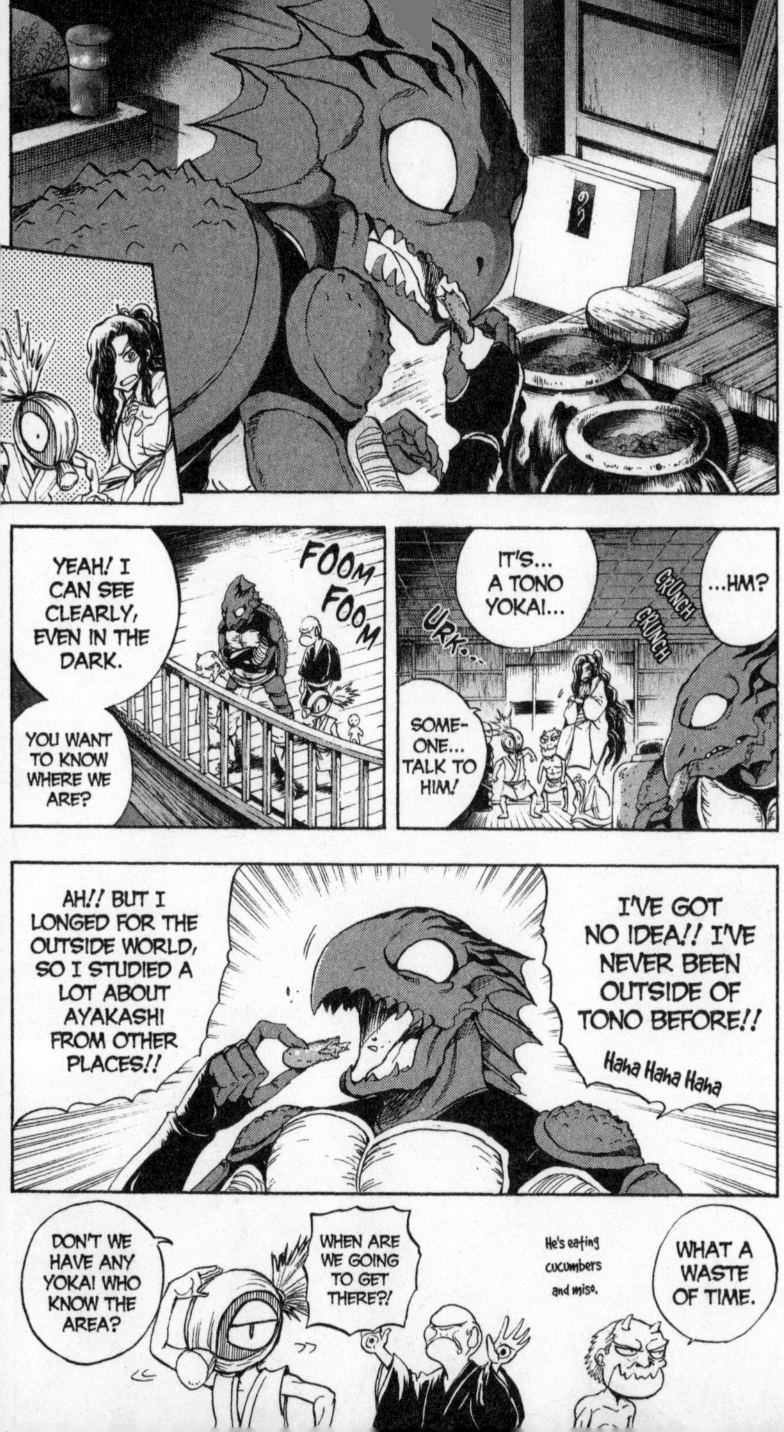
...HM?
CRUNCH CRUNCH
IT'S... A TONO YOKAI...
URK...
SOME-ONE... TALK TO HIM!
FOOM FOOM
YEAH! I CAN SEE CLEARLY, EVEN IN THE DARK.
YOU WANT TO KNOW WHERE WE ARE?
I'VE GOT NO IDEA!! I'VE NEVER BEEN OUTSIDE OF TONO BEFORE!!
Haha Haha Haha
AH!! BUT I LONGED FOR THE OUTSIDE WORLD, SO I STUDIED A LOT ABOUT AYAKASHI FROM OTHER PLACES!!
WHAT A WASTE OF TIME.
He's eating cucumbers and miso.
WHEN ARE WE GOING TO GET THERE?!
DON'T WE HAVE ANY YOKAI WHO KNOW THE AREA?

READ THIS WAY

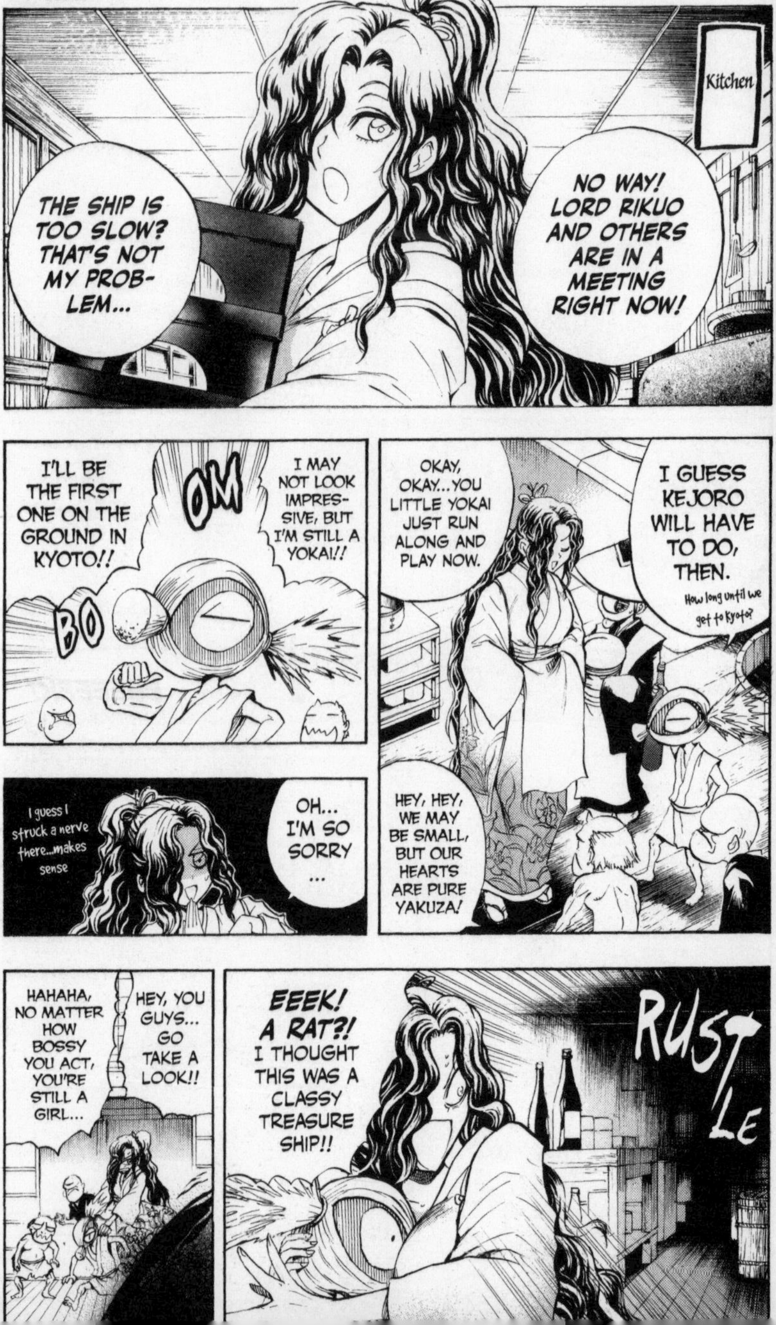
Kitchen
NO WAY! LORD RIKUO AND OTHERS ARE IN A MEETING RIGHT NOW!
THE SHIP IS TOO SLOW? THAT'S NOT MY PROB-LEM...
I GUESS KEJORO WILL HAVE TO DO, THEN.
How long until we get to Kyoto?
OKAY, OKAY... YOU LITTLE YOKAI JUST RUN ALONG AND PLAY NOW.
HEY, HEY, WE MAY BE SMALL, BUT OUR HEARTS ARE PURE YAKUZA!
I MAY NOT LOOK IMPRES-SIVE, BUT I'M STILL A YOKAI!!
OM
I'LL BE THE FIRST ONE ON THE GROUND IN KYOTO!!
BO
OH... I'M SO SORRY ...
I guess I struck a nerve there...makes sense
RUSTLE
EEEK! A RAT?! I THOUGHT THIS WAS A CLASSY TREASURE SHIP!!
HEY, YOU GUYS... GO TAKE A LOOK!!
HAHAHA, NO MATTER HOW BOSSY YOU ACT, YOU'RE STILL A GIRL...

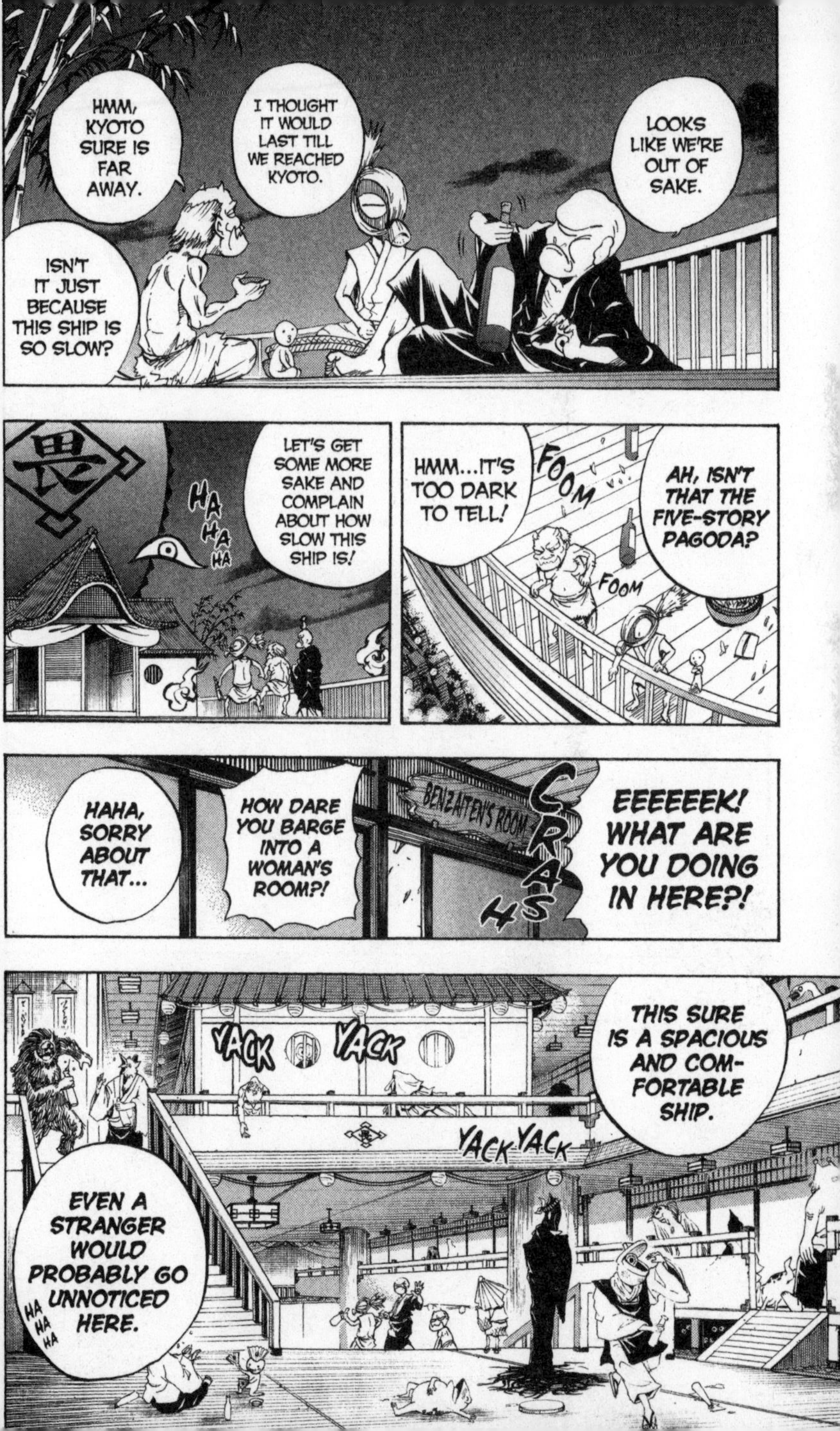
LOOKS LIKE WE'RE OUT OF SAKE.
I THOUGHT IT WOULD LAST TILL WE REACHED KYOTO.
HMM, KYOTO SURE IS FAR AWAY.
ISN'T IT JUST BECAUSE THIS SHIP IS SO SLOW?
AH, ISN'T THAT THE FIVE-STORY PAGODA?
FOOM
HMM...IT'S TOO DARK TO TELL!
FOOM
LET'S GET SOME MORE SAKE AND COMPLAIN ABOUT HOW SLOW THIS SHIP IS!
HA HA HA HA
EEEEEEK! WHAT ARE YOU DOING IN HERE?!
CRASH
BENZAITEN'S ROOM
HOW DARE YOU BARGE INTO A WOMAN'S ROOM?!
HAHA, SORRY ABOUT THAT...
THIS SURE IS A SPACIOUS AND COM-FORTABLE SHIP.
YACK YACK
YACK YACK
YACK
YACK
EVEN A STRANGER WOULD PROBABLY GO UNNOTICED HERE.
HA HA HA

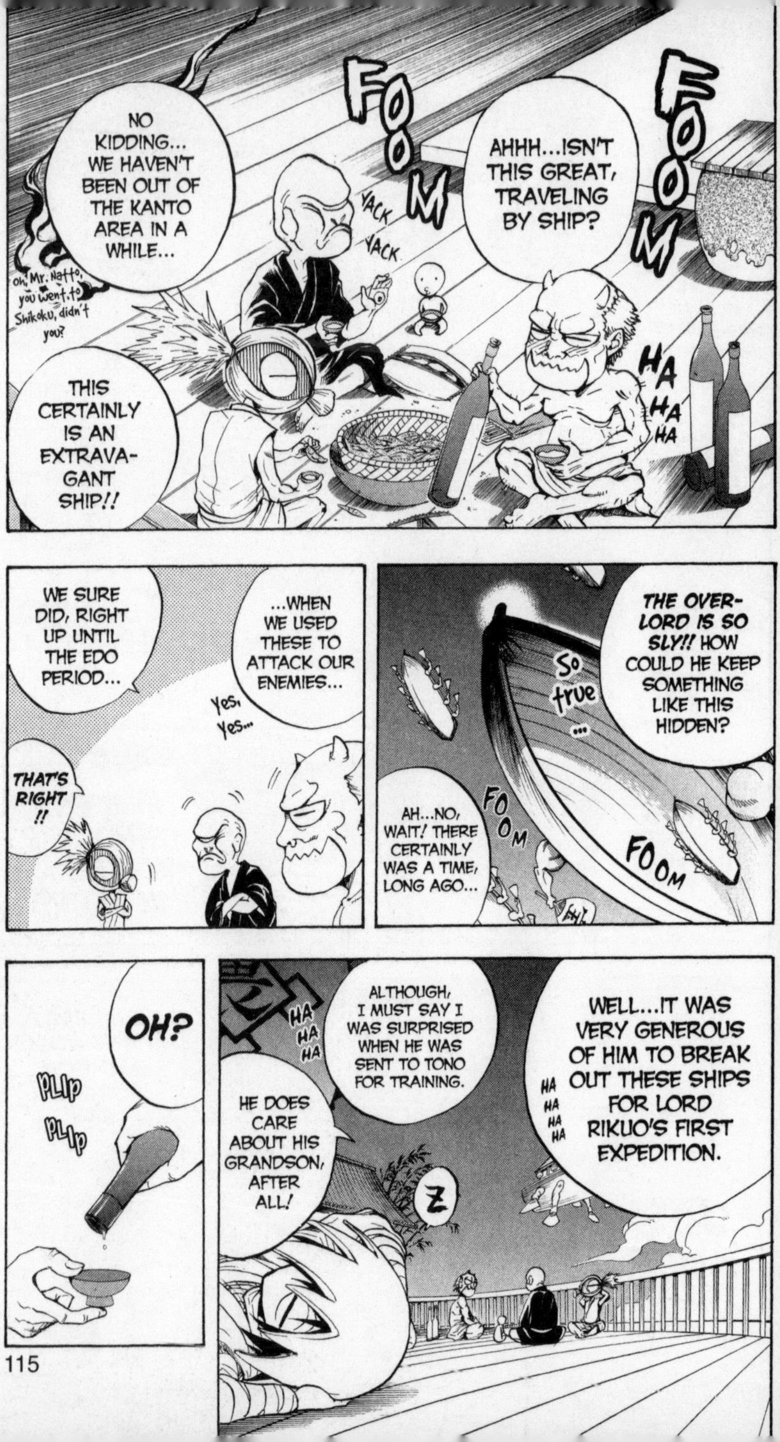
FOOM
FOOM
AHHH...ISN'T THIS GREAT, TRAVELING BY SHIP?
HA HA HA HA
NO KIDDING... WE HAVEN'T BEEN OUT OF THE KANTO AREA IN A WHILE...
YACK YACK
Oh, Mr. Natto, you went to Shikoku, didn't you?
THIS CERTAINLY IS AN EXTRAVAGANT SHIP!!
THE OVERLORD IS SO SLY!! HOW COULD HE KEEP SOMETHING LIKE THIS HIDDEN?
So true...
AH...NO, WAIT! THERE CERTAINLY WAS A TIME, LONG AGO...
FOOM
FOOM
...WHEN WE USED THESE TO ATTACK OUR ENEMIES...
WE SURE DID, RIGHT UP UNTIL THE EDO PERIOD...
Yes, yes...
THAT'S RIGHT!!
WELL...IT WAS VERY GENEROUS OF HIM TO BREAK OUT THESE SHIPS FOR LORD RIKUO'S FIRST EXPEDITION.
HA HA HA HA
ALTHOUGH, I MUST SAY I WAS SURPRISED WHEN HE WAS SENT TO TONO FOR TRAINING.
HA HA HA
HE DOES CARE ABOUT HIS GRANDSON, AFTER ALL!
Z
OH?
PLIP
PLIP

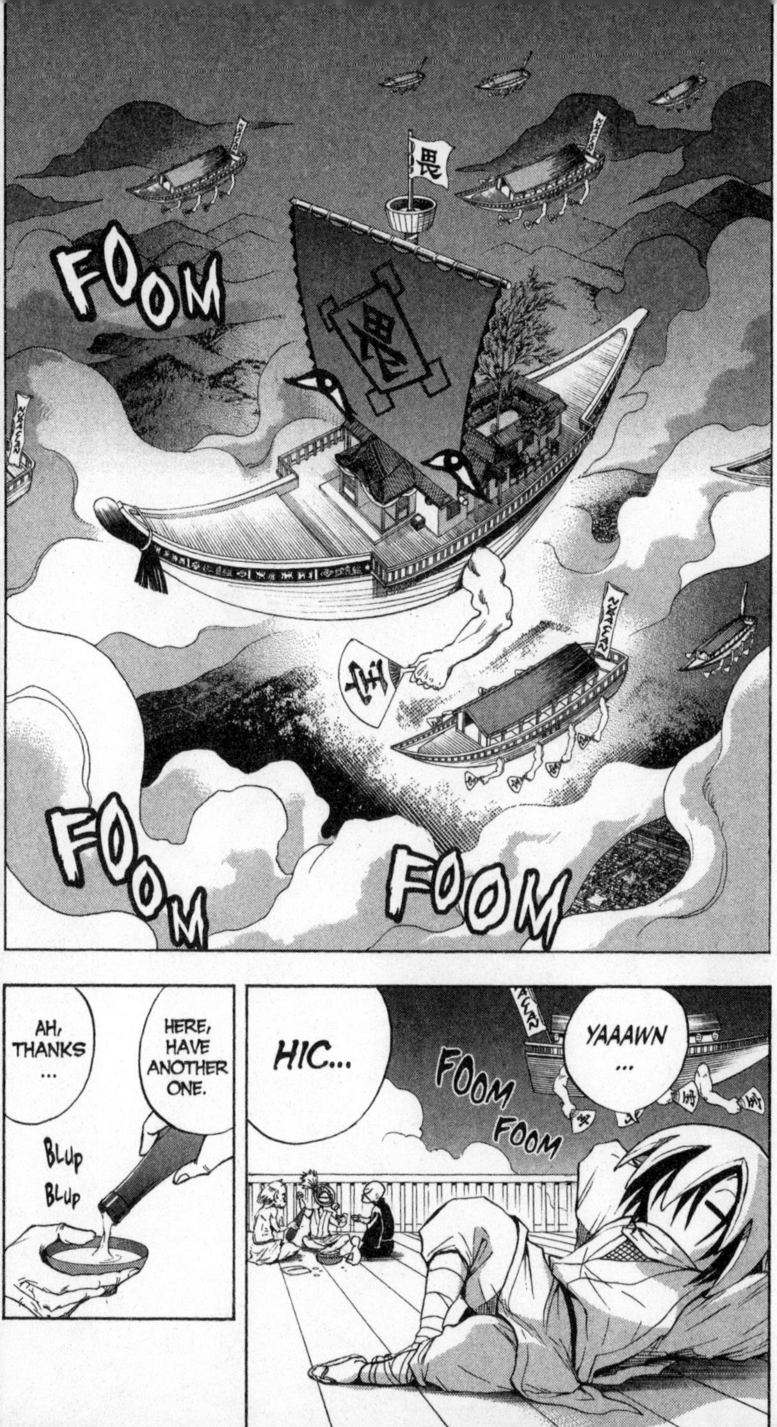
FOOM
FOOM
FOOM
YAAAWN ...
FOOM FOOM
HIC...
HERE, HAVE ANOTHER ONE.
AH, THANKS ...
BLUP BLUP

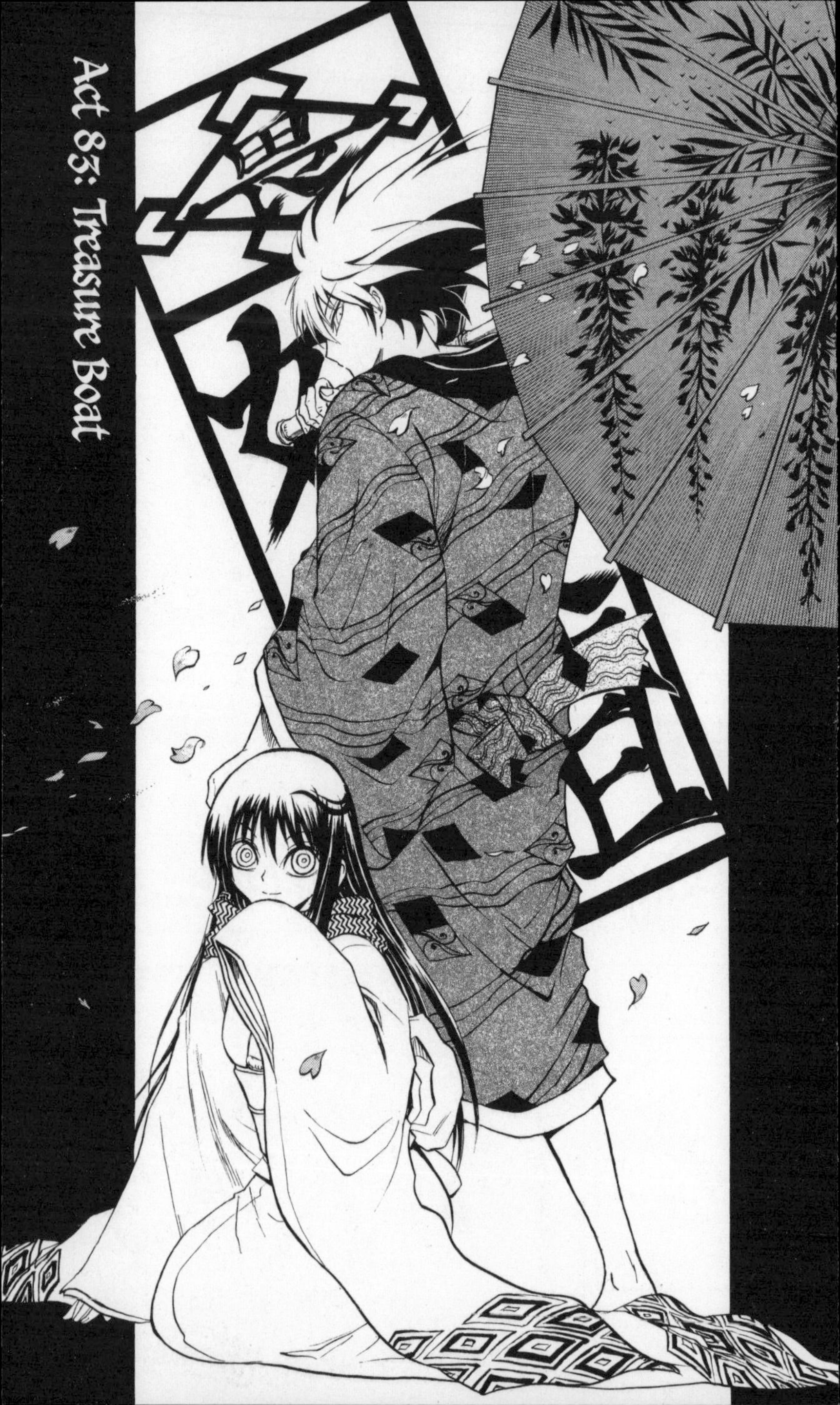
Act 83: Treasure Boat

NURA: RISE OF THE YOKAI CLAN

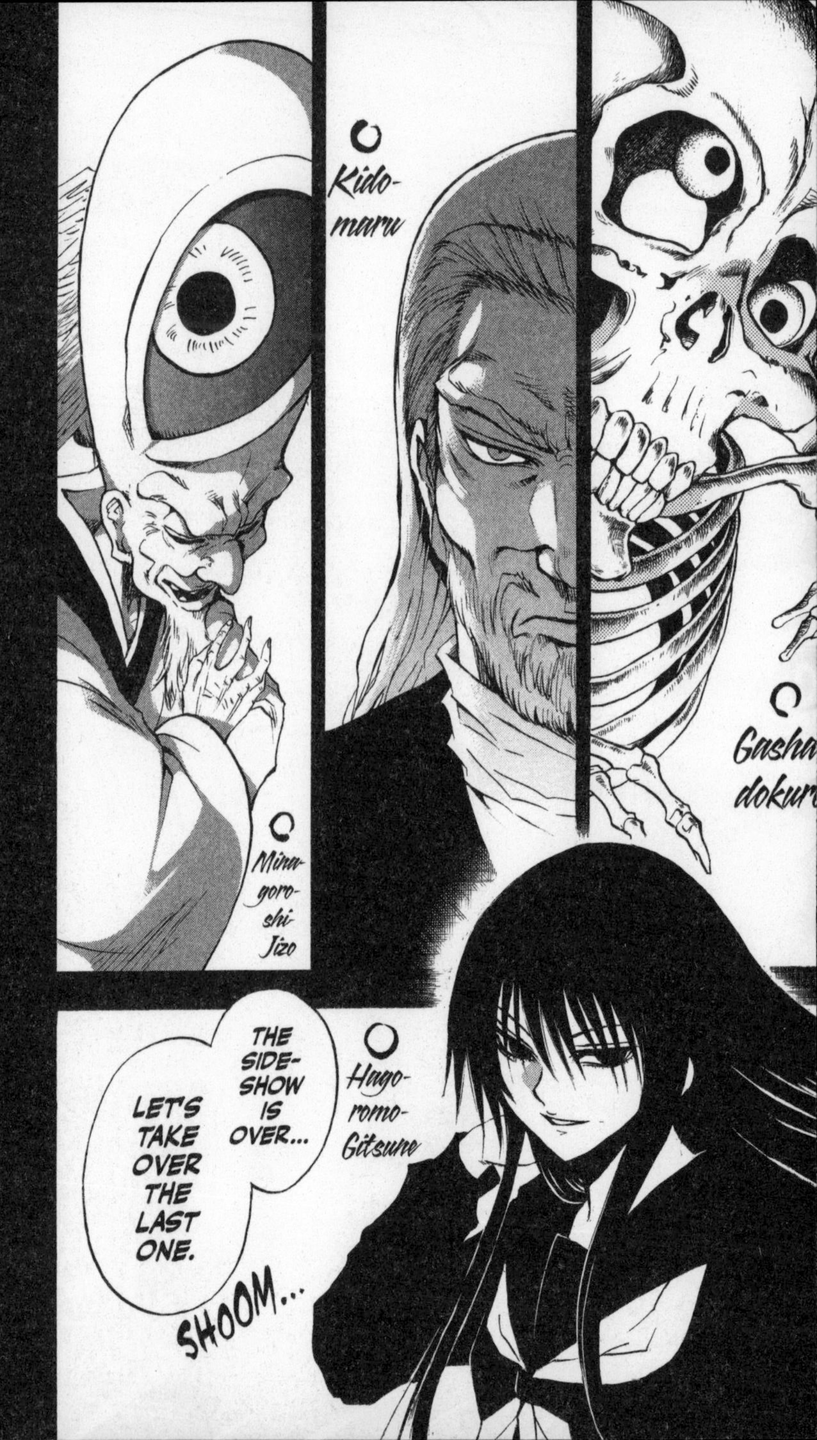
Gasha dokur
Kido-maru
Mina-goro-shi-Jizo
Hago-romo-Gitsune
THE SIDE-SHOW IS OVER...
LET'S TAKE OVER THE LAST ONE.
SHOOM...

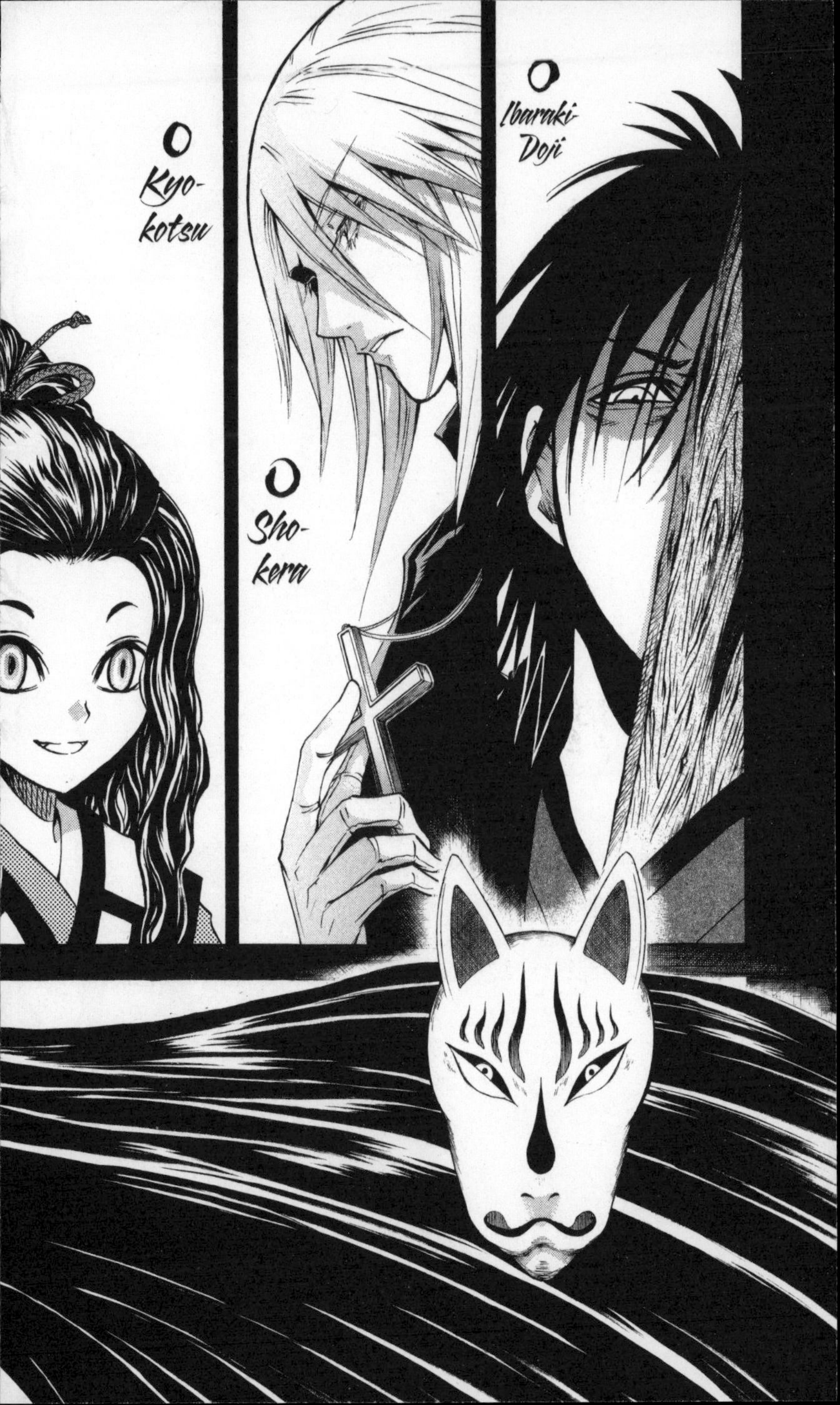
Ibaraki-Doji
Shokera
Kyokotsu

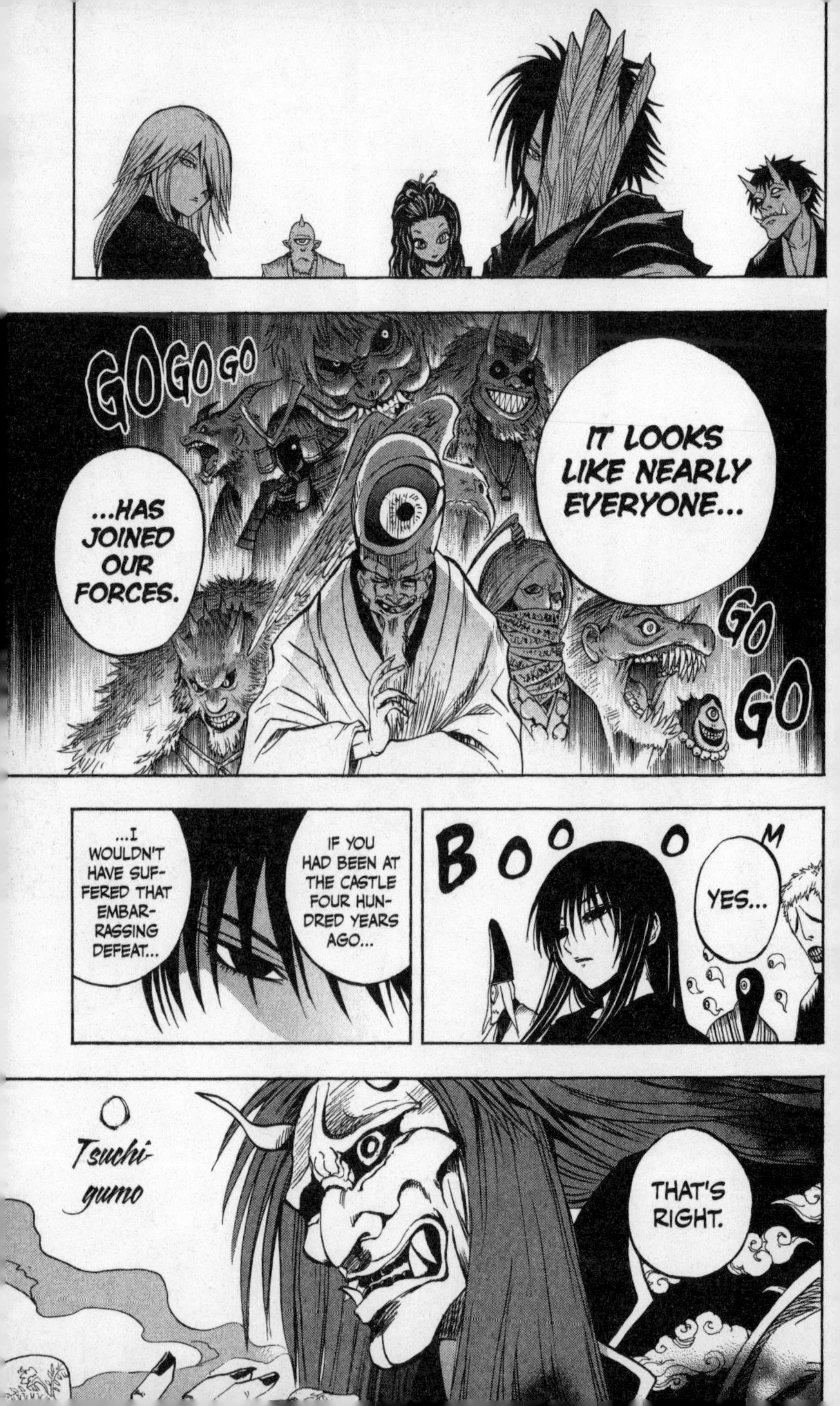

GO GO
GO
IT LOOKS LIKE NEARLY EVERYONE...
...HAS JOINED OUR FORCES.
GOGOGO
BOOOM
YES...
IF YOU HAD BEEN AT THE CASTLE FOUR HUN-DRED YEARS AGO...
...I WOULDN'T HAVE SUF-FERED THAT EMBAR-RASSING DEFEAT...
THAT'S RIGHT.
Tsuchigumo

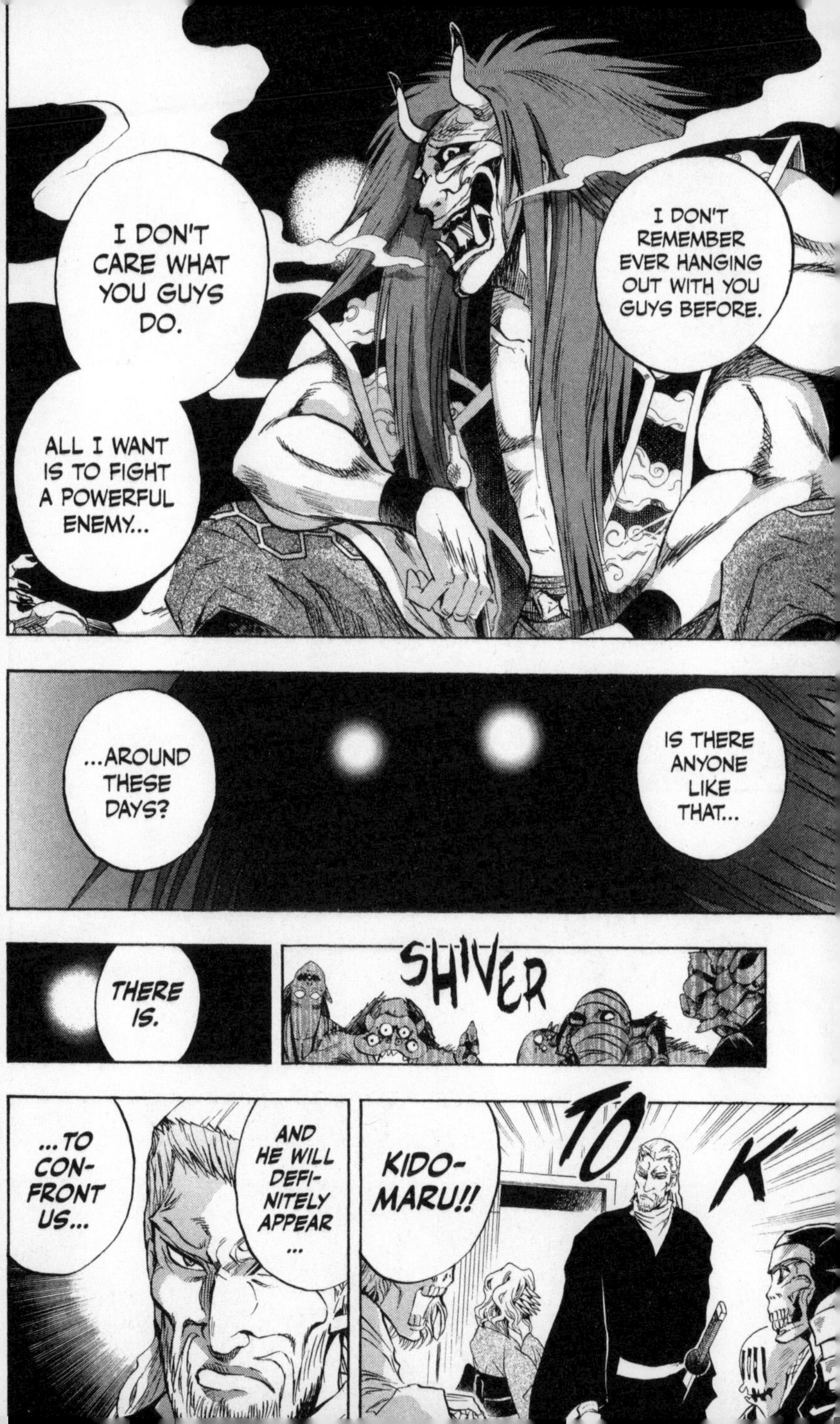
I DON'T REMEMBER EVER HANGING OUT WITH YOU GUYS BEFORE.
I DON'T CARE WHAT YOU GUYS DO.
ALL I WANT IS TO FIGHT A POWERFUL ENEMY...
IS THERE ANYONE LIKE THAT...
...AROUND THESE DAYS?
SHIVER
THERE IS.
TOK
KIDO-MARU!!
AND HE WILL DEFI-NITELY APPEAR ...
...TO CON-FRONT US...

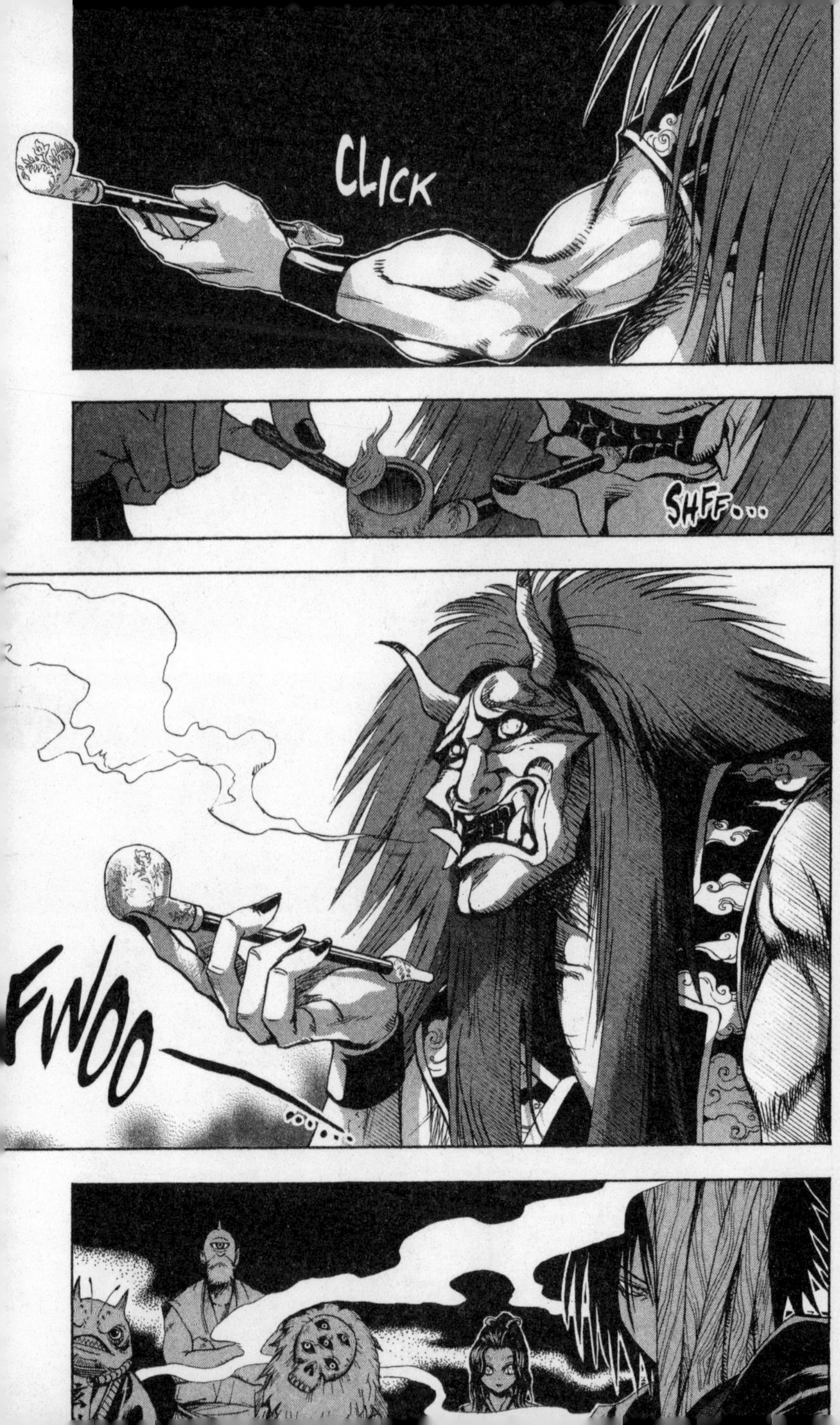
CLICK
SHFF...
FWOO

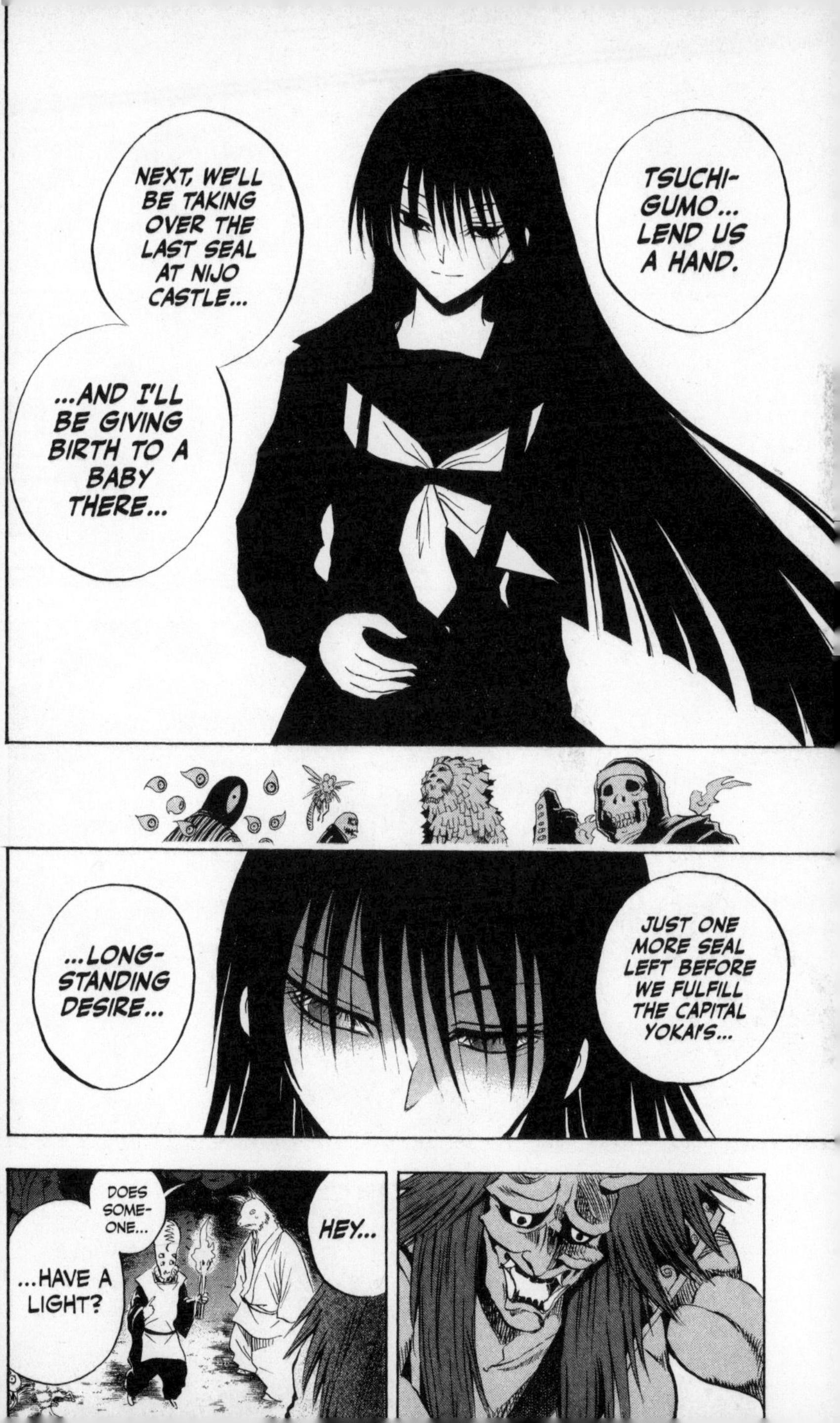
TSUCHI-GUMO... LEND US A HAND.
NEXT, WE'LL BE TAKING OVER THE LAST SEAL AT NIJO CASTLE...
...AND I'LL BE GIVING BIRTH TO A BABY THERE...
JUST ONE MORE SEAL LEFT BEFORE WE FULFILL THE CAPITAL YOKAI'S...
...LONG-STANDING DESIRE...
HEY...
DOES SOME-ONE...
...HAVE A LIGHT?

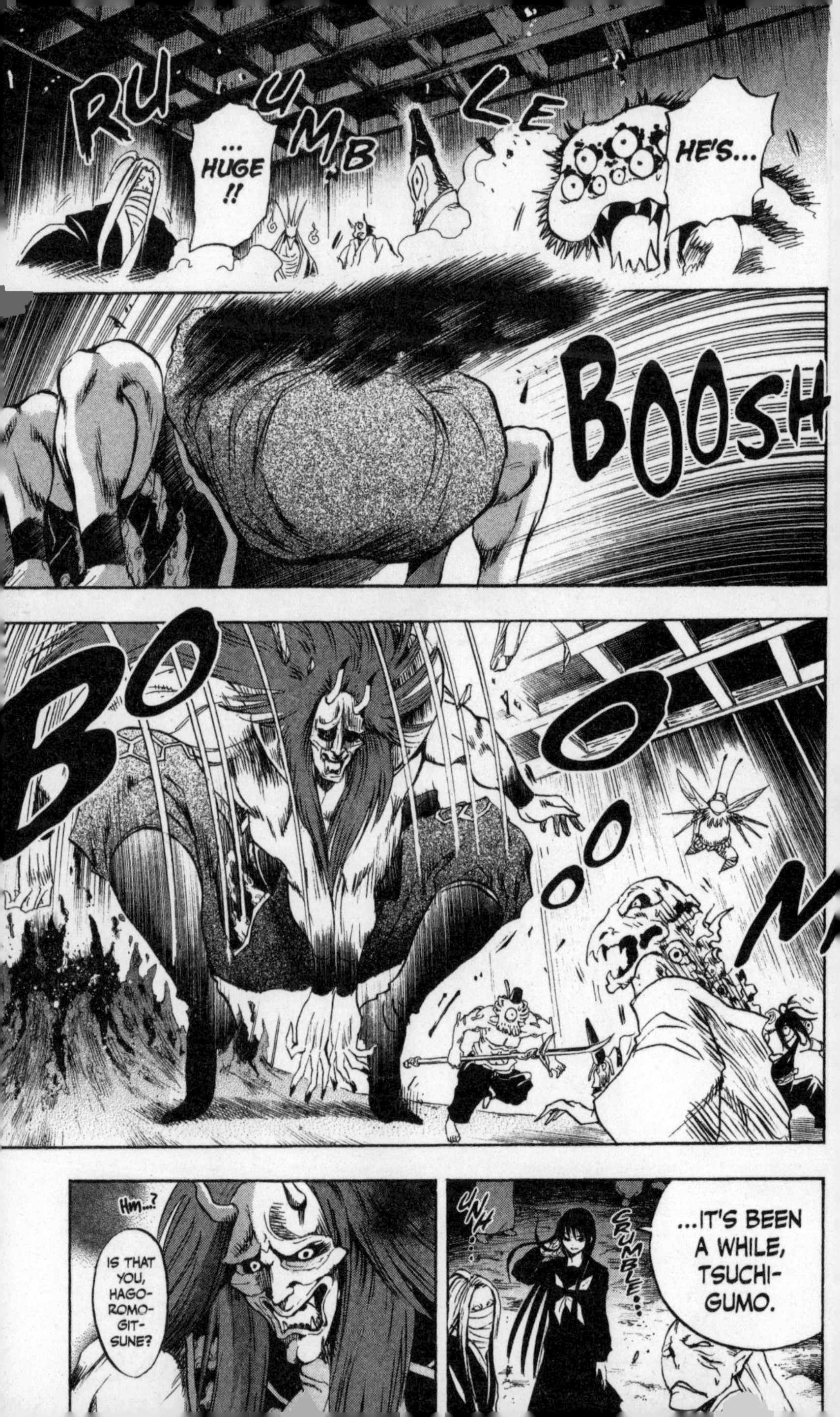
RUUMBLE
HE'S...
...HUGE!!
BOOSH
BOOOOOM
...IT'S BEEN A WHILE, TSUCHIGUMO.
CRUMBLE...
UNH...
Hm...?
IS THAT YOU, HAGOROMO-GITSUNE?

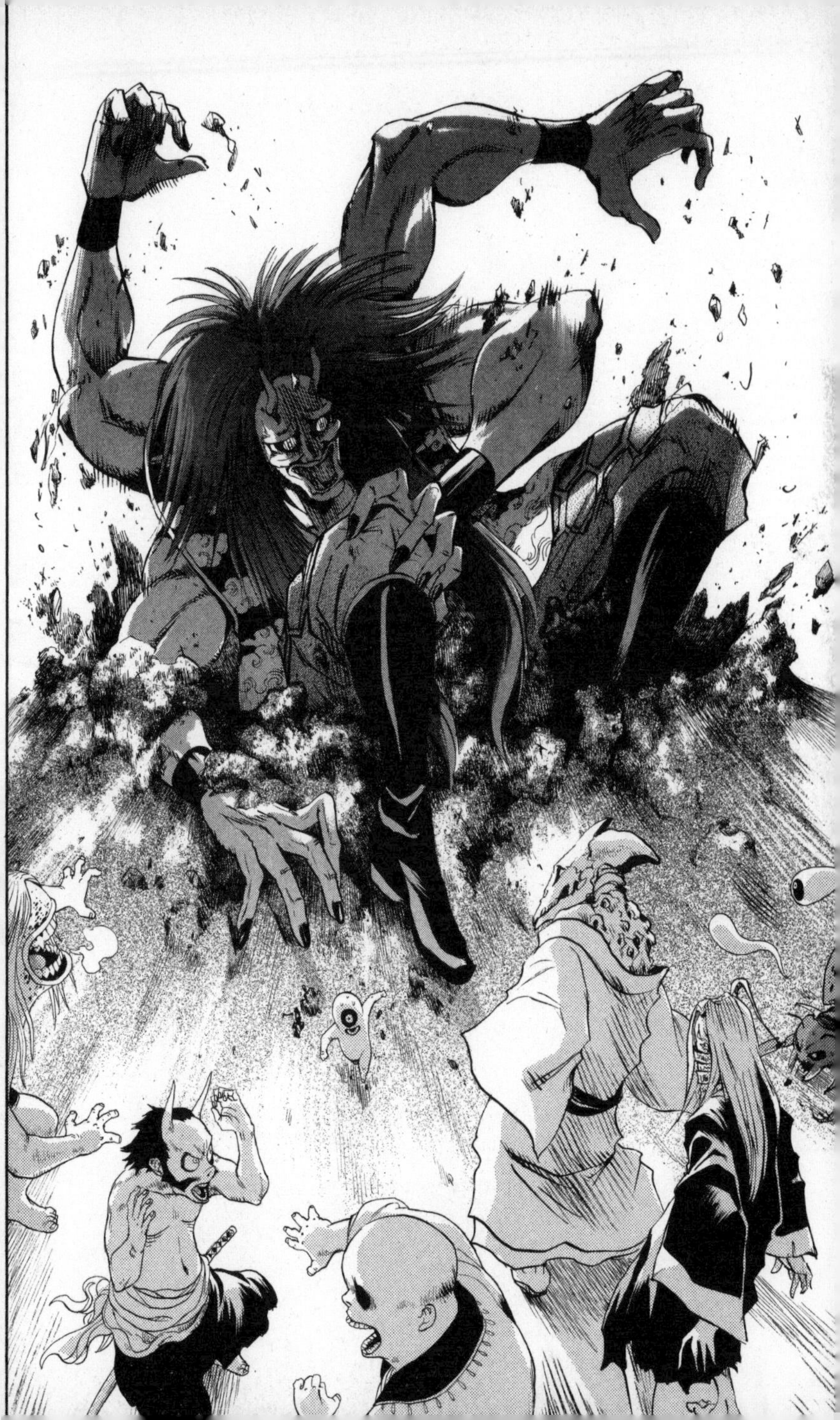

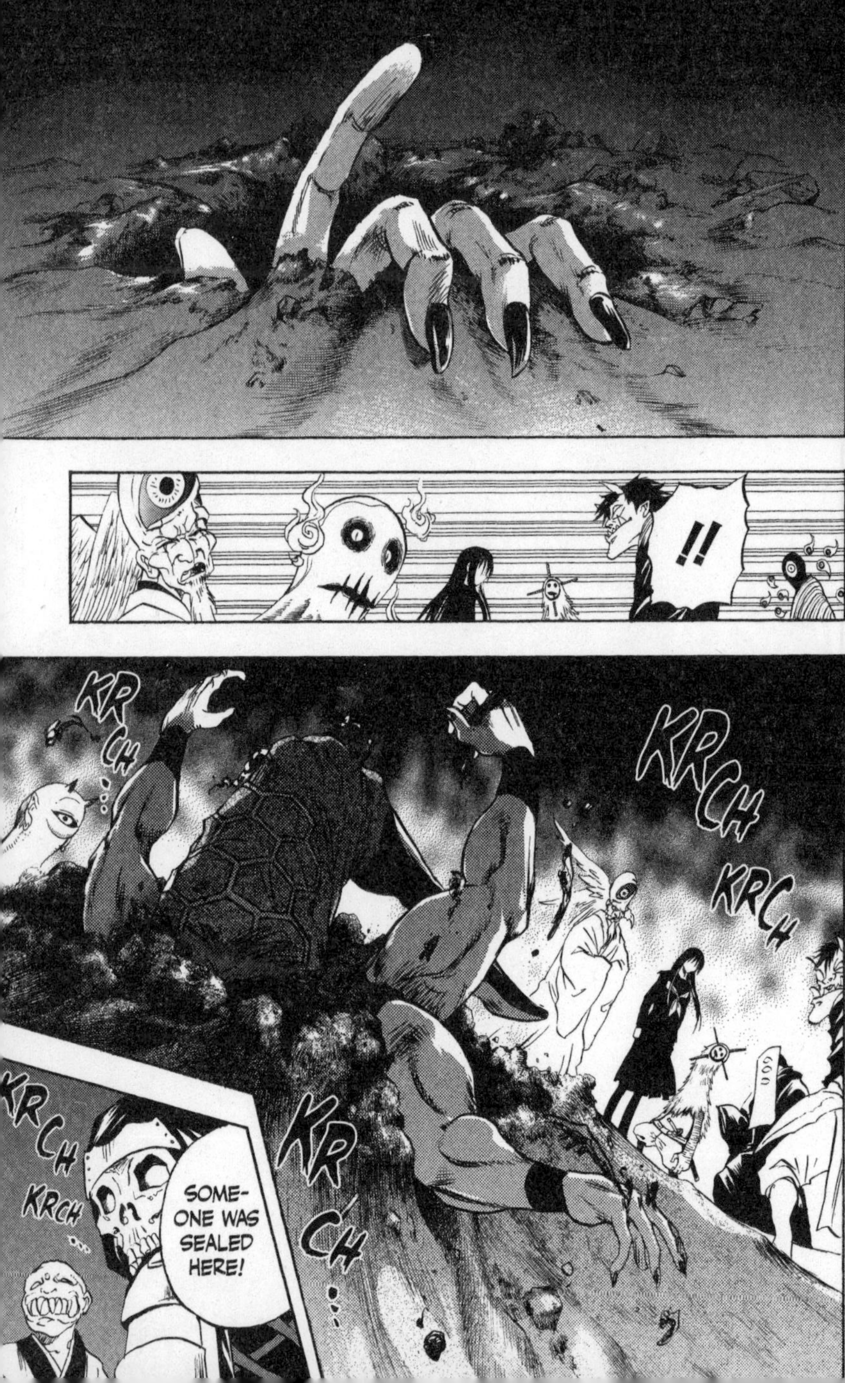
!!
KRCH
KRCH
KRCH...
KRCH
KRCH...
SOME-ONE WAS SEALED HERE!
KRCH...

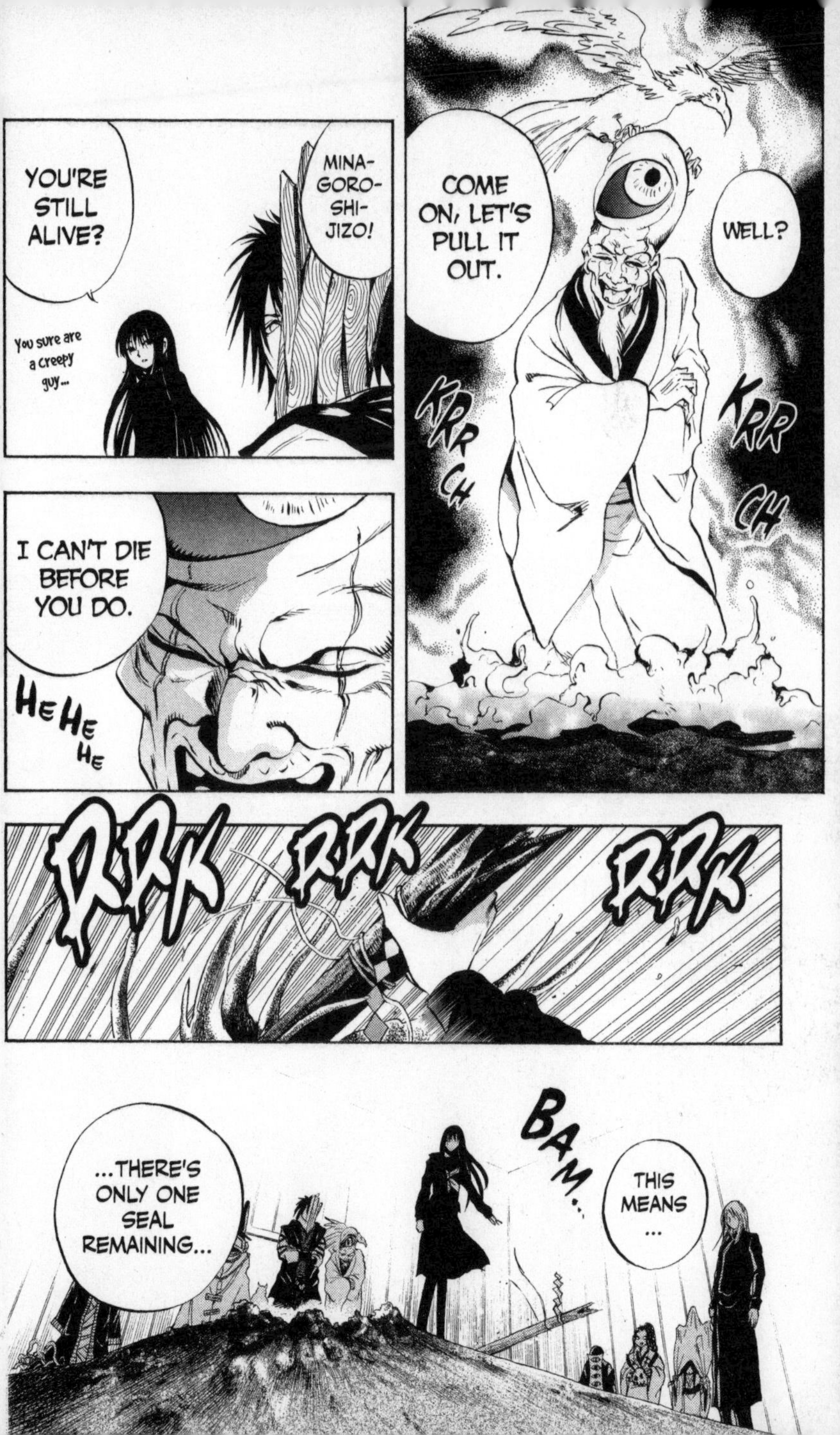
WELL?
COME ON, LET'S PULL IT OUT.
KRRCH
KRRCH
MINA-GORO-SHI-JIZO!
YOU'RE STILL ALIVE?
You sure are a creepy guy...
I CAN'T DIE BEFORE YOU DO.
HEHEHE
RRK
RRK
RRK
THIS MEANS...
BAM...
...THERE'S ONLY ONE SEAL REMAINING...

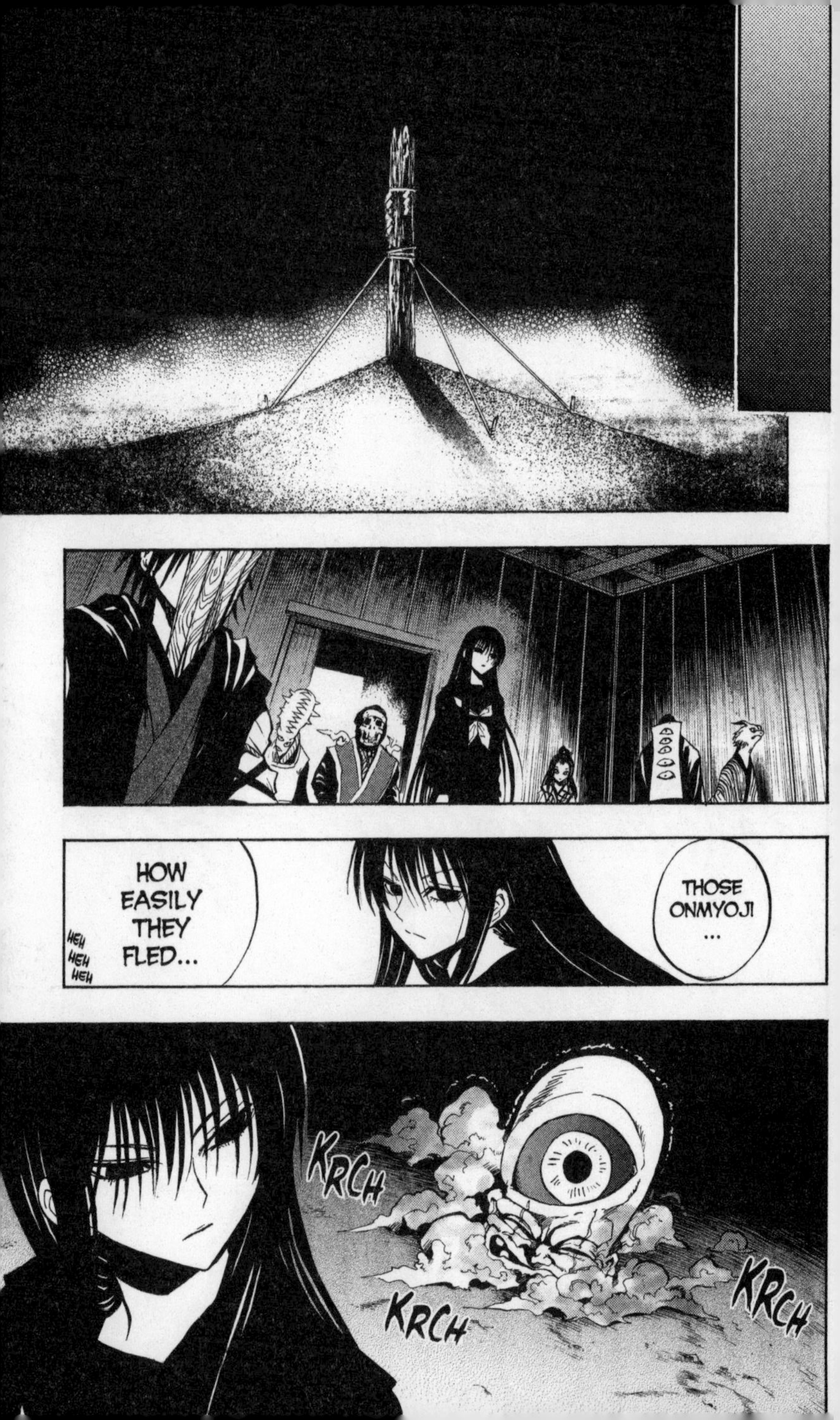
THOSE ONMYOJI ...
HOW EASILY THEY FLED...
HEH HEH HEH
KRCH
KRCH
KRCH

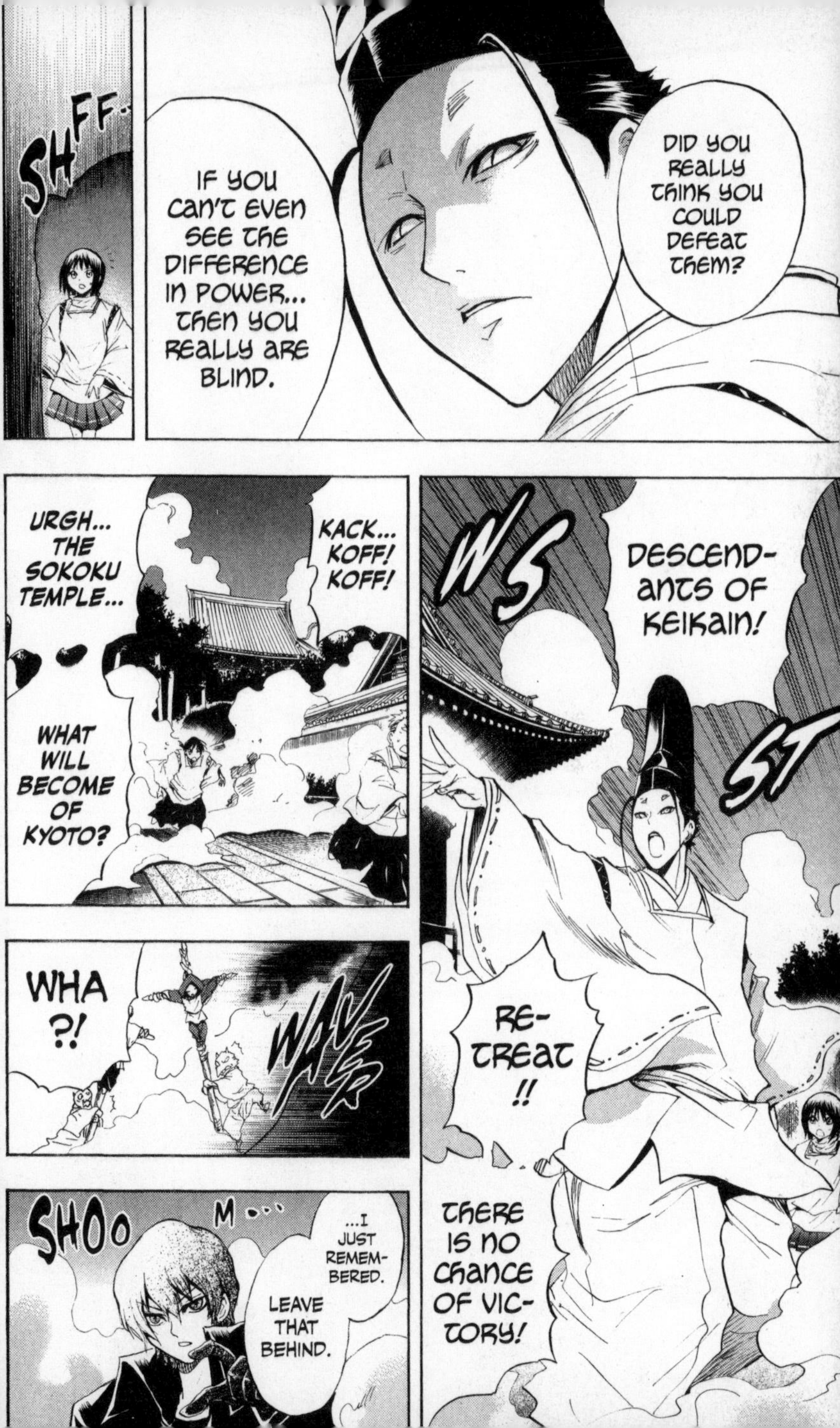
DID YOU REALLY THINK YOU COULD DEFEAT THEM?
IF YOU CAN'T EVEN SEE THE DIFFERENCE IN POWER... THEN YOU REALLY ARE BLIND.
SHFF..
WS
DESCEND-ANTS OF KEIKAIN!
ST
RE-TREAT!!
THERE IS NO CHANCE OF VIC-TORY!
KACK... KOFF! KOFF!
URGH... THE SOKOKU TEMPLE...
WHAT WILL BECOME OF KYOTO?
WAVER
WHA?!
...I JUST REMEM-BERED.
LEAVE THAT BEHIND.
SHOOM...

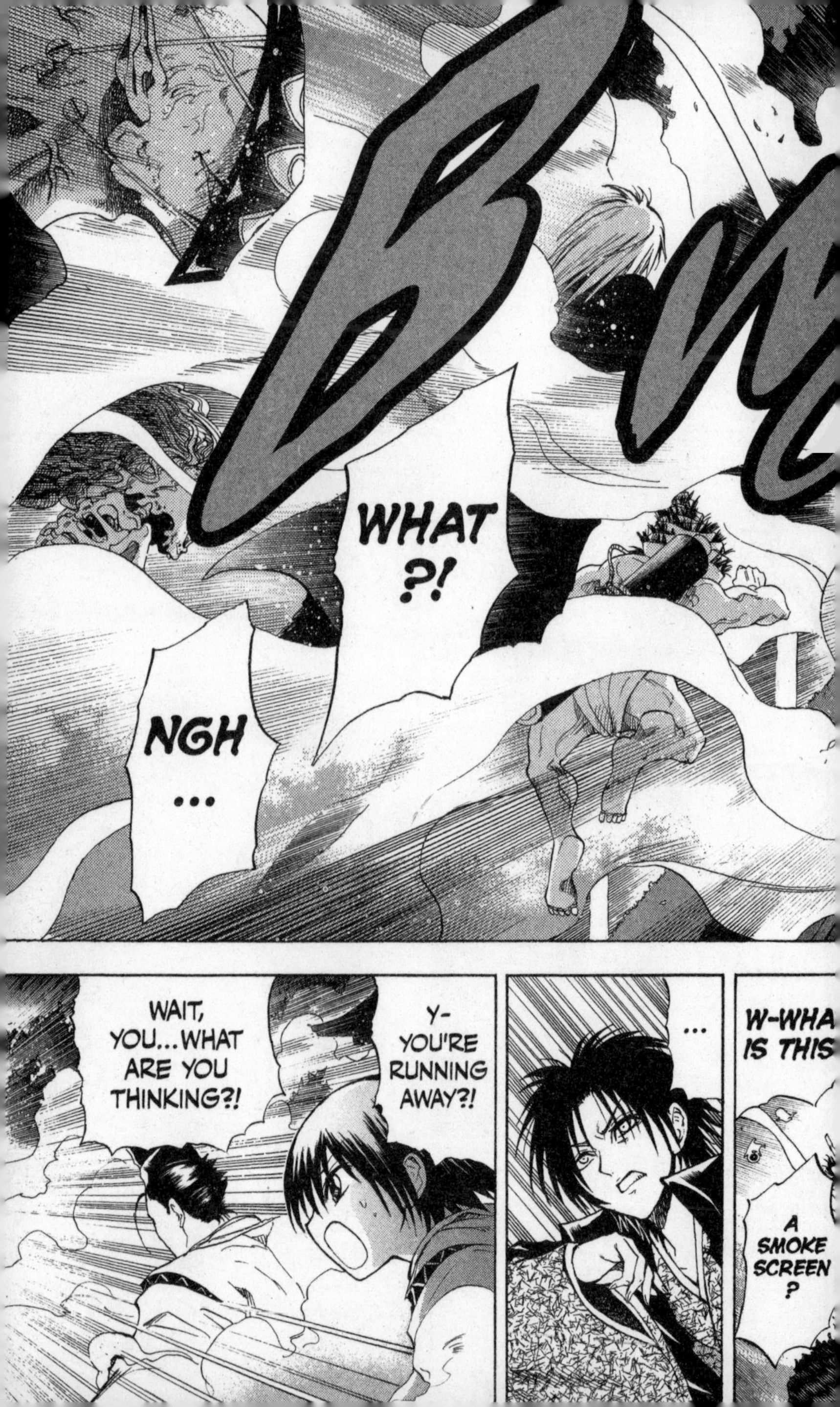
WHAT ?!
NGH ...
W-WHA IS THIS
A SMOKE SCREEN ?
...
Y- YOU'RE RUNNING AWAY?!
WAIT, YOU...WHAT ARE YOU THINKING?!

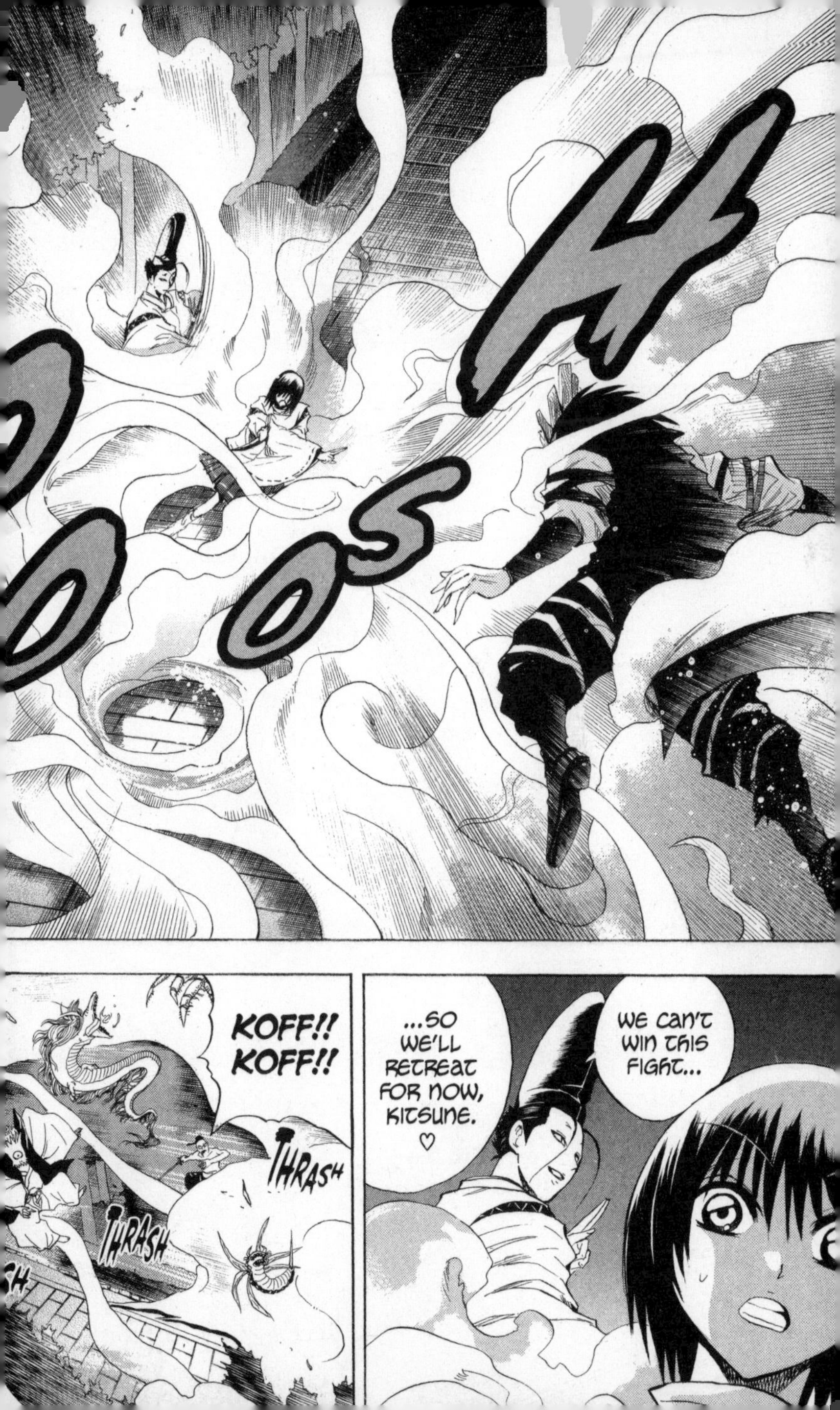
DOOSH
WE CAN'T WIN THIS FIGHT...
...SO WE'LL RETREAT FOR NOW, KITSUNE. ♡
KOFF!! KOFF!!
THRASH
THRASH

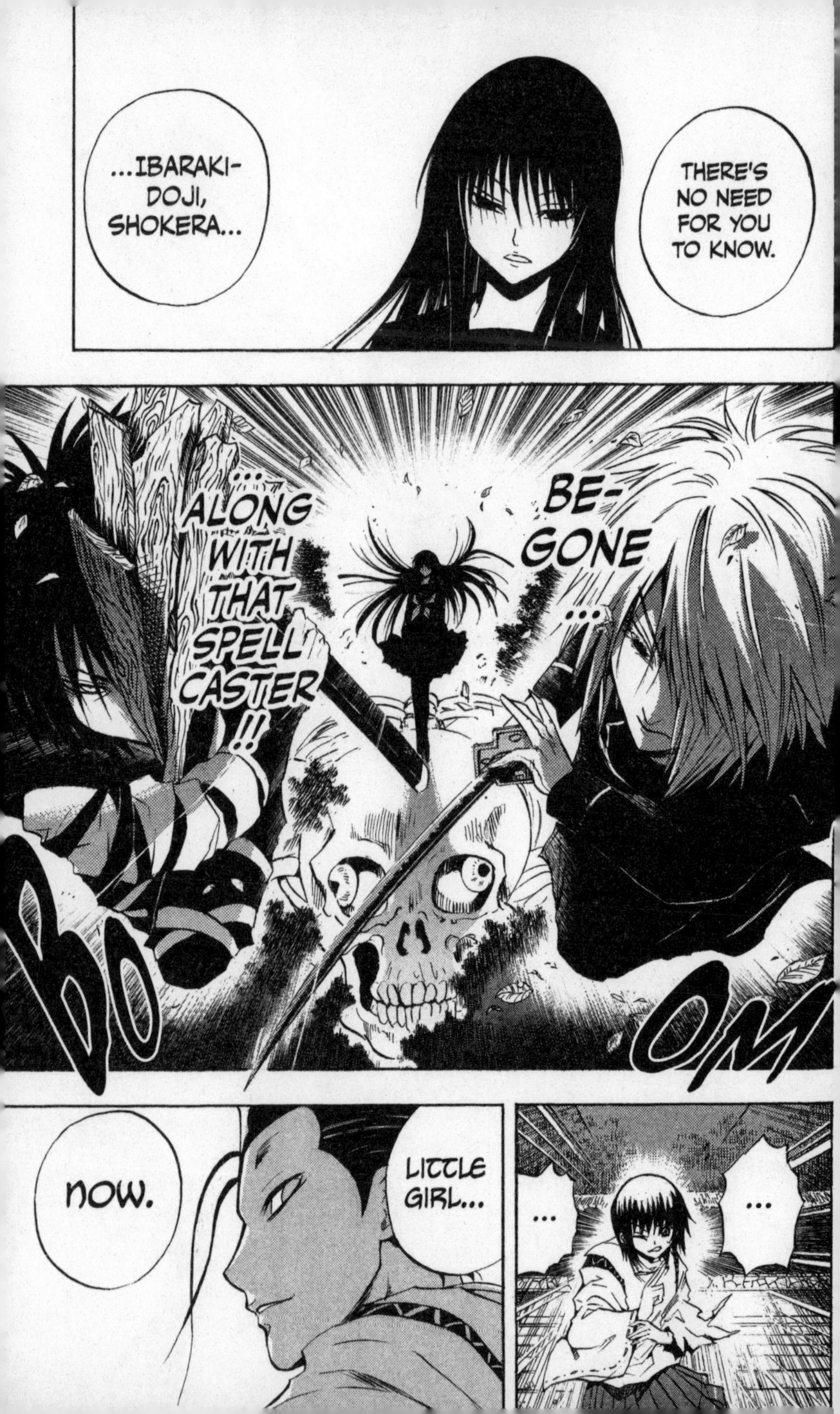
THERE'S NO NEED FOR YOU TO KNOW.
...IBARAKI-DOJI, SHOKERA...
BE-GONE...
...ALONG WITH THAT SPELL CASTER!!
BOOM
...
...
LITTLE GIRL...
now.

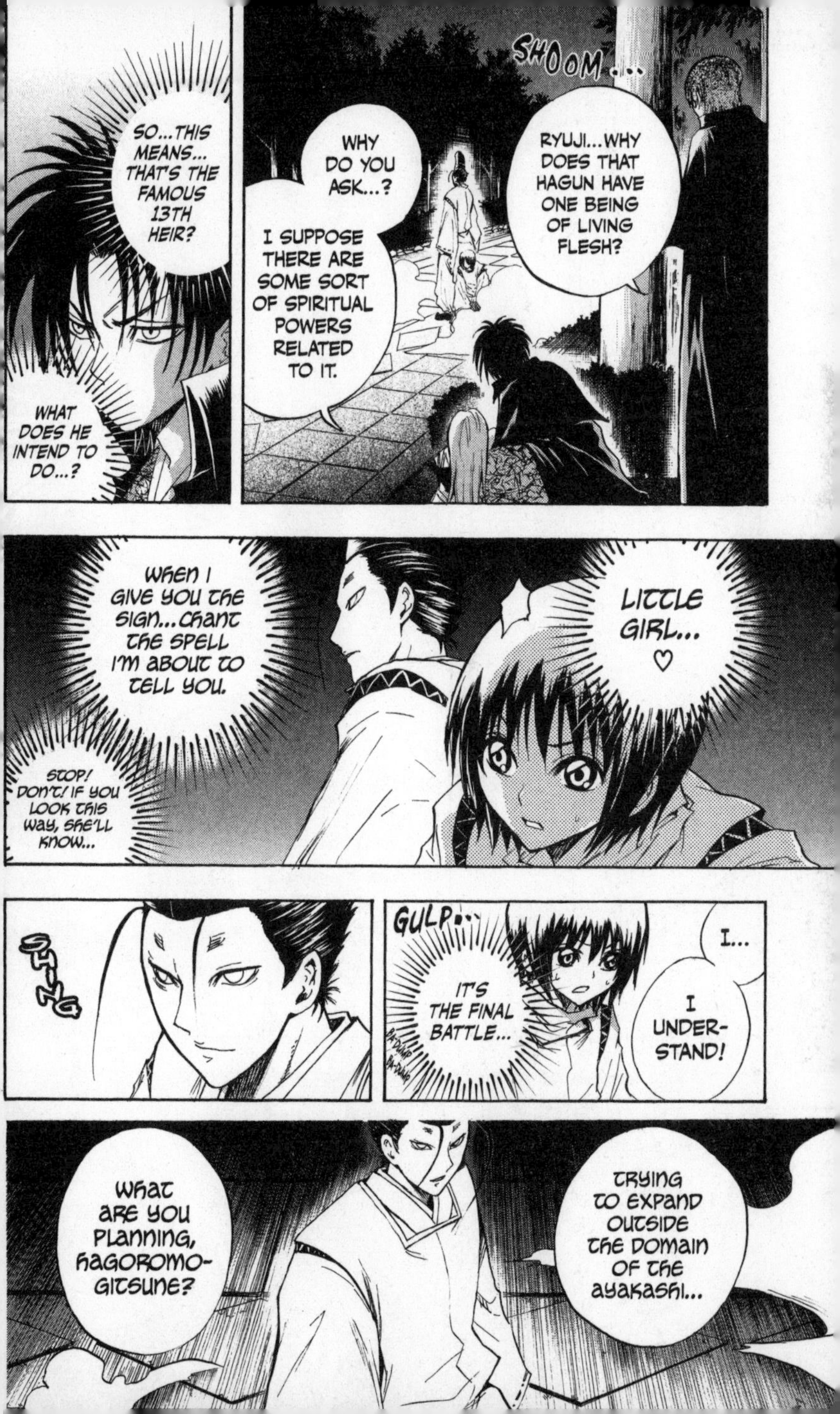
SHOOM...
RYUJI...WHY DOES THAT HAGUN HAVE ONE BEING OF LIVING FLESH?
WHY DO YOU ASK...?
I SUPPOSE THERE ARE SOME SORT OF SPIRITUAL POWERS RELATED TO IT.
SO...THIS MEANS... THAT'S THE FAMOUS 13TH HEIR?
WHAT DOES HE INTEND TO DO...?
LITTLE GIRL... ♡
WHEN I GIVE YOU THE SIGN...CHANT THE SPELL I'M ABOUT TO TELL YOU.
STOP! DON'T! IF YOU LOOK THIS WAY, SHE'LL KNOW...
GULP...
I...
I UNDERSTAND!
IT'S THE FINAL BATTLE...
BA-DUMP BA-DUMP
SHING
TRYING TO EXPAND OUTSIDE THE DOMAIN OF THE AYAKASHI...
WHAT ARE YOU PLANNING, HAGOROMO-GITSUNE?

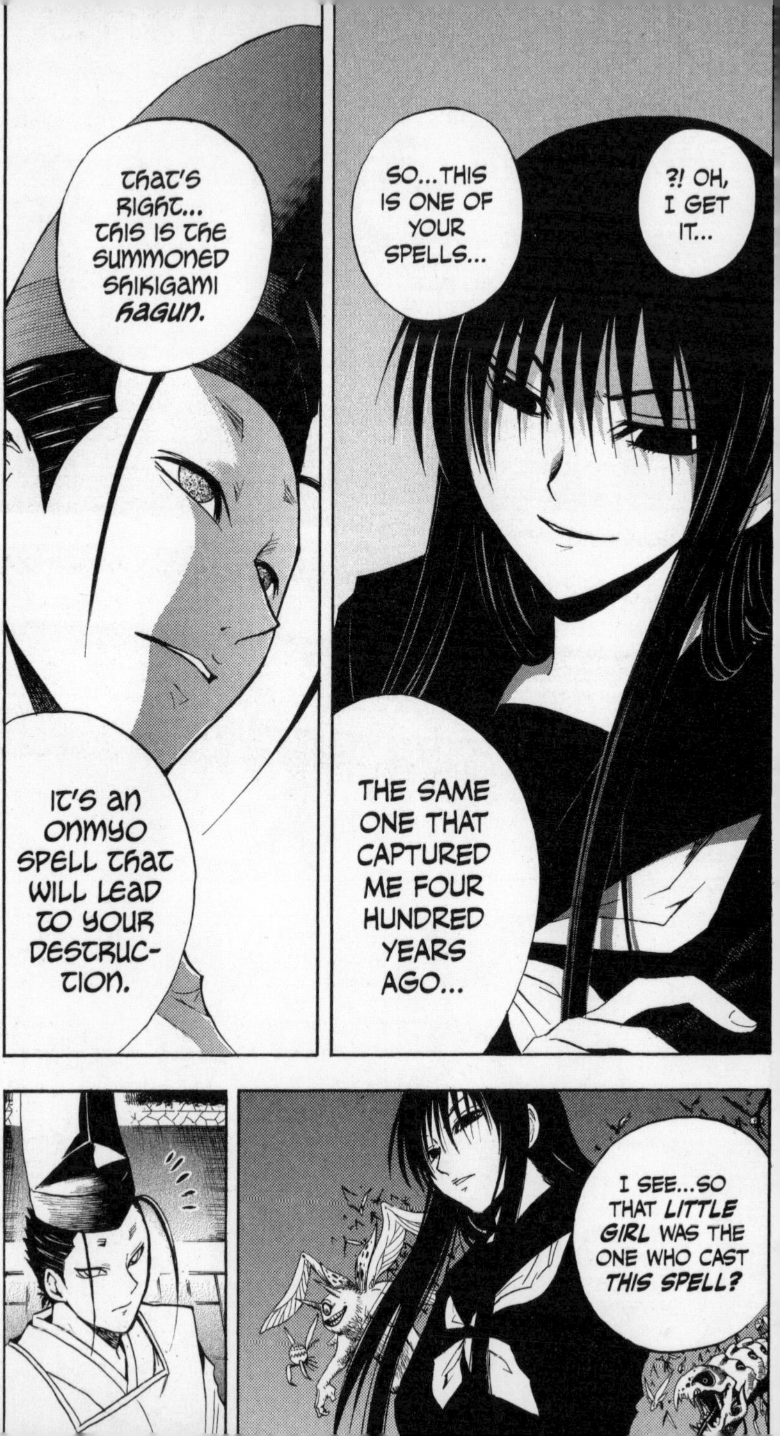
?! OH, I GET IT...
SO...THIS IS ONE OF YOUR SPELLS...
THE SAME ONE THAT CAPTURED ME FOUR HUNDRED YEARS AGO...
THAT'S RIGHT... THIS IS THE SUMMONED SHIKIGAMI HAGUN.
IT'S AN ONMYO SPELL THAT WILL LEAD TO YOUR DESTRUCTION.
I SEE...SO THAT LITTLE GIRL WAS THE ONE WHO CAST THIS SPELL?

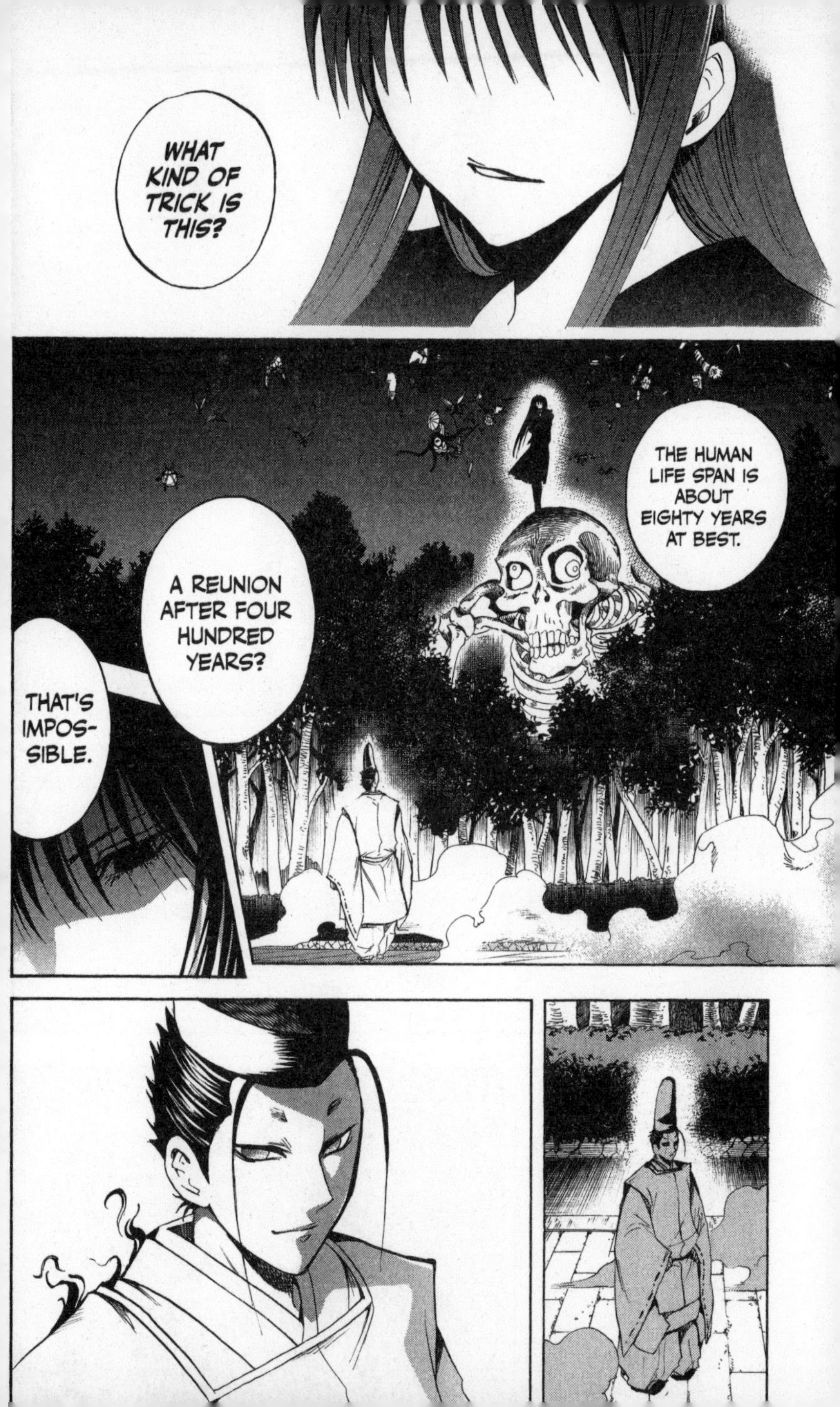
WHAT KIND OF TRICK IS THIS?
THE HUMAN LIFE SPAN IS ABOUT EIGHTY YEARS AT BEST.
A REUNION AFTER FOUR HUNDRED YEARS?
THAT'S IMPOS-SIBLE.

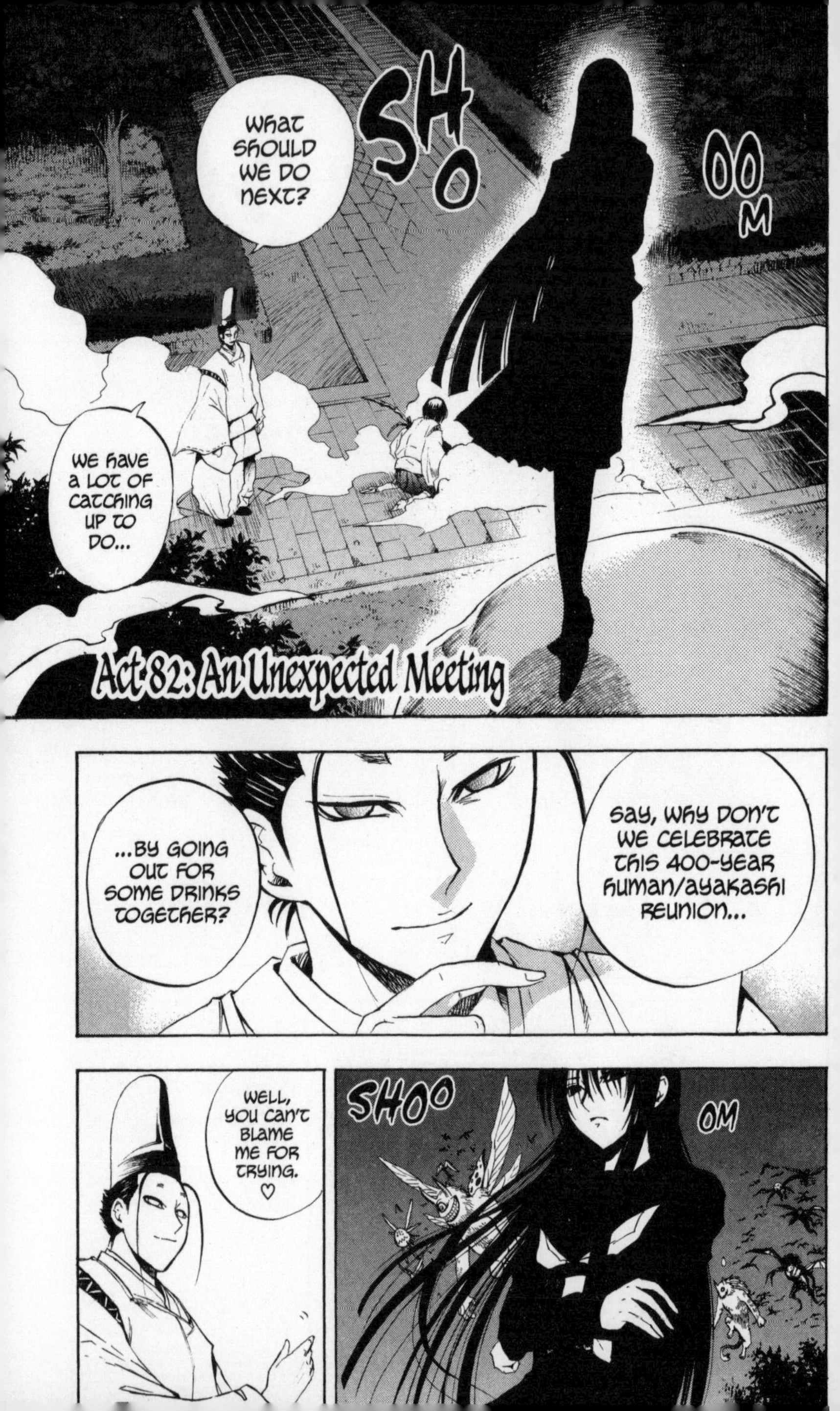

SHO
OOM
WHAT SHOULD WE DO NEXT?
WE HAVE A LOT OF CATCHING UP TO DO...
Act 82: An Unexpected Meeting
SAY, WHY DON'T WE CELEBRATE THIS 400-YEAR HUMAN/AYAKASHI REUNION...
...BY GOING OUT FOR SOME DRINKS TOGETHER?
SHOO
OM
WELL, YOU CAN'T BLAME ME FOR TRYING. ♡

FIELD TRIP EDITION #10 BY KIYO

KIYOTSUGU'S YOKAI BRAIN

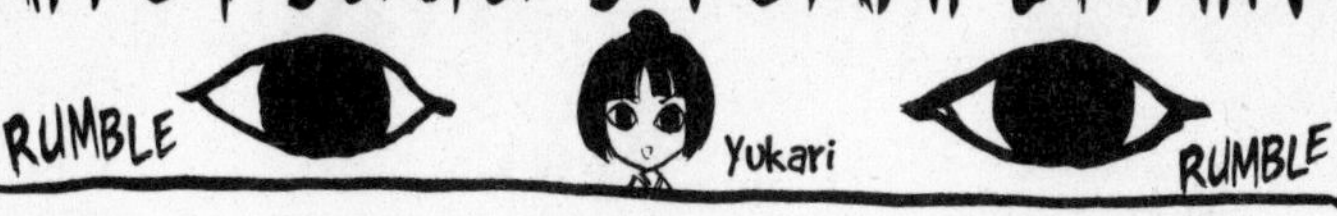
RUMBLE
Yukari
RUMBLE

Question 1: Who is the most popular, Kurotabo, Kubinashi or Rikuo? *—Benizakura, Gunma Prefecture*

Tsurara: It's Rikuo!!

Rikuo: R-really? I don't think it'd be me...

Tsurara: No, Waka is number one!!

Kejoro: Tsurara...don't you realize? Being popular means they're always surrounded by girls. Do you want Rikuo to be that way?

Tsurara: Rikuo is not popular!! He'll never be popular! Not ever!!

Rikuo: Th-that's...a little...

Question 2: How strong is Aotabo's grip? I'm curious about it, so please let me know!! *—Terubo, Tochigi Prefecture*

Aotabo: The strength of my grip is measured in entirely different units!!

Kurotabo: What do you mean by that, Ao? Don't tell me it's measured in tons.

Aotabo: No, it's measured in years!! It takes three years to fully recover from being crushed in my grip!!

Kurotabo: ...

Question 3: Which sports does Yukari like to do? *—Ranpu, Gunma Prefecture*

Yukari: The two-meter dash.

Question 4: Where does Kappa usually sleep? Is it in the mansion, or in the pond? *—Ayumi Sasaki, Miyagi Prefecture*

Kappa: Hmmm... I'd say the river. I sleep in the river, and look forward to finding out where I end up in the morning.

Question 5: About how many swords does Kurotabo have? *—Yosshii, Tokyo*

Kurotabo: Not quite 999 like Benkei would have, but there has to be at least 200 of them. I've never counted, though.

Question 6: Rikuo's sword is Nenekirimaru. What about Itaku's scythe? *—Minami Omoda, Ehime Prefecture*

Itaku: Cloth, Tree, Bamboo, Iron, Sword, and Frying Pan, a total of six. The names originate from their handles.

Question 7: In Act 54, Yura taped up the torn shikigami Tanro together and used it, but does shikigami paper need to be reused?

Yura: Tanro is in that charm...so I have to use that. Well, it's possible to transfer it to another paper, but the only paper I had handy was a receipt. Oh, by the way! That purse I use? It's a charm against evil spirits. Did you know that? It's not just an unfashionable-looking frog!!

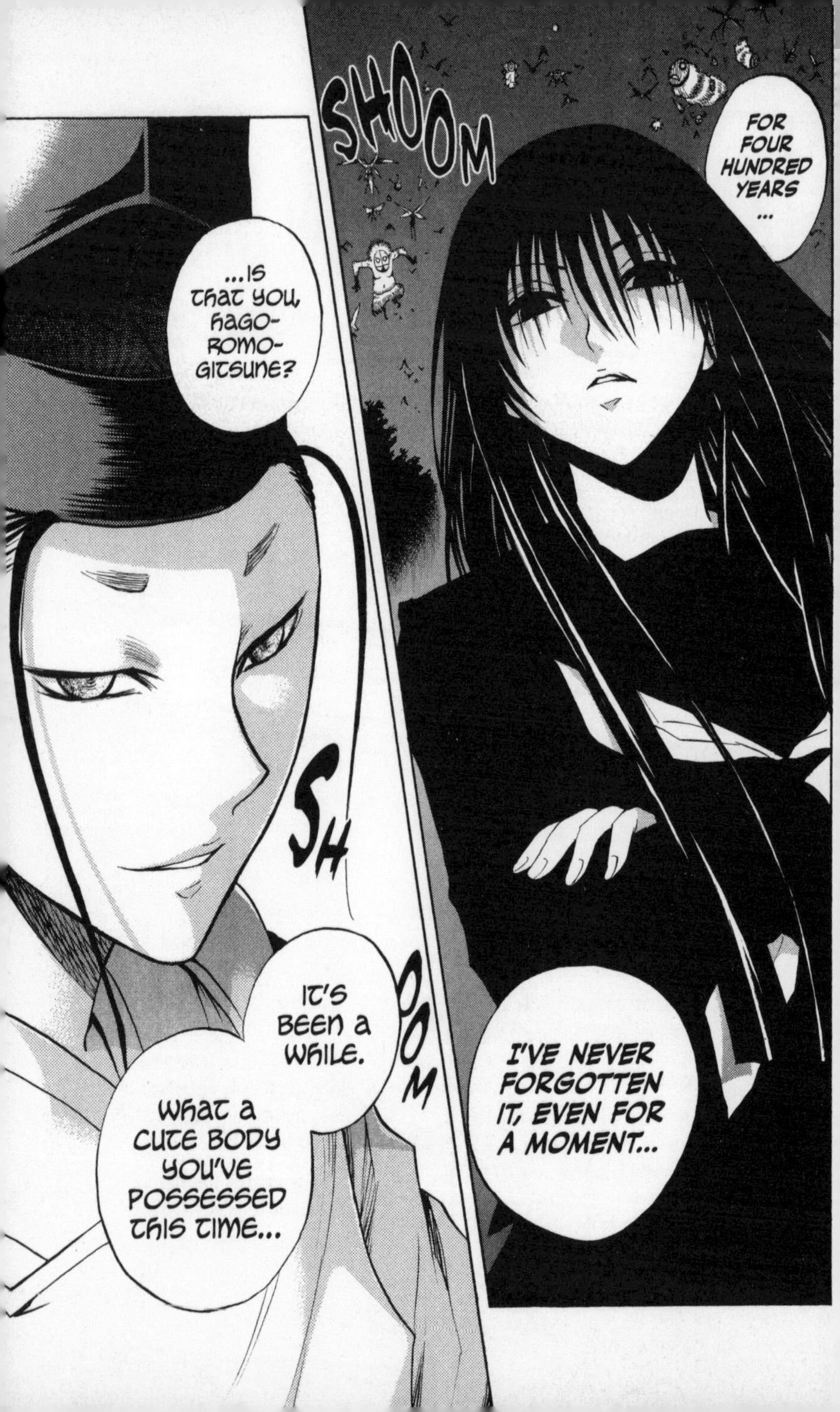
SHOOM
FOR FOUR HUNDRED YEARS...
I'VE NEVER FORGOTTEN IT, EVEN FOR A MOMENT...
...IS THAT YOU, HAGO-ROMO-GITSUNE?
SHOOM
IT'S BEEN A WHILE.
WHAT A CUTE BODY YOU'VE POSSESSED THIS TIME...

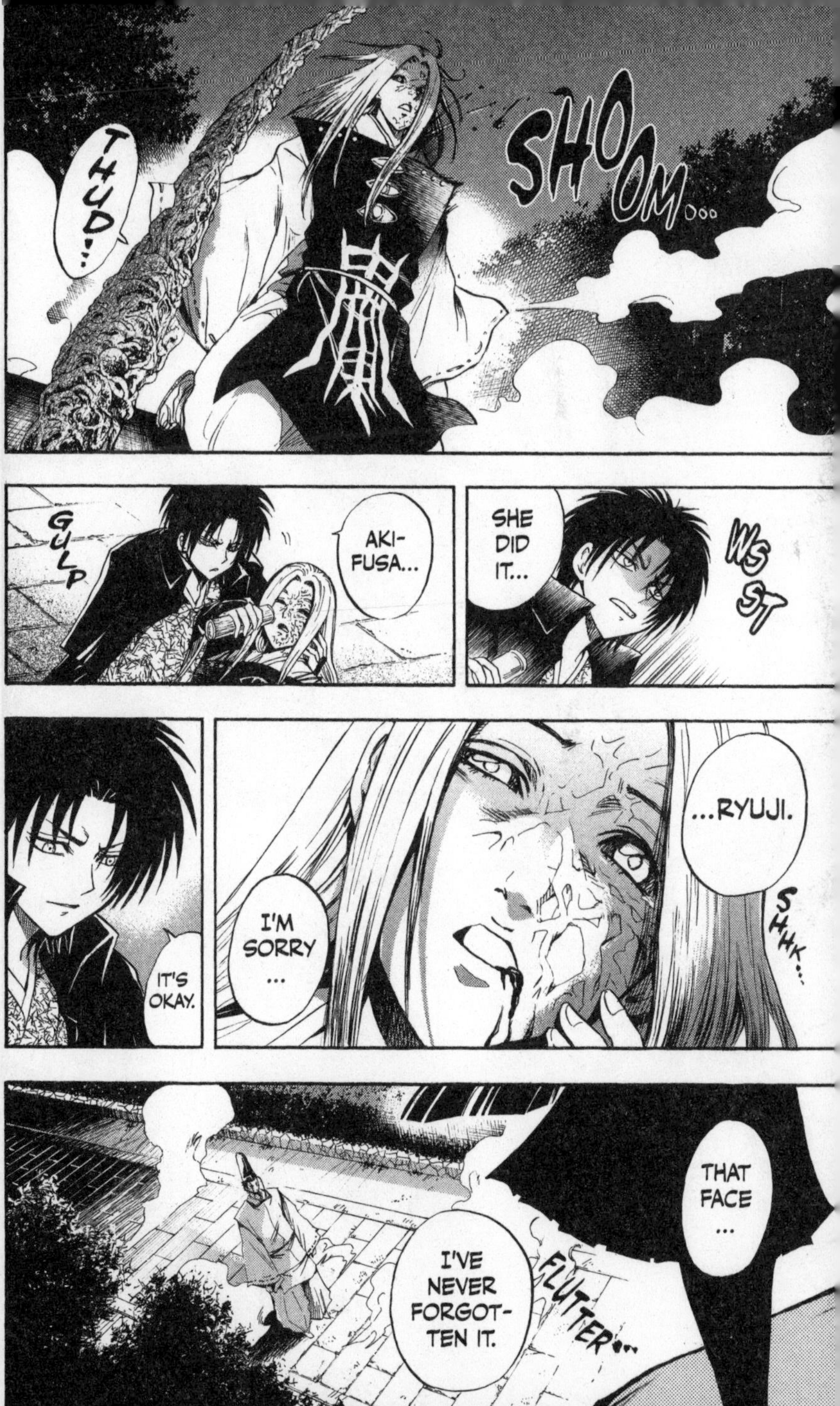
SHOOOM...
THUD...
WSST
SHE DID IT...
AKI-FUSA...
GULP
...RYUJI.
SHHK...
I'M SORRY ...
IT'S OKAY.
THAT FACE ...
FLUTTER...
I'VE NEVER FORGOT-TEN IT.

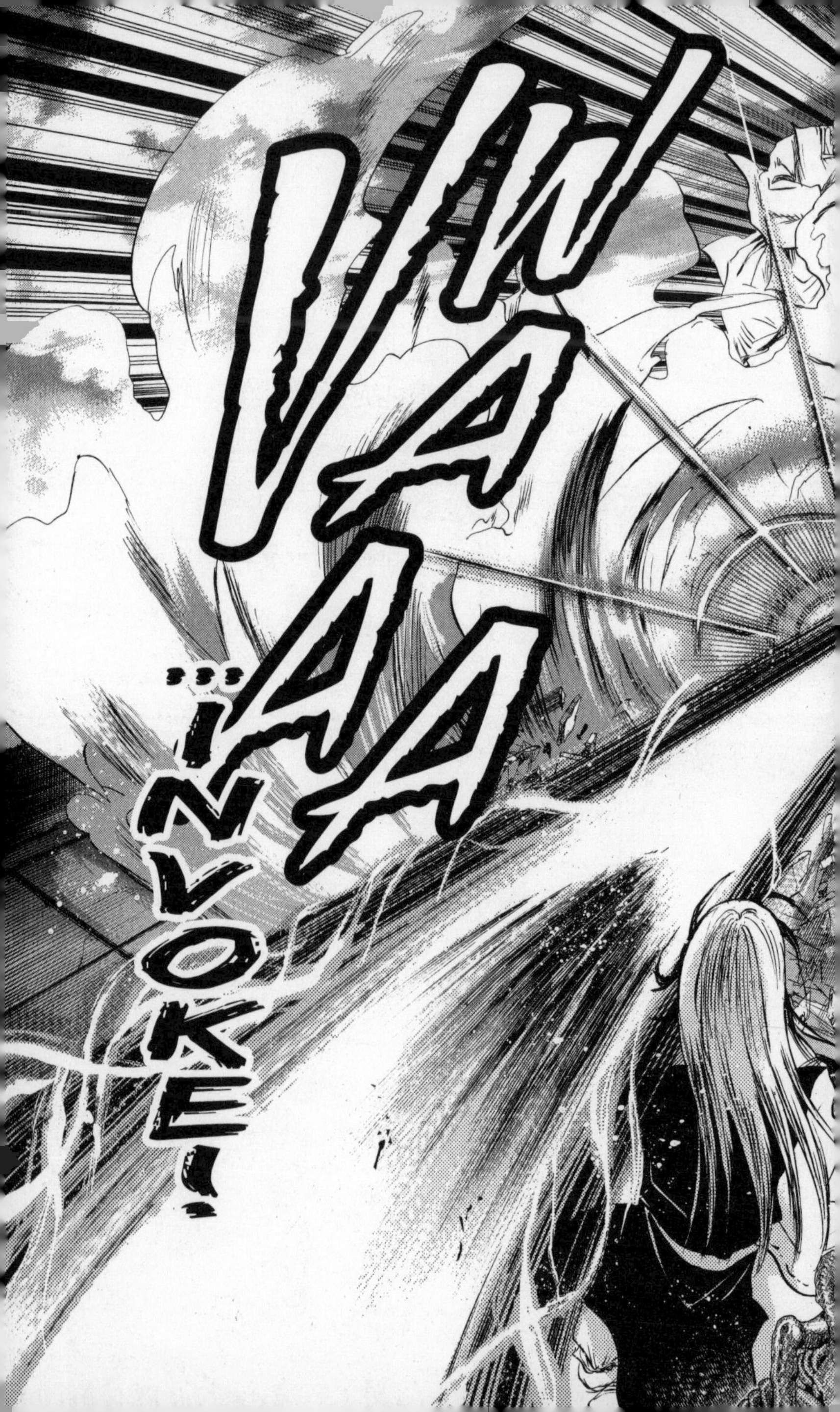
VWAAA
...INVOKE!

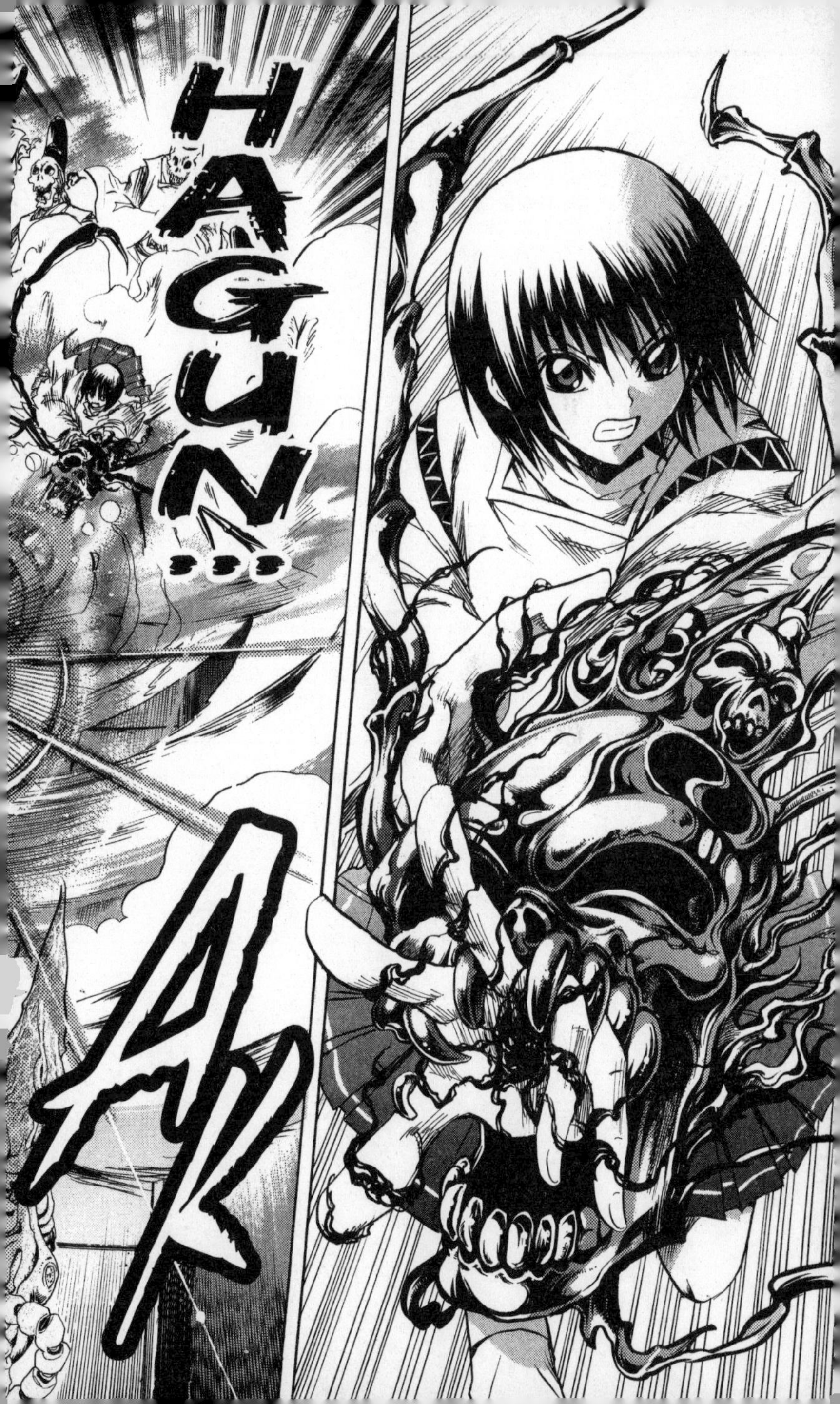
HAGUN...
A

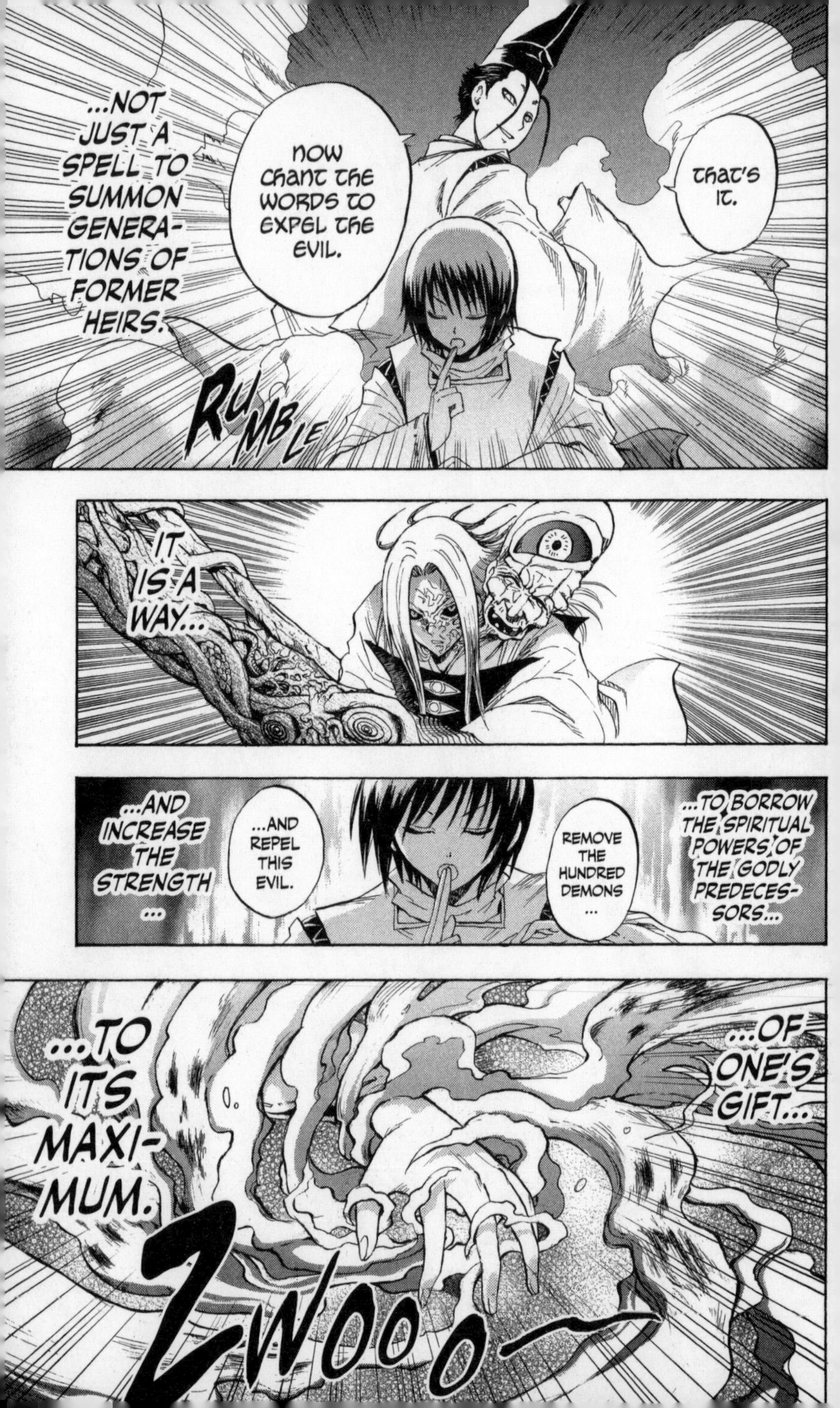
THAT'S IT.
NOW CHANT THE WORDS TO EXPEL THE EVIL.
...NOT JUST A SPELL TO SUMMON GENERA-TIONS OF FORMER HEIRS.
RUMBLE
IT IS A WAY...
...TO BORROW THE SPIRITUAL POWERS OF THE GODLY PREDECES-SORS...
REMOVE THE HUNDRED DEMONS ...
...AND REPEL THIS EVIL.
...AND INCREASE THE STRENGTH ...
...OF ONE'S GIFT...
...TO ITS MAXI-MUM.
ZWOOO—

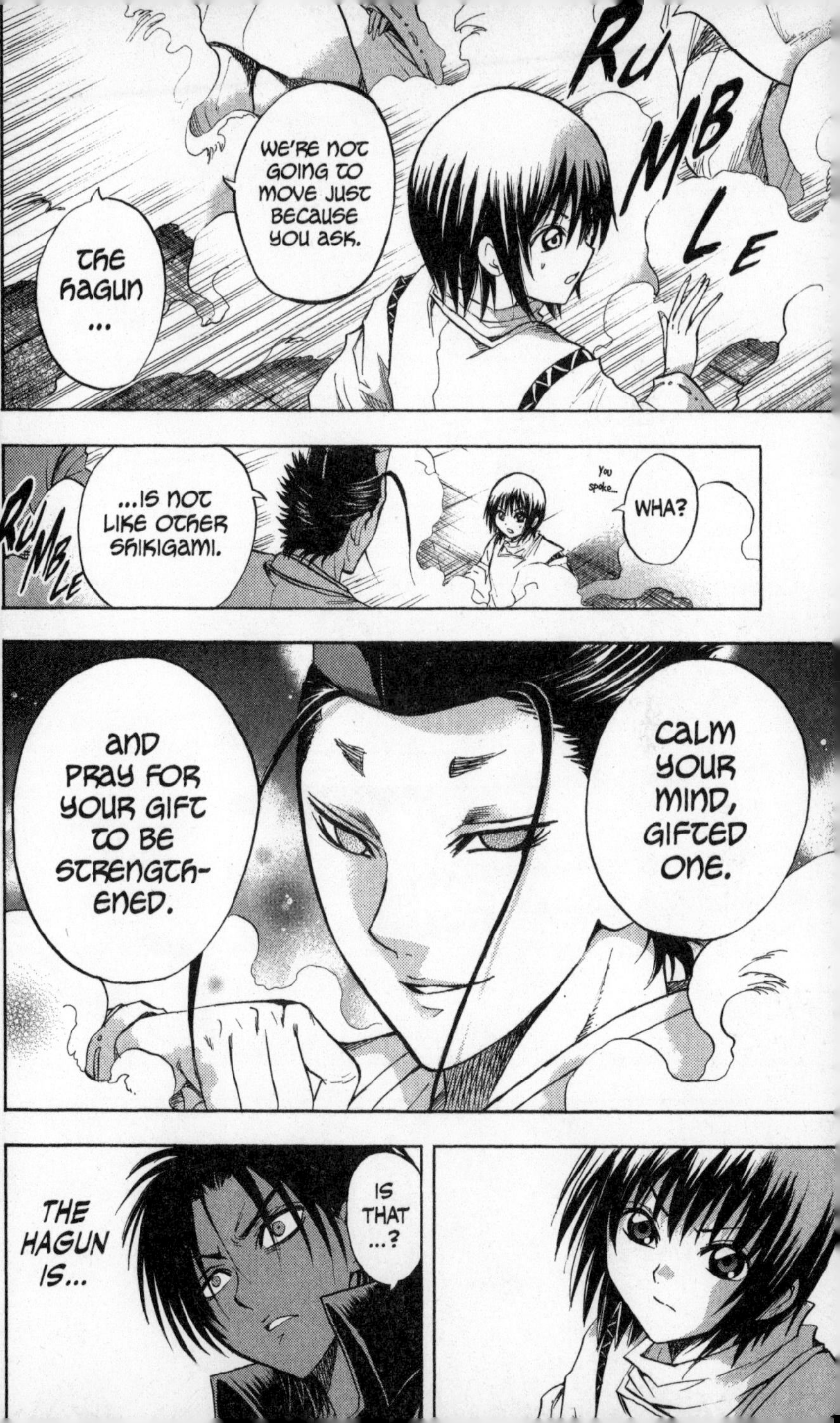
RUMBLE
WE'RE NOT GOING TO MOVE JUST BECAUSE YOU ASK.
THE HAGUN ...
WHA?
You spoke...
...IS NOT LIKE OTHER SHIKIGAMI.
RUMBLE
CALM YOUR MIND, GIFTED ONE.
AND PRAY FOR YOUR GIFT TO BE STRENGTH-ENED.
IS THAT ...?
THE HAGUN IS...

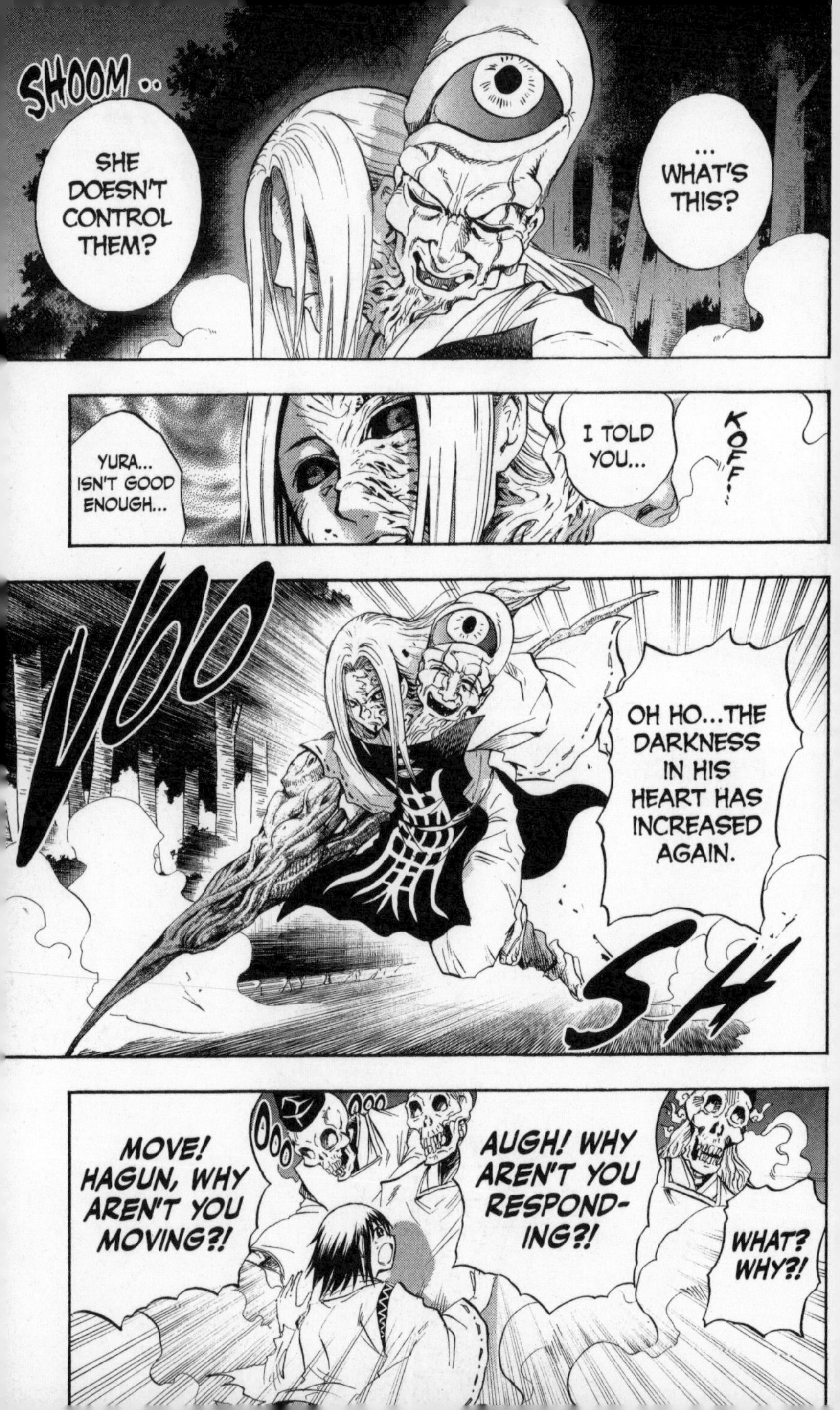

SHOOM ..
... WHAT'S THIS?
SHE DOESN'T CONTROL THEM?
KOFF!
I TOLD YOU...
YURA... ISN'T GOOD ENOUGH...
OH HO...THE DARKNESS IN HIS HEART HAS INCREASED AGAIN.
SH
VOO
WHAT? WHY?!
AUGH! WHY AREN'T YOU RESPOND-ING?!
MOVE! HAGUN, WHY AREN'T YOU MOVING?!

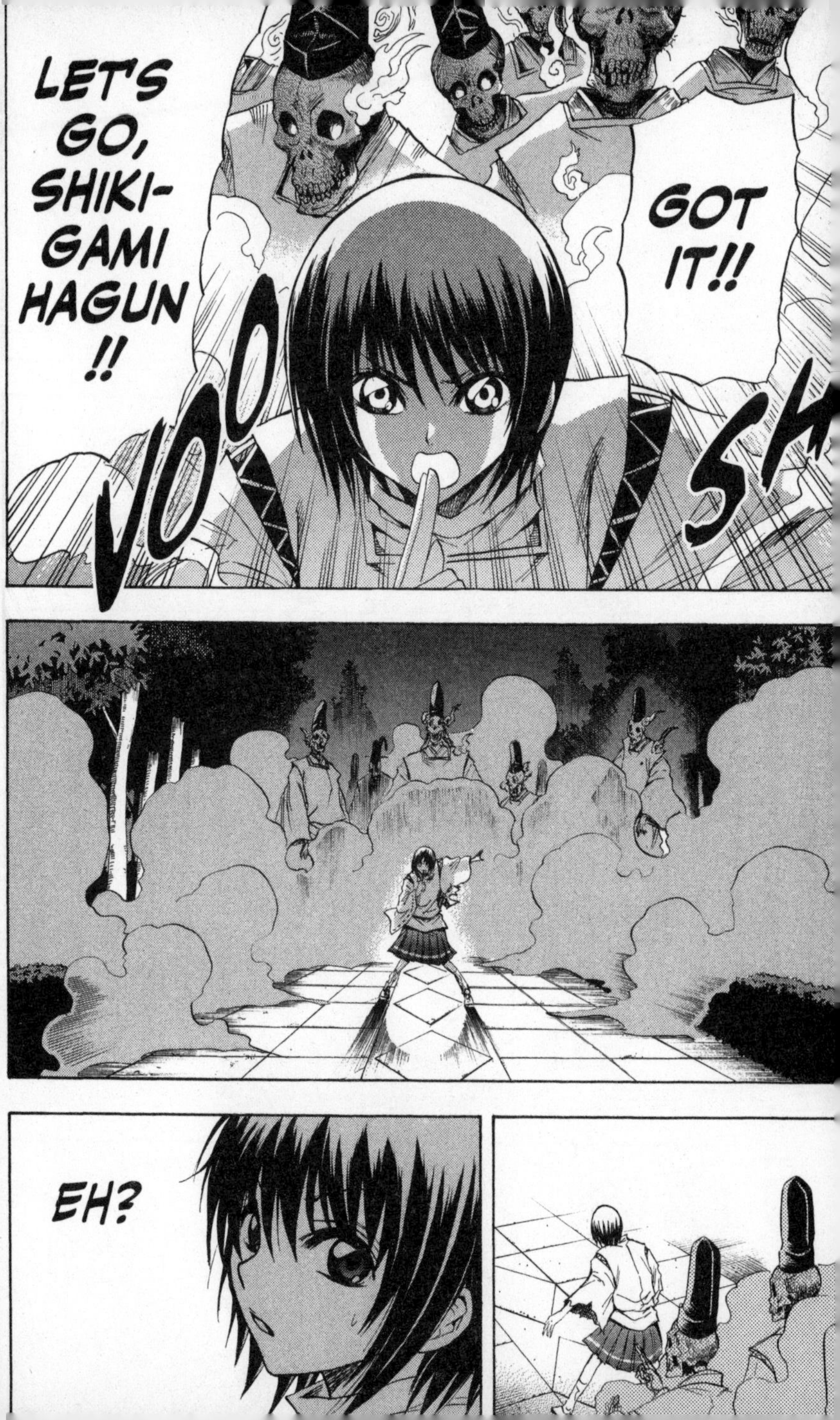
GOT IT!!
SH
LET'S GO, SHIKIGAMI HAGUN!!
VOOO
EH?

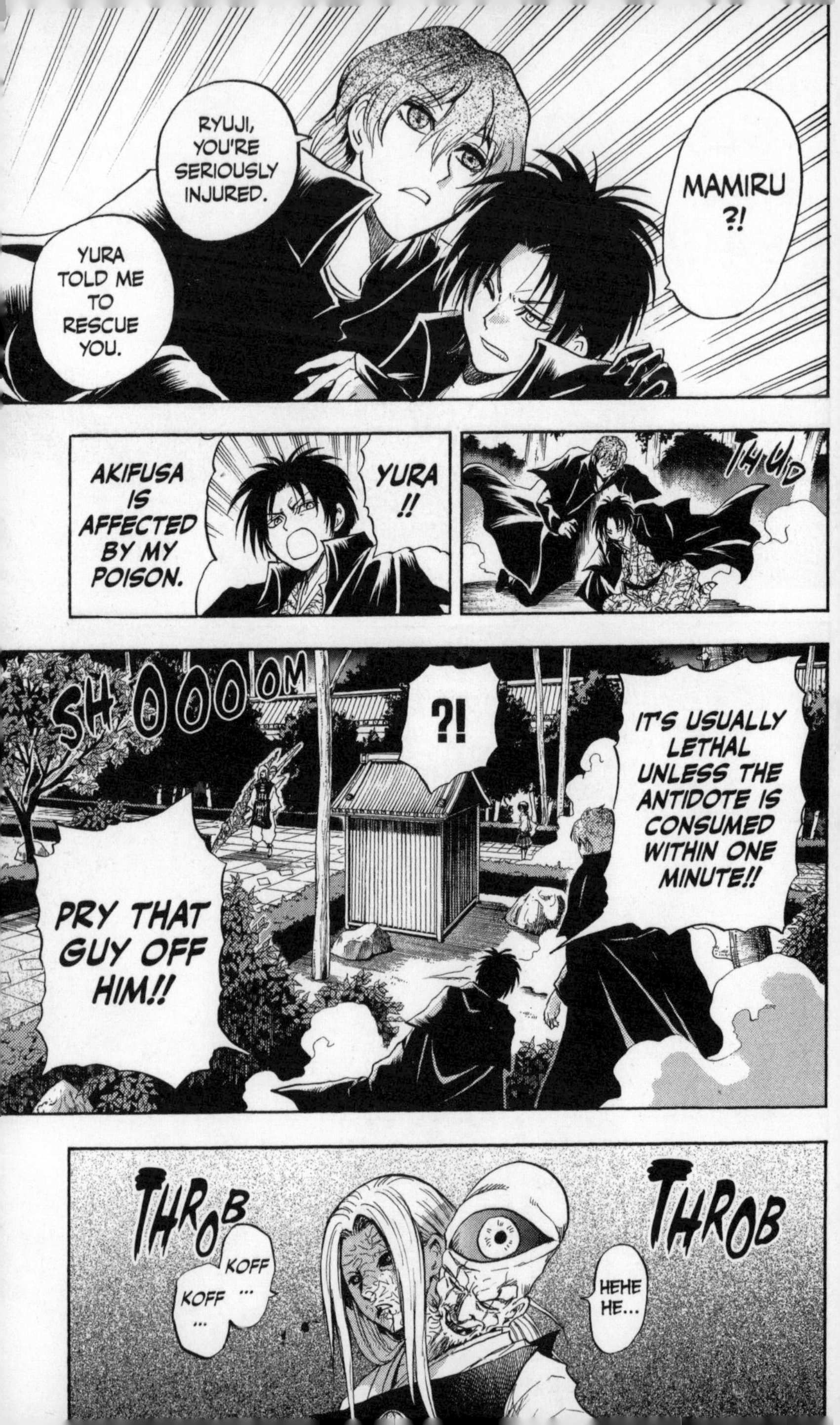
MAMIRU ?!
RYUJI, YOU'RE SERIOUSLY INJURED.
YURA TOLD ME TO RESCUE YOU.
THUD
YURA !!
AKIFUSA IS AFFECTED BY MY POISON.
IT'S USUALLY LETHAL UNLESS THE ANTIDOTE IS CONSUMED WITHIN ONE MINUTE!!
?!
SHOOOOM
PRY THAT GUY OFF HIM!!
THROB
HEHE HE...
THROB
KOFF ...
KOFF ...

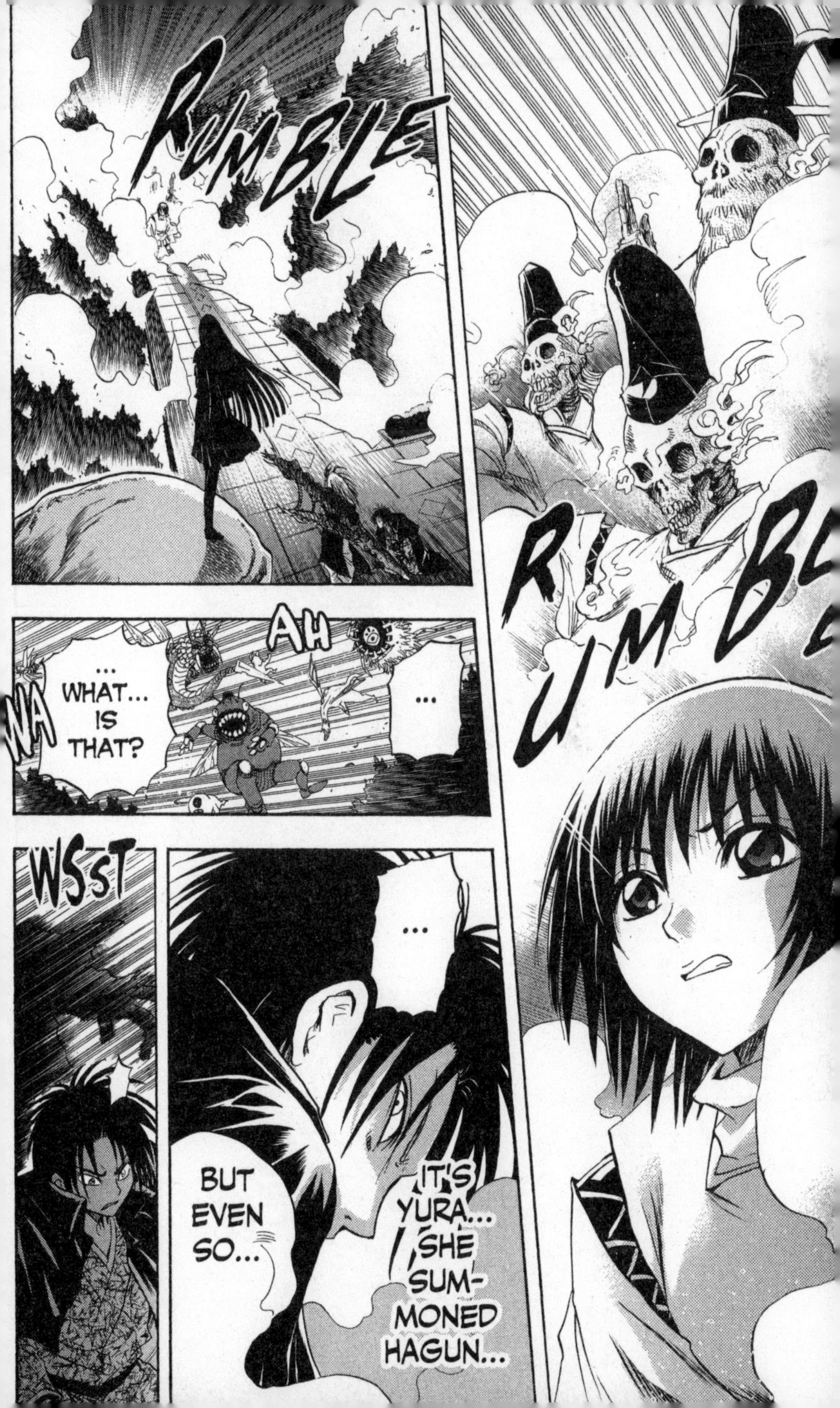

RUMB
RUMBLE
AH
...
... WHAT... IS THAT?
WA
...
IT'S YURA... SHE SUM-MONED HAGUN...
BUT EVEN SO...
WSST

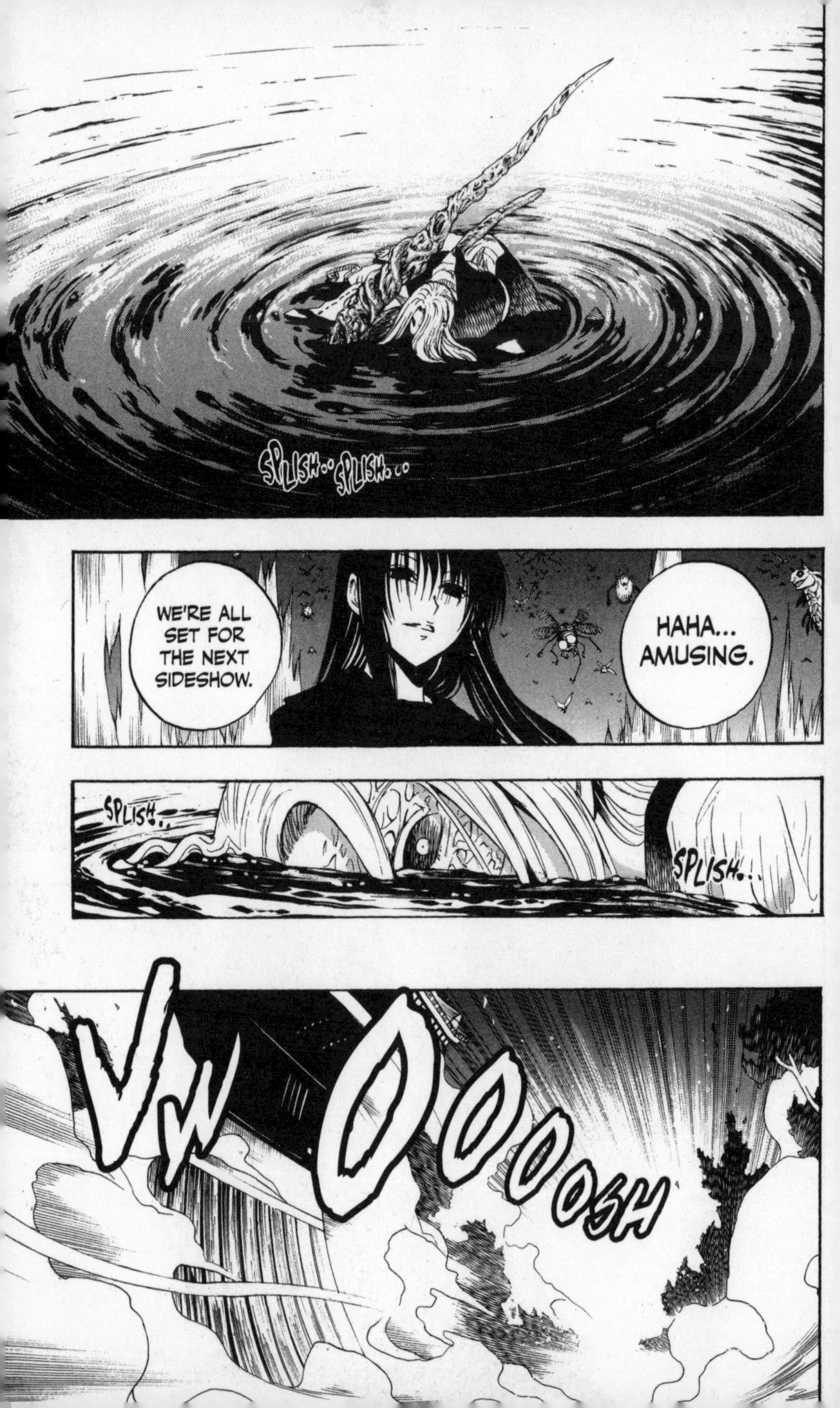
SPLISH... SPLISH...
HAHA... AMUSING.
WE'RE ALL SET FOR THE NEXT SIDESHOW.
SPLISH...
SPLISH...
VWOOOOSH

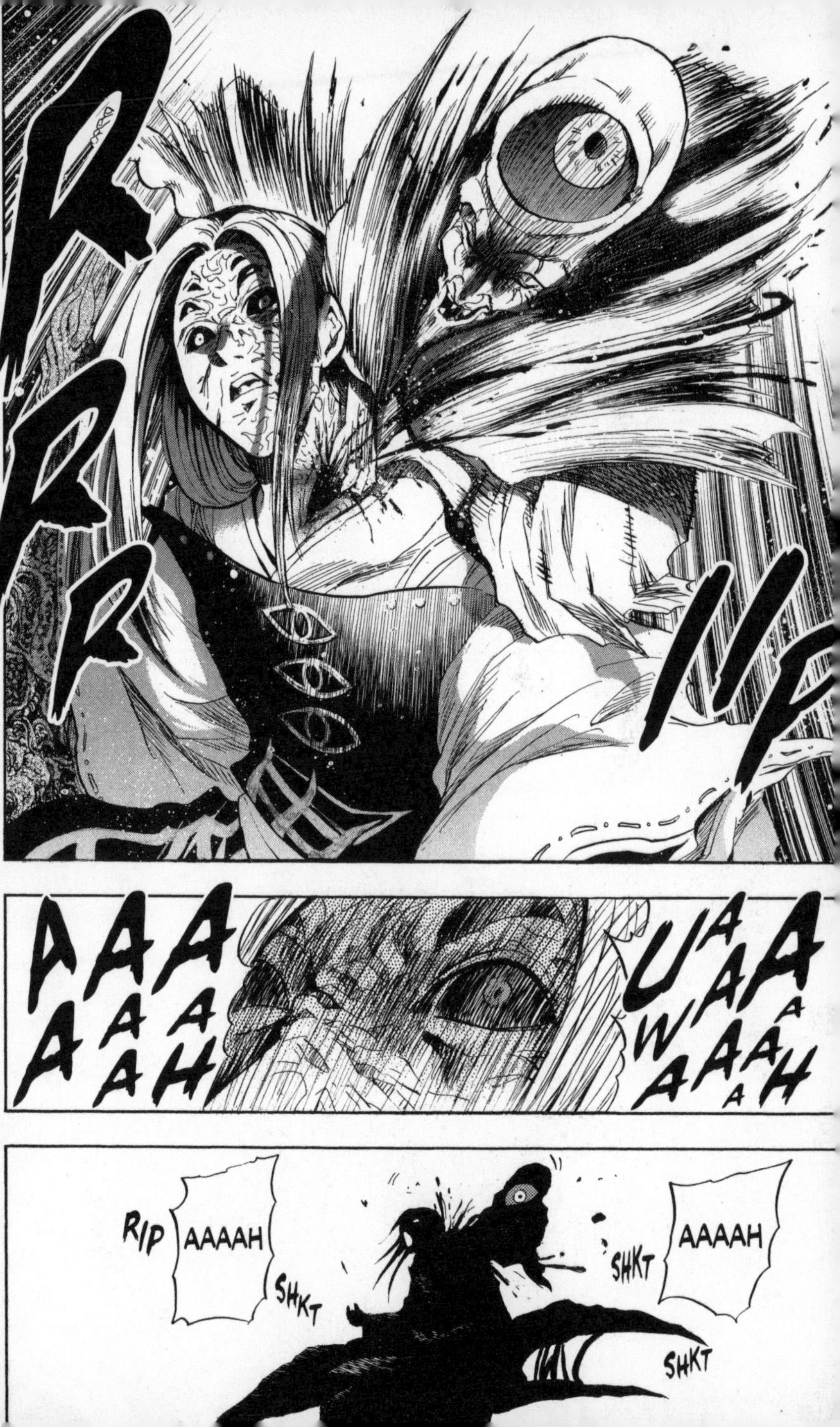
AAAAAAAAH
AAAAH
SHKT
SHKT
AAAAH
RIP
SHKT

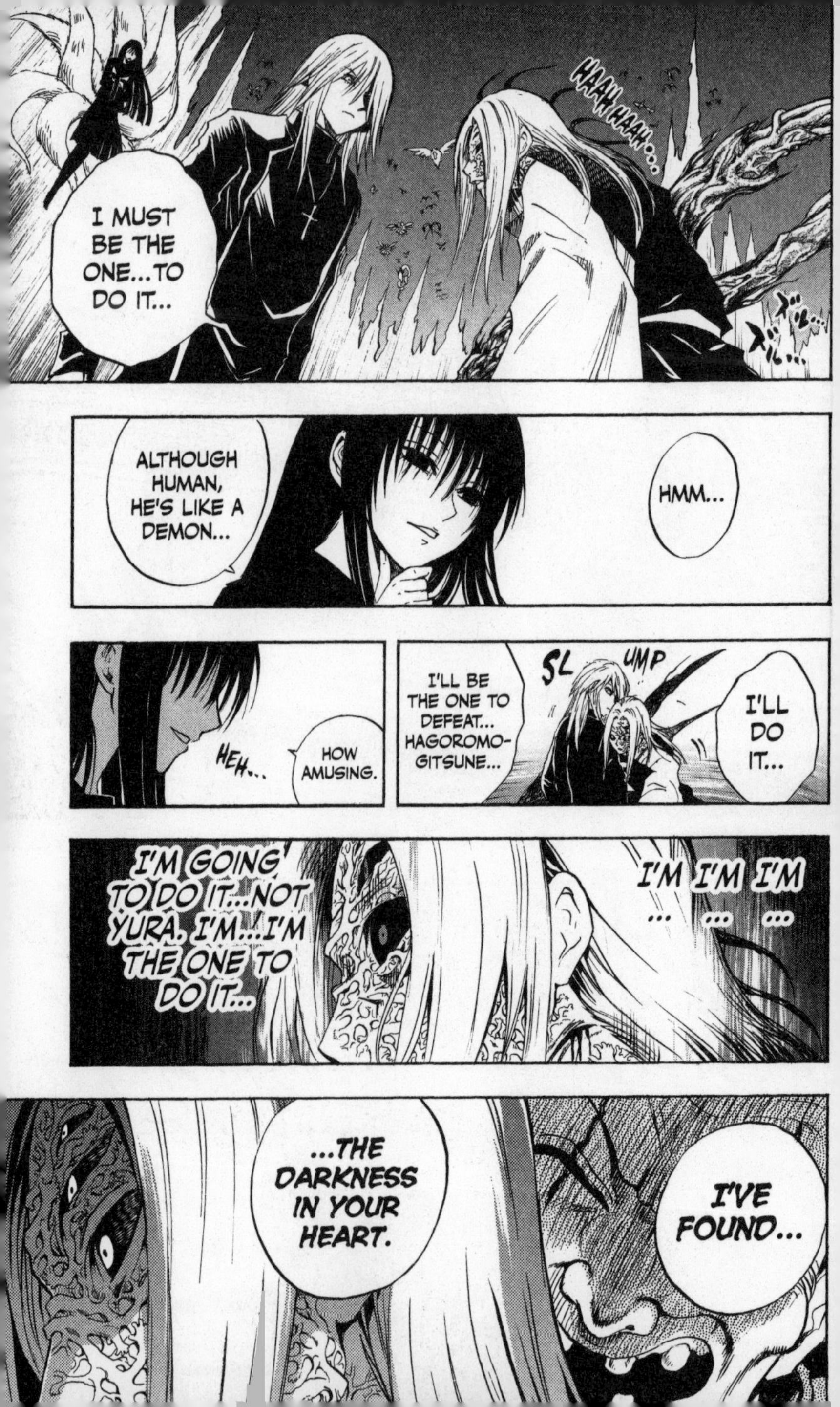
HAAH HAAH...
I MUST BE THE ONE...TO DO IT...
HMM...
ALTHOUGH HUMAN, HE'S LIKE A DEMON...
I'LL DO IT...
SLUMP
I'LL BE THE ONE TO DEFEAT... HAGOROMO-GITSUNE...
HOW AMUSING.
HEH...
I'M I'M I'M ... ...
I'M GOING TO DO IT...NOT YURA. I'M...I'M THE ONE TO DO IT...
I'VE FOUND...
...THE DARKNESS IN YOUR HEART.

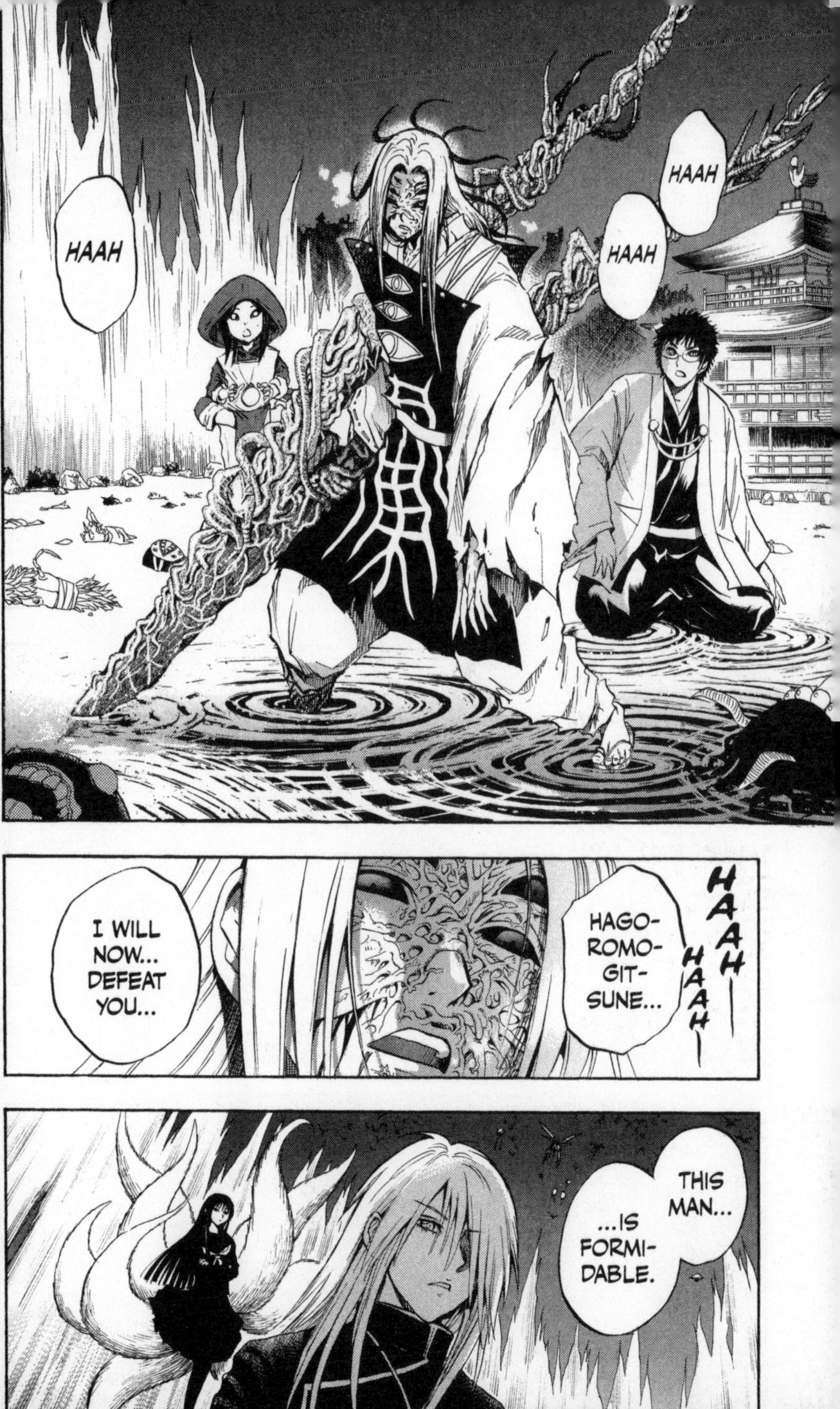
HAAH
HAAH
HAAH
HAAH HAAH
HAGO-ROMO-GIT-SUNE...
I WILL NOW... DEFEAT YOU...
THIS MAN...
...IS FORMIDABLE.

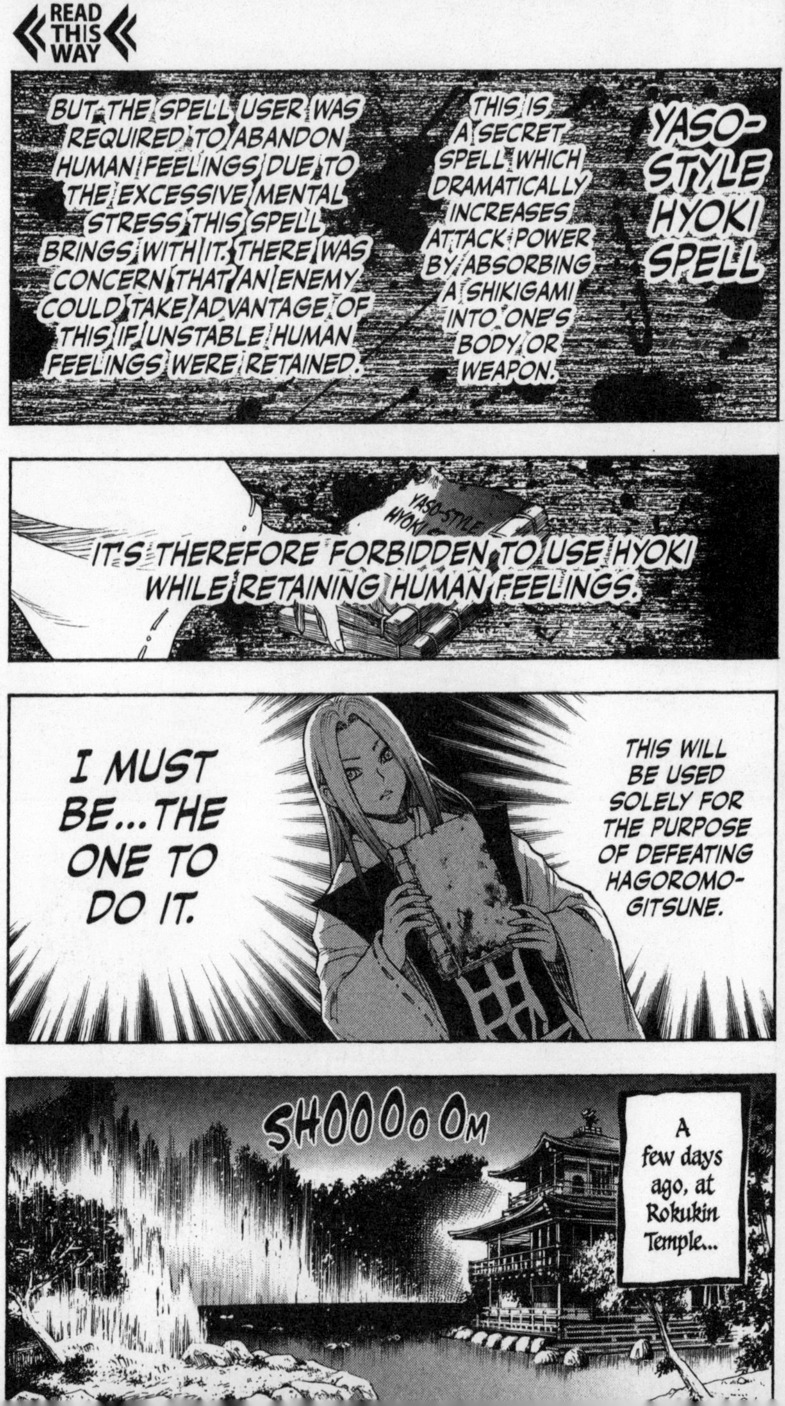
READ THIS WAY
YASO-STYLE HYOKI SPELL
THIS IS A SECRET SPELL WHICH DRAMATICALLY INCREASES ATTACK POWER BY ABSORBING A SHIKIGAMI INTO ONE'S BODY OR WEAPON.
BUT THE SPELL USER WAS REQUIRED TO ABANDON HUMAN FEELINGS DUE TO THE EXCESSIVE MENTAL STRESS THIS SPELL BRINGS WITH IT. THERE WAS CONCERN THAT AN ENEMY COULD TAKE ADVANTAGE OF THIS IF UNSTABLE HUMAN FEELINGS WERE RETAINED.
YASO-STYLE HYOKI
IT'S THEREFORE FORBIDDEN TO USE HYOKI WHILE RETAINING HUMAN FEELINGS.
THIS WILL BE USED SOLELY FOR THE PURPOSE OF DEFEATING HAGOROMO-GITSUNE.
I MUST BE...THE ONE TO DO IT.
A few days ago, at Rokukin Temple...
SHOOOoOM

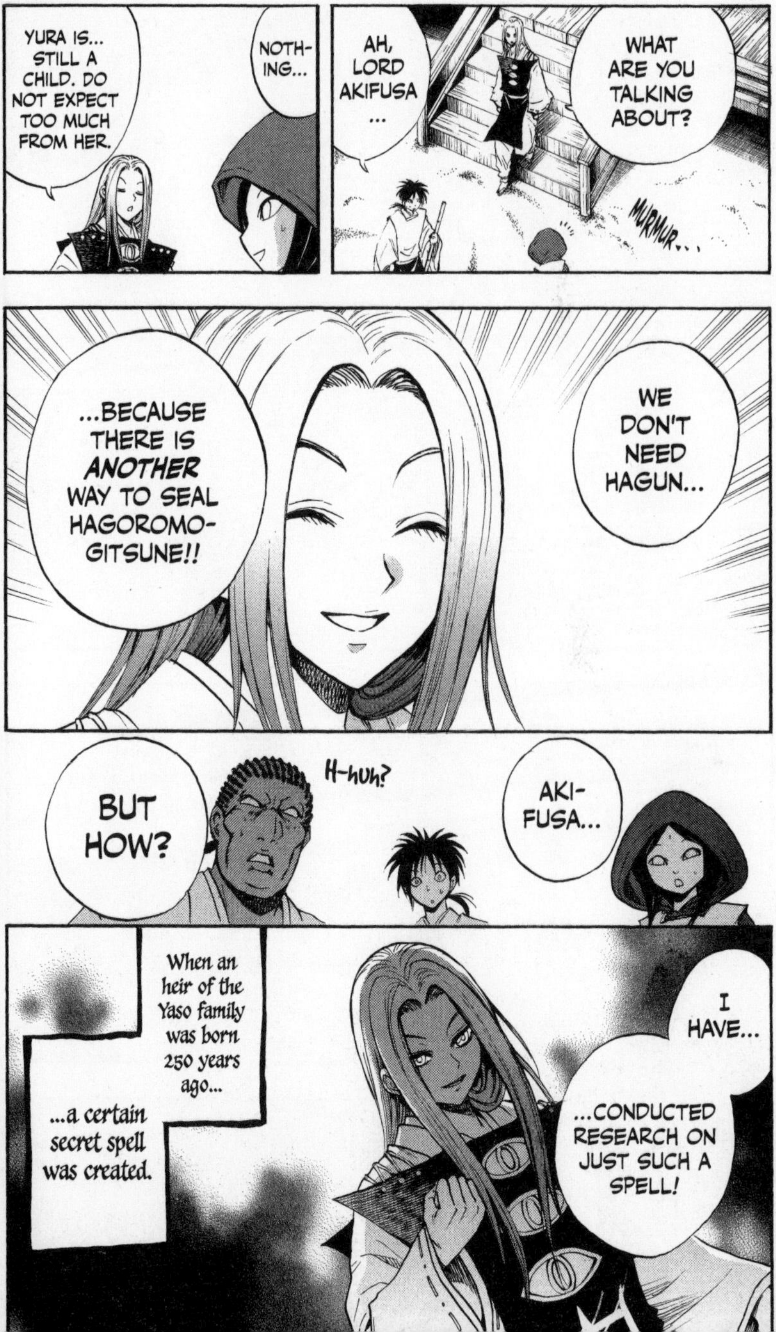
WHAT ARE YOU TALKING ABOUT?
AH, LORD AKIFUSA...
MURMUR...
NOTH-ING...
YURA IS... STILL A CHILD. DO NOT EXPECT TOO MUCH FROM HER.
WE DON'T NEED HAGUN...
...BECAUSE THERE IS ANOTHER WAY TO SEAL HAGOROMO-GITSUNE!!
AKI-FUSA...
H-huh?
BUT HOW?
I HAVE...
...CONDUCTED RESEARCH ON JUST SUCH A SPELL!
When an heir of the Yaso family was born 250 years ago...
...a certain secret spell was created.

READ THIS WAY

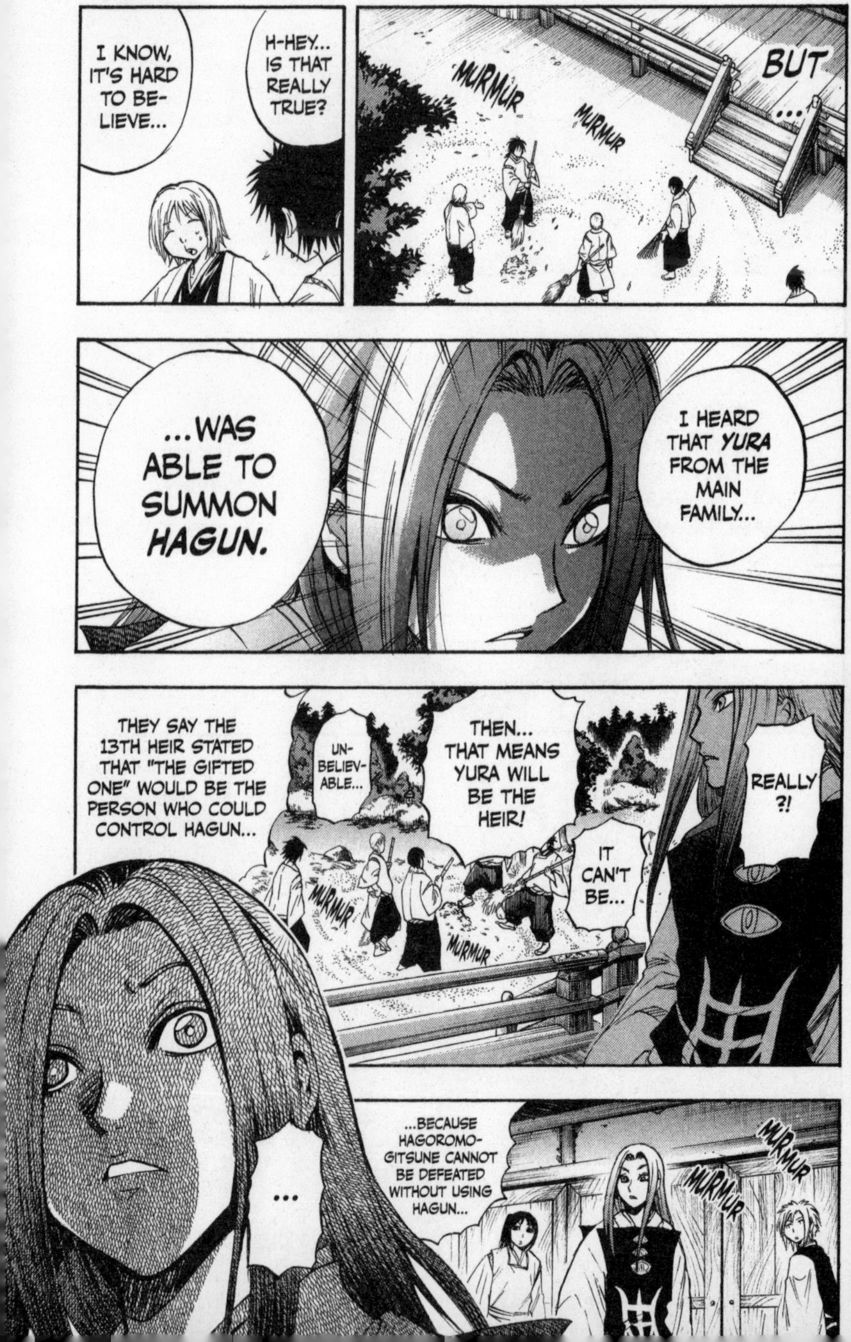
MURMUR
MURMUR
BUT...
H-HEY... IS THAT REALLY TRUE?
I KNOW, IT'S HARD TO BE-LIEVE...
I HEARD THAT YURA FROM THE MAIN FAMILY...
...WAS ABLE TO SUMMON HAGUN.
REALLY?!
IT CAN'T BE...
THEN... THAT MEANS YURA WILL BE THE HEIR!
UN-BELIEV-ABLE...
MURMUR
MURMUR
THEY SAY THE 13TH HEIR STATED THAT "THE GIFTED ONE" WOULD BE THE PERSON WHO COULD CONTROL HAGUN...
MURMUR
MURMUR
...BECAUSE HAGOROMO-GITSUNE CANNOT BE DEFEATED WITHOUT USING HAGUN...
...

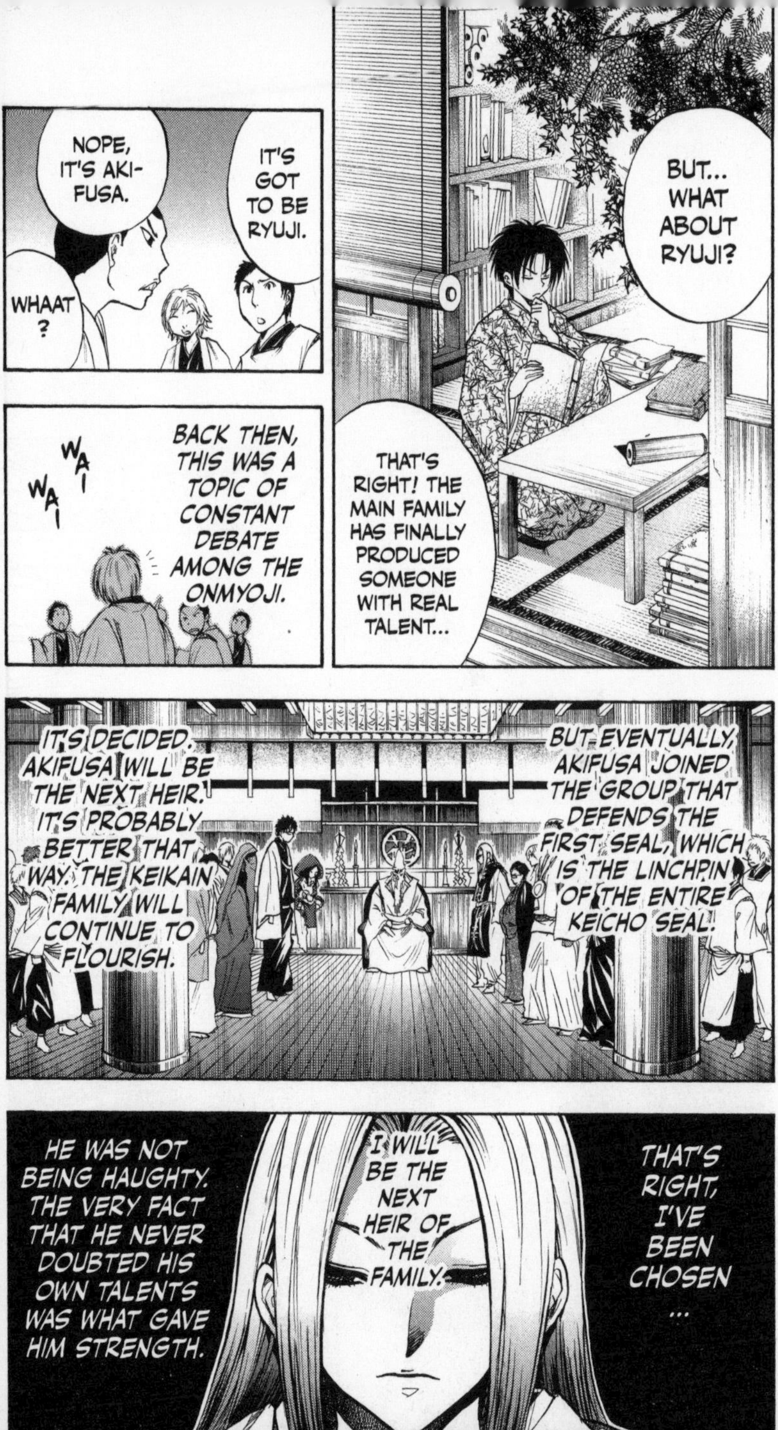
BUT... WHAT ABOUT RYUJI?
THAT'S RIGHT! THE MAIN FAMILY HAS FINALLY PRODUCED SOMEONE WITH REAL TALENT...
IT'S GOT TO BE RYUJI.
NOPE, IT'S AKI-FUSA.
WHAAT?
BACK THEN, THIS WAS A TOPIC OF CONSTANT DEBATE AMONG THE ONMYOJI.
WAI
WAI
BUT EVENTUALLY, AKIFUSA JOINED THE GROUP THAT DEFENDS THE FIRST SEAL, WHICH IS THE LINCHPIN OF THE ENTIRE KEICHO SEAL!
IT'S DECIDED. AKIFUSA WILL BE THE NEXT HEIR. IT'S PROBABLY BETTER THAT WAY. THE KEIKAIN FAMILY WILL CONTINUE TO FLOURISH.
THAT'S RIGHT, I'VE BEEN CHOSEN...
I WILL BE THE NEXT HEIR OF THE FAMILY.
HE WAS NOT BEING HAUGHTY. THE VERY FACT THAT HE NEVER DOUBTED HIS OWN TALENTS WAS WHAT GAVE HIM STRENGTH.

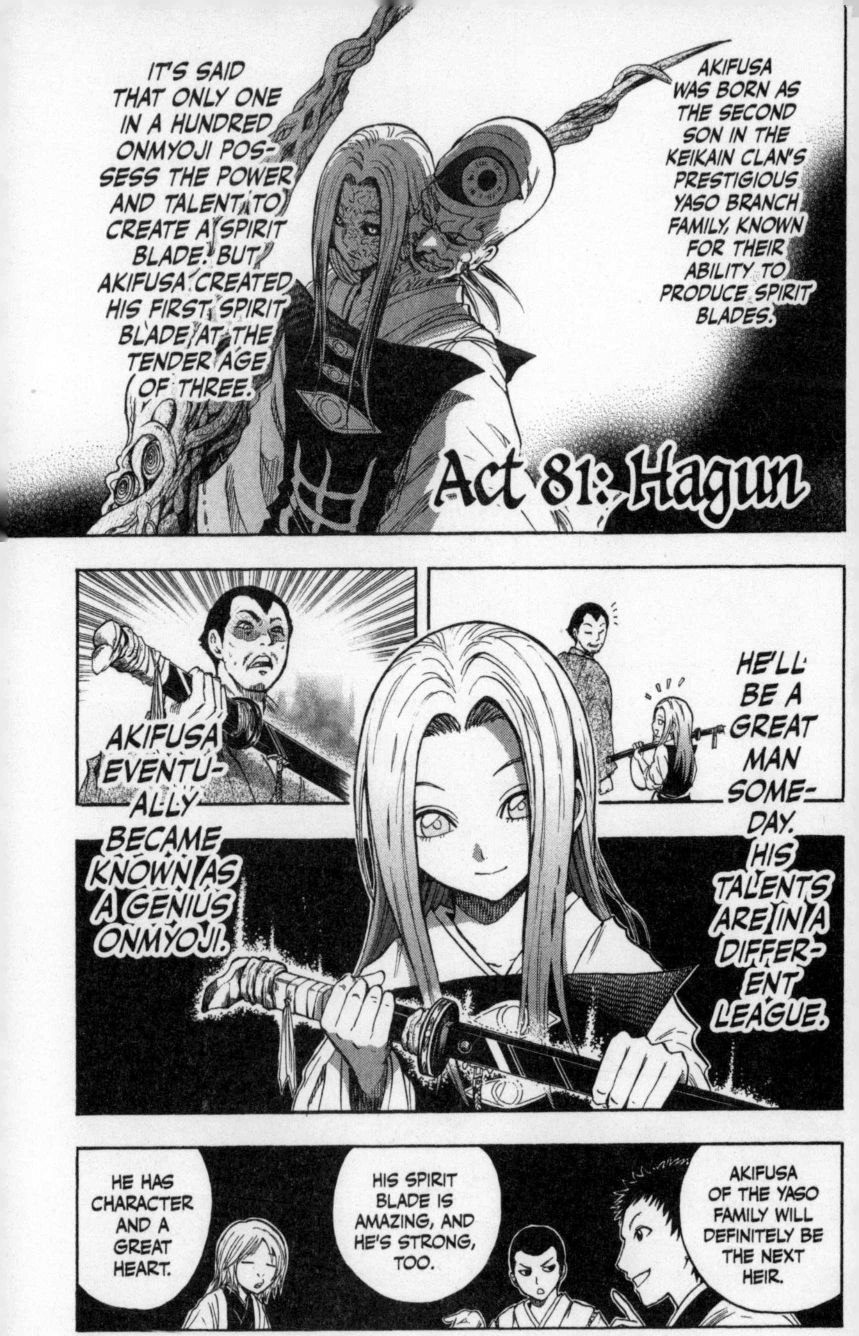
AKIFUSA WAS BORN AS THE SECOND SON IN THE KEIKAIN CLAN'S PRESTIGIOUS YASO BRANCH FAMILY, KNOWN FOR THEIR ABILITY TO PRODUCE SPIRIT BLADES.
IT'S SAID THAT ONLY ONE IN A HUNDRED ONMYOJI POS-SESS THE POWER AND TALENT TO CREATE A SPIRIT BLADE. BUT AKIFUSA CREATED HIS FIRST SPIRIT BLADE AT THE TENDER AGE OF THREE.
Act 81: Hagun
HE'LL BE A GREAT MAN SOME-DAY. HIS TALENTS ARE IN A DIFFER-ENT LEAGUE.
AKIFUSA EVENTU-ALLY BECAME KNOWN AS A GENIUS ONMYOJI.
AKIFUSA OF THE YASO FAMILY WILL DEFINITELY BE THE NEXT HEIR.
HIS SPIRIT BLADE IS AMAZING, AND HE'S STRONG, TOO.
HE HAS CHARACTER AND A GREAT HEART.

other characters with one vote in popularity voting (characters...?)

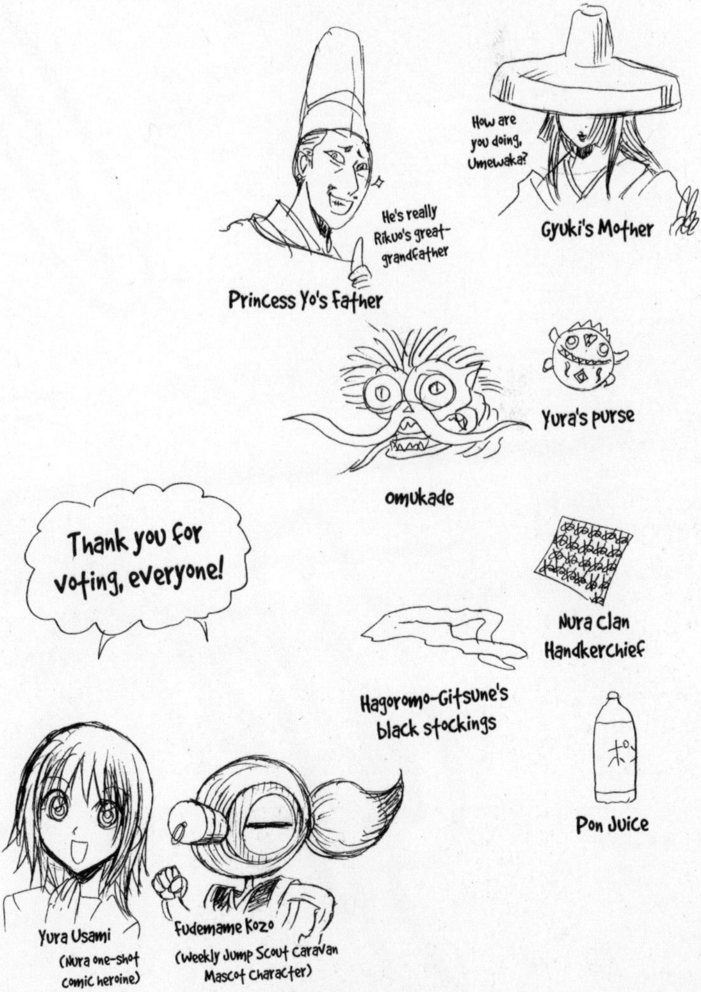

How are you doing, Umewaka?
Gyuki's Mother
He's really Rikuo's great-grandfather
Princess Yo's Father
Yura's purse
omukade
Thank you for voting, everyone!
Nura Clan Handkerchief
Hagoromo-Gitsune's black stockings
ポン
Pon Juice
Yura Usami
(Nura one-shot comic heroine)
Fudemame Kozo
(Weekly Jump Scout Caravan Mascot Character)

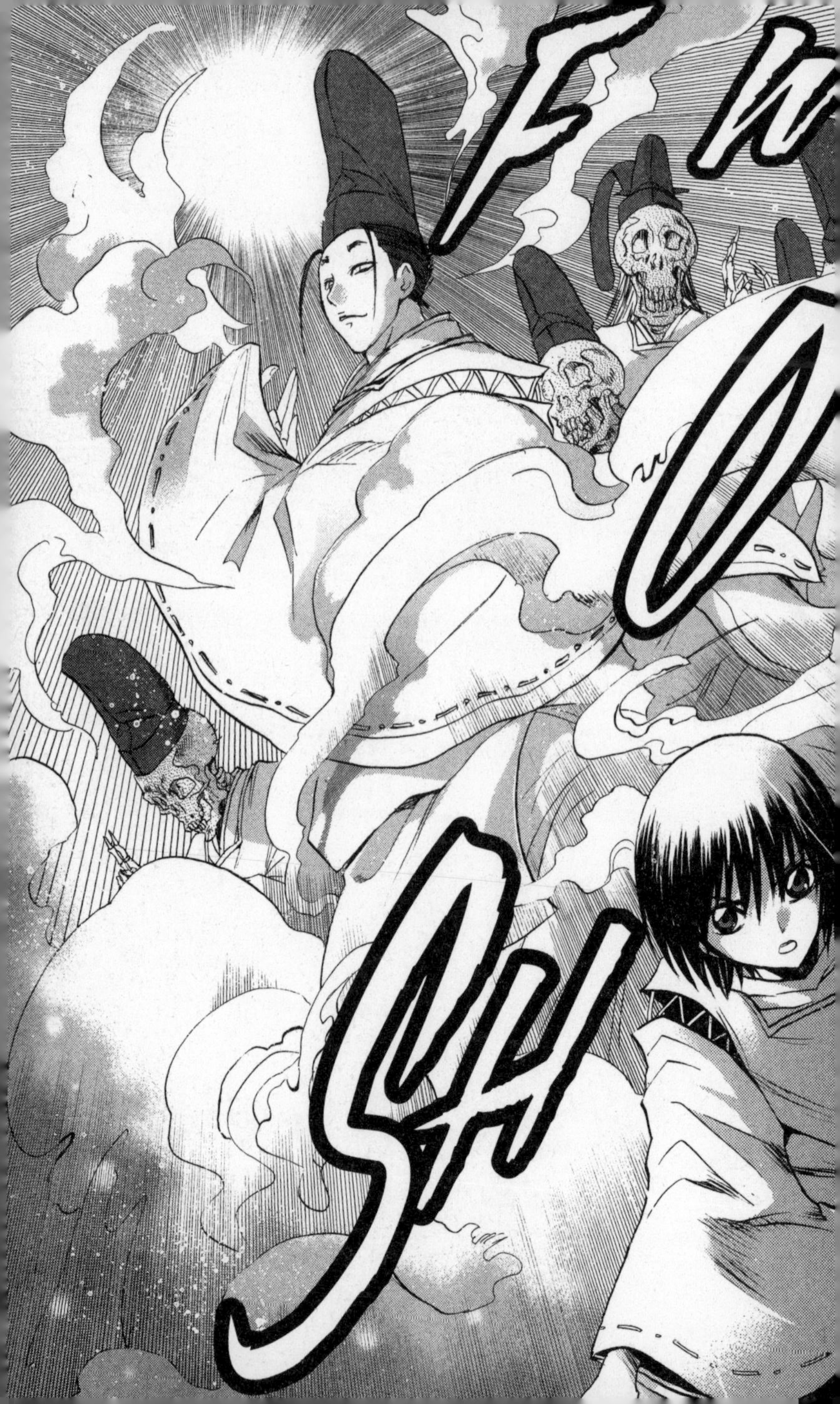

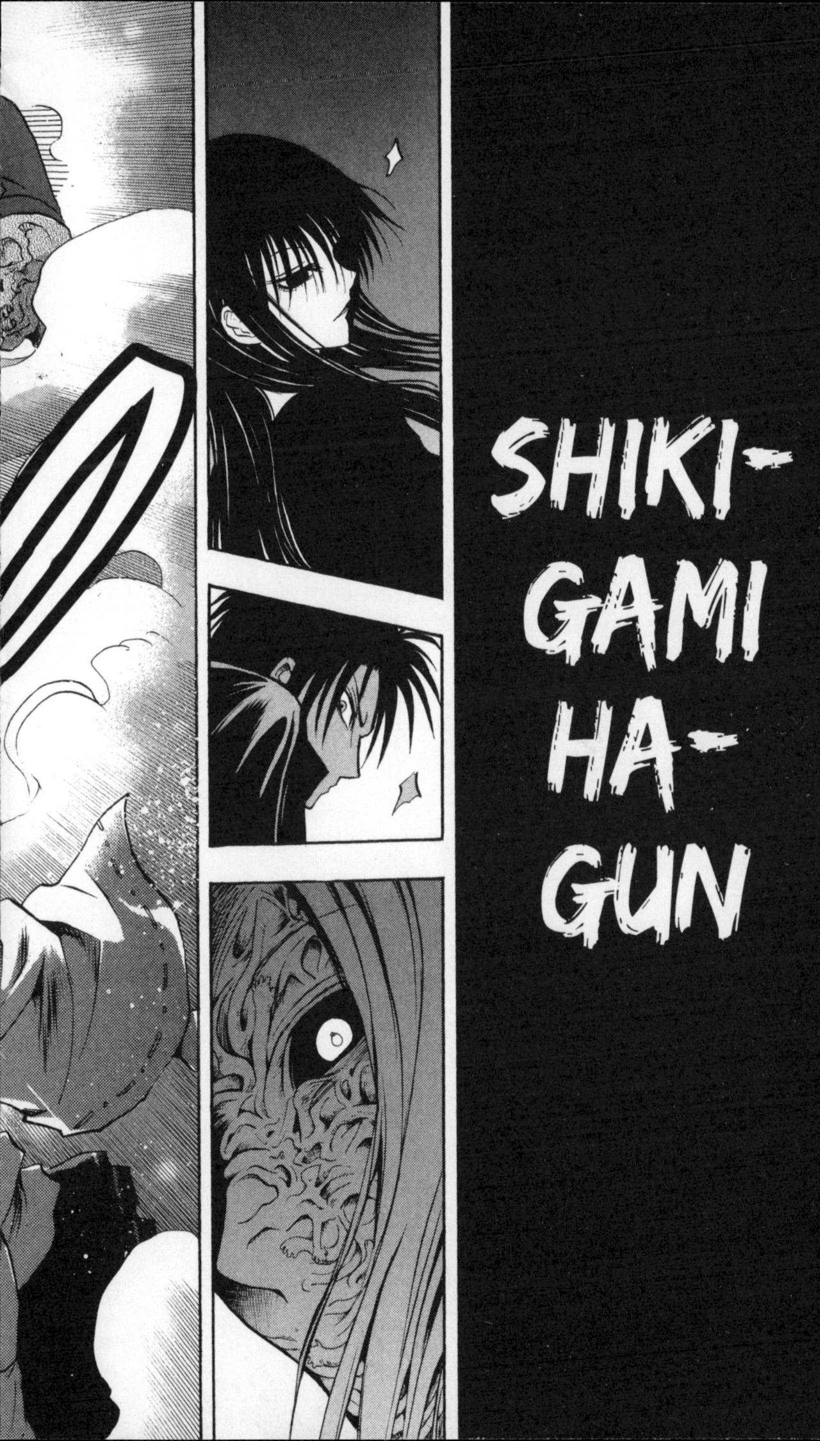
SHIKI-GAMI HA-GUN

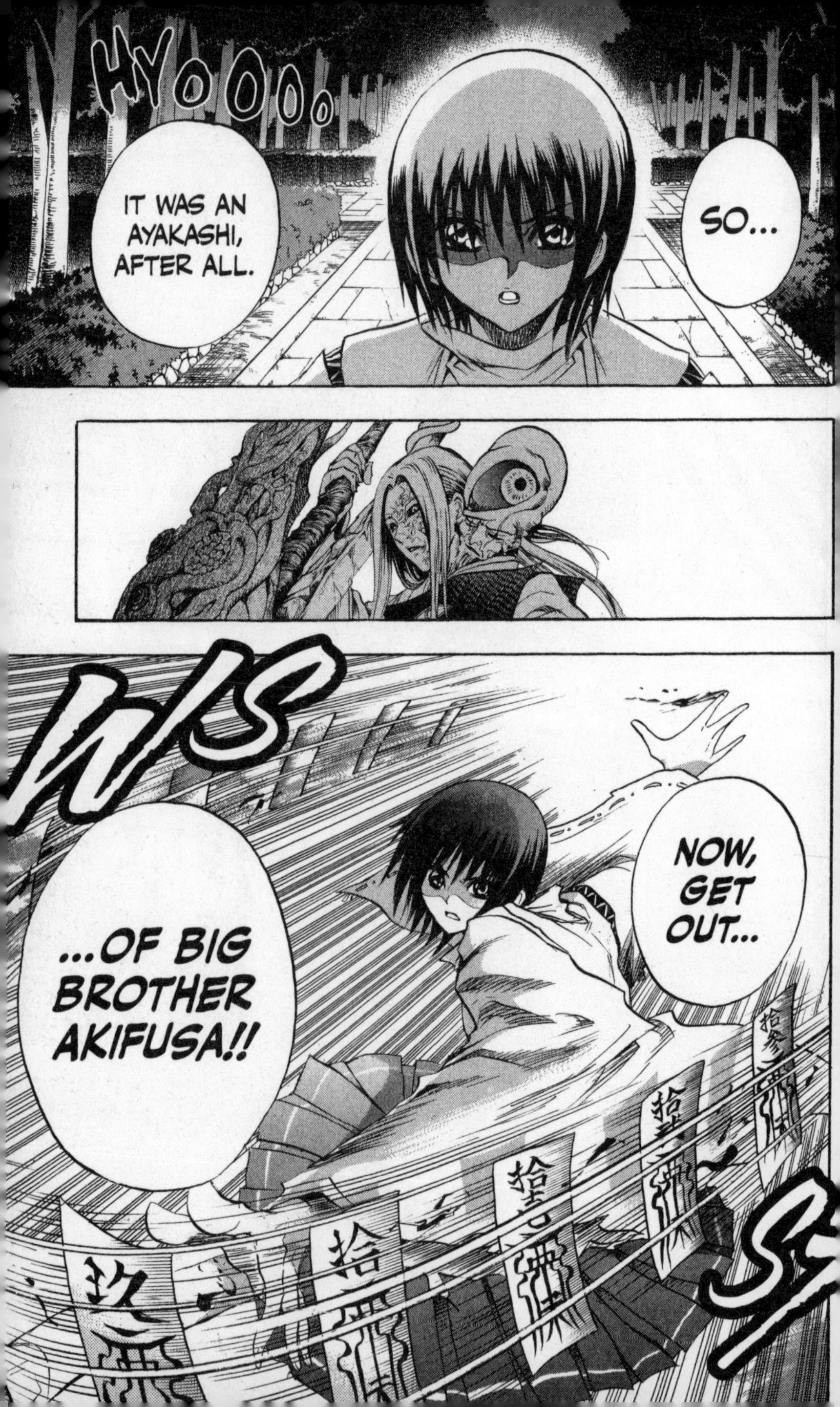
HYOOOo
SO...
IT WAS AN AYAKASHI, AFTER ALL.
NOW, GET OUT...
...OF BIG BROTHER AKIFUSA!!

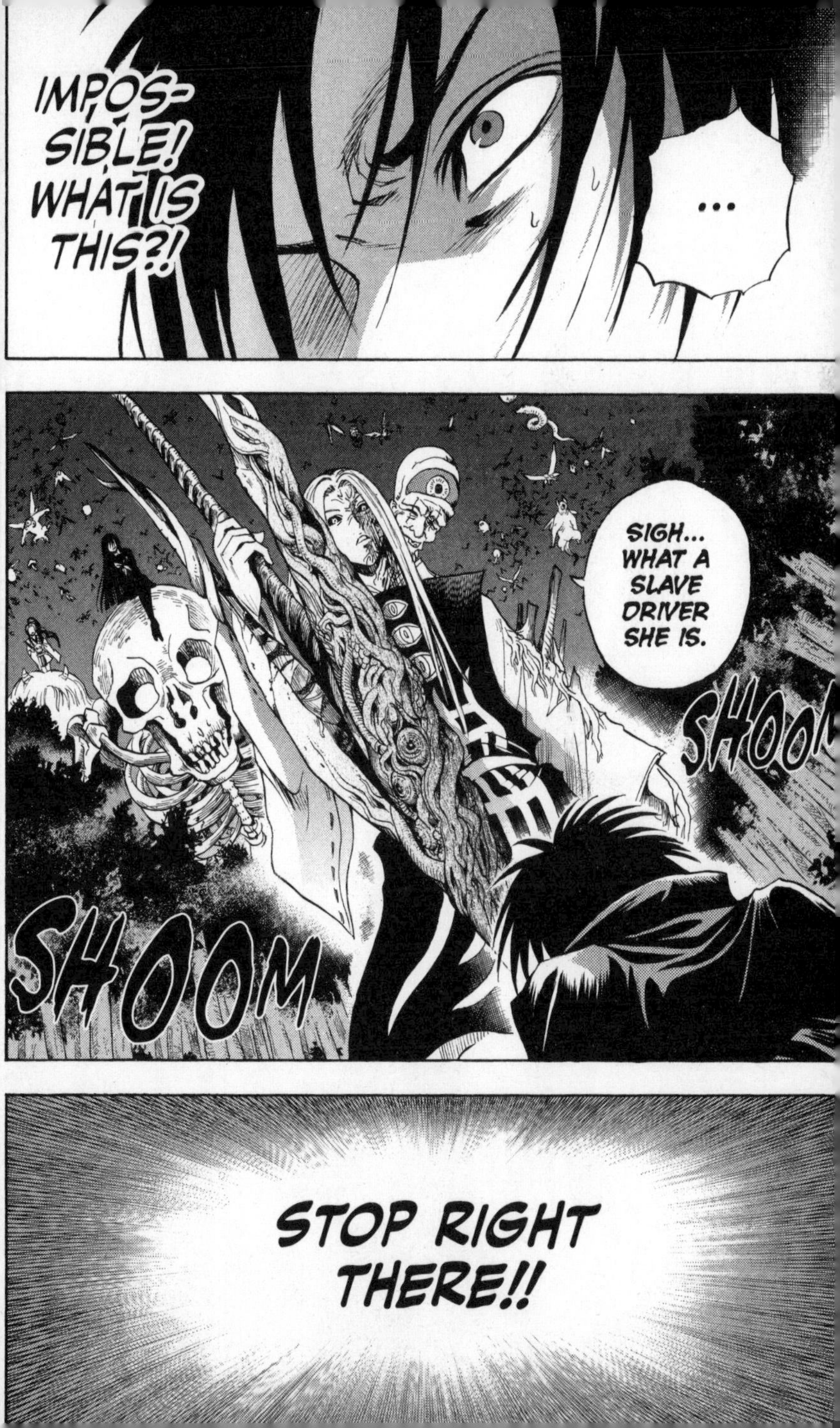
...
IMPOS-SIBLE! WHAT IS THIS?!
SHOO
SIGH... WHAT A SLAVE DRIVER SHE IS.
SHOOM
STOP RIGHT THERE!!

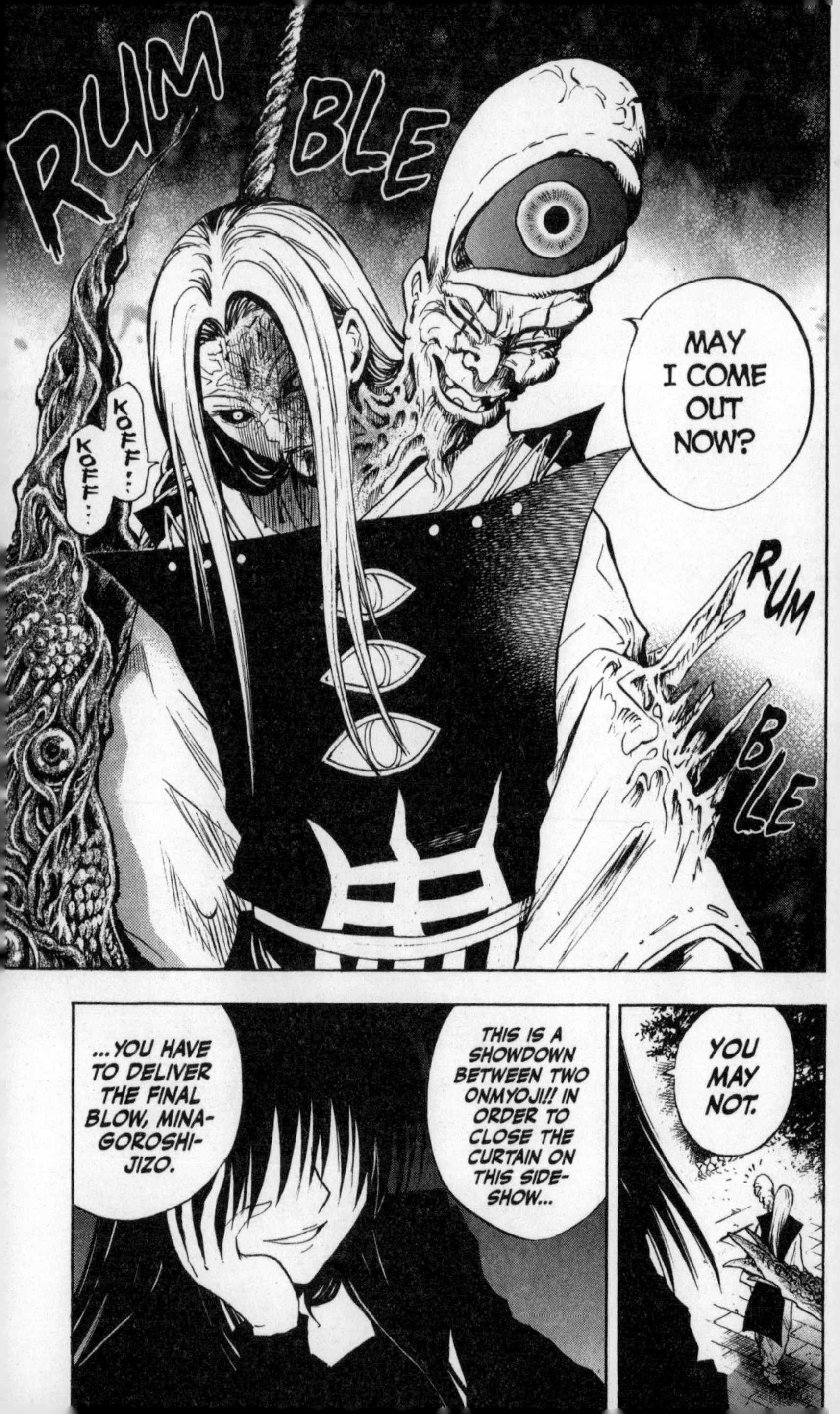
RUMBLE
MAY I COME OUT NOW?
KOFF!! KOFF...
RUMBLE
YOU MAY NOT.
THIS IS A SHOWDOWN BETWEEN TWO ONMYOJI!! IN ORDER TO CLOSE THE CURTAIN ON THIS SIDE-SHOW...
...YOU HAVE TO DELIVER THE FINAL BLOW, MINA-GOROSHI-JIZO.

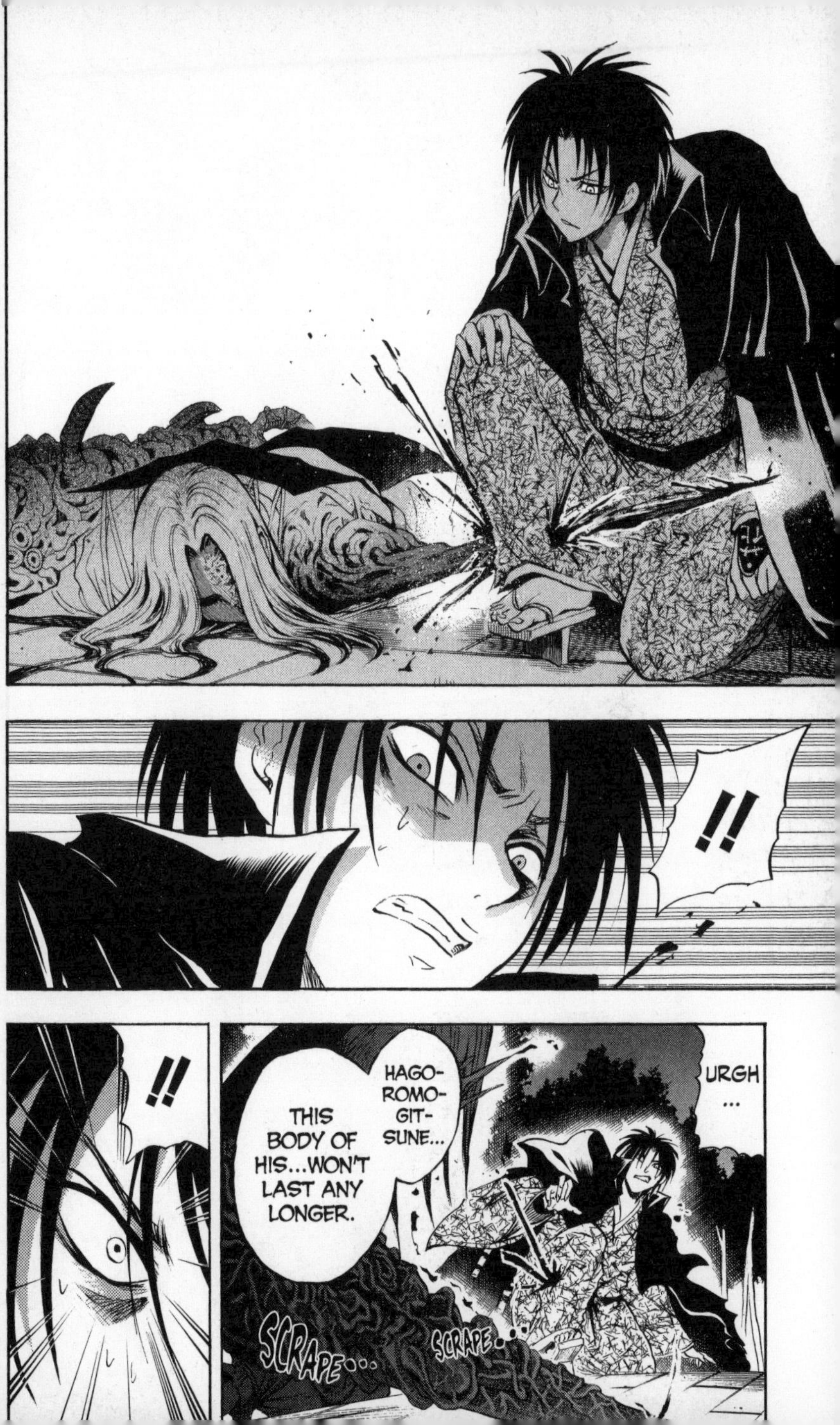
!!
!!
URGH...
HAGO-ROMO-GIT-SUNE...
THIS BODY OF HIS...WON'T LAST ANY LONGER.
SCRAPE...
SCRAPE...

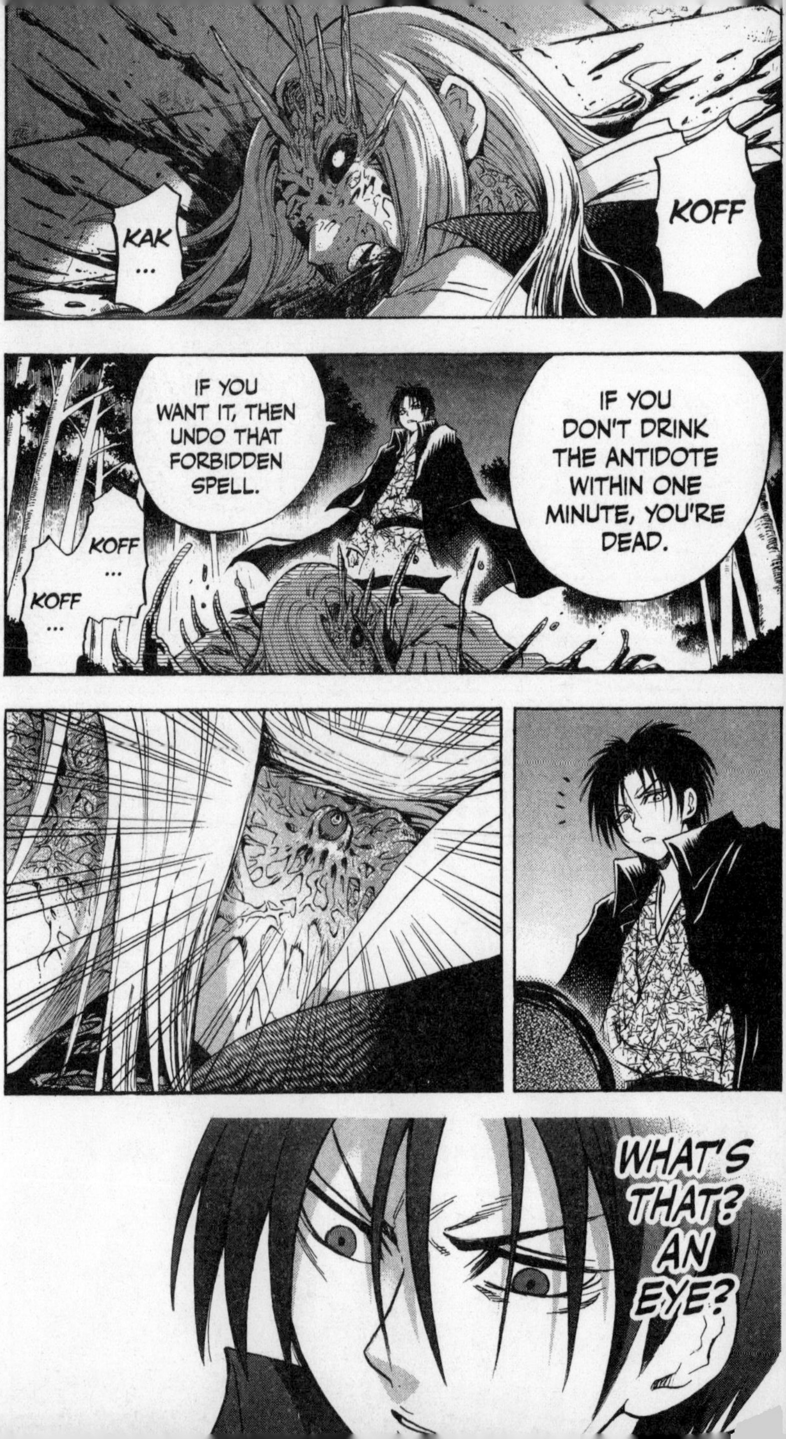
KOFF
KAK ...
IF YOU DON'T DRINK THE ANTIDOTE WITHIN ONE MINUTE, YOU'RE DEAD.
IF YOU WANT IT, THEN UNDO THAT FORBIDDEN SPELL.
KOFF ...
KOFF ...
WHAT'S THAT? AN EYE?

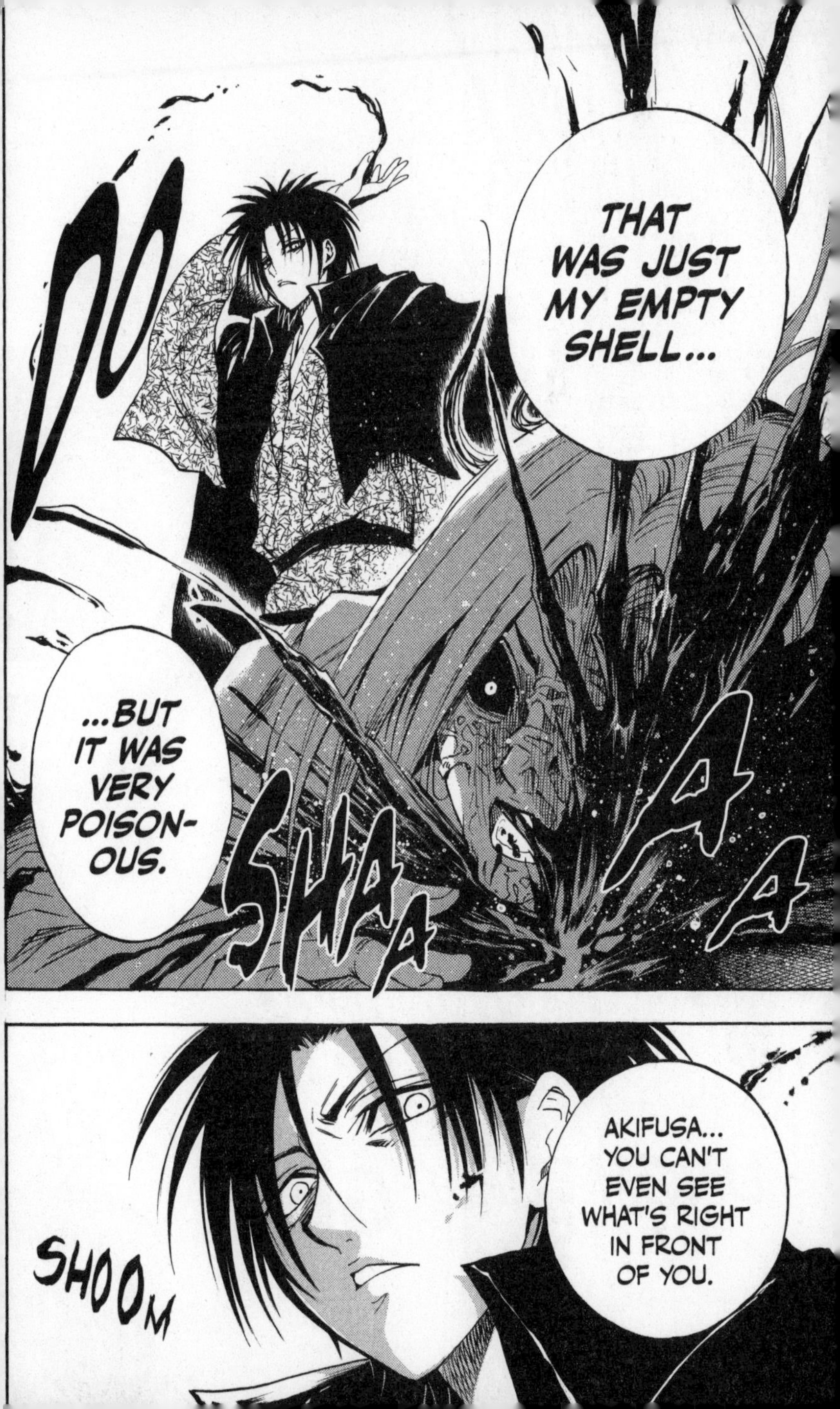
THAT WAS JUST MY EMPTY SHELL...
DO
...BUT IT WAS VERY POISON-OUS.
SHAAAA
AKIFUSA... YOU CAN'T EVEN SEE WHAT'S RIGHT IN FRONT OF YOU.
SHOOM

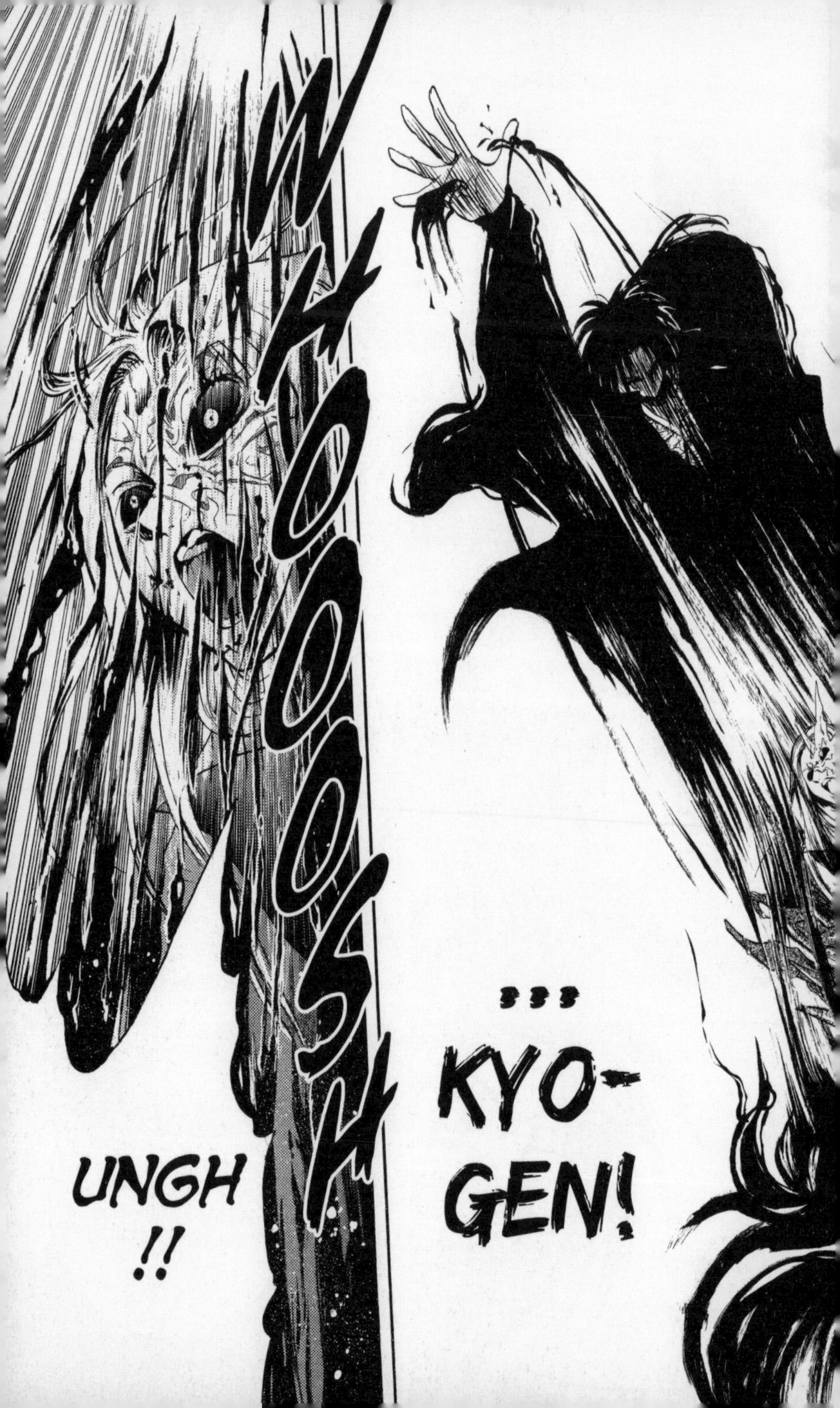
...KYO-
GEN!
SWOOOOSH
UNGH
!!

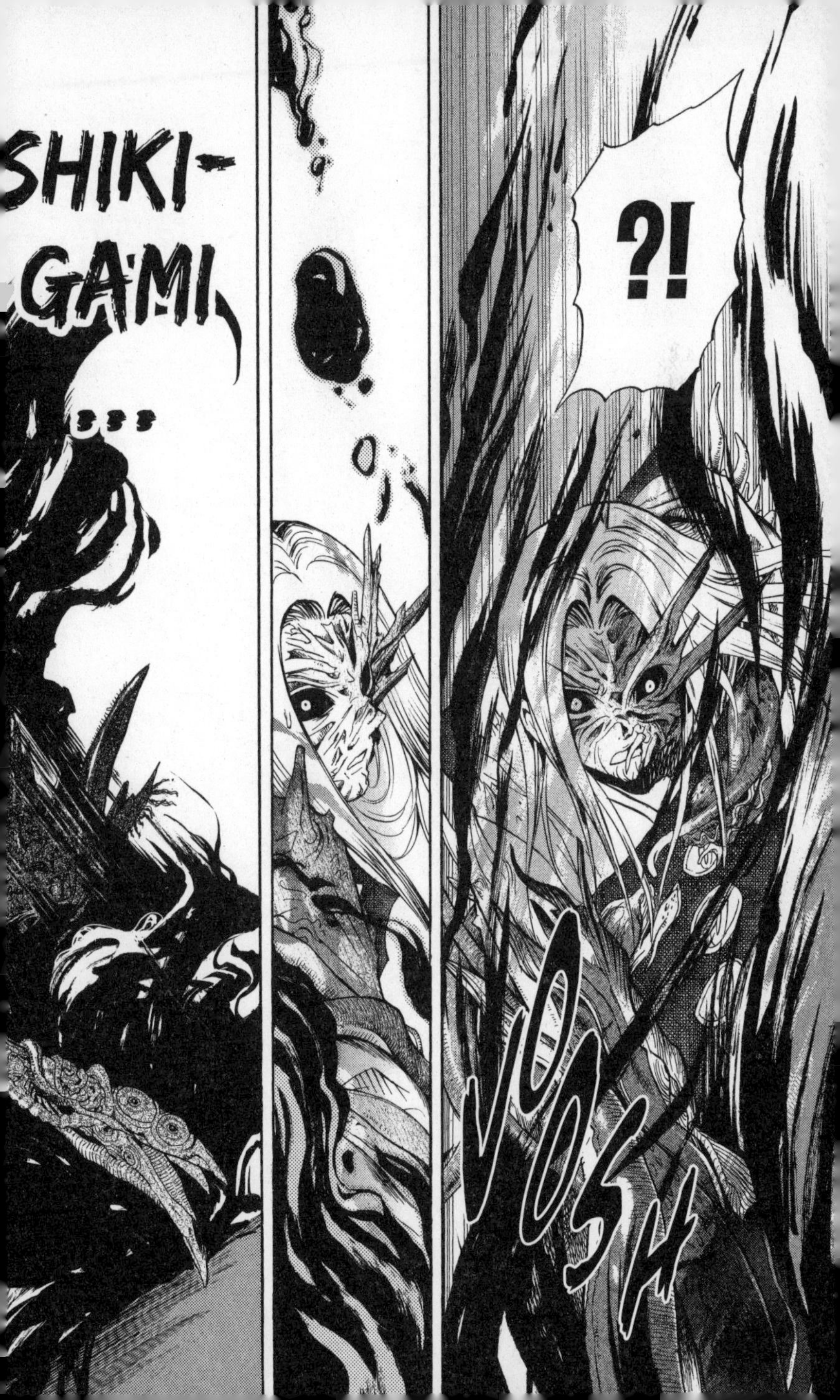
?!
VOOSH
SHIKI-GAMI...

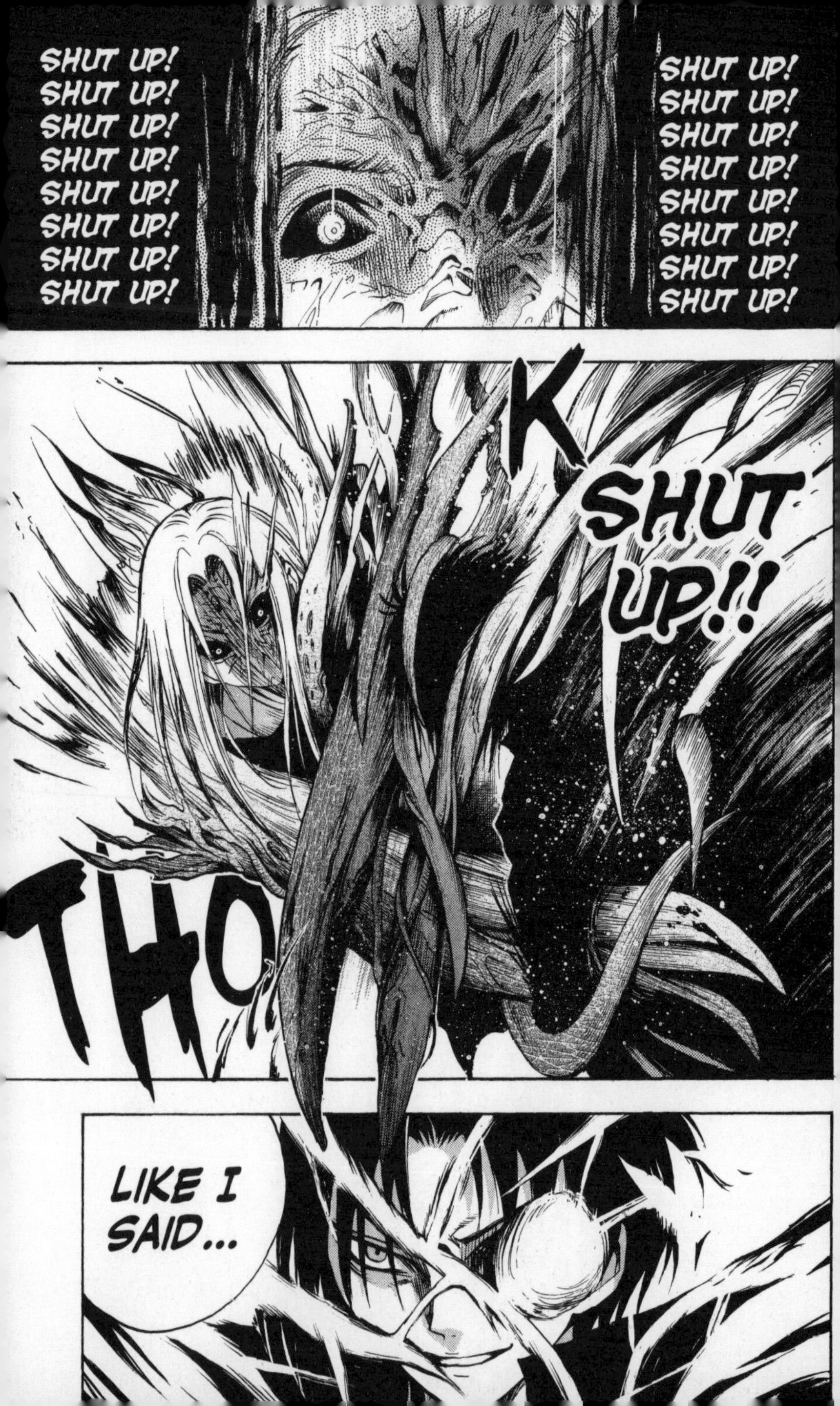
SHUT UP!
SHUT UP!
SHUT UP!
SHUT UP!
SHUT UP!
SHUT UP!
SHUT UP!
SHUT UP!
SHUT UP!
SHUT UP!
SHUT UP!
SHUT UP!
SHUT UP!
SHUT UP!
SHUT UP!
SHUT UP!
SHUT UP!!
THOK
LIKE I SAID...

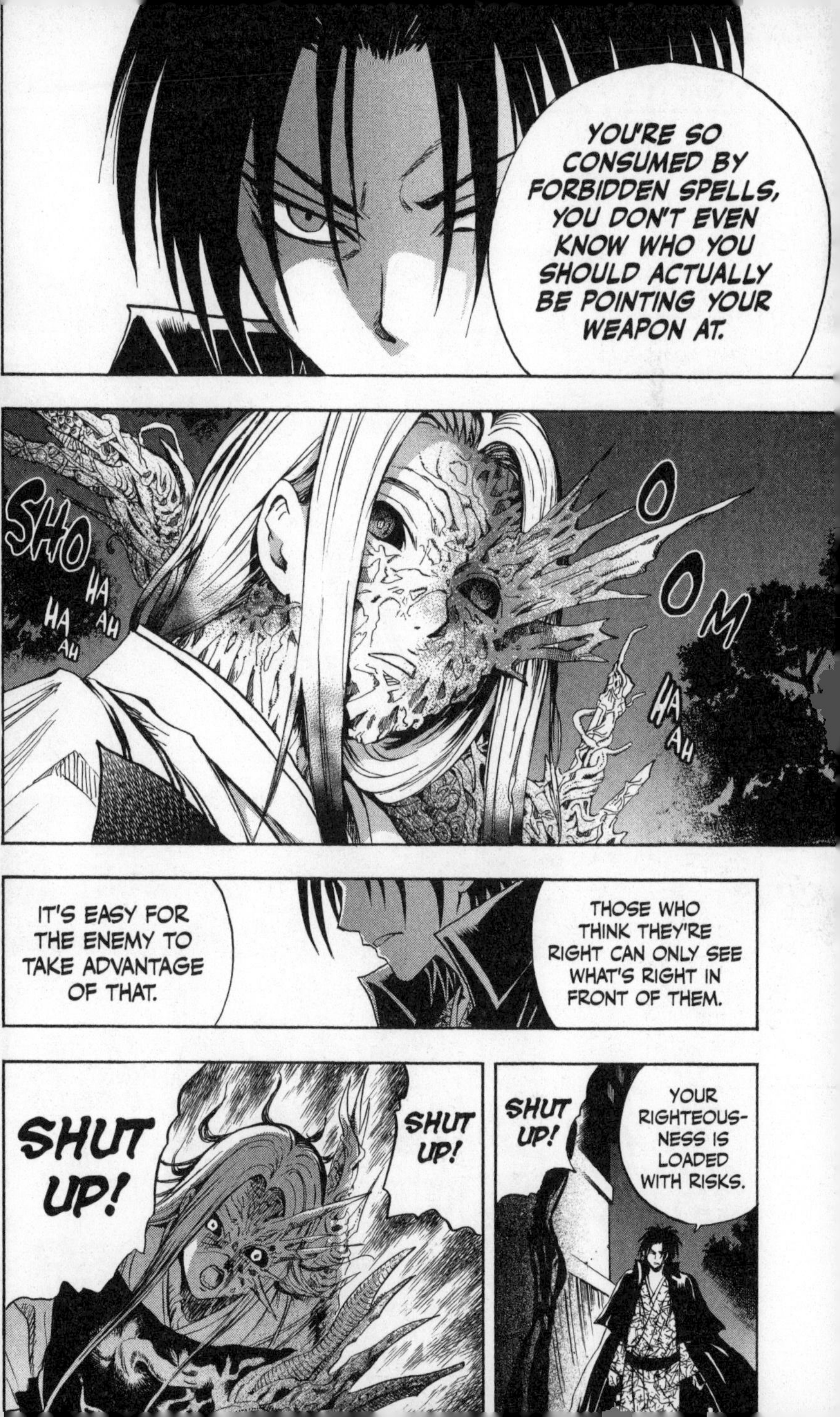
YOU'RE SO CONSUMED BY FORBIDDEN SPELLS, YOU DON'T EVEN KNOW WHO YOU SHOULD ACTUALLY BE POINTING YOUR WEAPON AT.
OOOM
HA AH
SHO
HA AH
HA AH
THOSE WHO THINK THEY'RE RIGHT CAN ONLY SEE WHAT'S RIGHT IN FRONT OF THEM.
IT'S EASY FOR THE ENEMY TO TAKE ADVANTAGE OF THAT.
YOUR RIGHTEOUS-NESS IS LOADED WITH RISKS.
SHUT UP!
SHUT UP!
SHUT UP!

READ THIS WAY

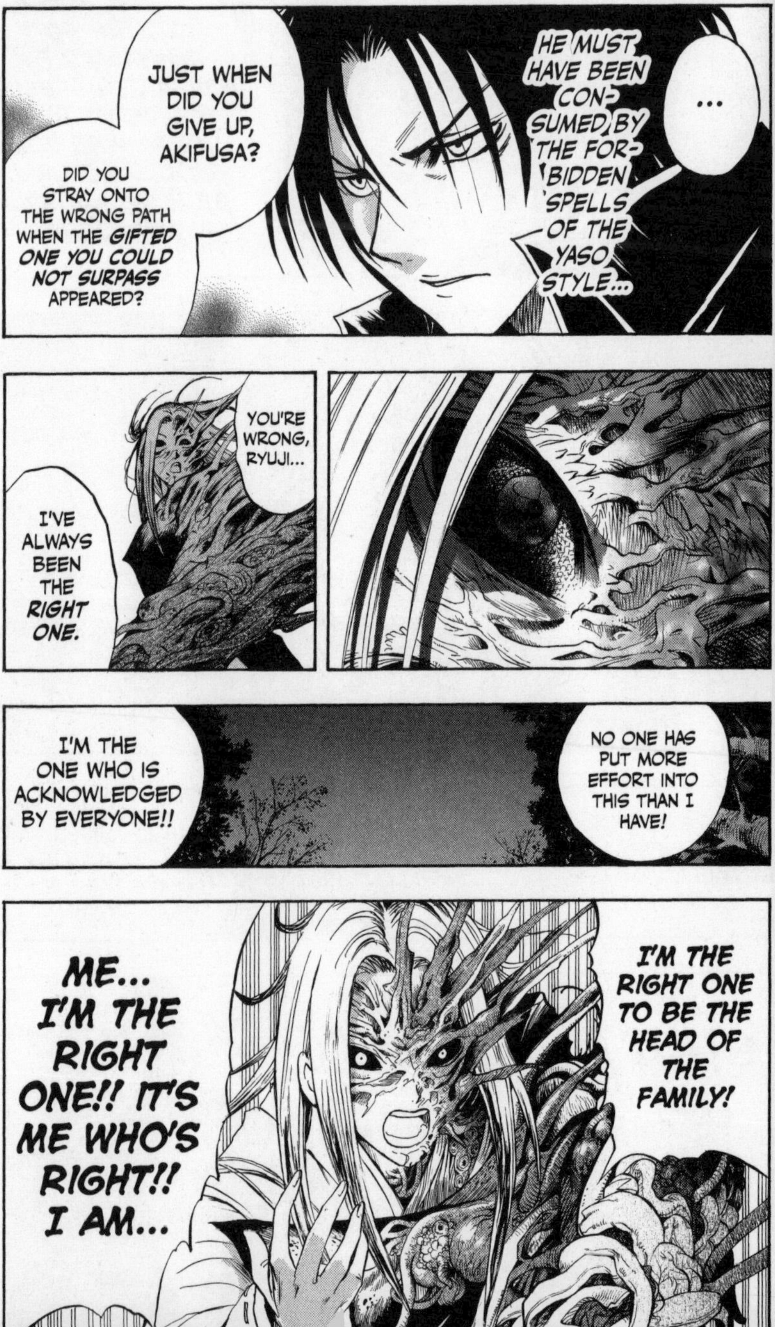
...
HE MUST HAVE BEEN CONSUMED BY THE FORBIDDEN SPELLS OF THE YASO STYLE...
JUST WHEN DID YOU GIVE UP, AKIFUSA?
DID YOU STRAY ONTO THE WRONG PATH WHEN THE *GIFTED ONE YOU COULD NOT SURPASS* APPEARED?
YOU'RE WRONG, RYUJI...
I'VE ALWAYS BEEN THE *RIGHT ONE.*
NO ONE HAS PUT MORE EFFORT INTO THIS THAN I HAVE!
I'M THE ONE WHO IS ACKNOWLEDGED BY EVERYONE!!
I'M THE RIGHT ONE TO BE THE HEAD OF THE FAMILY!
ME... I'M THE RIGHT ONE!! IT'S ME WHO'S RIGHT!! I AM...

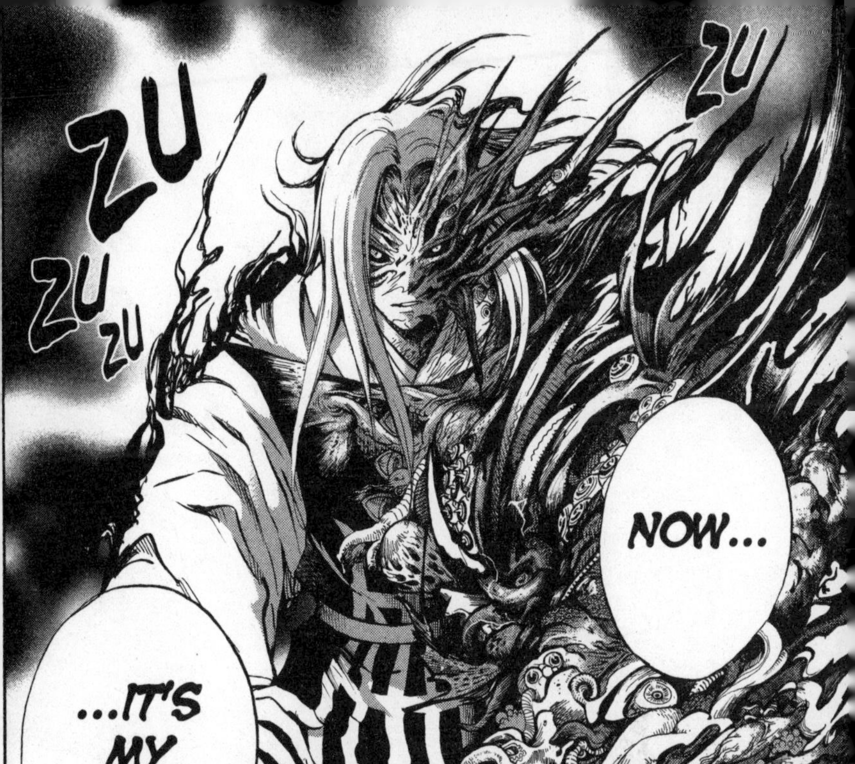
ZU
NOW...
ZU ZU ZU
...IT'S MY TURN...
ZU

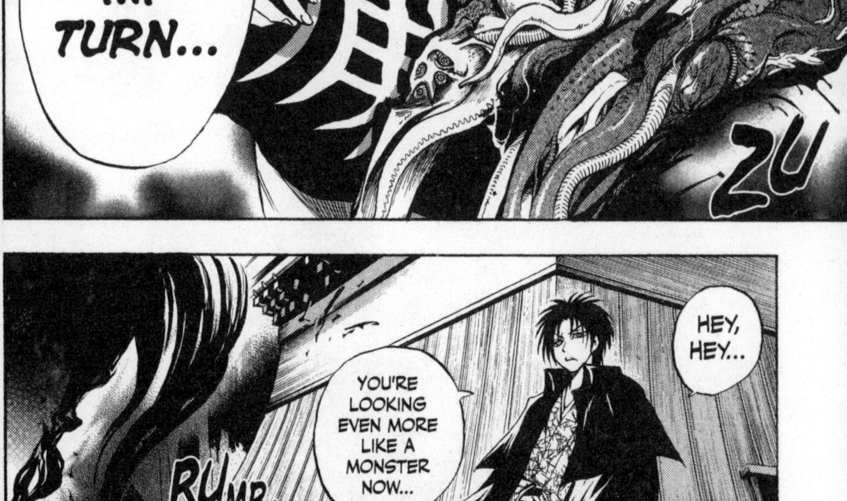
HEY, HEY...
YOU'RE LOOKING EVEN MORE LIKE A MONSTER NOW...
RUMBLE

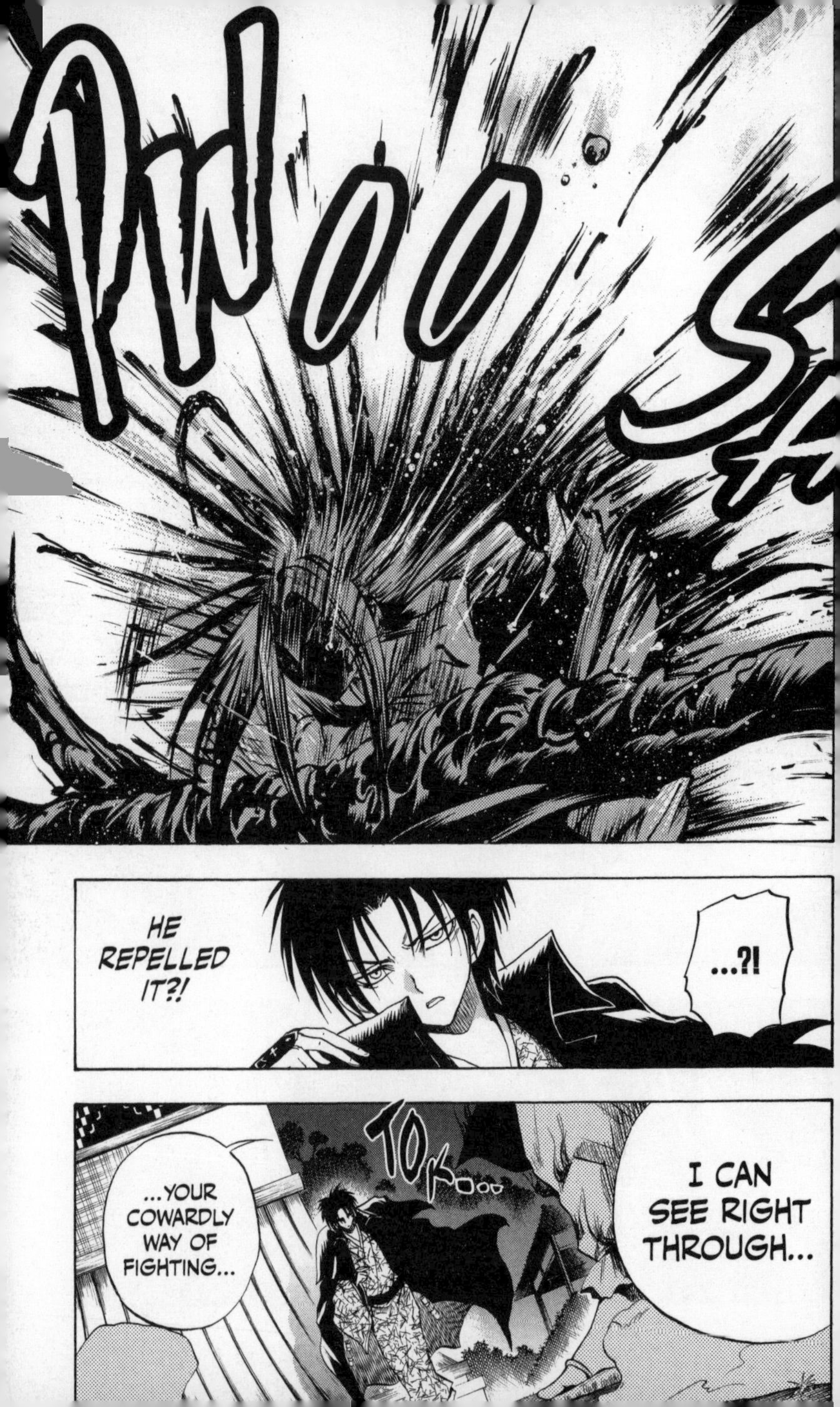
PWOOSH
...?!
HE REPELLED IT?!
I CAN SEE RIGHT THROUGH...
TOK...
...YOUR COWARDLY WAY OF FIGHTING...

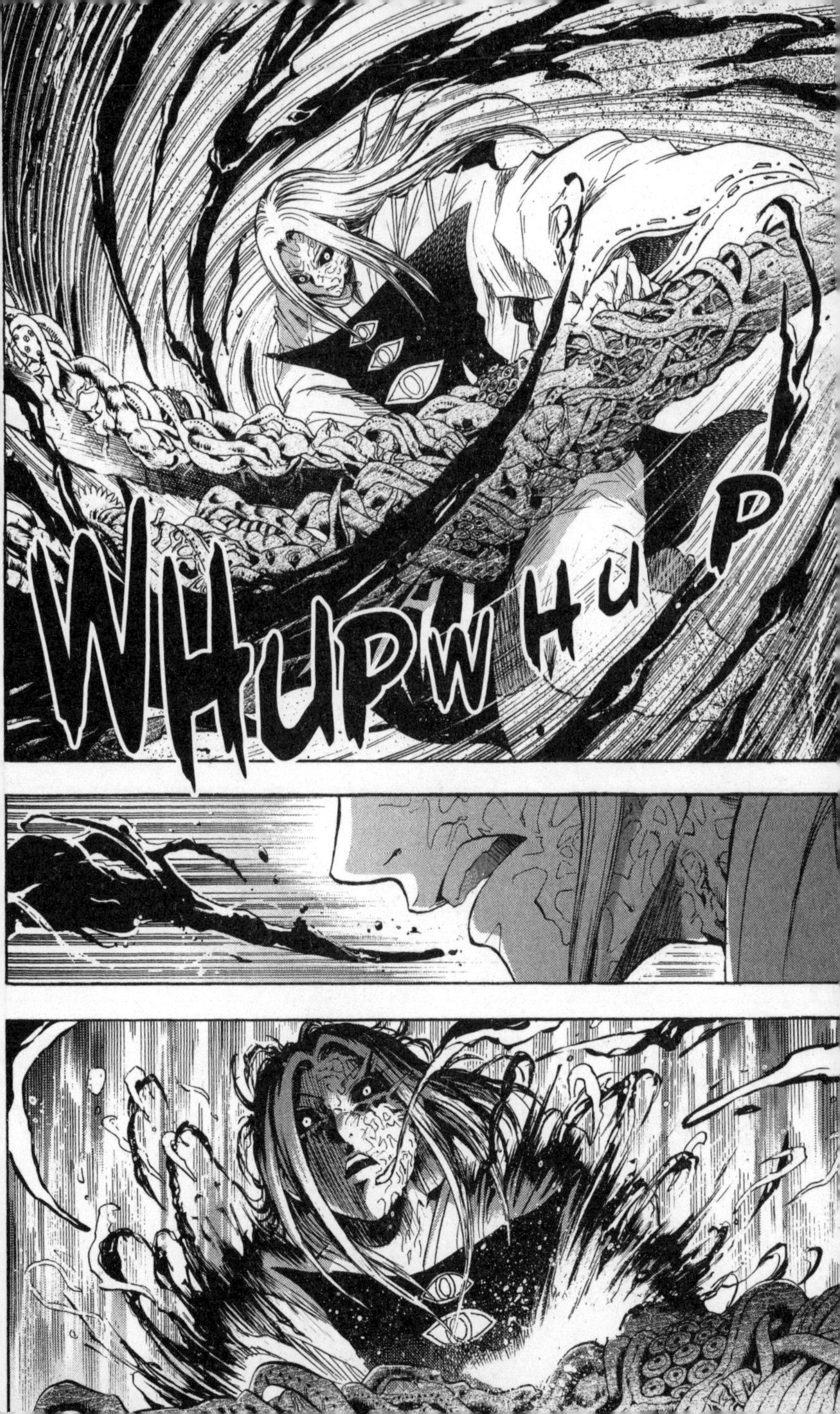
WHUPWHUP!

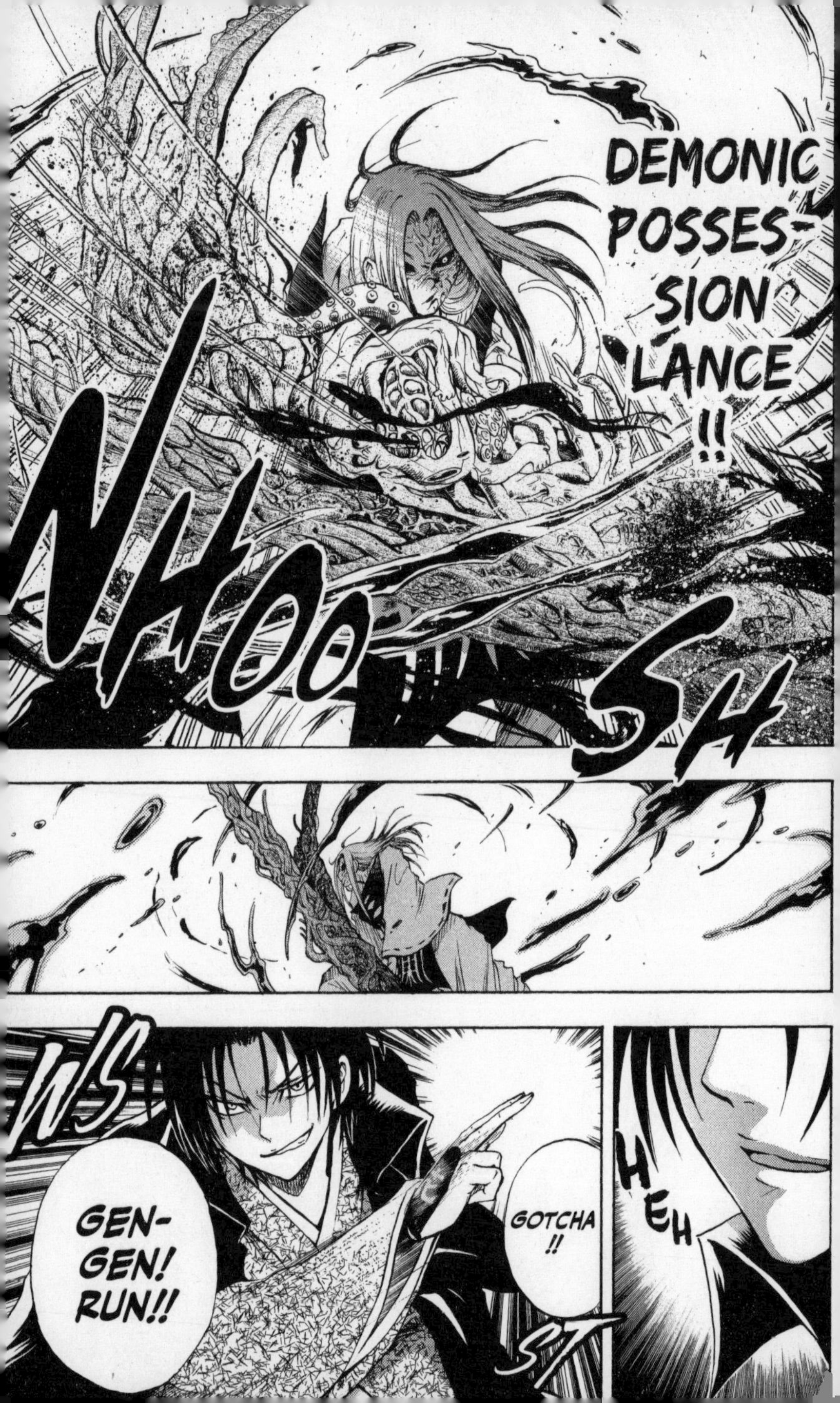
DEMONIC POSSES-SION LANCE!!
WHOOSH
HEH
GOTCHA!!
GEN-GEN! RUN!!

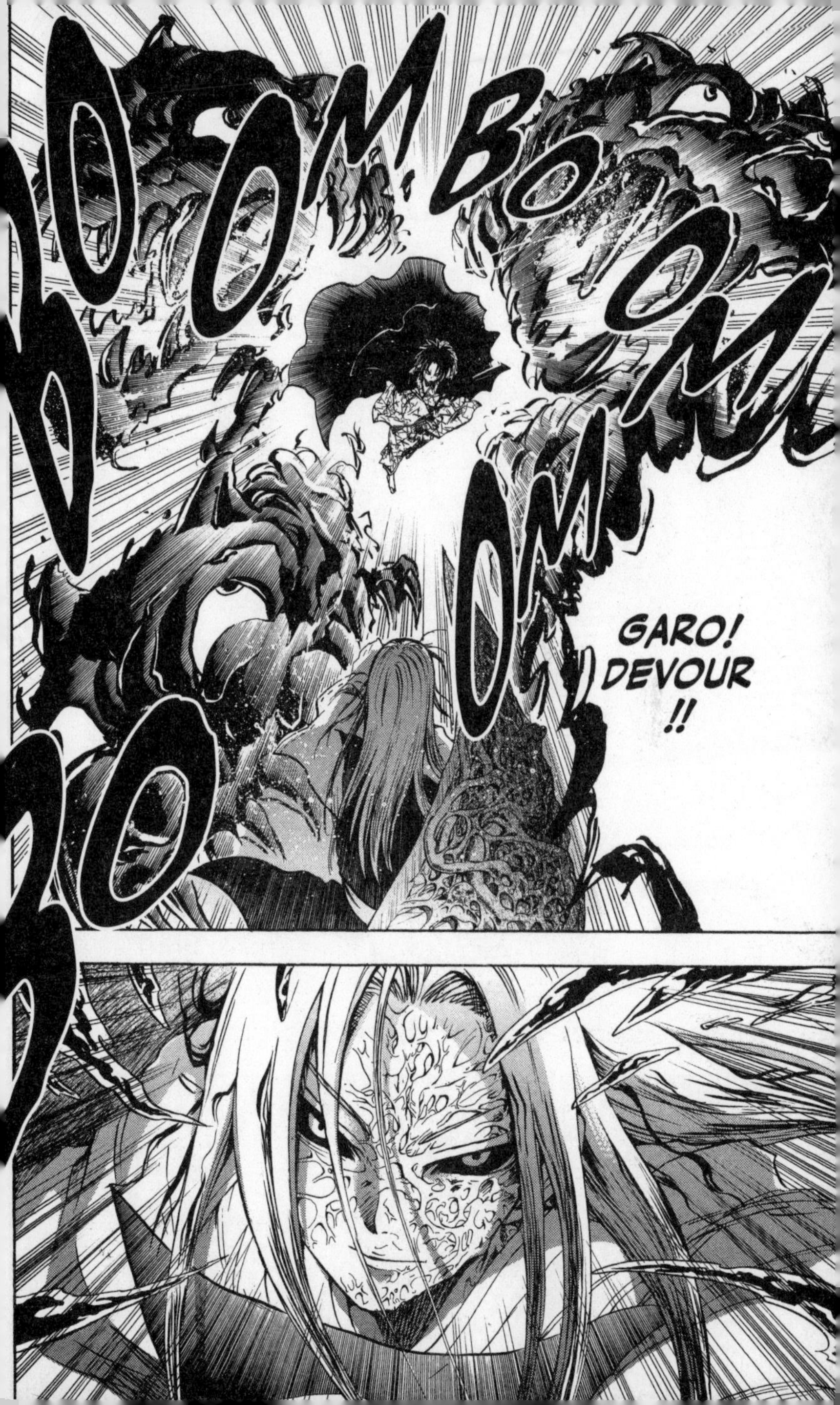
GARO! DEVOUR !!
BOOOM BOOOM
BOOOM

READ THIS WAY

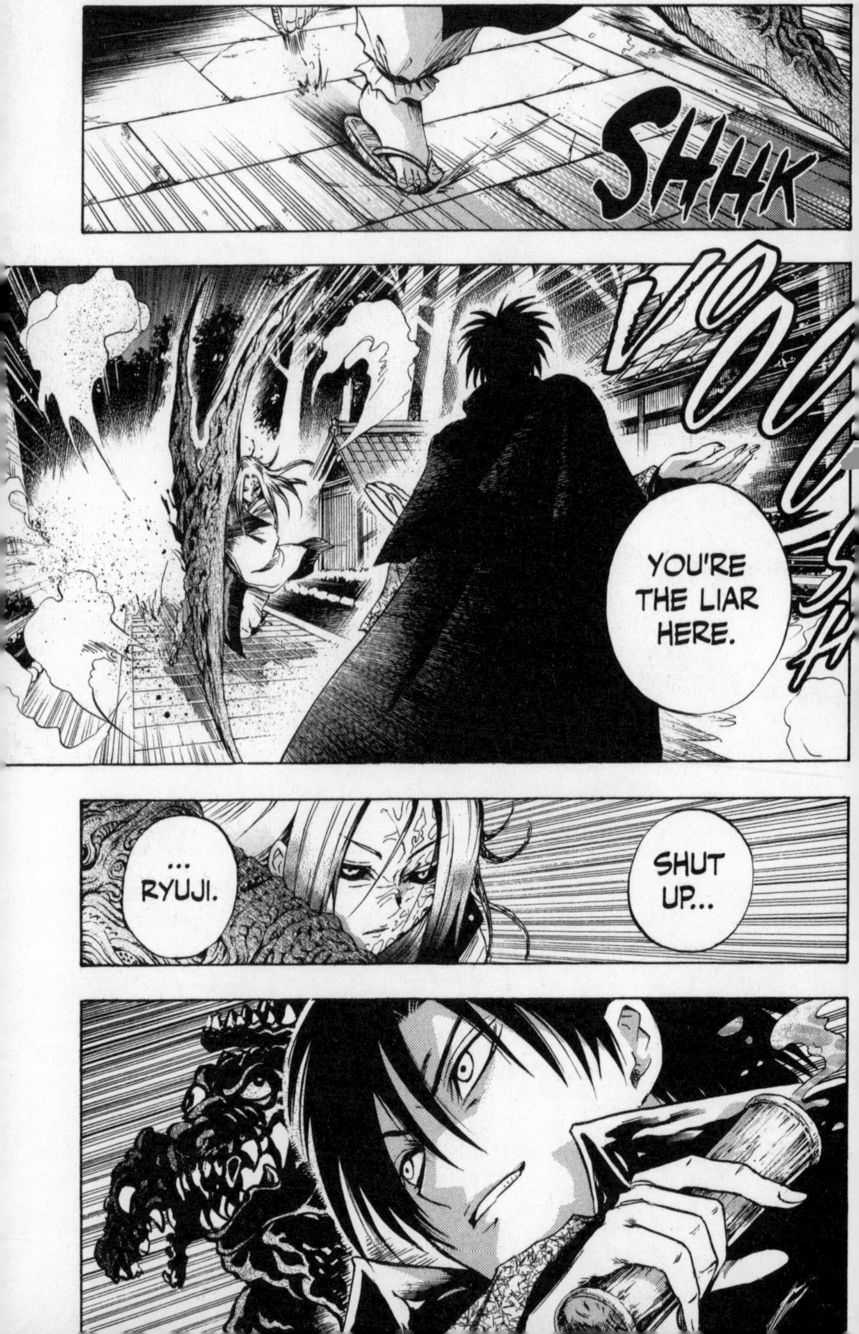

SHHK
YOU'RE THE LIAR HERE.
SHUT UP...
... RYUJI.

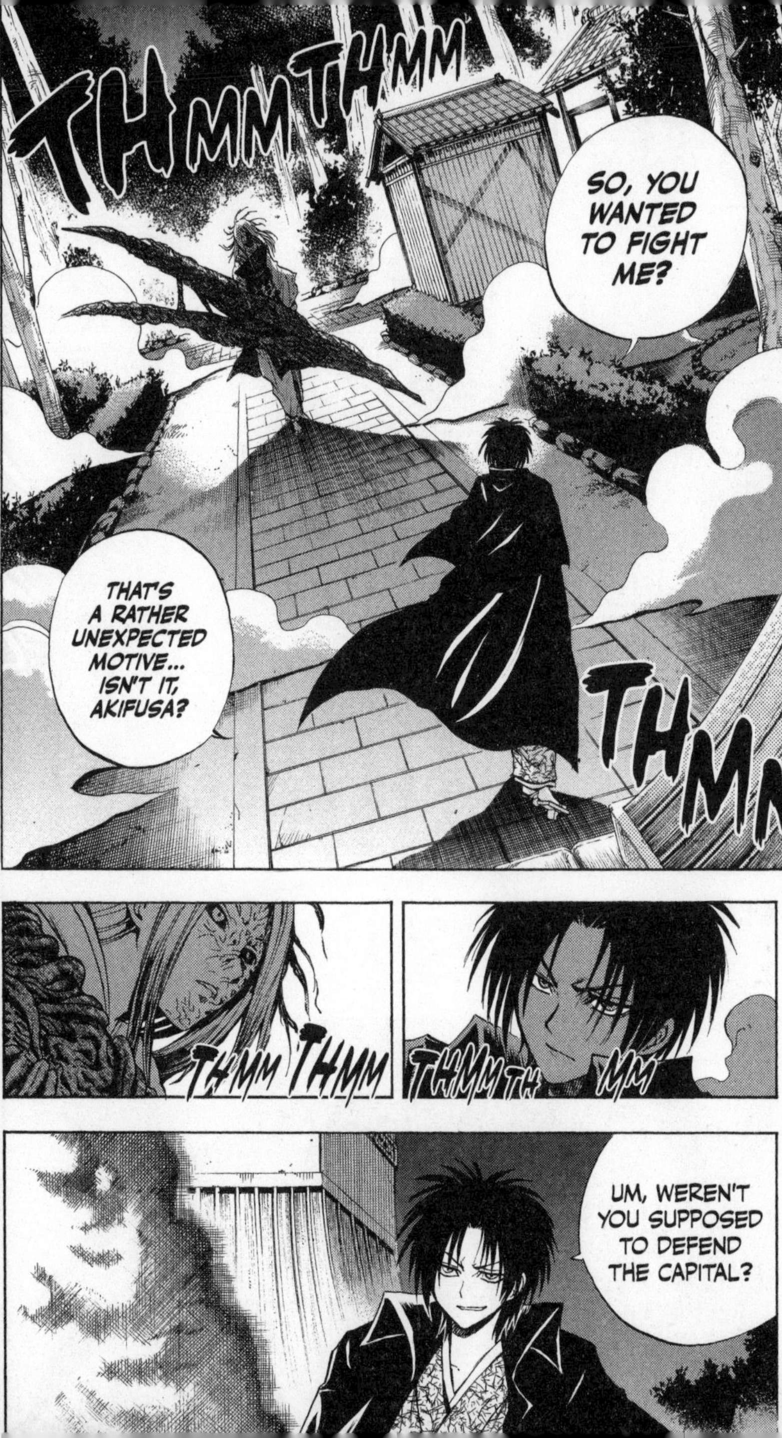
SO, YOU WANTED TO FIGHT ME?
THMM THMM
THMM
THAT'S A RATHER UNEXPECTED MOTIVE... ISN'T IT, AKIFUSA?
THMM TH MM
THMM THMM
UM, WEREN'T YOU SUPPOSED TO DEFEND THE CAPITAL?

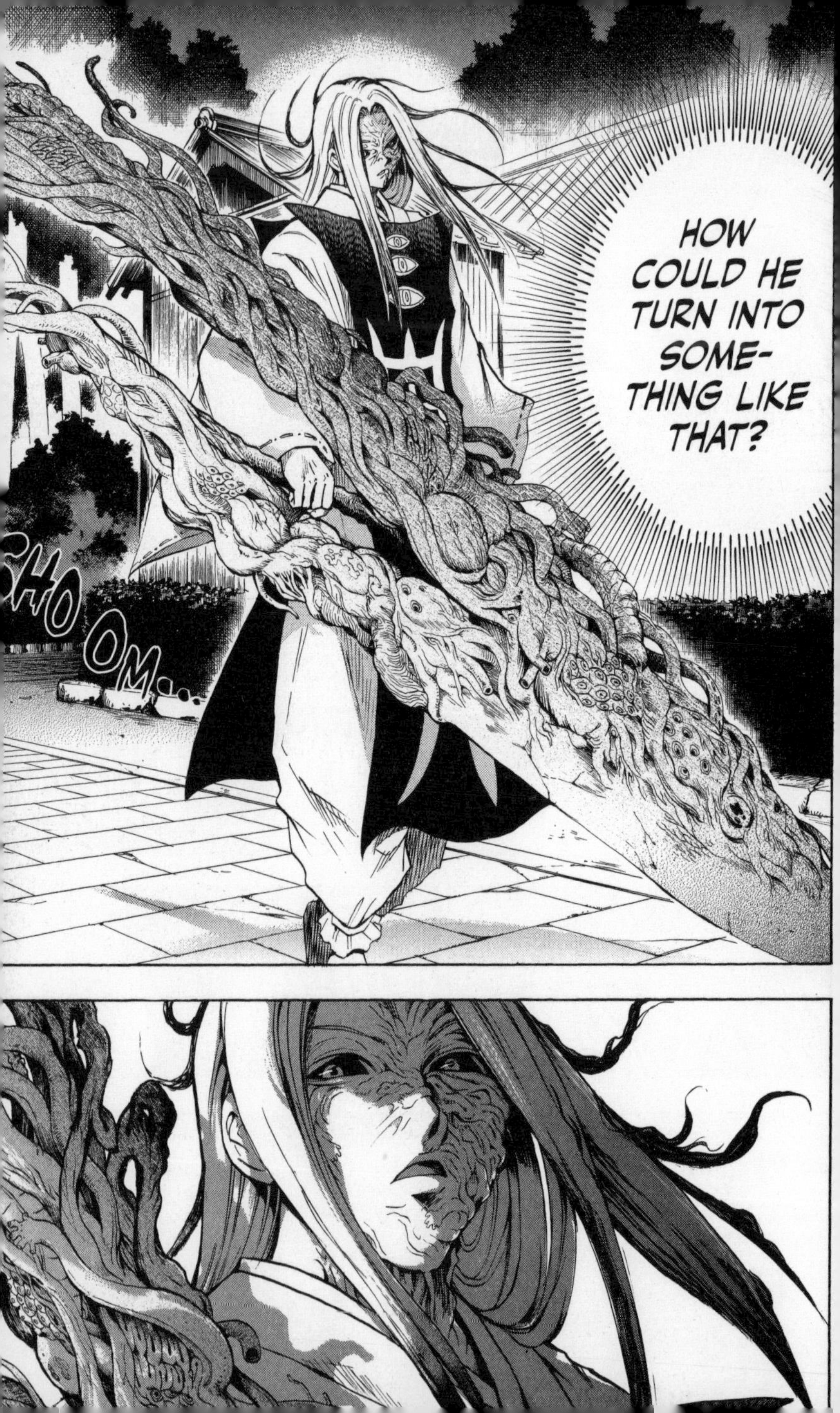
HOW COULD HE TURN INTO SOME-THING LIKE THAT?
SHOOM...

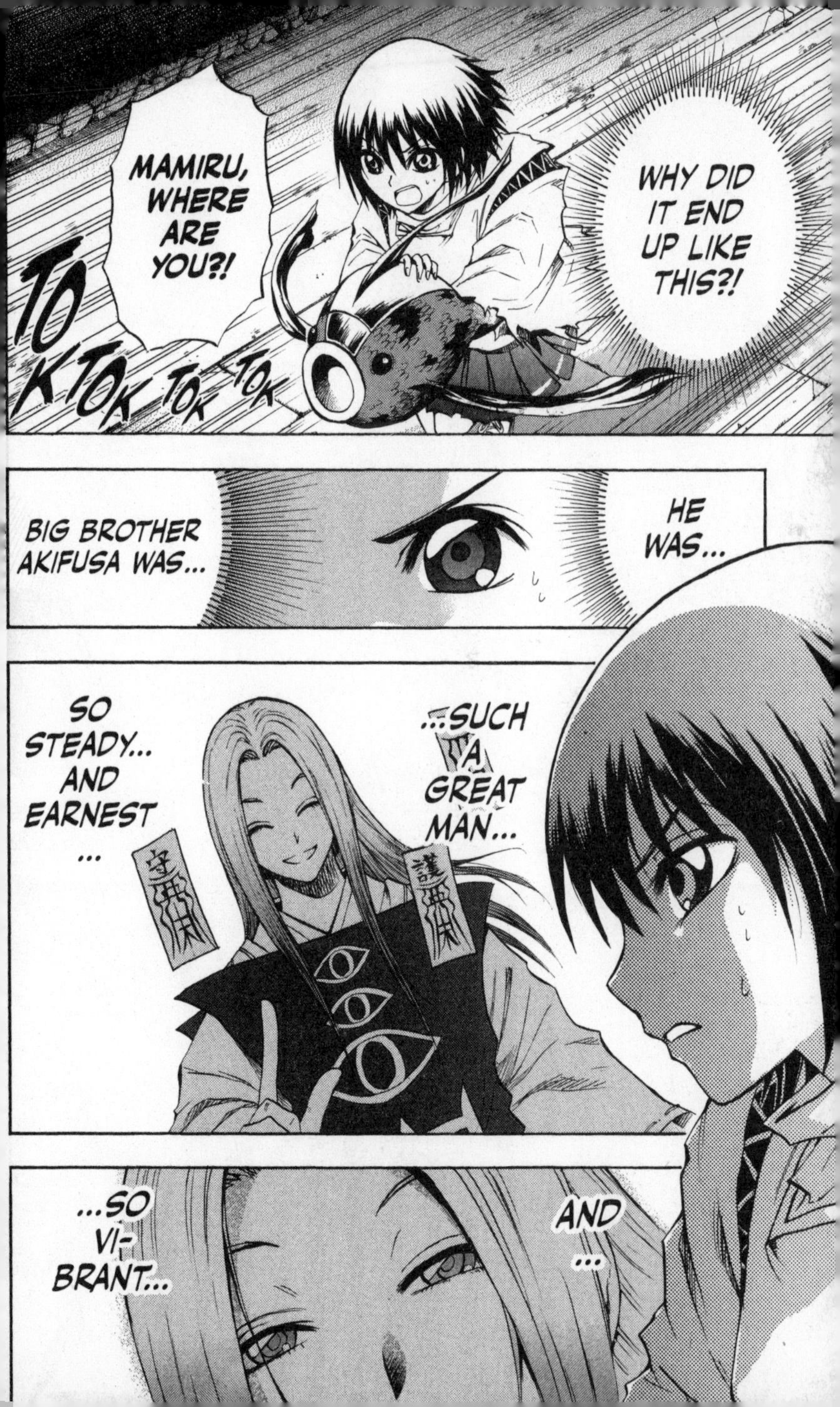
WHY DID IT END UP LIKE THIS?!
MAMIRU, WHERE ARE YOU?!
TOK
TOK
TOK
TOK
HE WAS...
BIG BROTHER AKIFUSA WAS...
...SUCH A GREAT MAN...
SO STEADY... AND EARNEST...
AND...
...SO VI-BRANT...

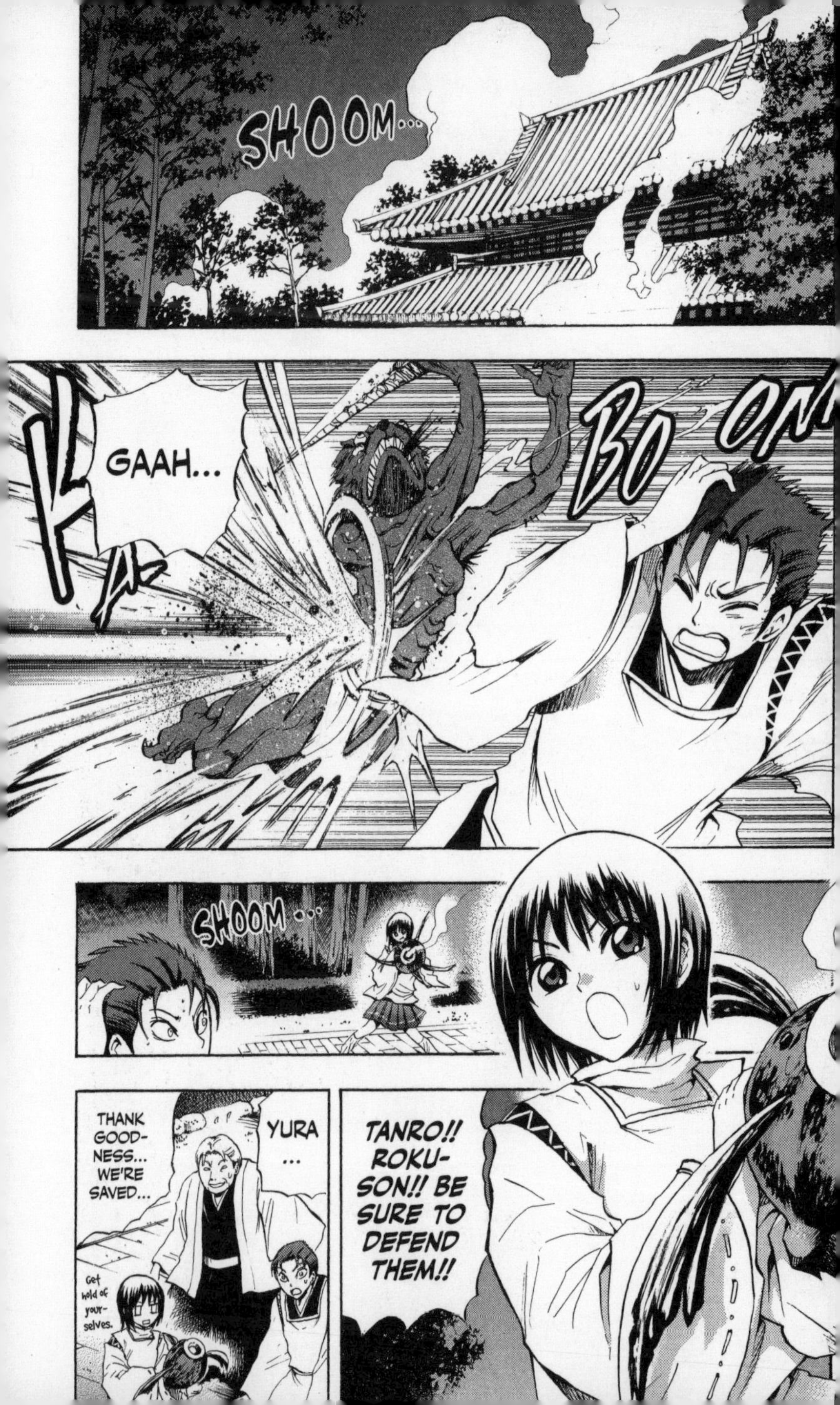
SHOOM...
GAAH...
TANRO!! ROKUSON!! BE SURE TO DEFEND THEM!!
SHOOM...
YURA...
THANK GOODNESS... WE'RE SAVED...
Get hold of yourselves.

Keikain Confidential

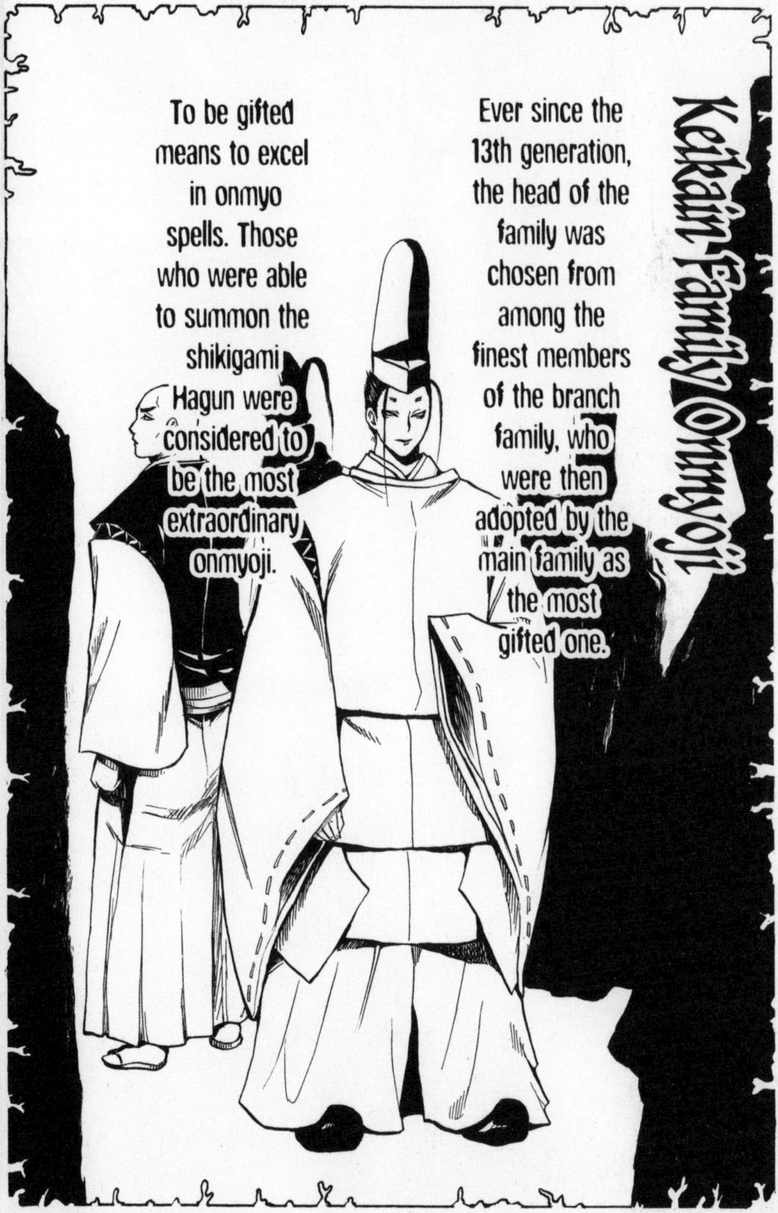

Keikain Family Onmyoji
Ever since the 13th generation, the head of the family was chosen from among the finest members of the branch family, who were then adopted by the main family as the most gifted one.
To be gifted means to excel in onmyo spells. Those who were able to summon the shikigami Hagun were considered to be the most extraordinary onmyoji.

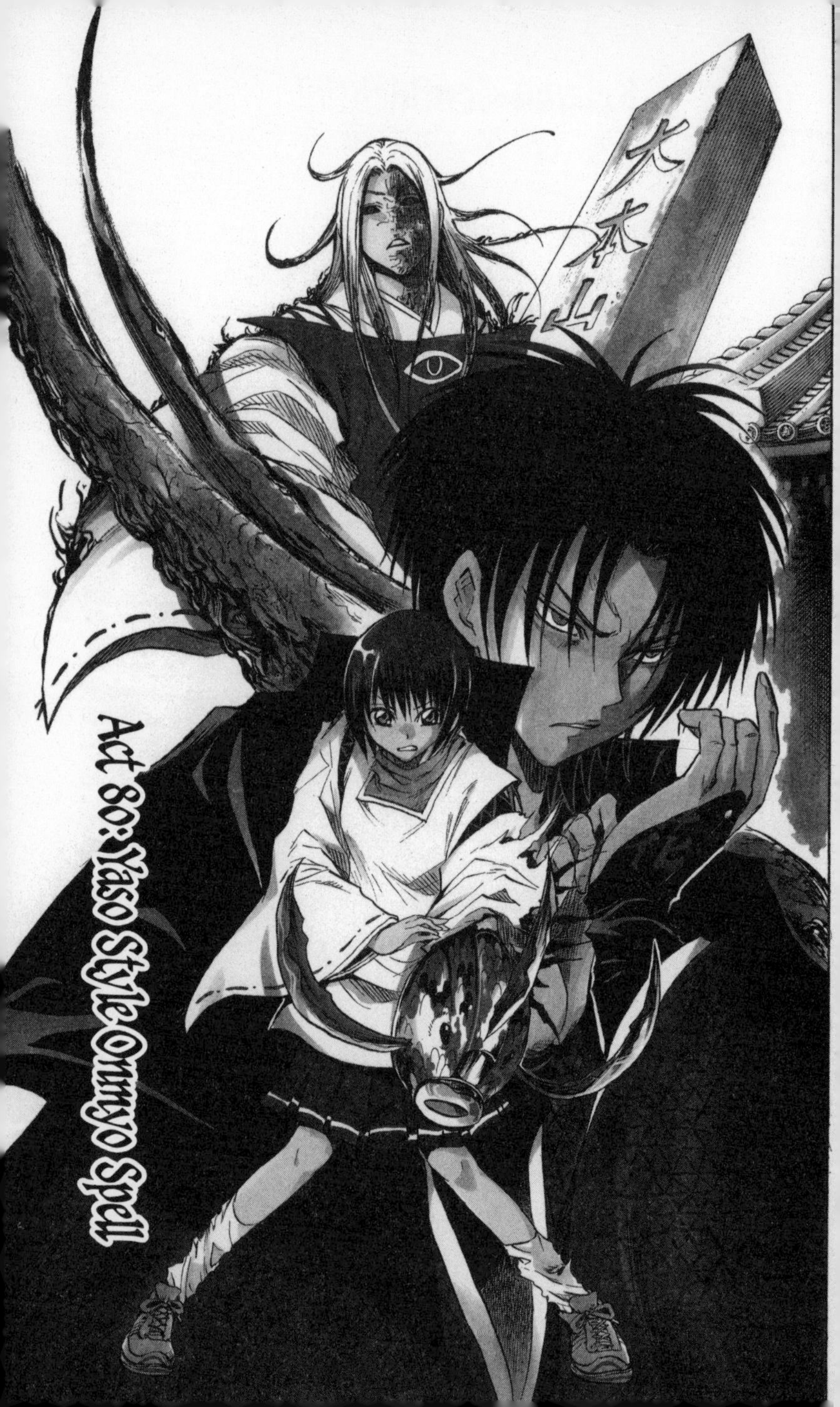
大本山
Act 80: Yaso Style Onmyo Spell

Announcing the results of
the first popularity vote!!

TKG (1 vote)

Tamapippi (1 vote)

Kaki-pii (1 vote)

Aotabo imposter
(1 vote)

Mr. Hasebe
(1 vote)

Kurotabo imposter
(1 vote)

To be
continued!

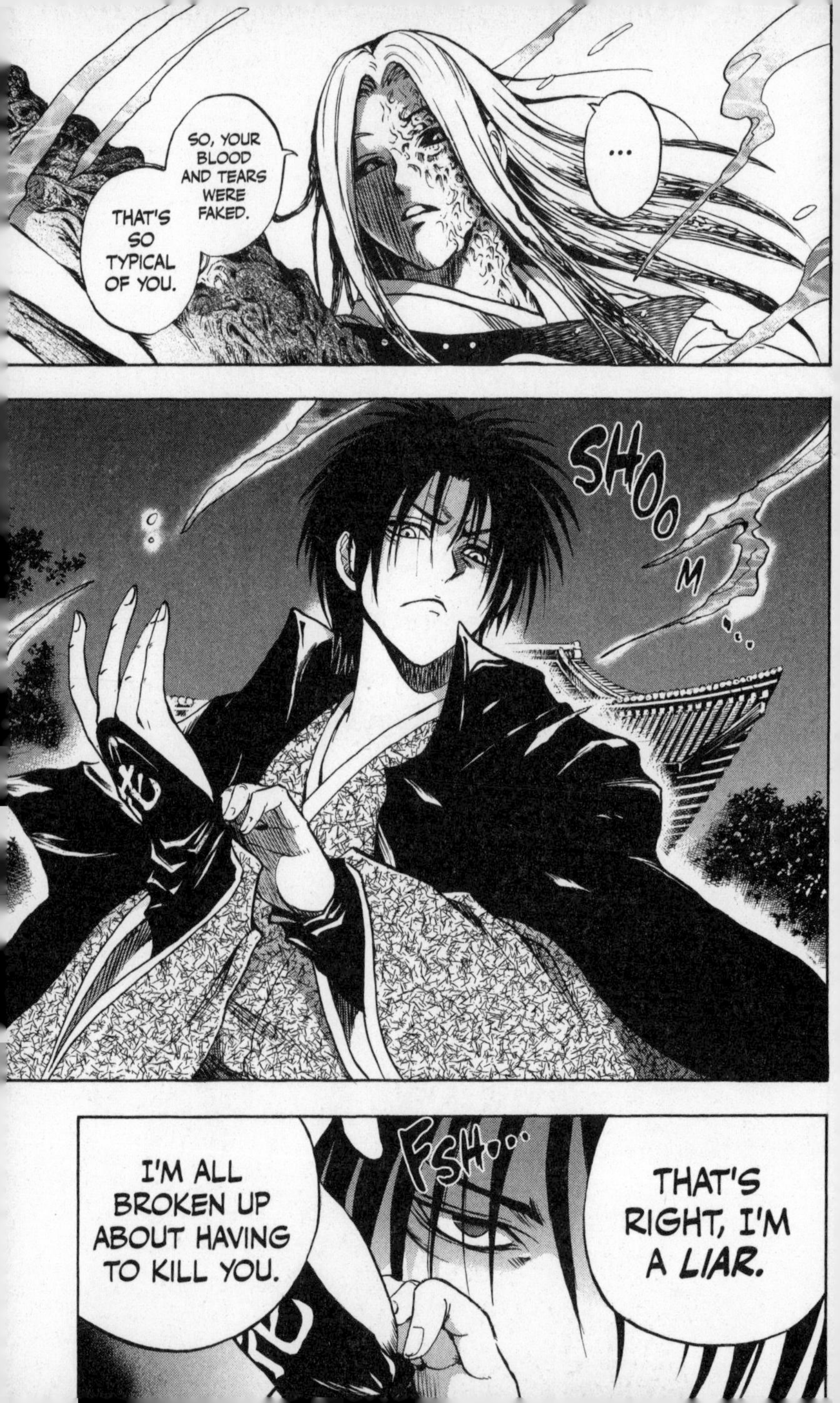
...
SO, YOUR BLOOD AND TEARS WERE FAKED.
THAT'S SO TYPICAL OF YOU.
SHOOM...
THAT'S RIGHT, I'M A *LIAR.*
FSH...
I'M ALL BROKEN UP ABOUT HAVING TO KILL YOU.

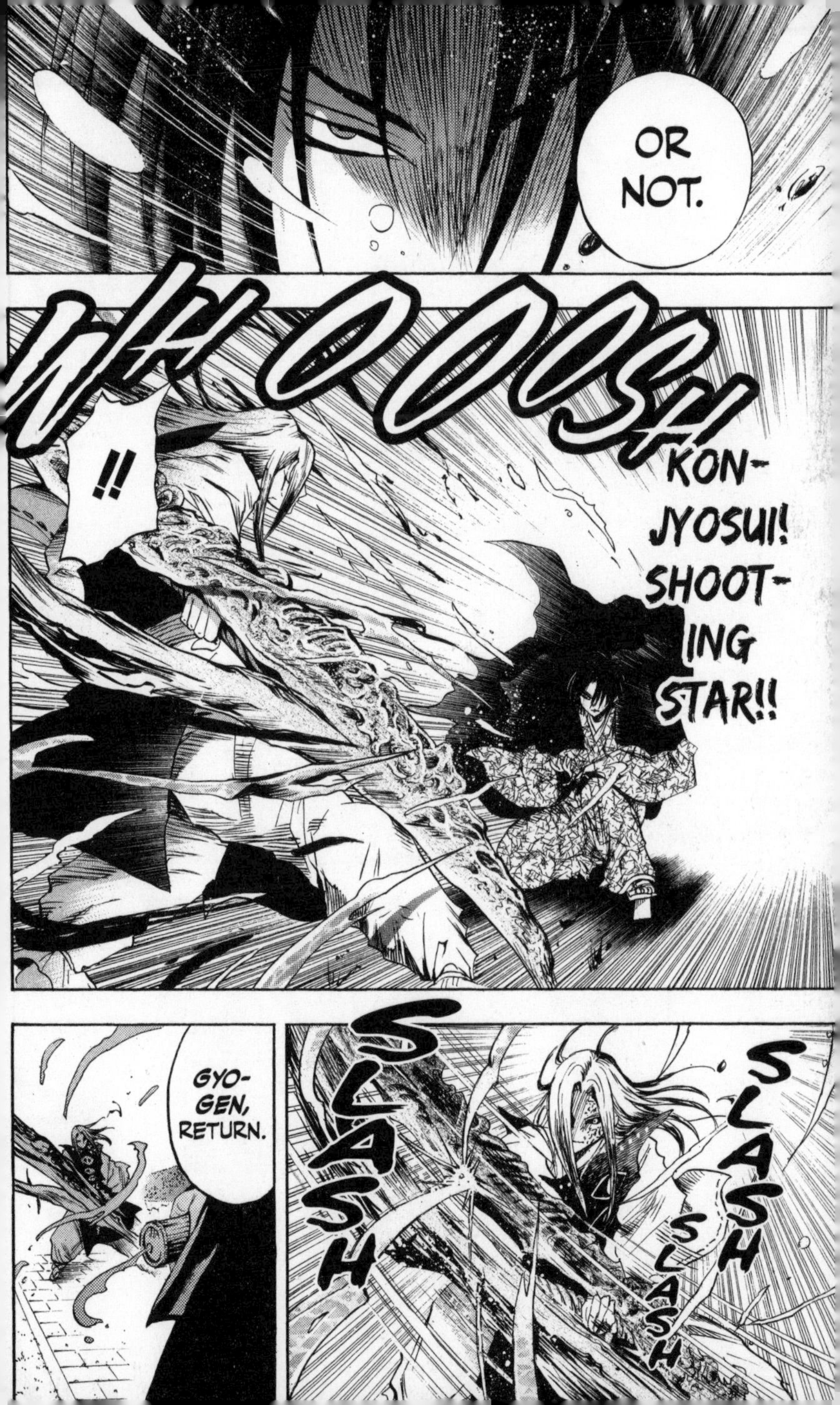
OR NOT.
WHOOOSH
!!
KON-JYOSUI! SHOOTING STAR!!
GYO-GEN, RETURN.
SLASH
SLASH
SLASH

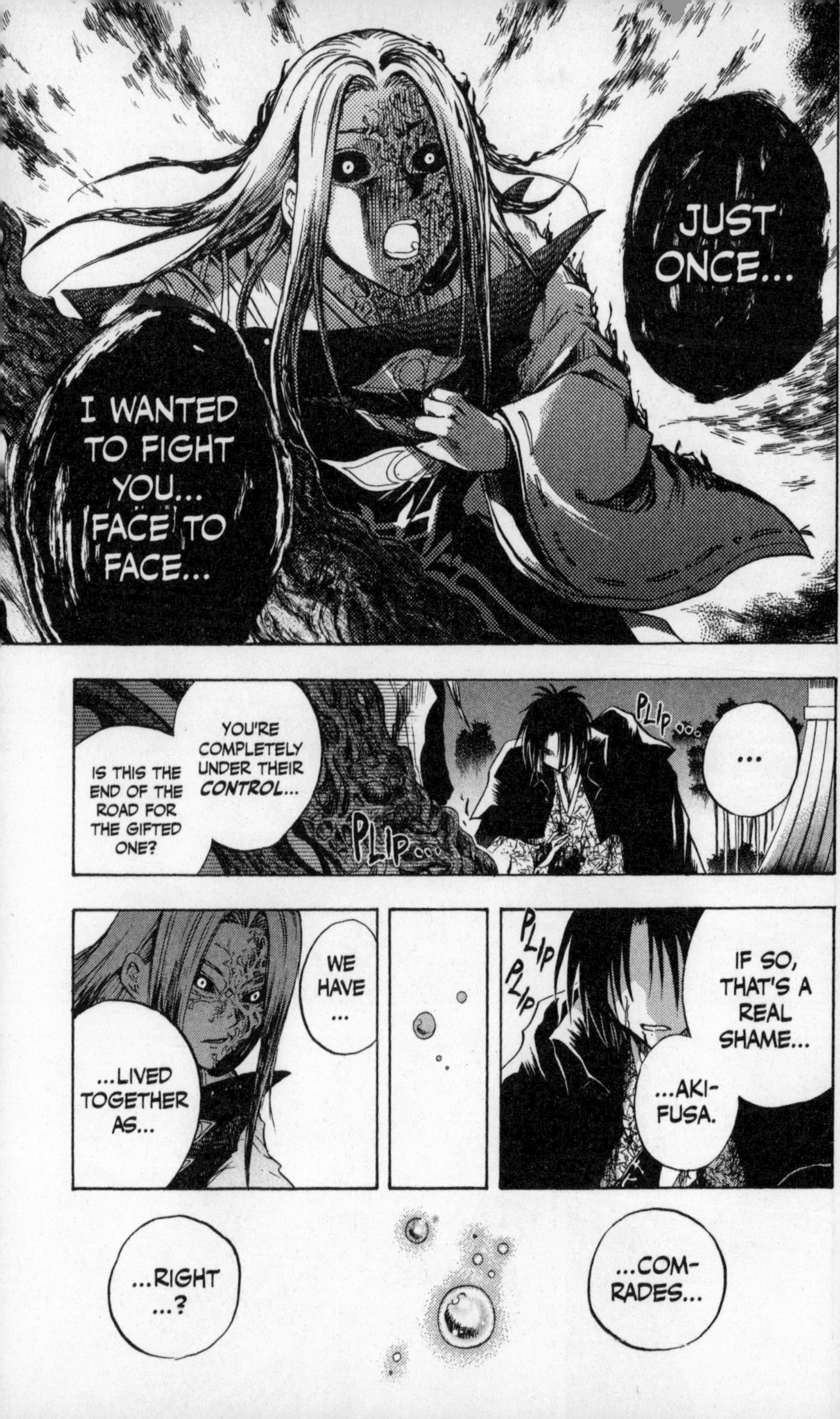
JUST ONCE...
I WANTED TO FIGHT YOU... FACE TO FACE...
PLIP...
...
YOU'RE COMPLETELY UNDER THEIR *CONTROL*...
IS THIS THE END OF THE ROAD FOR THE GIFTED ONE?
PLIP...
PLIP
PLIP
IF SO, THAT'S A REAL SHAME...
...AKI-FUSA.
WE HAVE ...
...LIVED TOGETHER AS...
...COM-RADES...
...RIGHT ...?

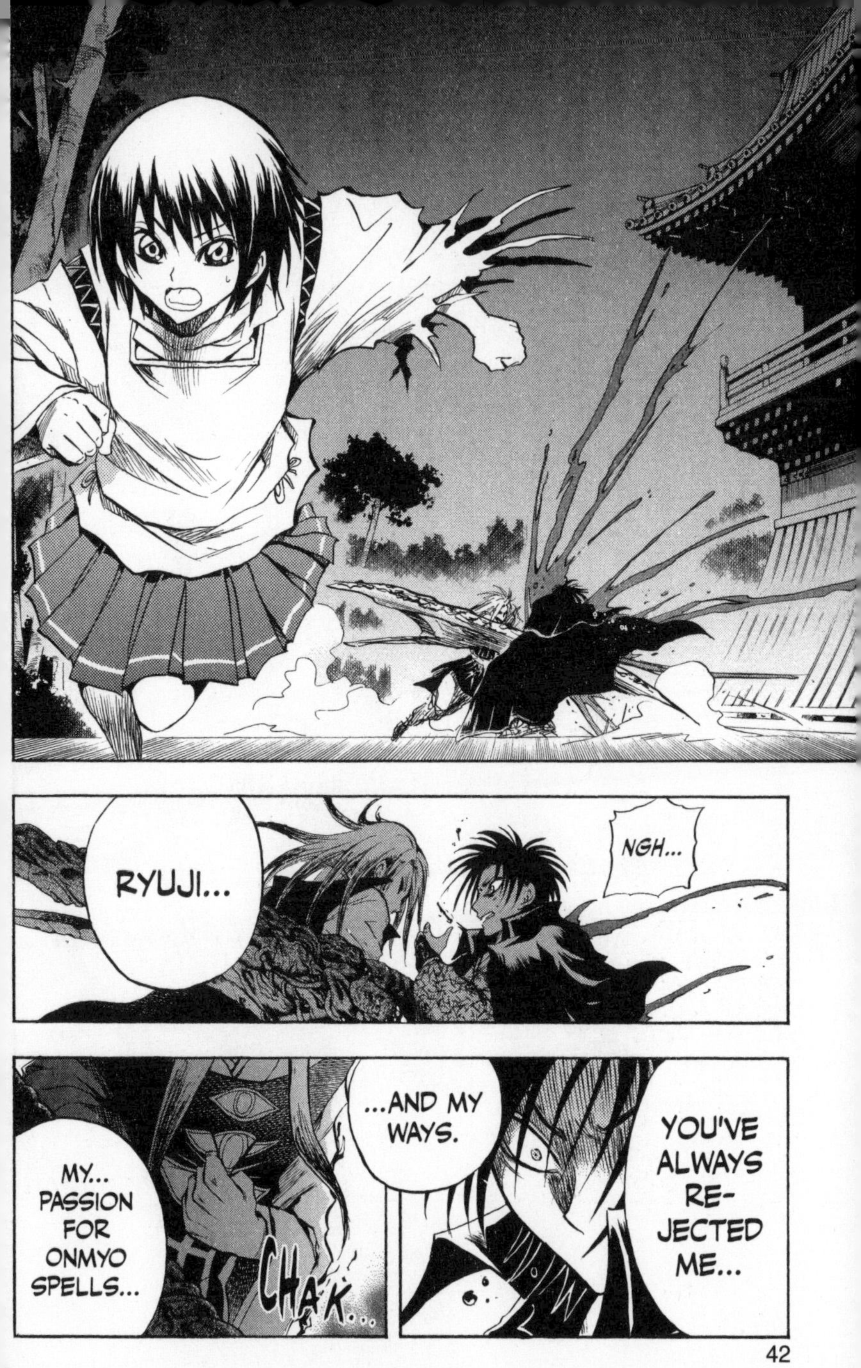
NGH...
RYUJI...
YOU'VE ALWAYS RE-JECTED ME...
MY... PASSION FOR ONMYO SPELLS...
...AND MY WAYS.
CHAK...

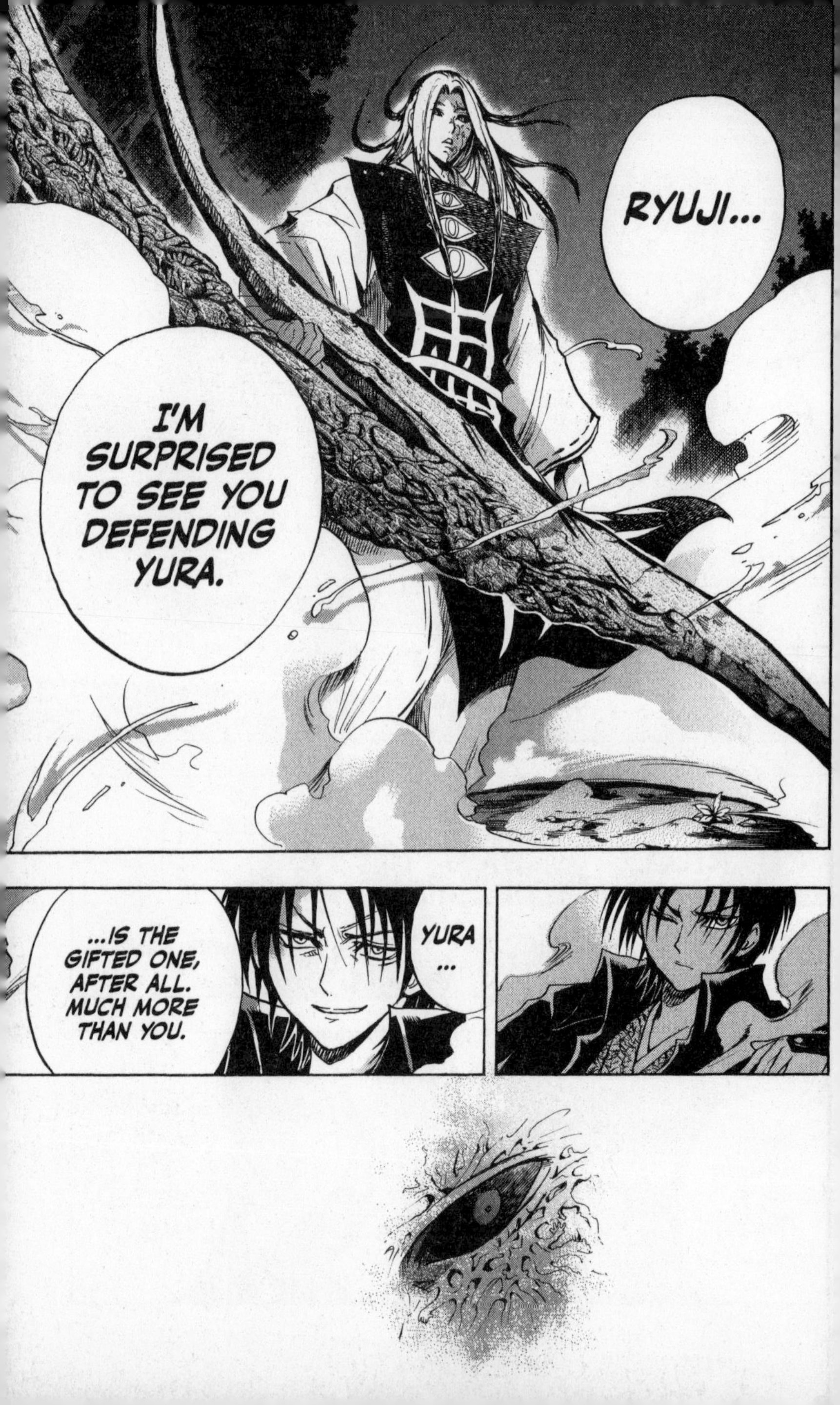
RYUJI...
I'M SURPRISED TO SEE YOU DEFENDING YURA.
YURA ...
...IS THE GIFTED ONE, AFTER ALL. MUCH MORE THAN YOU.

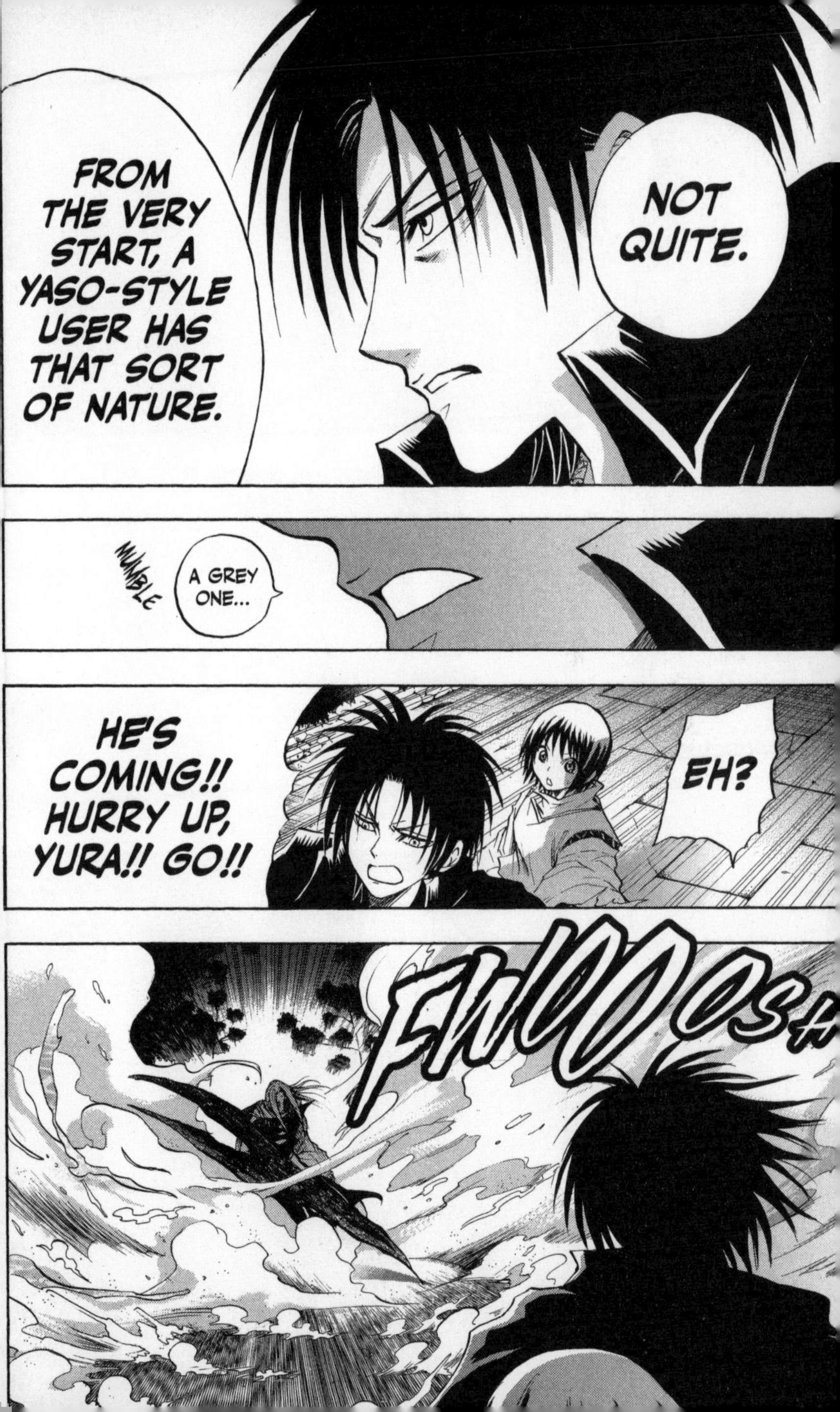
NOT QUITE.
FROM THE VERY START, A YASO-STYLE USER HAS THAT SORT OF NATURE.
A GREY ONE...
MUMBLE
EH?
HE'S COMING!! HURRY UP, YURA!! GO!!
FWOOOSH

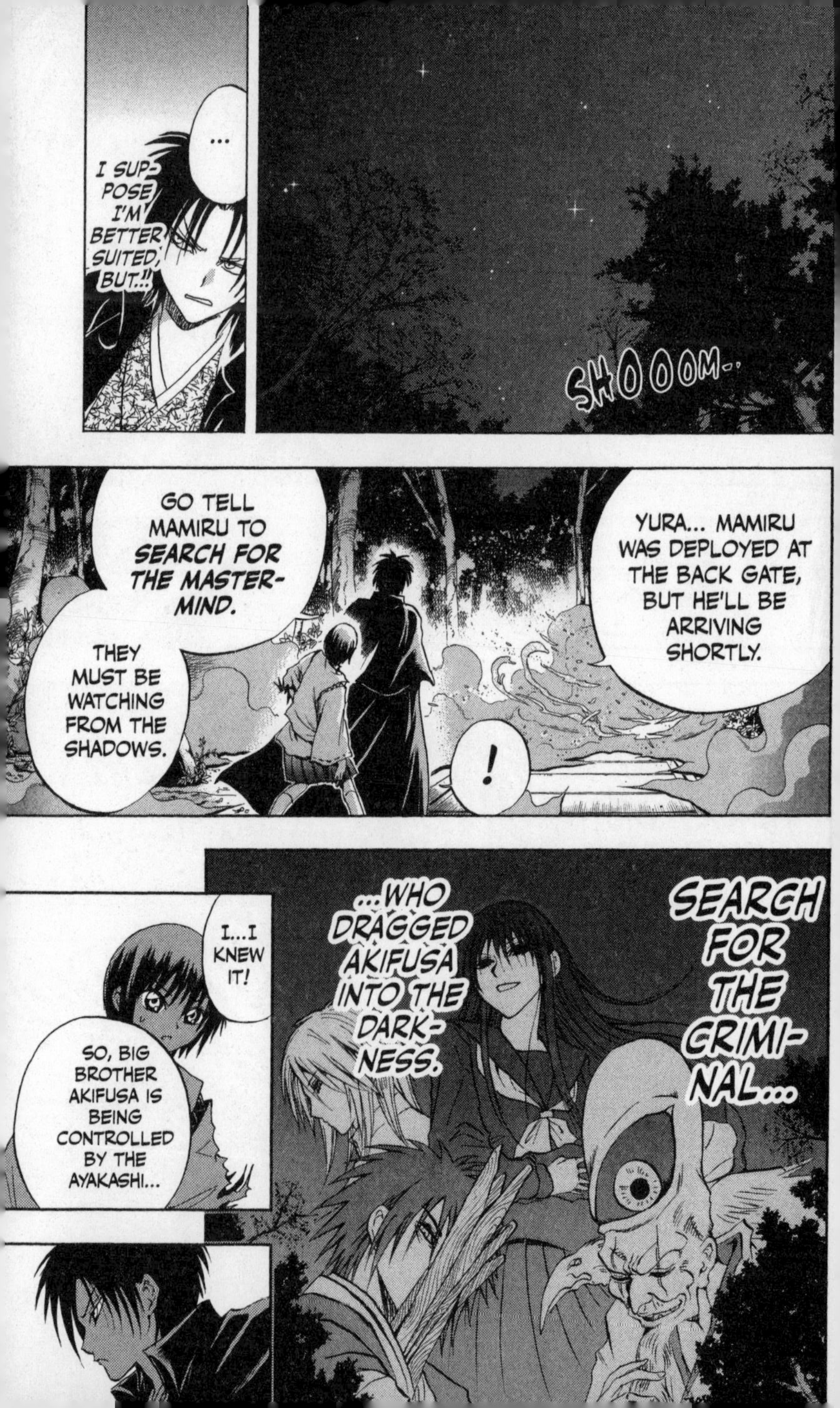
SHOOOM...
...
I SUPPOSE I'M BETTER SUITED, BUT...!!
YURA... MAMIRU WAS DEPLOYED AT THE BACK GATE, BUT HE'LL BE ARRIVING SHORTLY.
!
GO TELL MAMIRU TO SEARCH FOR THE MASTERMIND.
THEY MUST BE WATCHING FROM THE SHADOWS.
SEARCH FOR THE CRIMINAL...
...WHO DRAGGED AKIFUSA INTO THE DARKNESS.
I...I KNEW IT!
SO, BIG BROTHER AKIFUSA IS BEING CONTROLLED BY THE AYAKASHI...

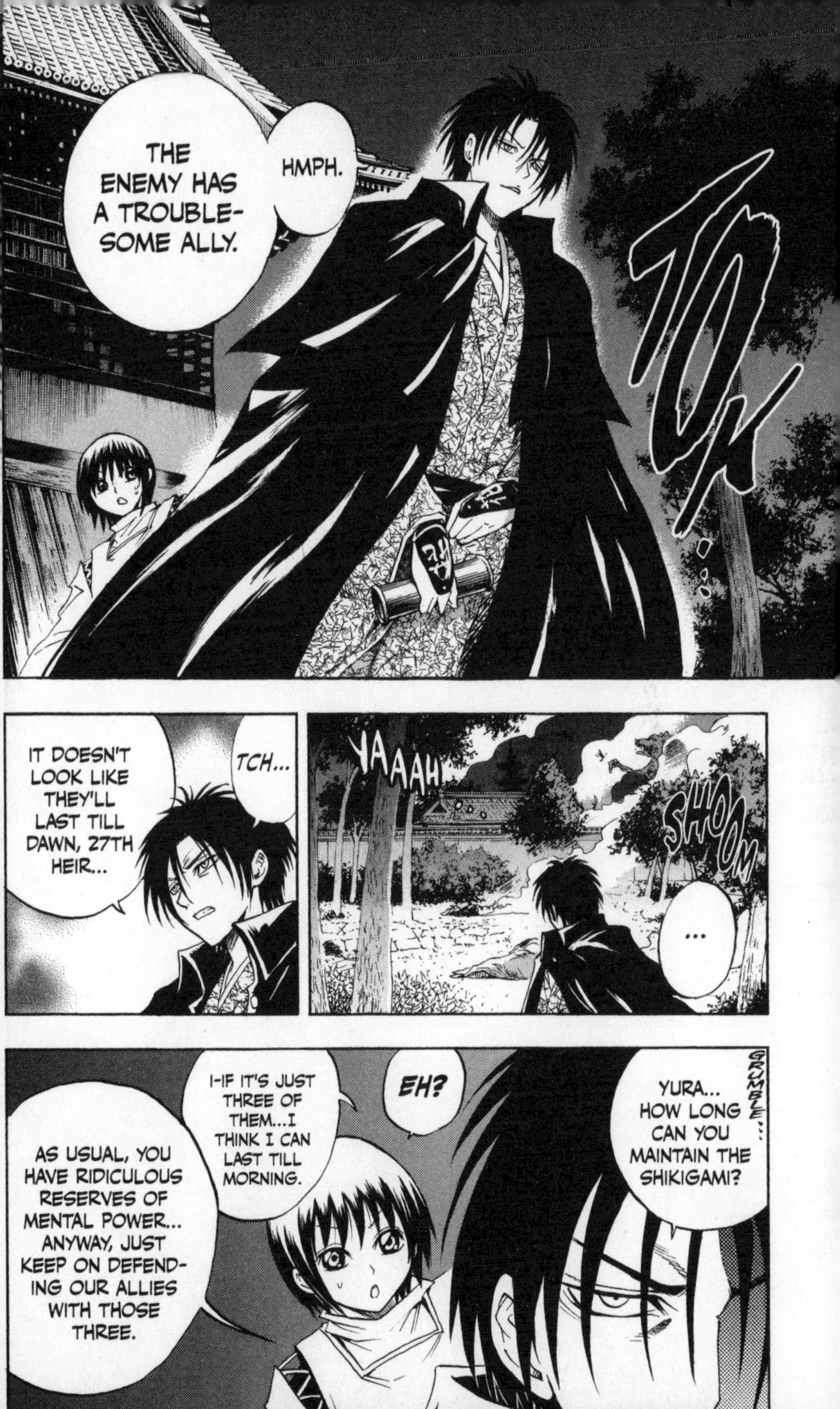
HMPH.
THE ENEMY HAS A TROUBLE-SOME ALLY.
TOK...
YAAAH
SHOOM
...
TCH...
IT DOESN'T LOOK LIKE THEY'LL LAST TILL DAWN, 27TH HEIR...
GRUMBLE...
YURA... HOW LONG CAN YOU MAINTAIN THE SHIKIGAMI?
EH?
I-IF IT'S JUST THREE OF THEM...I THINK I CAN LAST TILL MORNING.
AS USUAL, YOU HAVE RIDICULOUS RESERVES OF MENTAL POWER... ANYWAY, JUST KEEP ON DEFEND-ING OUR ALLIES WITH THOSE THREE.

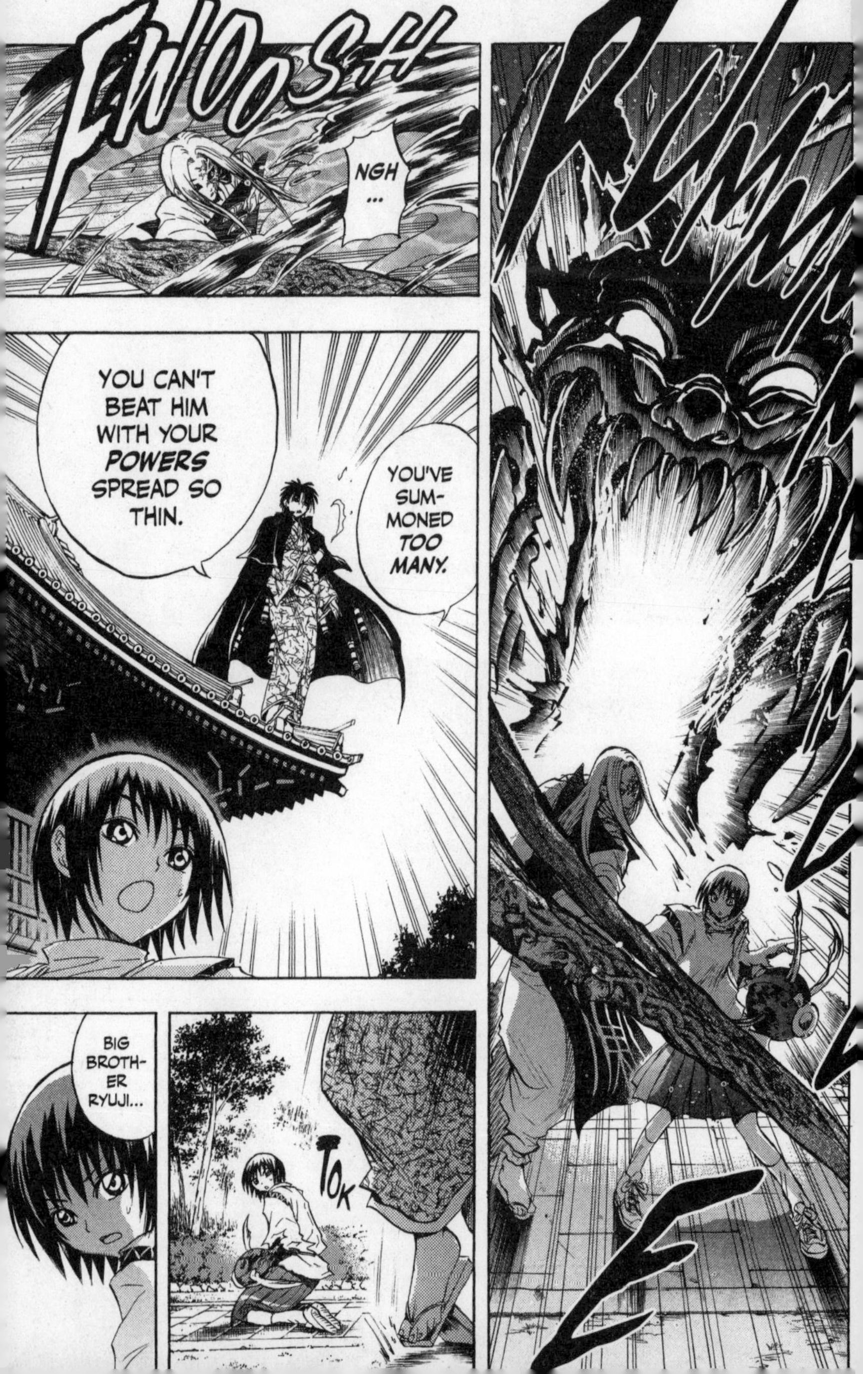
FWOOSH
NGH ...
YOU CAN'T BEAT HIM WITH YOUR *POWERS* SPREAD SO THIN.
YOU'VE SUM-MONED *TOO MANY.*
TOK
BIG BROTH-ER RYUJI...

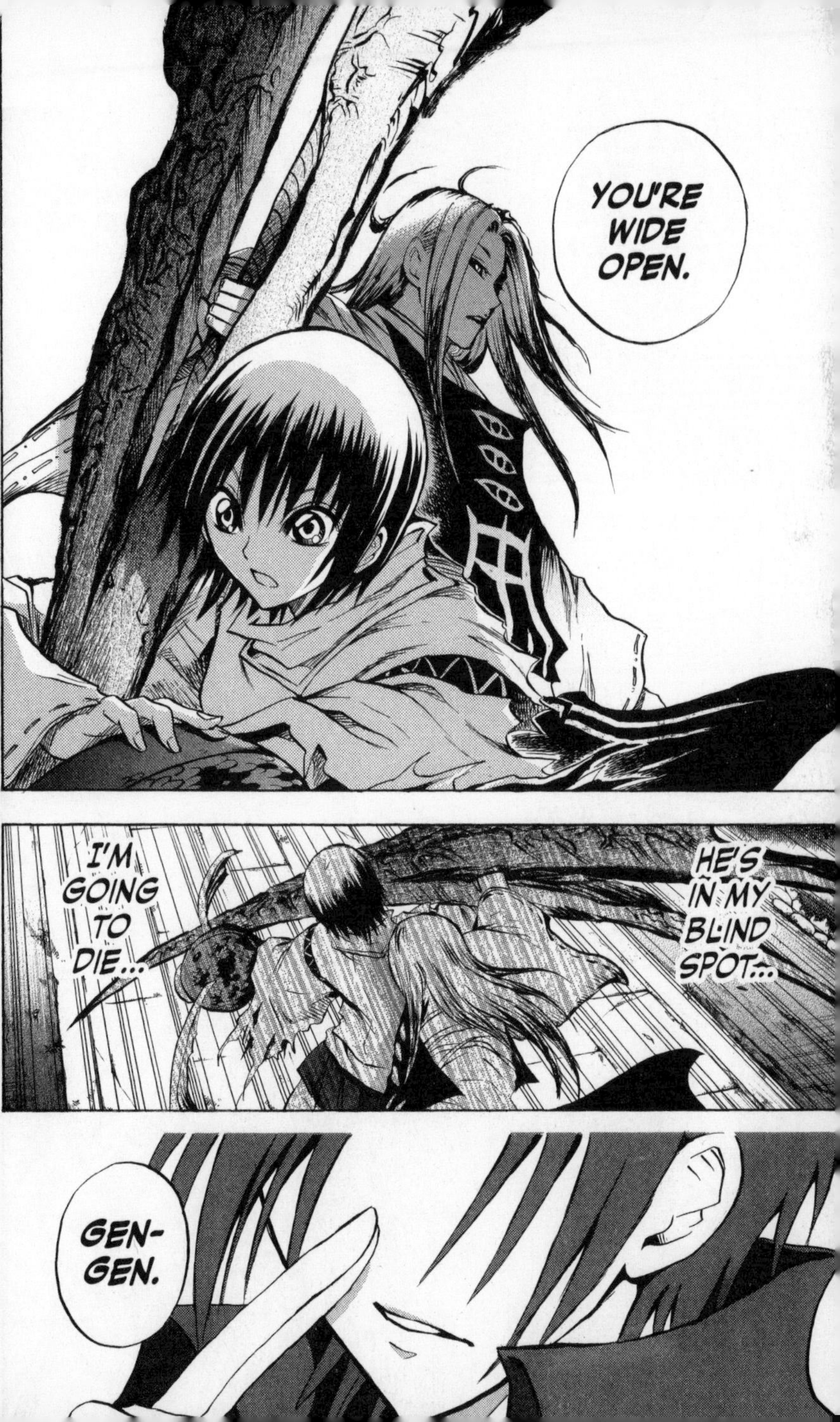
YOU'RE WIDE OPEN.
HE'S IN MY BLIND SPOT...
I'M GOING TO DIE...
GEN-GEN.

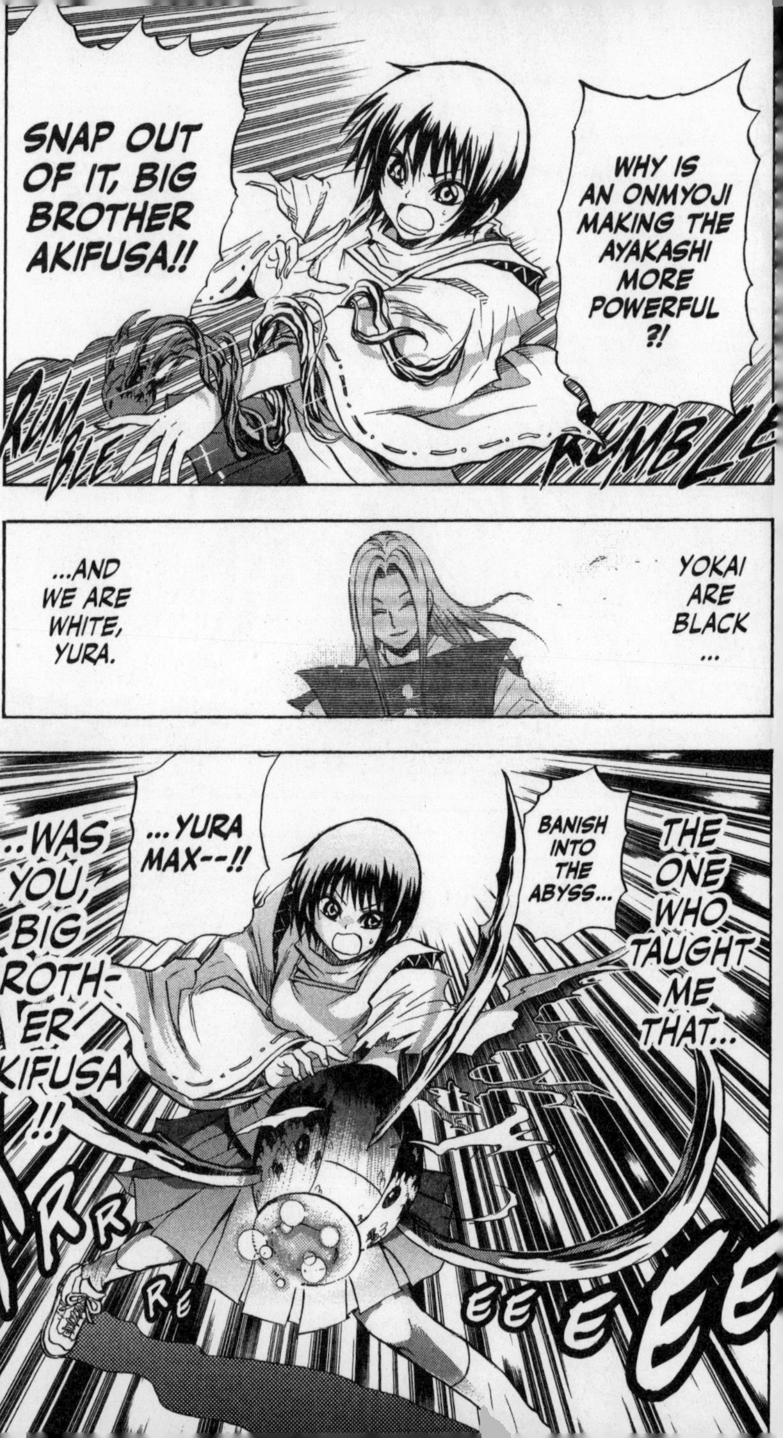
WHY IS AN ONMYOJI MAKING THE AYAKASHI MORE POWERFUL ?!
SNAP OUT OF IT, BIG BROTHER AKIFUSA!!
RUMBLE
RUMBLE
YOKAI ARE BLACK ...
...AND WE ARE WHITE, YURA.
THE ONE WHO TAUGHT ME THAT...
BANISH INTO THE ABYSS...
...YURA MAX--!!
...WAS YOU, BIG BROTH-ER AKIFUSA !!
EE E EE
ARR RE

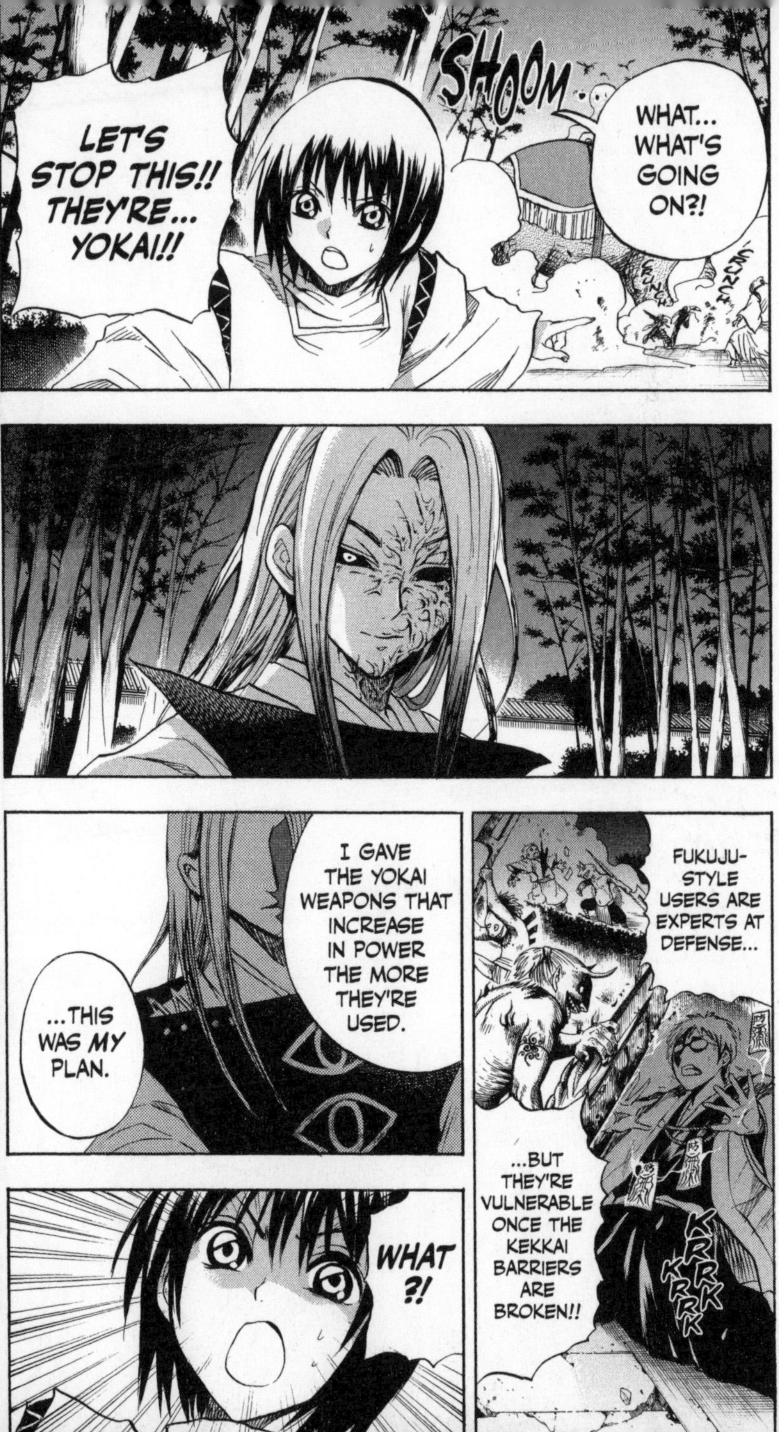
SHOOM
WHAT... WHAT'S GOING ON?!
LET'S STOP THIS!! THEY'RE... YOKAI!!
CRUNCH
CRUNCH
FUKUJU-STYLE USERS ARE EXPERTS AT DEFENSE...
...BUT THEY'RE VULNERABLE ONCE THE KEKKAI BARRIERS ARE BROKEN!!
KRRK KRRK
I GAVE THE YOKAI WEAPONS THAT INCREASE IN POWER THE MORE THEY'RE USED.
...THIS WAS MY PLAN.
WHAT?!

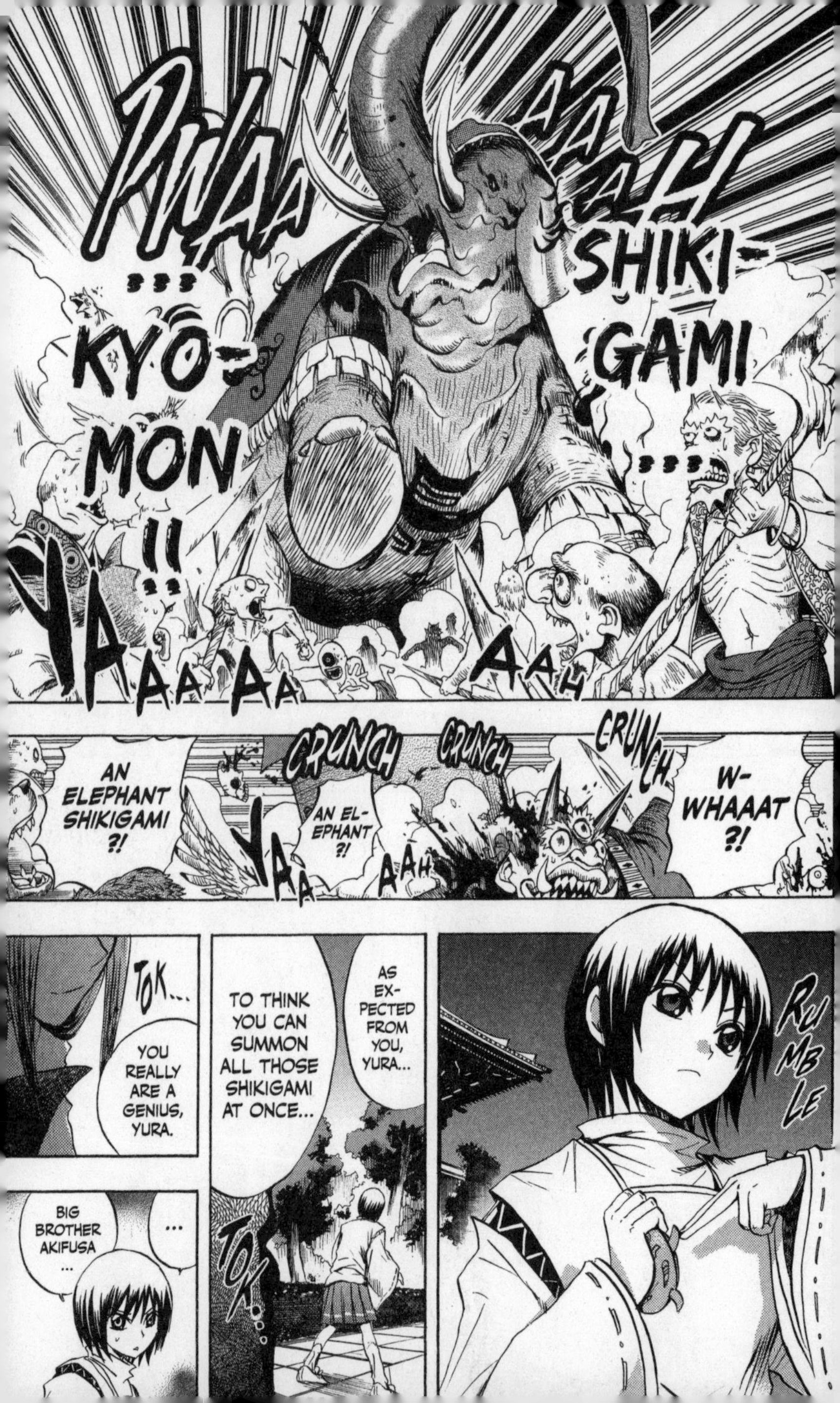
SHIKI-GAMI...
KYŌ-MON!!
YAAAAAAH
AAH
W-WHAAAT?!
CRUNCH
CRUNCH
CRUNCH
AN EL-EPHANT?!
AAH
YAAA
AN ELEPHANT SHIKIGAMI?!
RUMBLE
AS EX-PECTED FROM YOU, YURA...
TO THINK YOU CAN SUMMON ALL THOSE SHIKIGAMI AT ONCE...
TOK...
TOK...
YOU REALLY ARE A GENIUS, YURA.
...
BIG BROTHER AKIFUSA ...

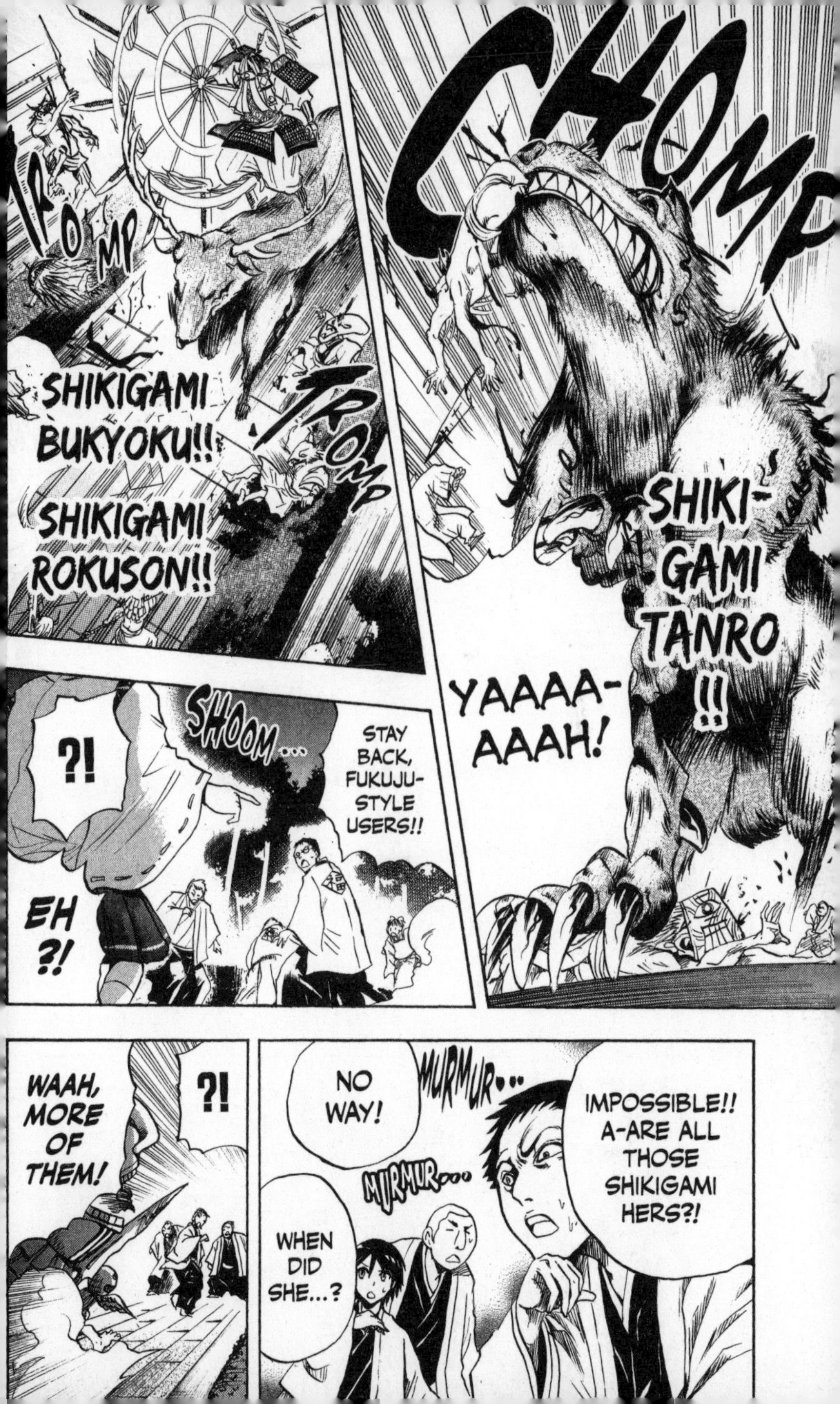
CHOMP
SHIKI-GAMI TANRO!!
YAAAA-AAAH!
TROMP
SHIKIGAMI BUKYOKU!!
SHIKIGAMI ROKUSON!!
TROMP
SHOOM...
STAY BACK, FUKUJU-STYLE USERS!!
?!
EH?!
IMPOSSIBLE!! A-ARE ALL THOSE SHIKIGAMI HERS?!
MURMUR...
NO WAY!
MURMUR...
WHEN DID SHE...?
?!
WAAH, MORE OF THEM!

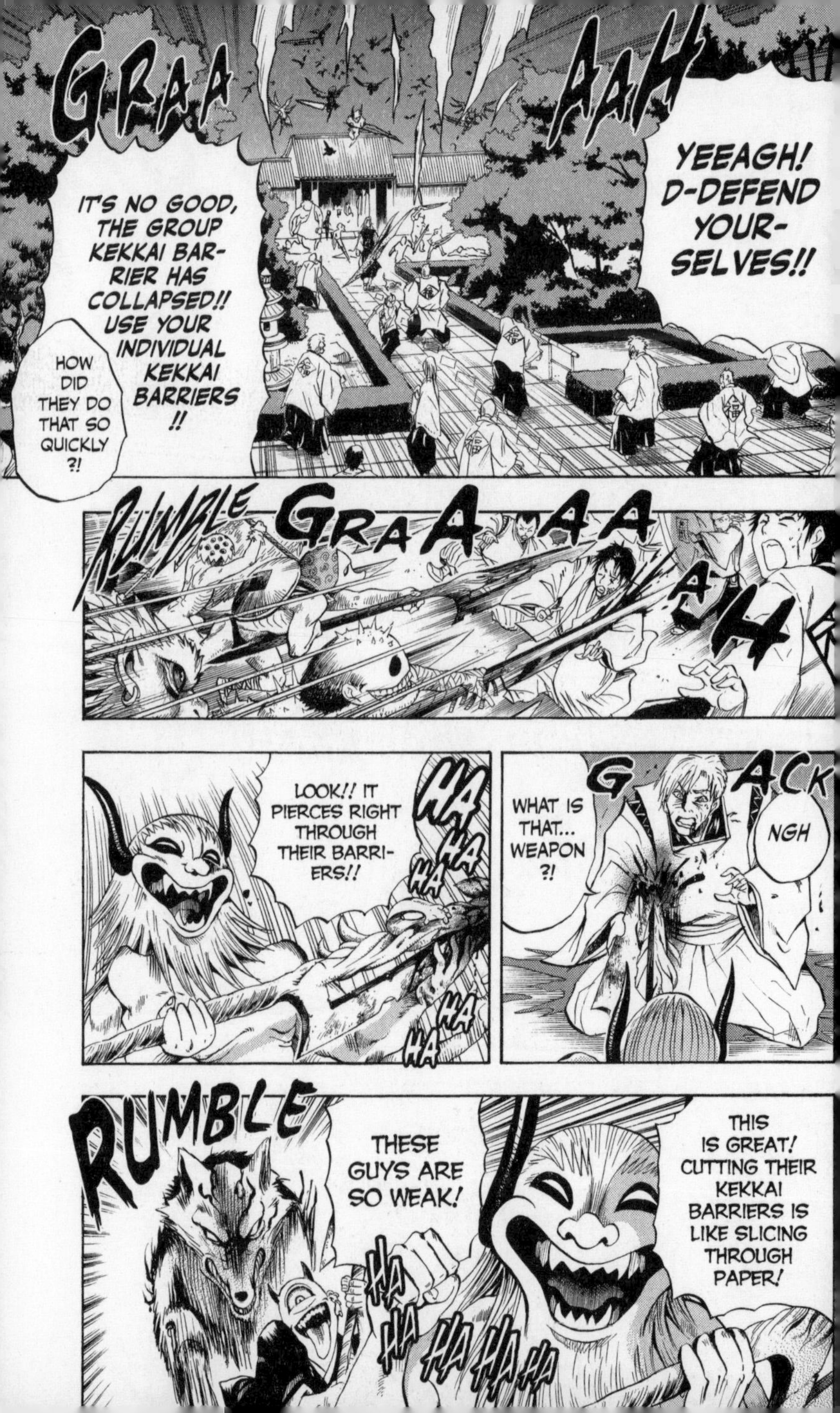
GRAAAAH
YEEAGH! D-DEFEND YOUR-SELVES!!
IT'S NO GOOD, THE GROUP KEKKAI BAR-RIER HAS COLLAPSED!! USE YOUR INDIVIDUAL KEKKAI BARRIERS!!
HOW DID THEY DO THAT SO QUICKLY?!
RUMBLE
GRAAAAAH
GACK
NGH
WHAT IS THAT... WEAPON?!
LOOK!! IT PIERCES RIGHT THROUGH THEIR BARRI-ERS!!
HA HA HA
HA HA
THIS IS GREAT! CUTTING THEIR KEKKAI BARRIERS IS LIKE SLICING THROUGH PAPER!
THESE GUYS ARE SO WEAK!
RUMBLE
HA HA HA HA HA HA

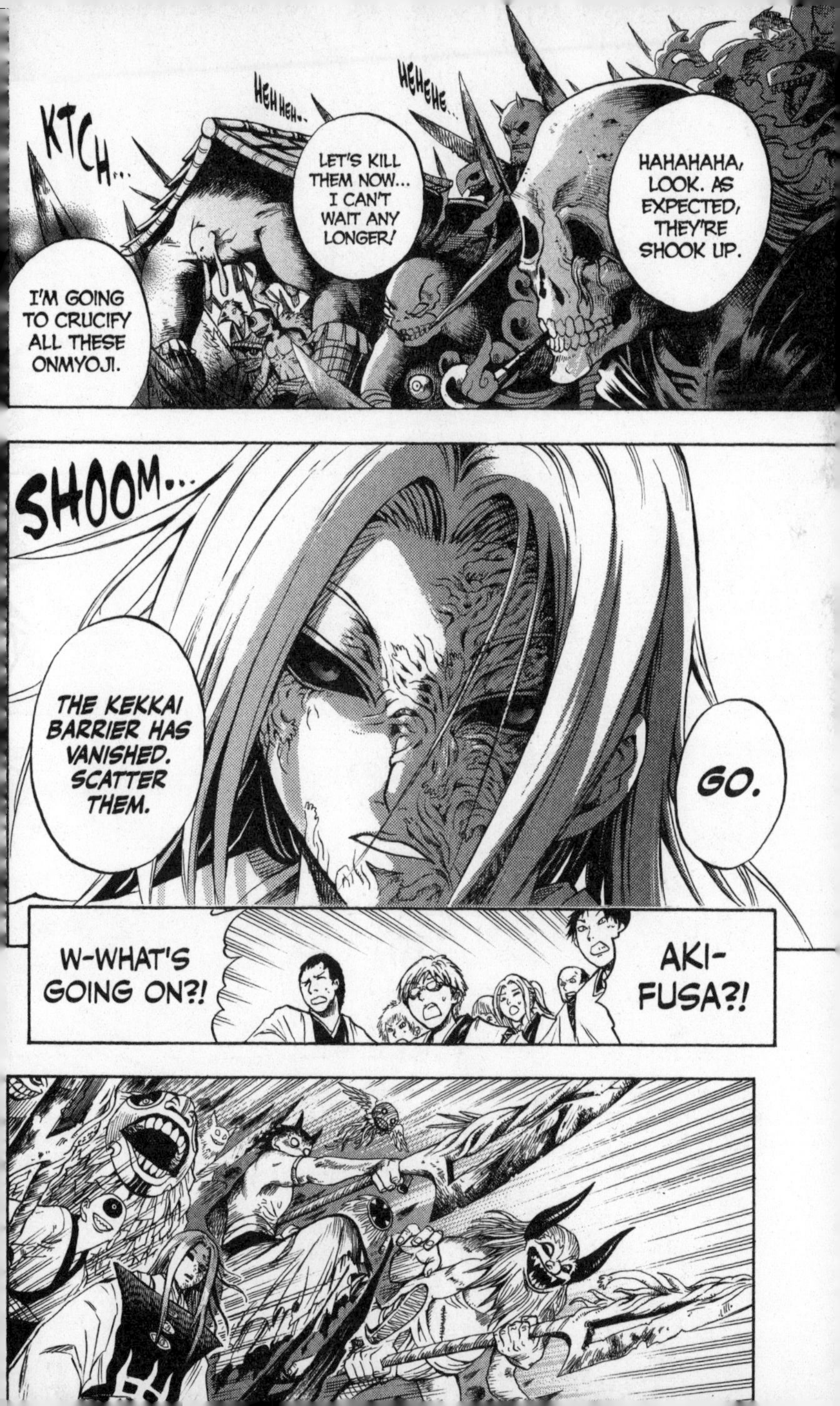
HAHAHAHA, LOOK. AS EXPECTED, THEY'RE SHOOK UP.
HEHEHE...
LET'S KILL THEM NOW... I CAN'T WAIT ANY LONGER!
HEH HEH...
KTCH...
I'M GOING TO CRUCIFY ALL THESE ONMYOJI.
GO.
THE KEKKAI BARRIER HAS VANISHED. SCATTER THEM.
SHOOM...
AKI-FUSA?!
W-WHAT'S GOING ON?!

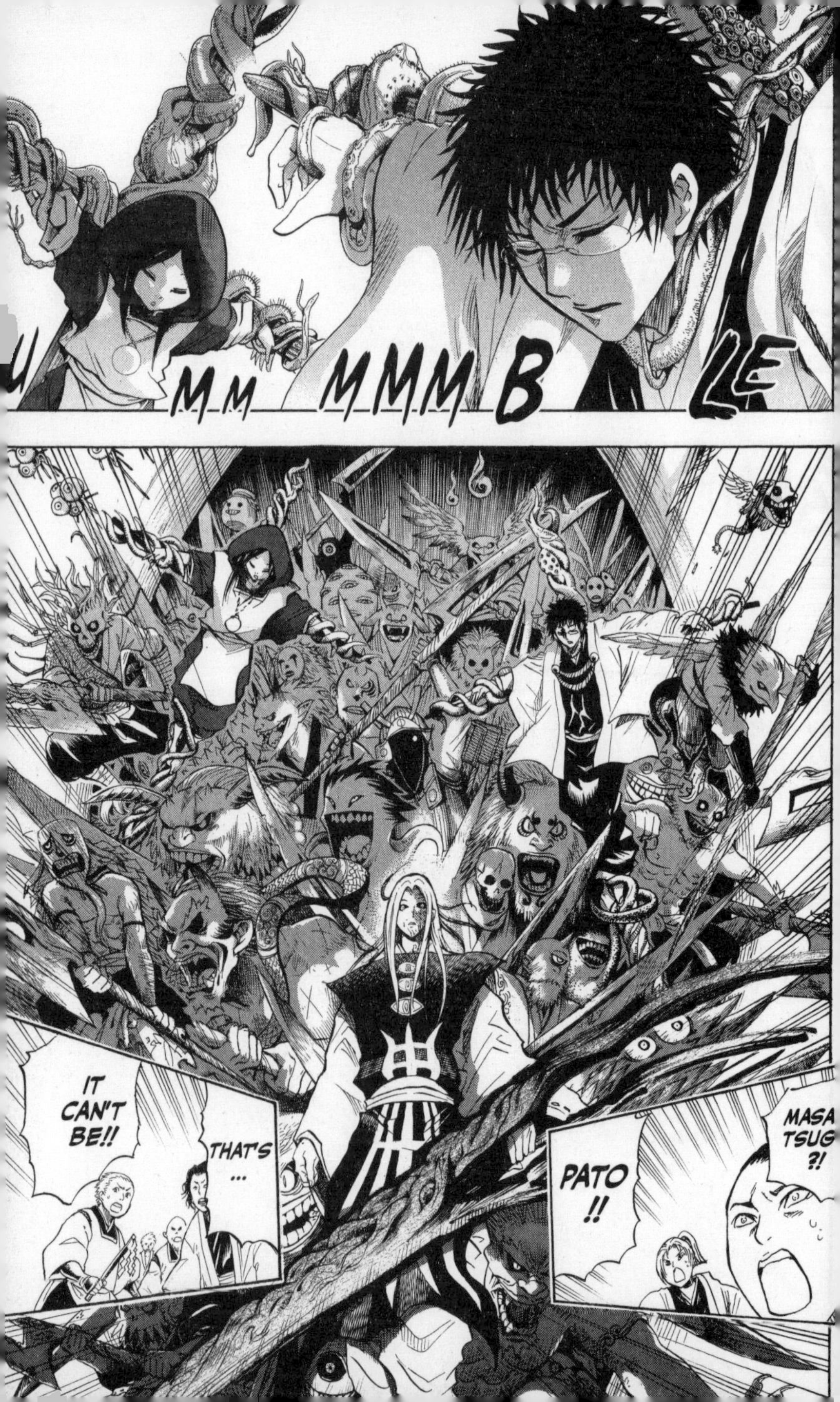
UMMMMMBLE
MASA TSUG ?!
PATO !!
THAT'S ...
IT CAN'T BE!!

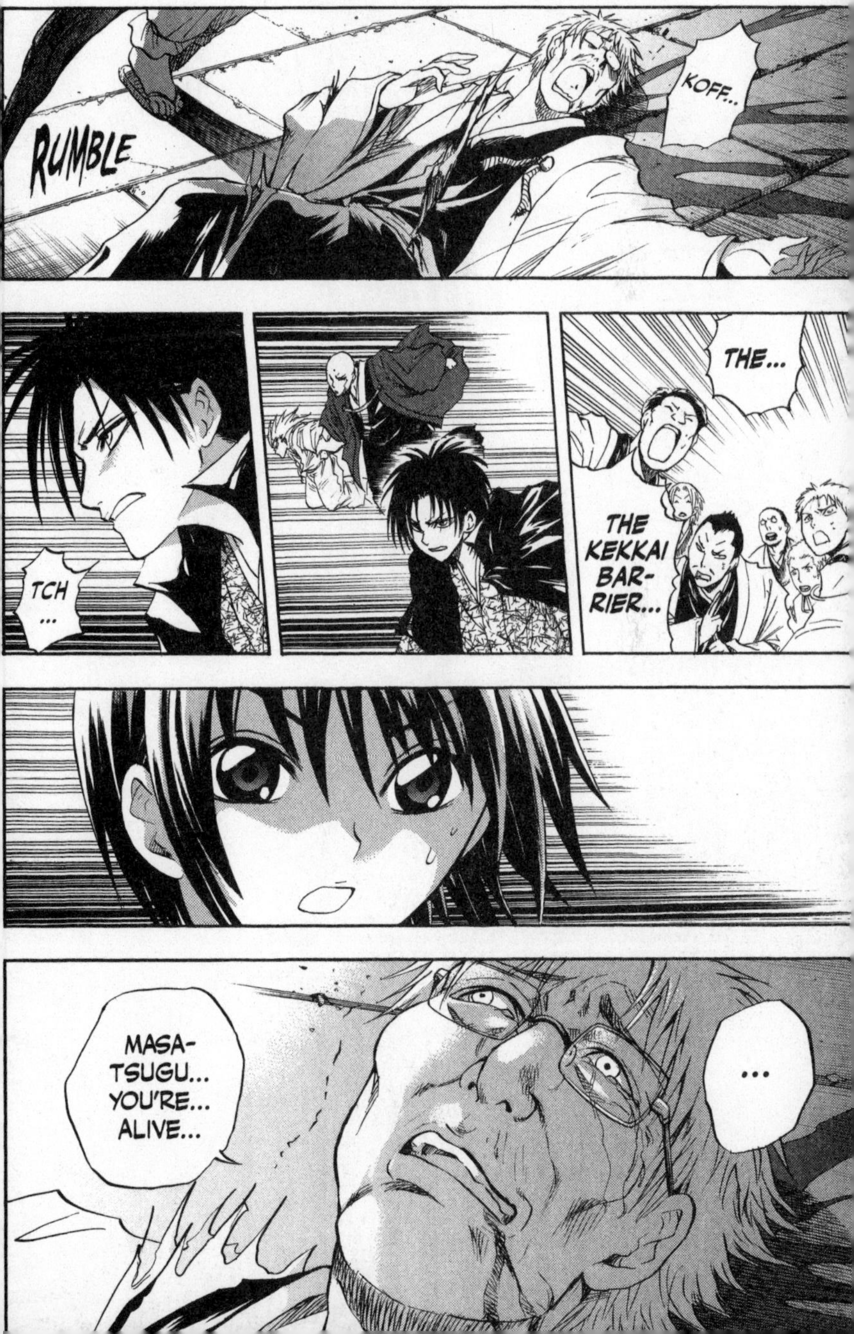
KOFF...
RUMBLE
THE...
THE KEKKAI BAR-RIER...
TCH ...
...
MASA-TSUGU... YOU'RE... ALIVE...

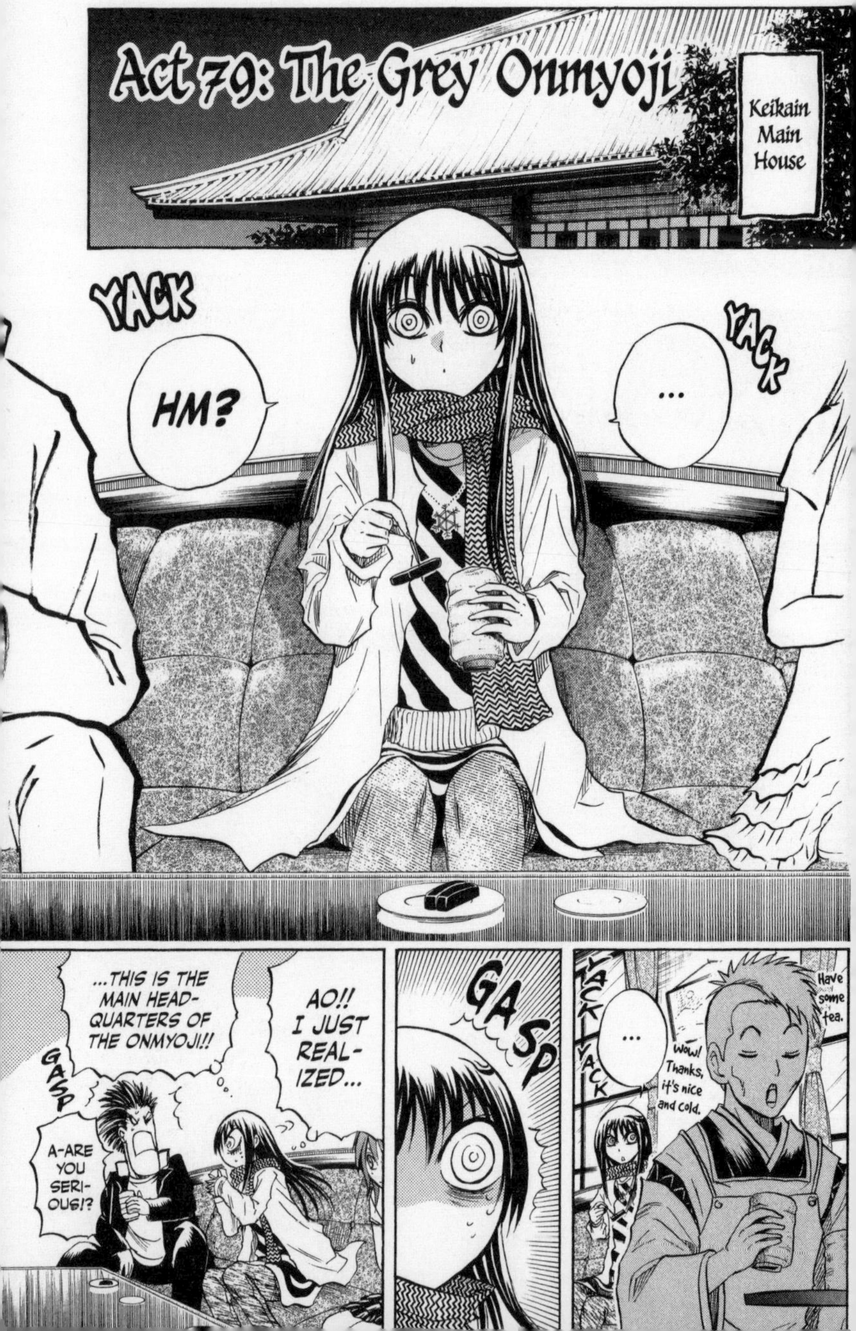
Keikain Main House
Act 79: The Grey Onmyoji
YACK
...
YACK
HM?
Have some tea.
YACK YACK
...
Wow! Thanks, it's nice and cold.
GASP
AO!! I JUST REAL-IZED...
...THIS IS THE MAIN HEAD-QUARTERS OF THE ONMYOJI!!
GASP
A-ARE YOU SERI-OUS!?

NURA: RISE OF THE YOKAI CLAN

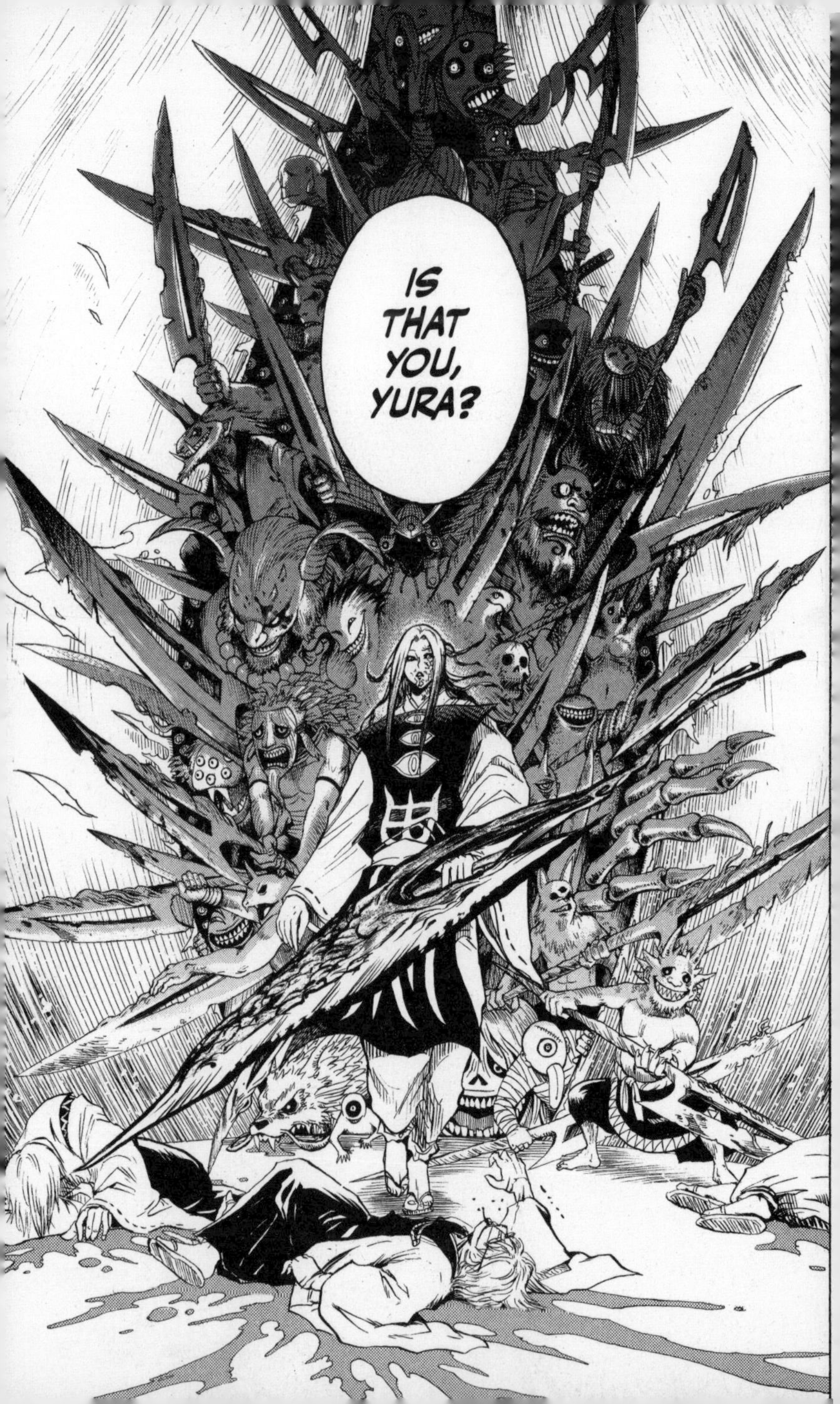
IS THAT YOU, YURA?

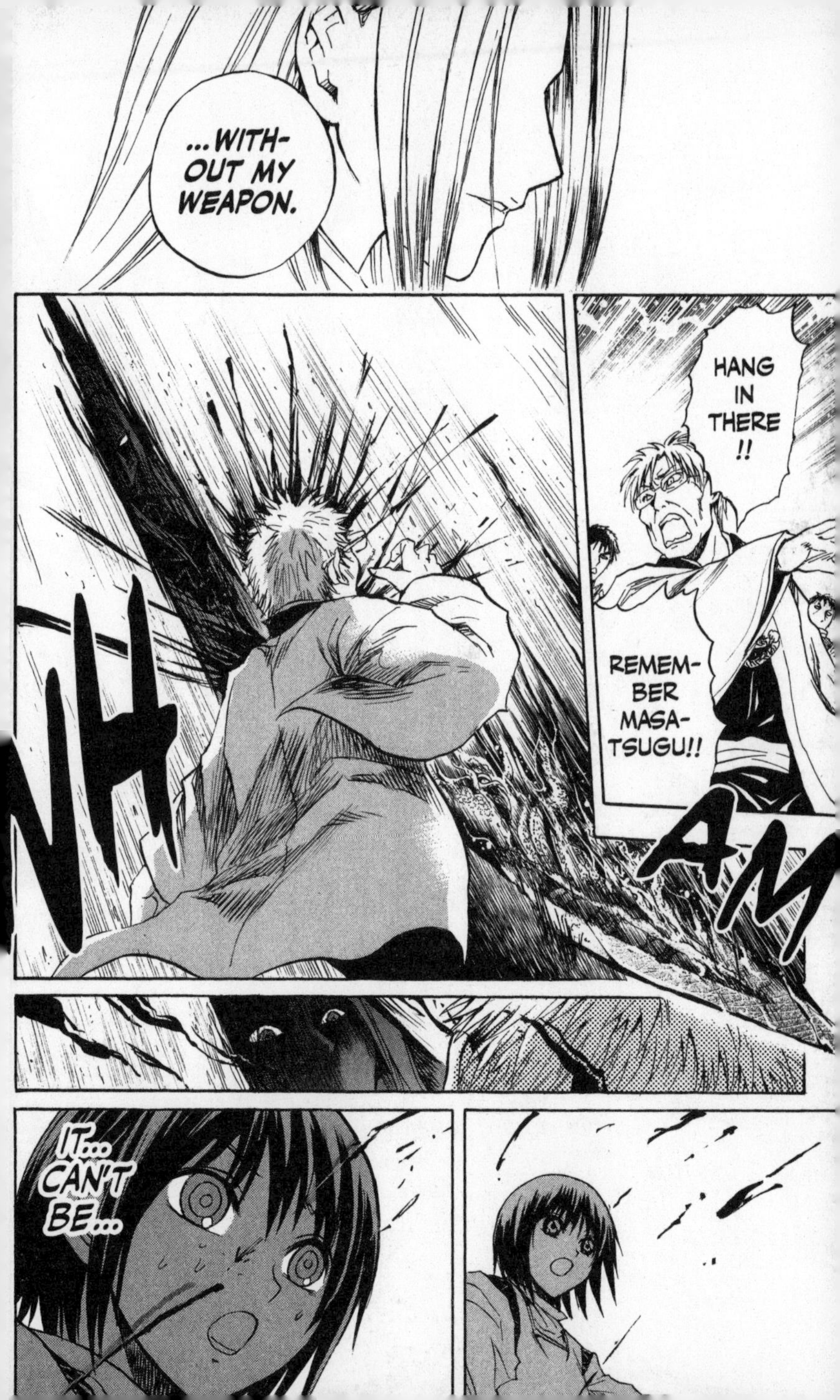
...WITH-OUT MY WEAPON.
HANG IN THERE!!
REMEM-BER MASA-TSUGU!!
IT... CAN'T BE...

BIG BROTHER AKIFUSA...
HE TAUGHT ME WHAT IT MEANS TO BE AN ONMYOJI, AND WAS THE MOST TALENTED OF US ALL.
TO THINK HE WAS DE-FEATED!
I STILL CAN'T BELIEVE IT.
ISN'T IT POSSIBLE HE'S STILL ALIVE?
HERE!!
THEY'RE HERE!!
IT'S THEM!
GAH!
?!
THE BARRIER HAS TRAPPED THEM!!
ZZZT
CRACKLE
ZZZT
GOOD! DON'T LET YOUR GUARD DOWN!!
ZZZT
ZZZT
ARGH... WE CAN'T GET IN?!
WHAT'S GOING ON!?
THIS IS...
...FUKUJU STYLE. IT'S A BARRIER CREATED BY AT LEAST THIRTY, AND IT WON'T BREAK THAT EASILY...
ZZZT

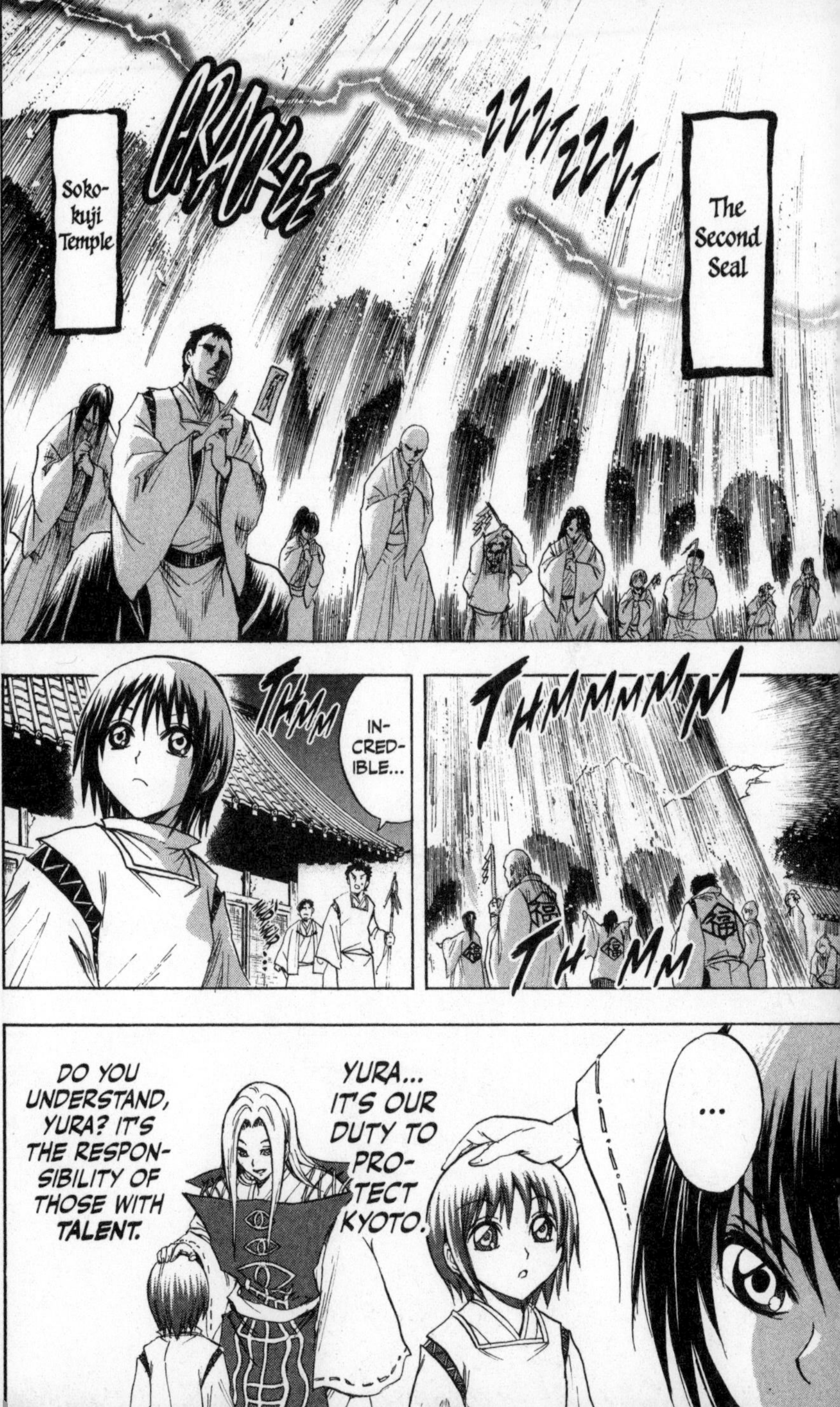
The Second Seal
ZZZT ZZZT
CRACKLE
Soko-kuji Temple
THMMMMM
THMM
THMM
IN-CRED-IBLE...
...
YURA... IT'S OUR DUTY TO PRO-TECT KYOTO.
DO YOU UNDERSTAND, YURA? IT'S THE RESPON-SIBILITY OF THOSE WITH TALENT.

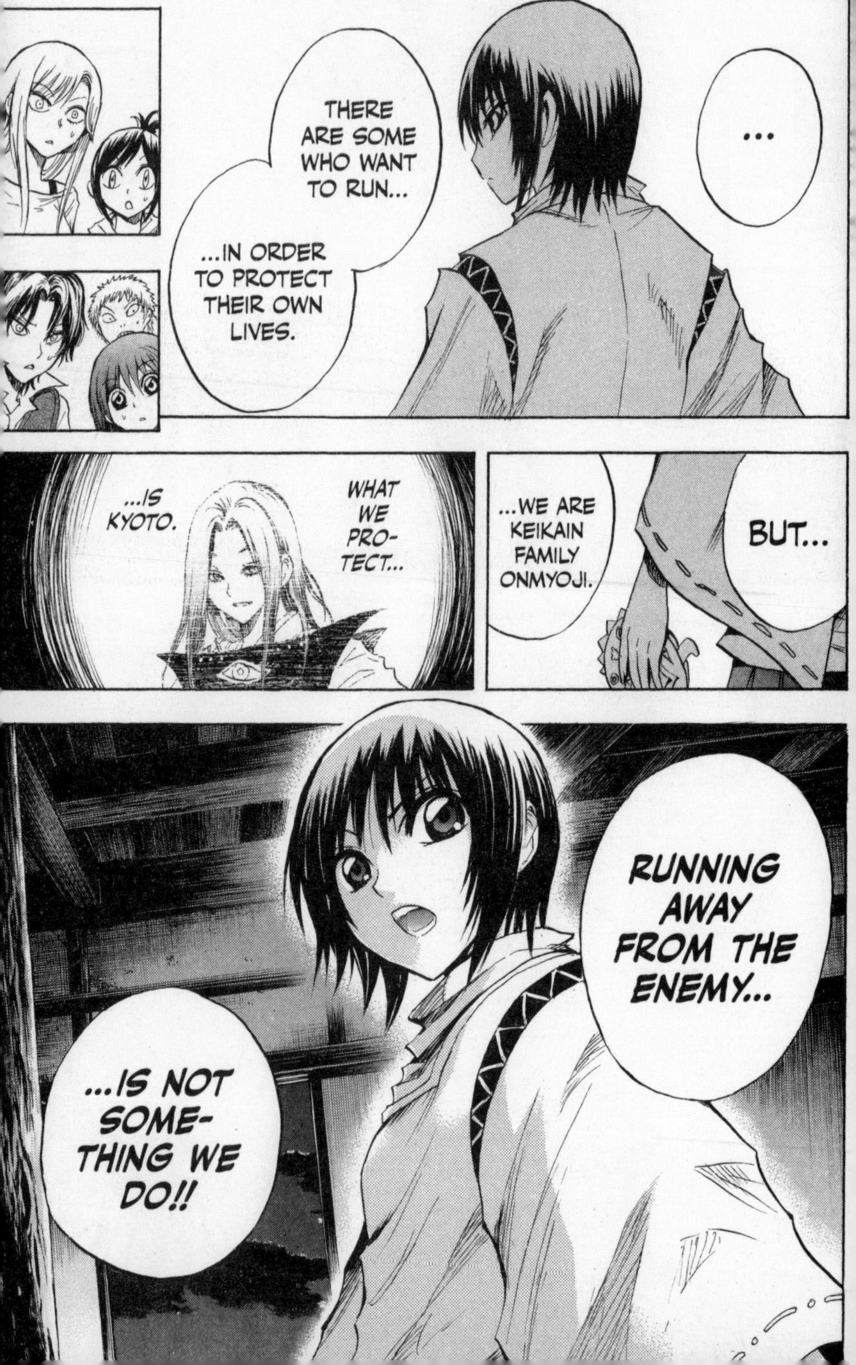
...
THERE ARE SOME WHO WANT TO RUN...
...IN ORDER TO PROTECT THEIR OWN LIVES.
BUT...
...WE ARE KEIKAIN FAMILY ONMYOJI.
WHAT WE PRO-TECT...
...IS KYOTO.
RUNNING AWAY FROM THE ENEMY...
...IS NOT SOME-THING WE DO!!

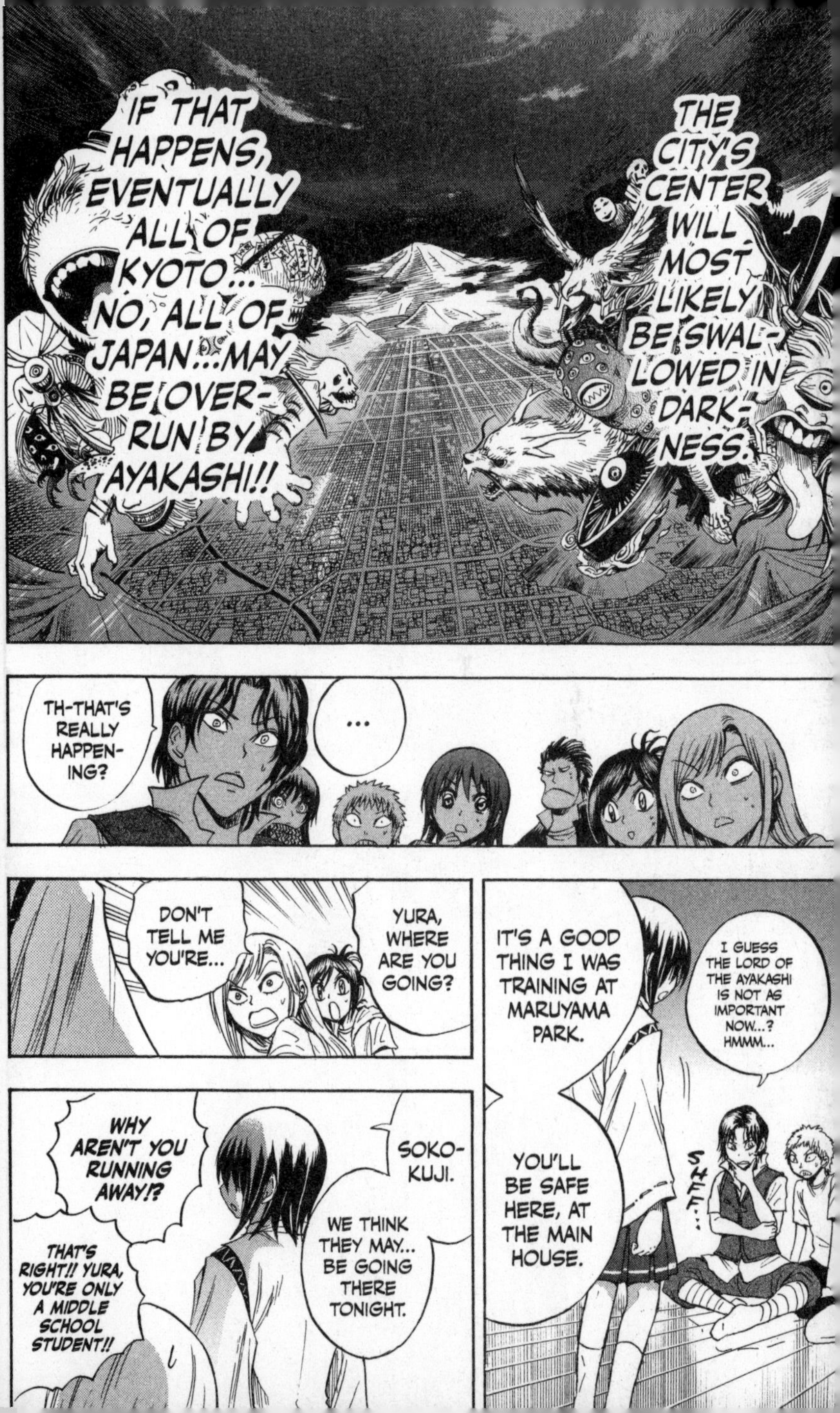
THE CITY'S CENTER WILL MOST LIKELY BE SWAL-LOWED IN DARK-NESS.
IF THAT HAPPENS, EVENTUALLY ALL OF KYOTO... NO, ALL OF JAPAN...MAY BE OVER-RUN BY AYAKASHI!!
...
TH-THAT'S REALLY HAPPEN-ING?
IT'S A GOOD THING I WAS TRAINING AT MARUYAMA PARK.
I GUESS THE LORD OF THE AYAKASHI IS NOT AS IMPORTANT NOW...? HMMM...
YOU'LL BE SAFE HERE, AT THE MAIN HOUSE.
SHFF...
YURA, WHERE ARE YOU GOING?
DON'T TELL ME YOU'RE...
SOKO-KUJI.
WE THINK THEY MAY... BE GOING THERE TONIGHT.
WHY AREN'T YOU RUNNING AWAY!?
THAT'S RIGHT!! YURA, YOU'RE ONLY A MIDDLE SCHOOL STUDENT!!

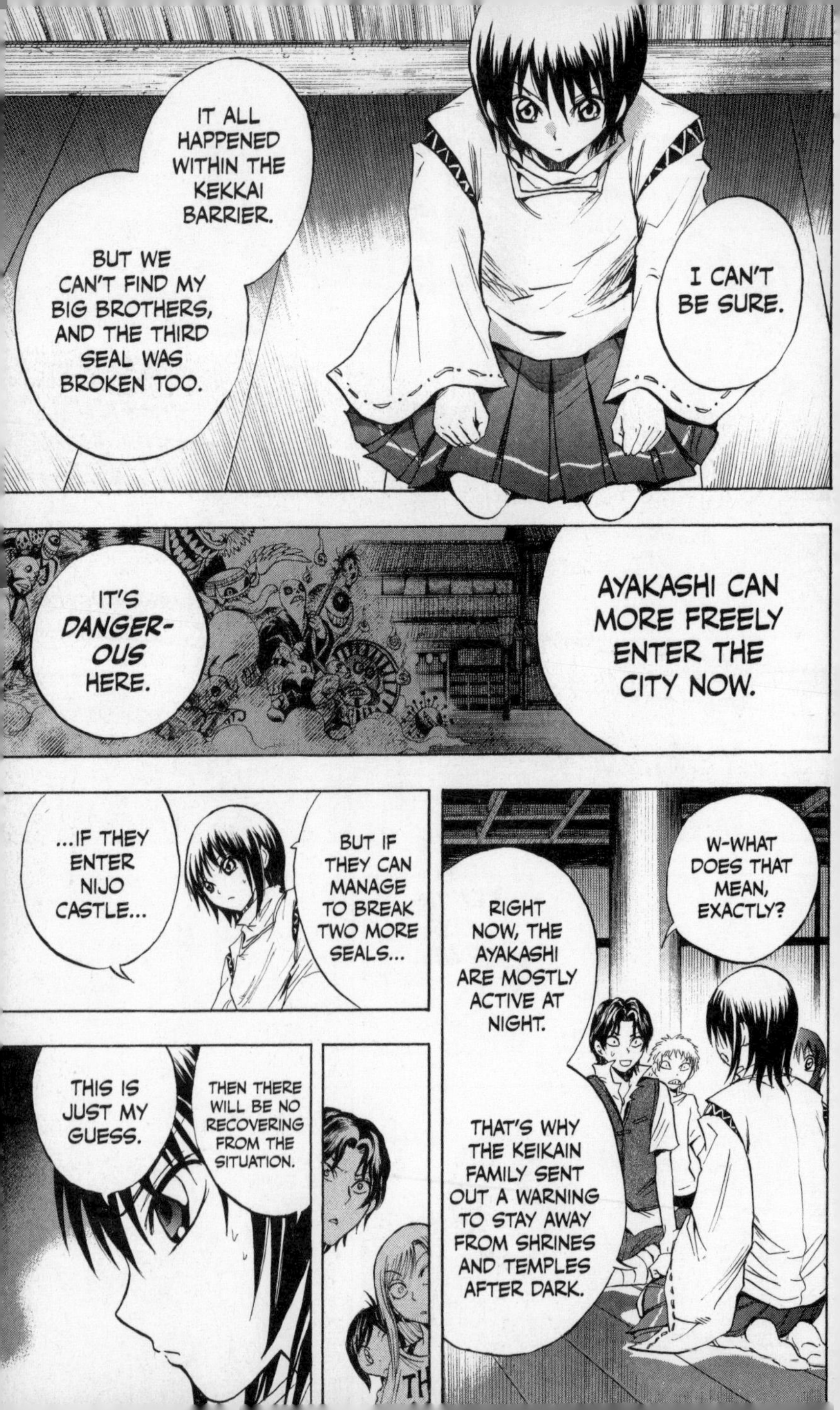
I CAN'T BE SURE.
IT ALL HAPPENED WITHIN THE KEKKAI BARRIER.
BUT WE CAN'T FIND MY BIG BROTHERS, AND THE THIRD SEAL WAS BROKEN TOO.
AYAKASHI CAN MORE FREELY ENTER THE CITY NOW.
IT'S *DANGEROUS* HERE.
W-WHAT DOES THAT MEAN, EXACTLY?
RIGHT NOW, THE AYAKASHI ARE MOSTLY ACTIVE AT NIGHT.
THAT'S WHY THE KEIKAIN FAMILY SENT OUT A WARNING TO STAY AWAY FROM SHRINES AND TEMPLES AFTER DARK.
BUT IF THEY CAN MANAGE TO BREAK TWO MORE SEALS...
...IF THEY ENTER NIJO CASTLE...
THEN THERE WILL BE NO RECOVERING FROM THE SITUATION.
THIS IS JUST MY GUESS.

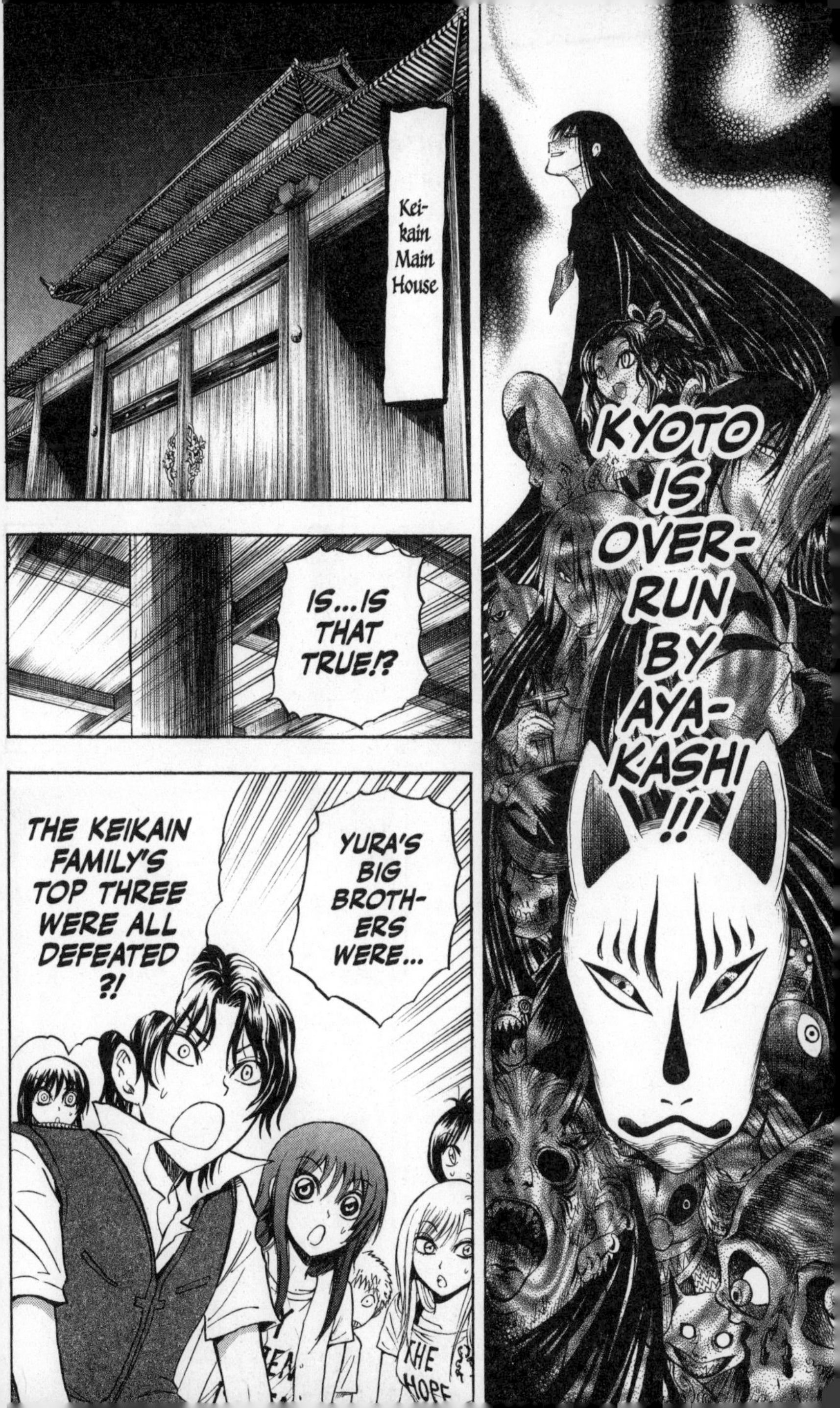

KYOTO IS OVER-RUN BY AYA-KASHI!!
Kei-kain Main House
IS...IS THAT TRUE!?
YURA'S BIG BROTH-ERS WERE...
THE KEIKAIN FAMILY'S TOP THREE WERE ALL DEFEATED?!
THE HOPE

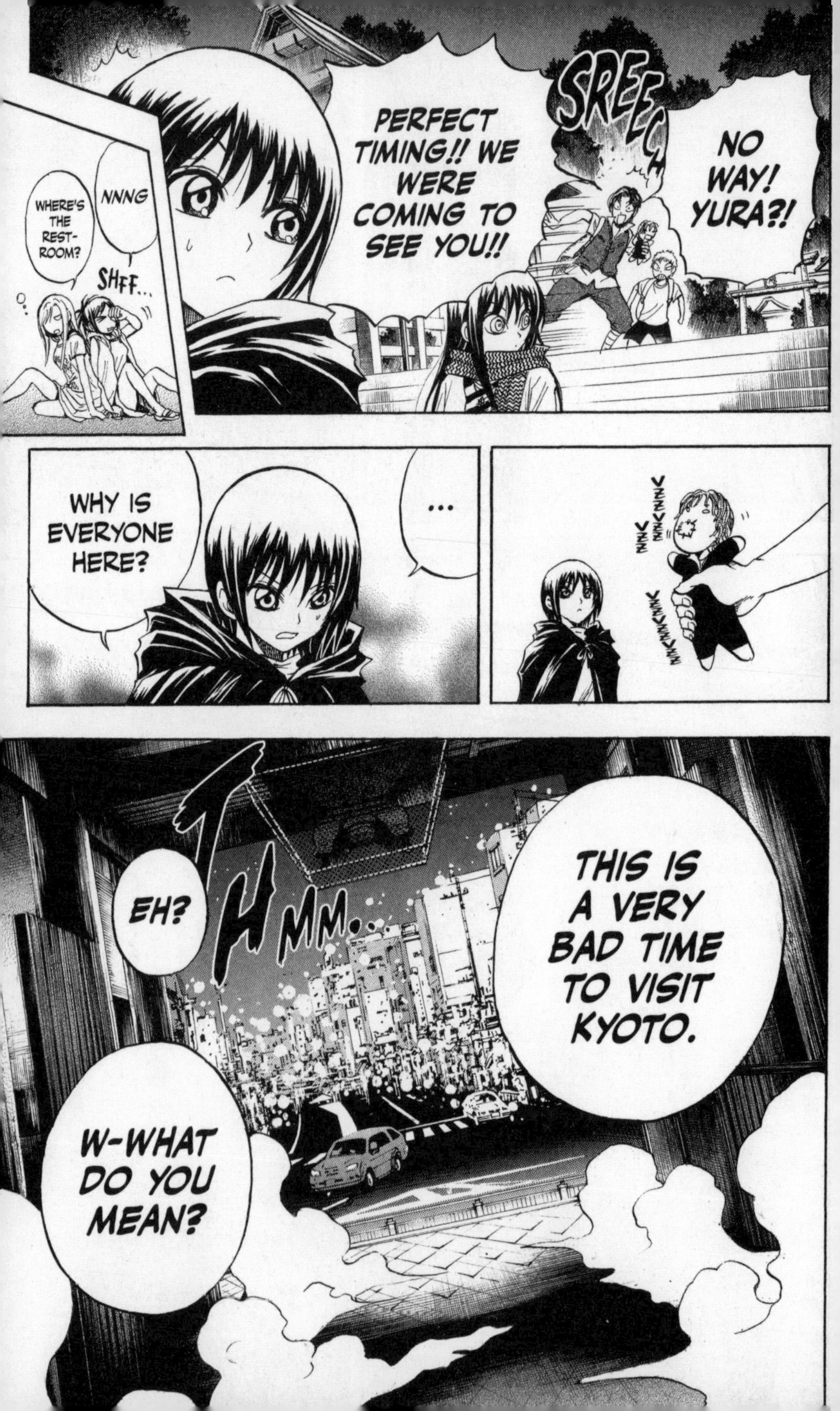

NO WAY! YURA?!
SREEECH
PERFECT TIMING!! WE WERE COMING TO SEE YOU!!
NNNG
WHERE'S THE REST-ROOM?
SHFF...
...
WHY IS EVERYONE HERE?
THIS IS A VERY BAD TIME TO VISIT KYOTO.
THMM..
EH?
W-WHAT DO YOU MEAN?

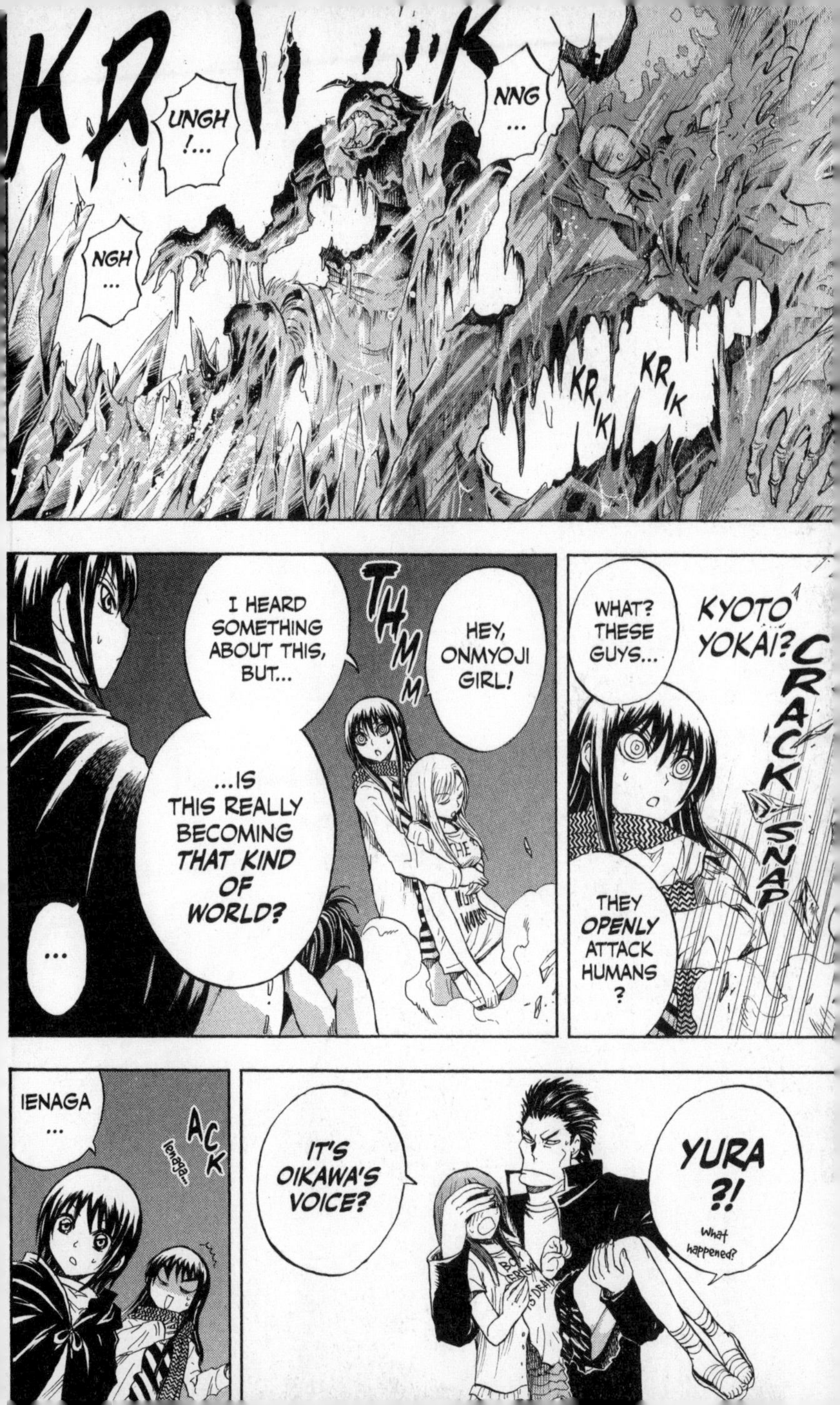
NNG ...
KRIIIK
UNGH !...
NGH ...
KRIK KRIK
KYOTO YOKAI?
WHAT? THESE GUYS...
CRACK SNAP
THEY OPENLY ATTACK HUMANS ?
HEY, ONMYOJI GIRL!
THMM
I HEARD SOMETHING ABOUT THIS, BUT...
...IS THIS REALLY BECOMING THAT KIND OF WORLD?
...
YURA ?!
What happened?
IT'S OIKAWA'S VOICE?
ACK
Ienaga...
IENAGA ...

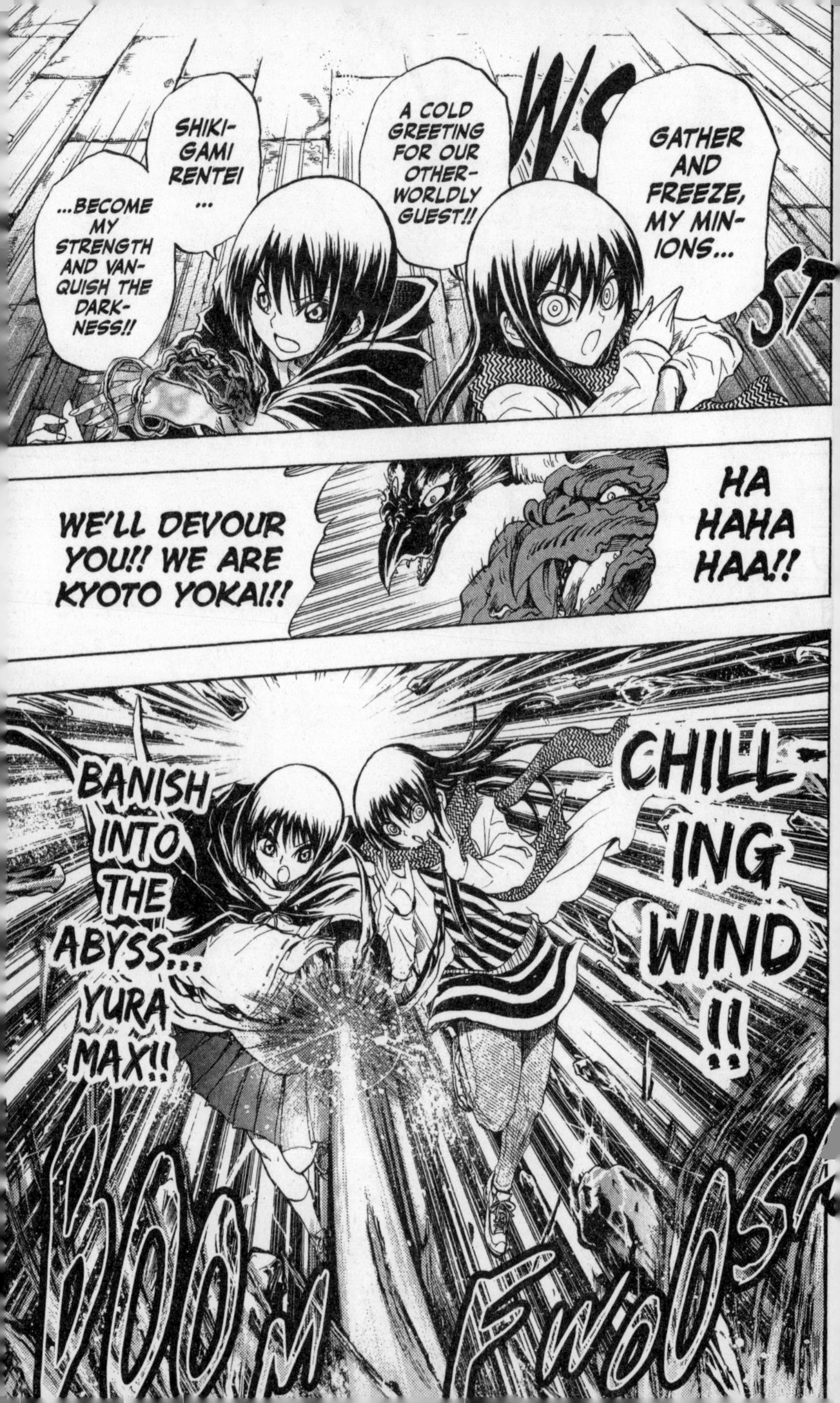
GATHER AND FREEZE, MY MINIONS...
WS
ST
A COLD GREETING FOR OUR OTHER-WORLDLY GUEST!!
SHIKI-GAMI RENTEI...
...BECOME MY STRENGTH AND VAN-QUISH THE DARK-NESS!!
HA HAHA HAA!!
WE'LL DEVOUR YOU!! WE ARE KYOTO YOKAI!!
CHILL-ING WIND!!
BANISH INTO THE ABYSS... YURA MAX!!
FWOOSH
BOOM

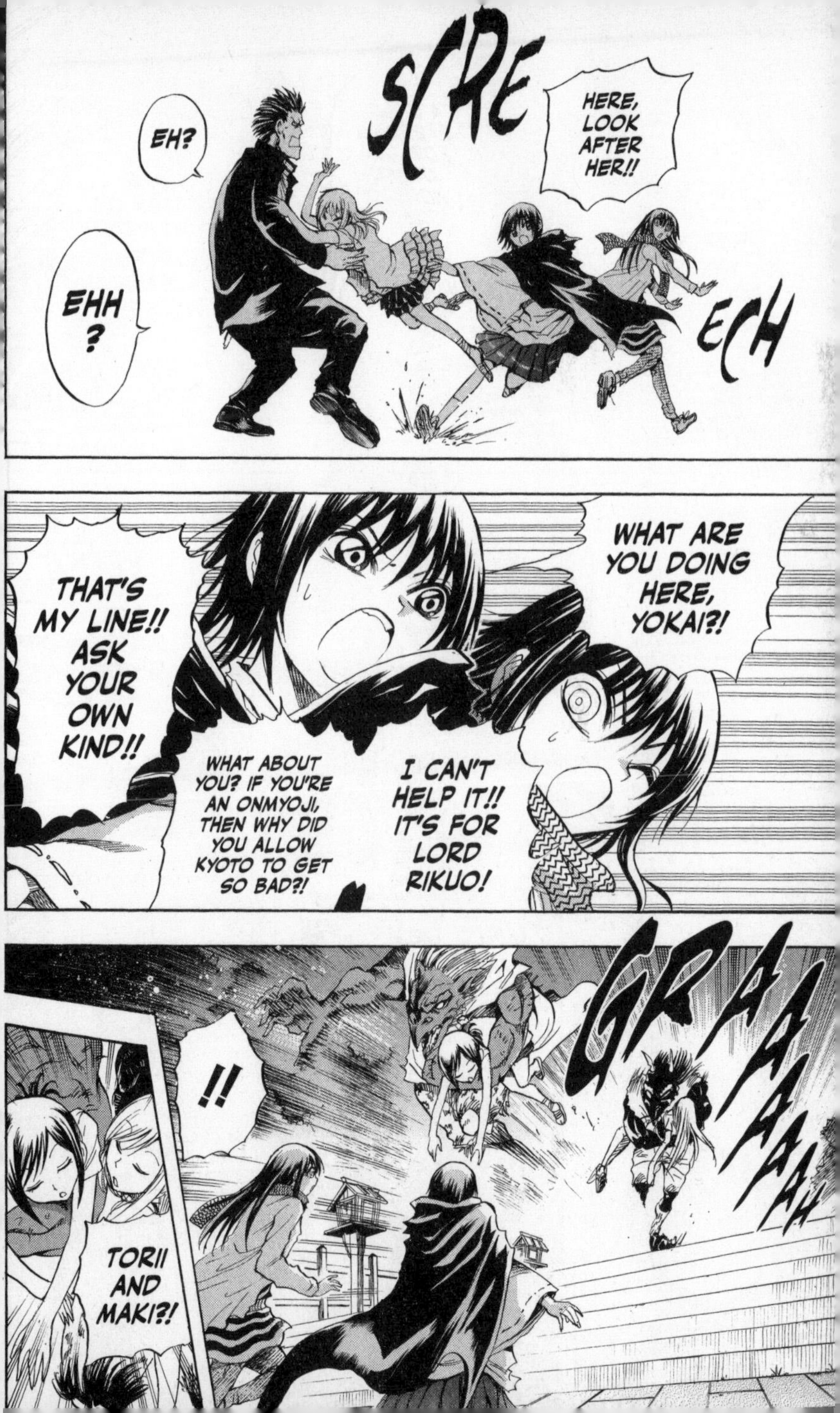
HERE, LOOK AFTER HER!!
SCRE
ECH
EH?
EHH ?
WHAT ARE YOU DOING HERE, YOKAI?!
THAT'S MY LINE!! ASK YOUR OWN KIND!!
I CAN'T HELP IT!! IT'S FOR LORD RIKUO!
WHAT ABOUT YOU? IF YOU'RE AN ONMYOJI, THEN WHY DID YOU ALLOW KYOTO TO GET SO BAD?!
GRAAAAAH
!!
TORII AND MAKI?!

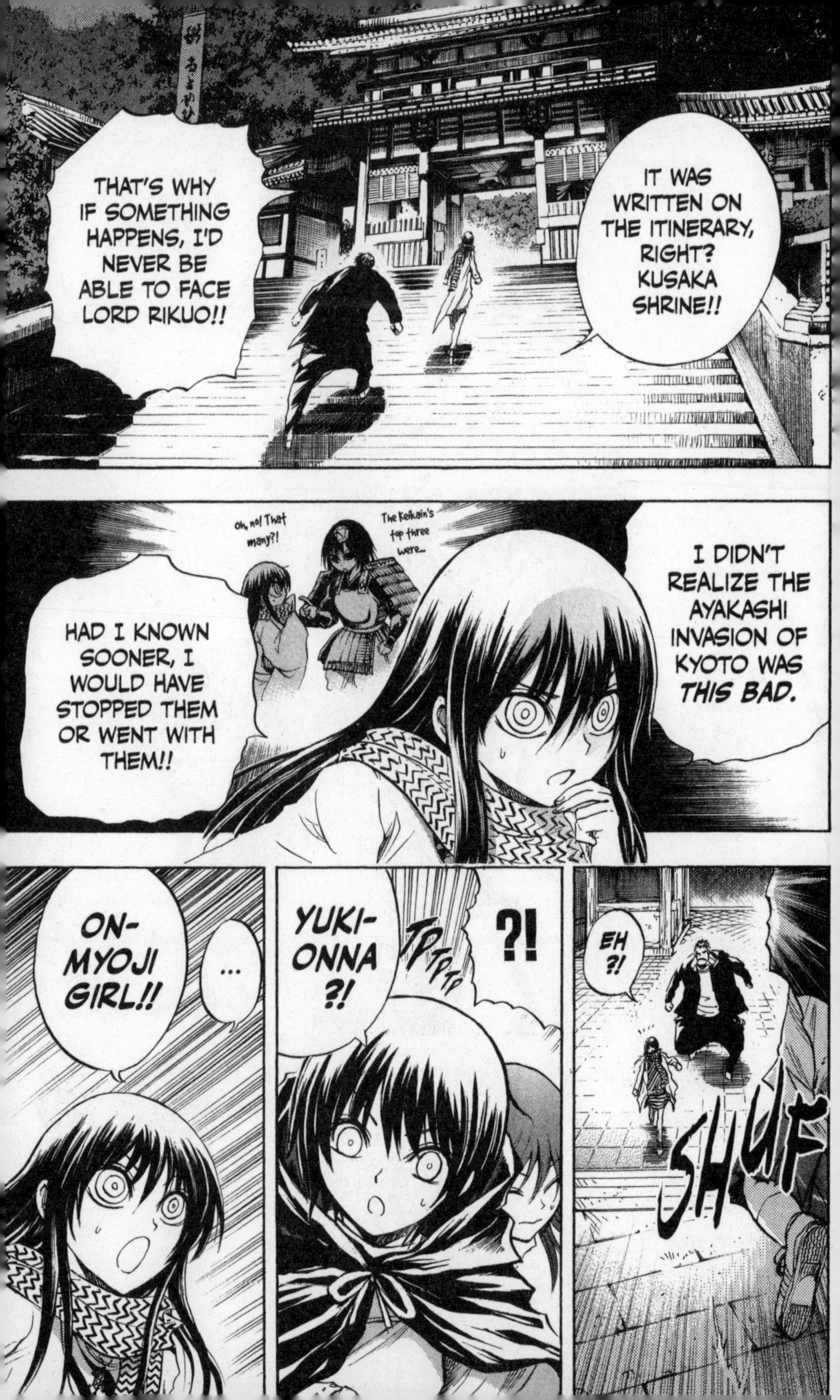
IT WAS WRITTEN ON THE ITINERARY, RIGHT? KUSAKA SHRINE!!
THAT'S WHY IF SOMETHING HAPPENS, I'D NEVER BE ABLE TO FACE LORD RIKUO!!
I DIDN'T REALIZE THE AYAKASHI INVASION OF KYOTO WAS *THIS BAD.*
The Keikain's top three were...
Oh, no! That many?!
HAD I KNOWN SOONER, I WOULD HAVE STOPPED THEM OR WENT WITH THEM!!
EH ?!
SHUF
?!
TPTPTP
YUKI-ONNA ?!
...
ON-MYOJI GIRL!!

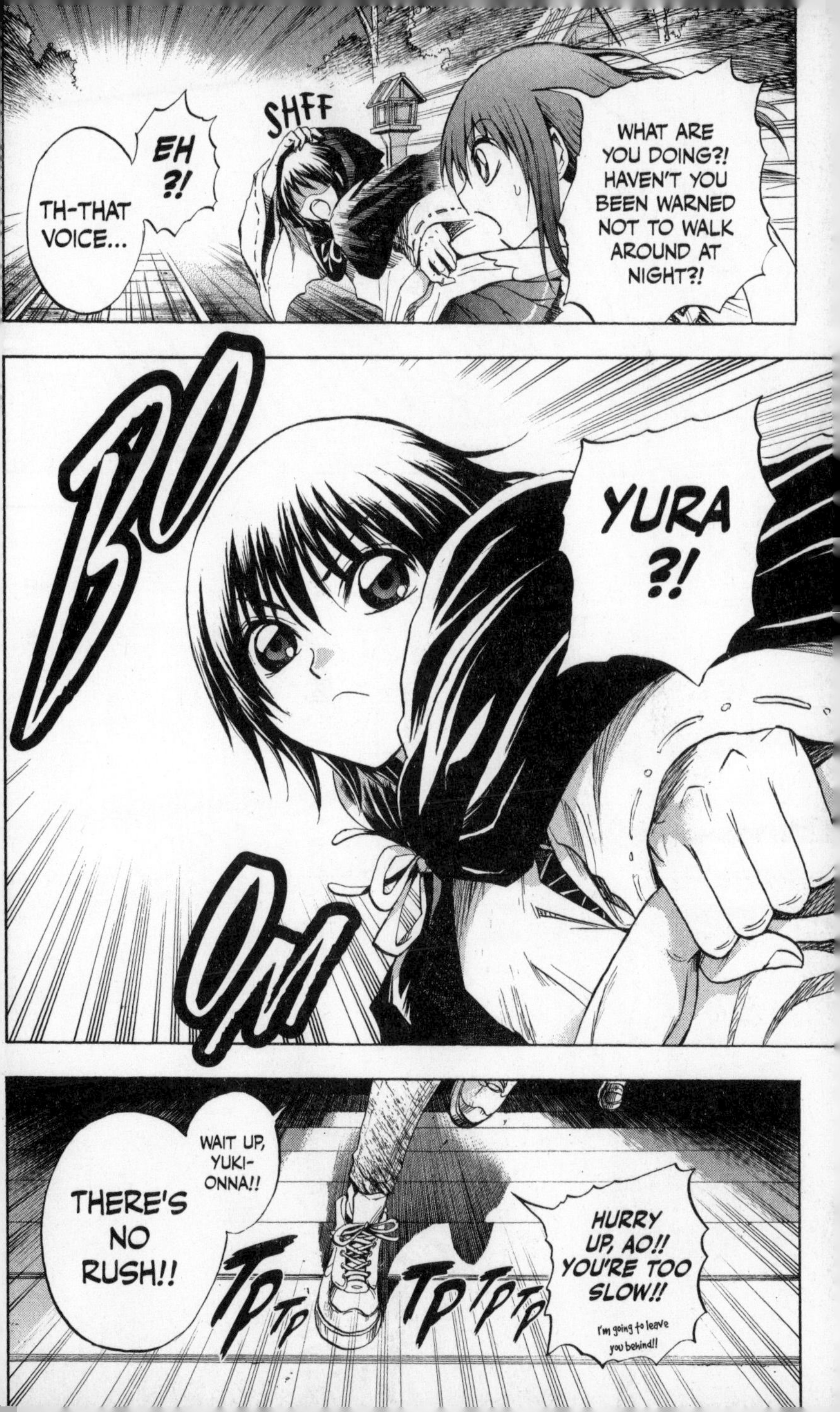
WHAT ARE YOU DOING?! HAVEN'T YOU BEEN WARNED NOT TO WALK AROUND AT NIGHT?!
SHFF
EH ?!
TH-THAT VOICE...
YURA ?!
BOOM
HURRY UP, AO!! YOU'RE TOO SLOW!!
I'm going to leave you behind!!
TP TP TP TP TP TP
WAIT UP, YUKI-ONNA!!
THERE'S NO RUSH!!

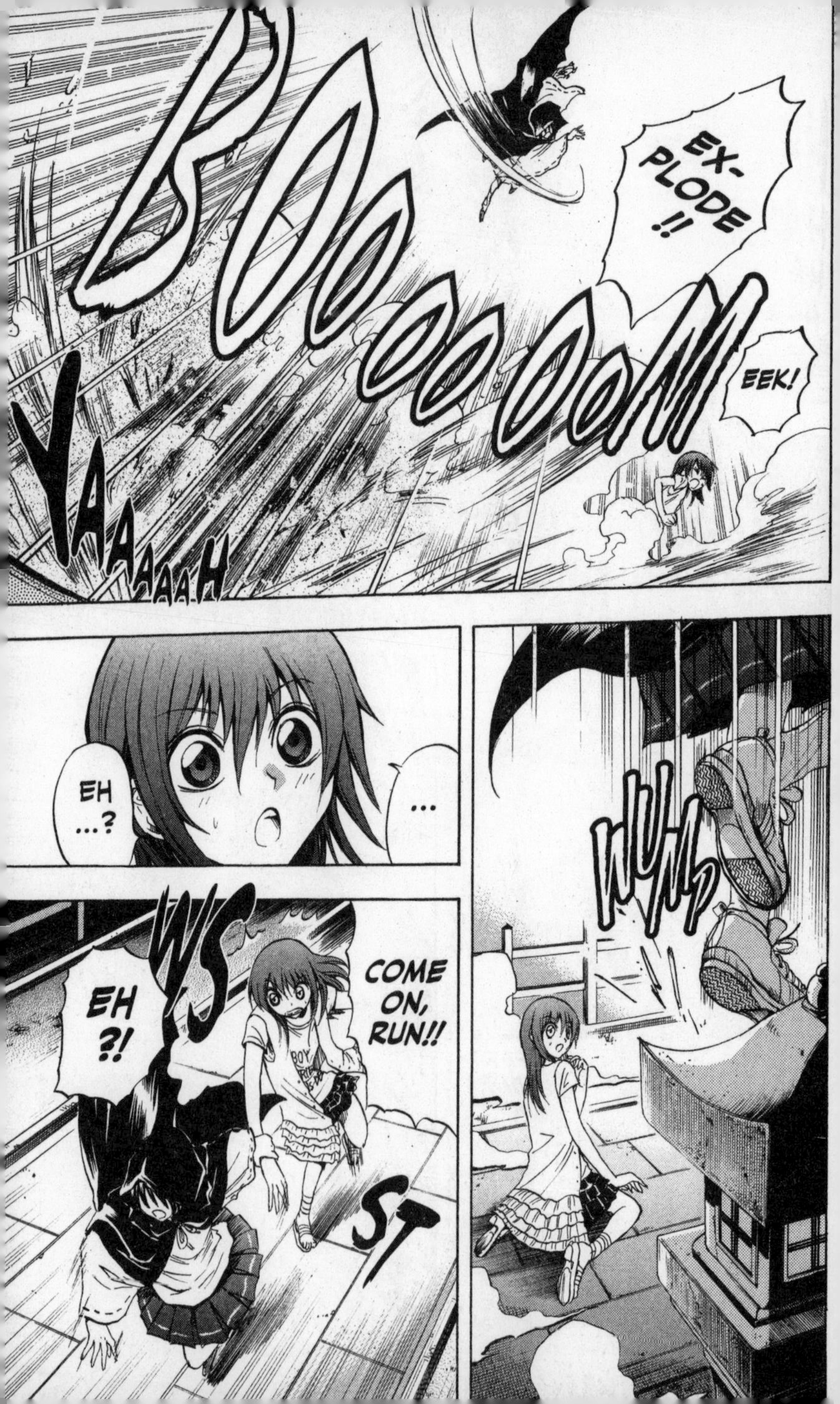
EX-PLODE !!
BOOOOOOM
EEK!
YAAAAAH
WUMP
...
EH ...?
COME ON, RUN!!
WS
EH ?!
ST

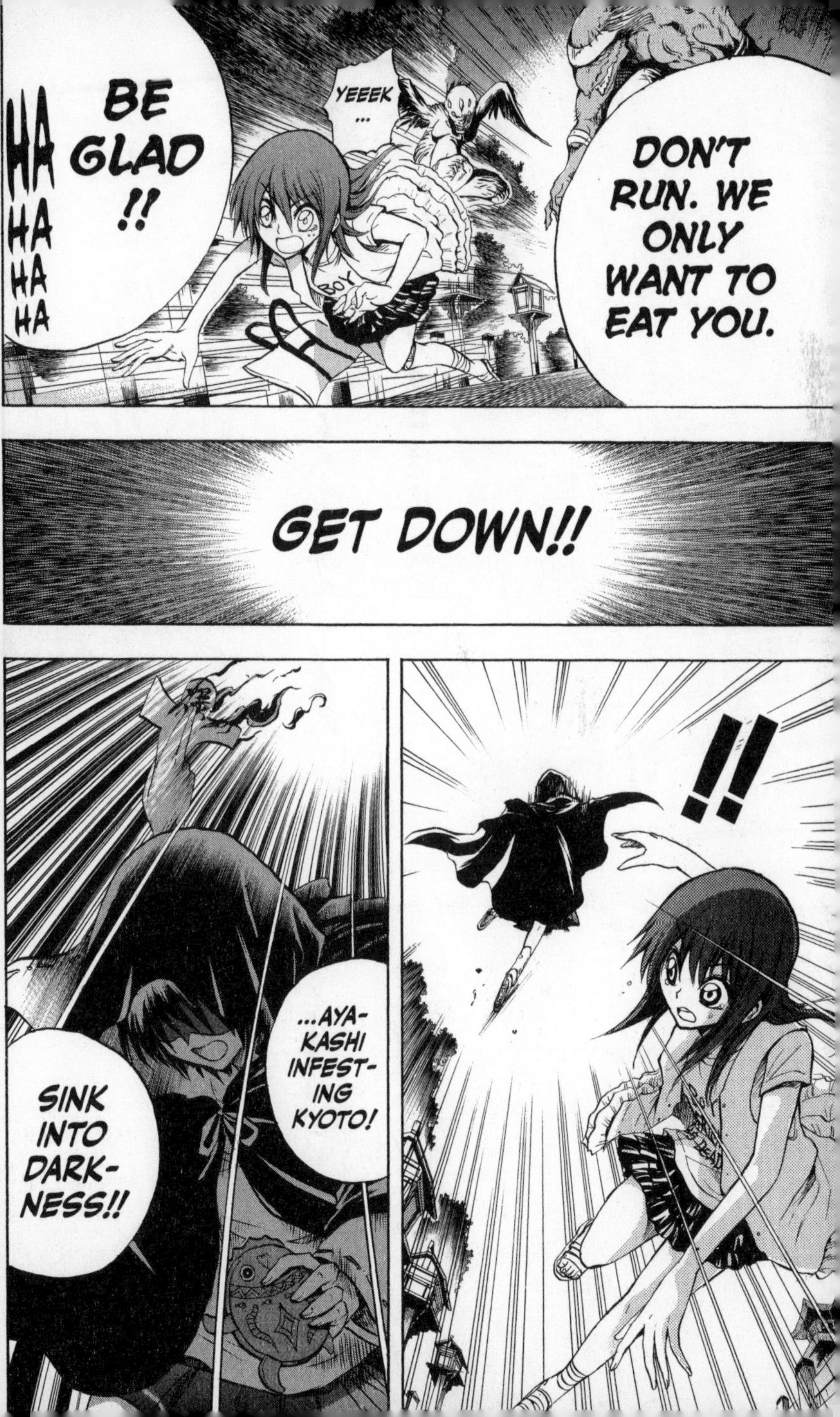
DON'T RUN. WE ONLY WANT TO EAT YOU.
YEEEK ...
BE GLAD!!
HA HA HA HA HA HA
GET DOWN!!
!!
...AYA-KASHI INFEST-ING KYOTO!
SINK INTO DARK-NESS!!

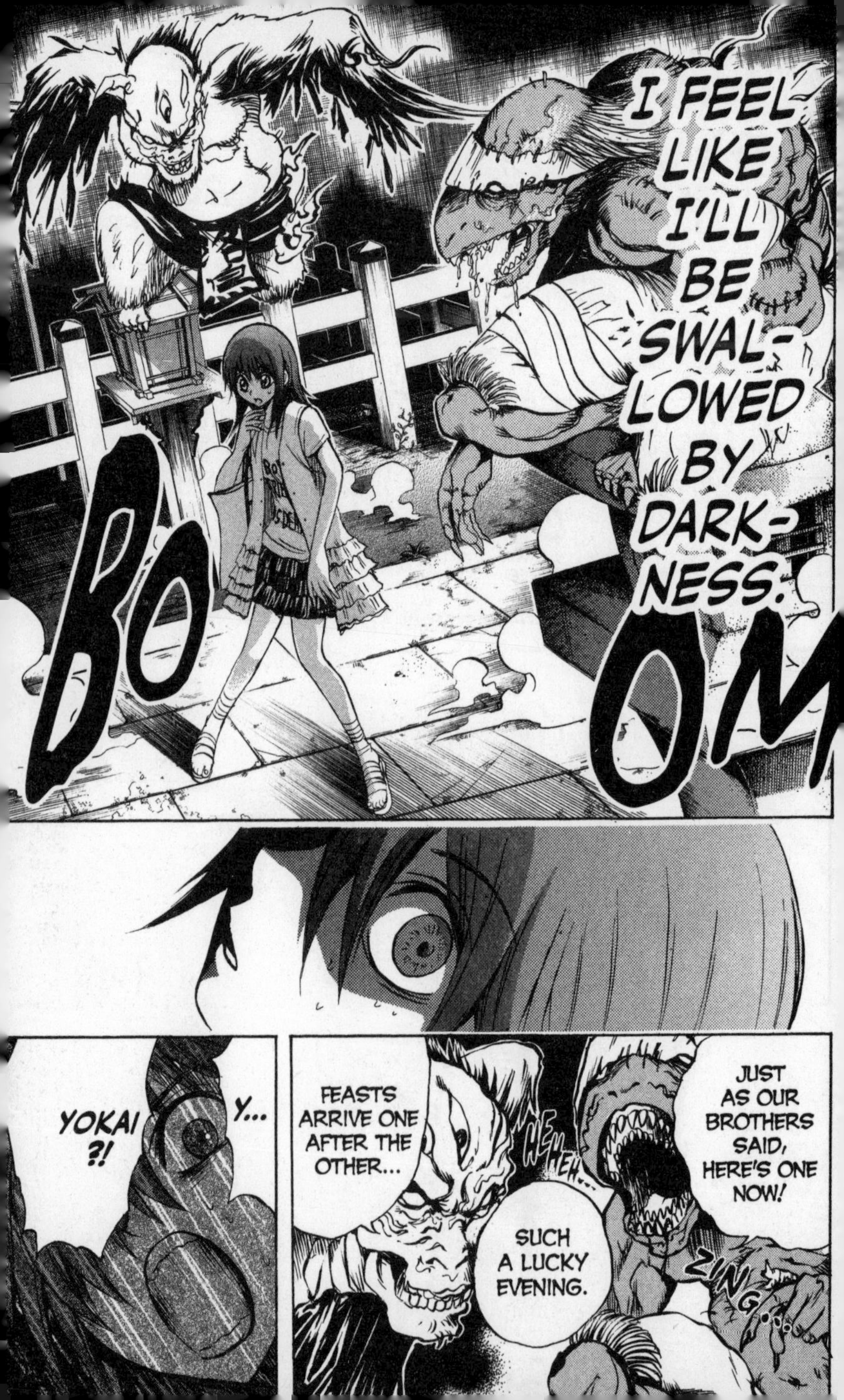
I FEEL LIKE I'LL BE SWAL-LOWED BY DARK-NESS.
BOOM
JUST AS OUR BROTHERS SAID, HERE'S ONE NOW!
HEH HEH...
FEASTS ARRIVE ONE AFTER THE OTHER...
SUCH A LUCKY EVENING.
ZING...
Y...
YOKAI ?!

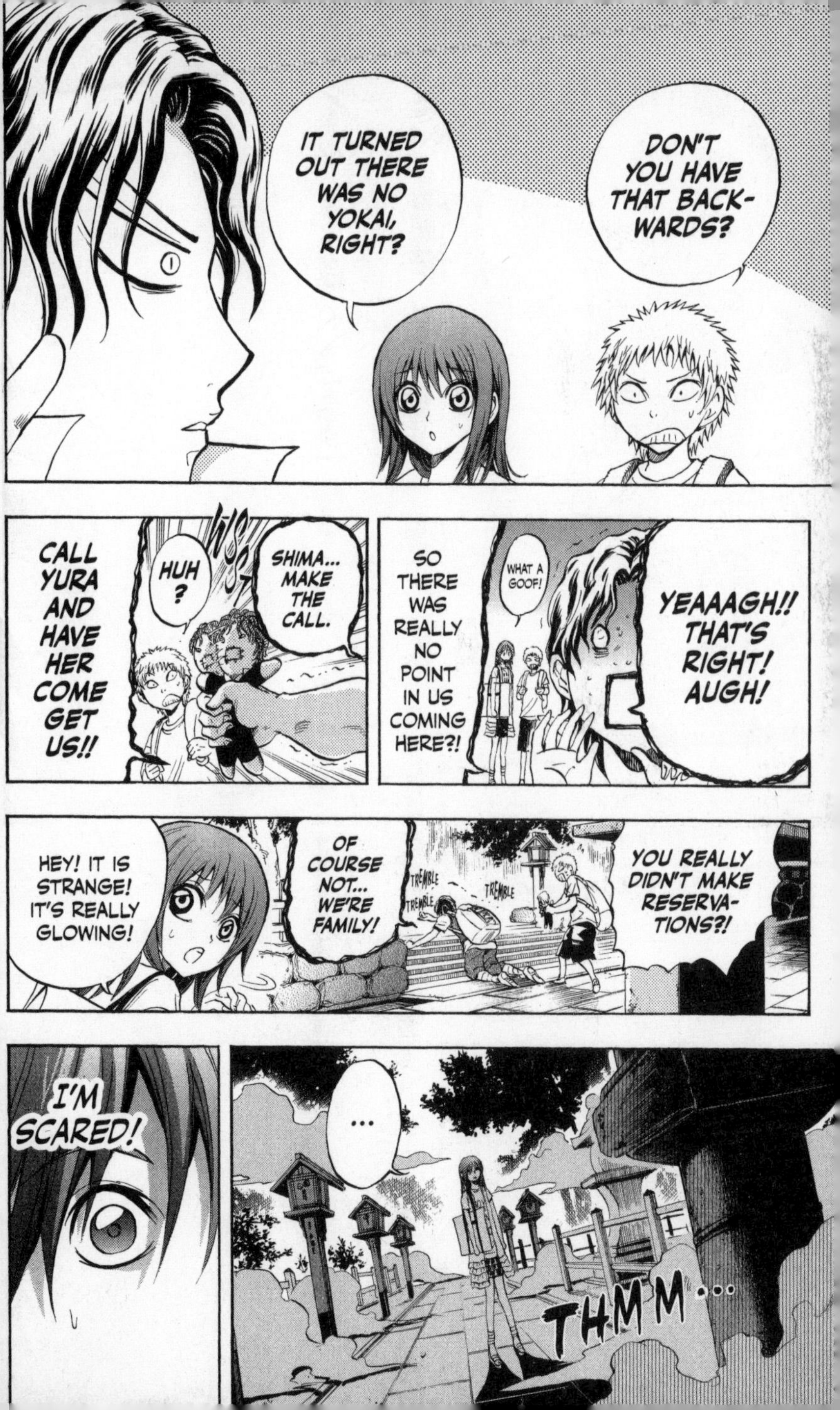
IT TURNED OUT THERE WAS NO YOKAI, RIGHT?
DON'T YOU HAVE THAT BACK-WARDS?
YEAAAGH!! THAT'S RIGHT! AUGH!
WHAT A GOOF!
SO THERE WAS REALLY NO POINT IN US COMING HERE?!
SHIMA... MAKE THE CALL.
WSS
HUH?
CALL YURA AND HAVE HER COME GET US!!
YOU REALLY DIDN'T MAKE RESERVA-TIONS?!
TREMBLE
TREMBLE
TREMBLE
OF COURSE NOT... WE'RE FAMILY!
HEY! IT IS STRANGE! IT'S REALLY GLOWING!
...
THMM...
I'M SCARED!

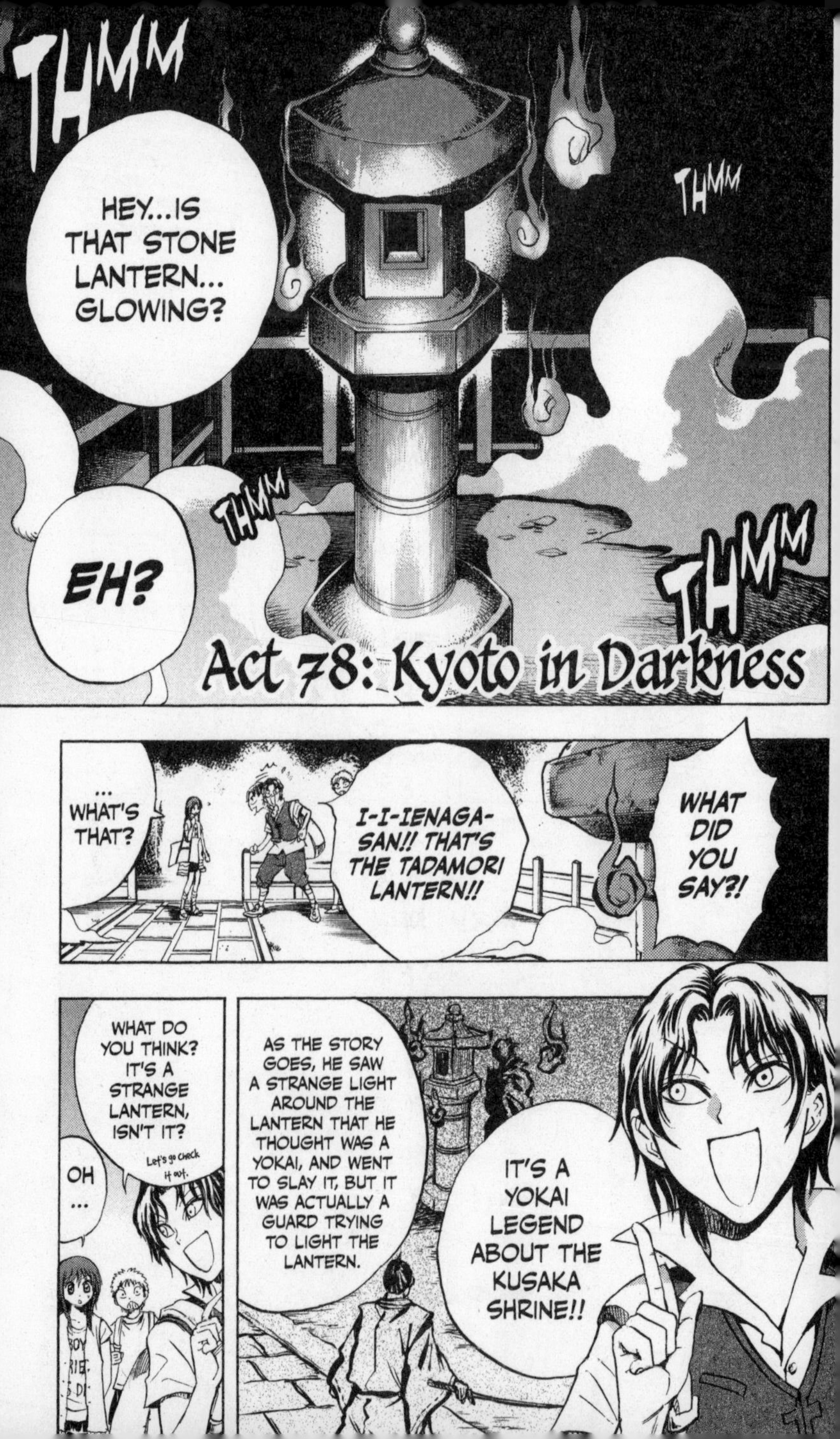
THMM
THMM
HEY...IS THAT STONE LANTERN... GLOWING?
THMM
THMM
EH?
Act 78: Kyoto in Darkness
WHAT DID YOU SAY?!
I-I-IENAGA-SAN!! THAT'S THE TADAMORI LANTERN!!
... WHAT'S THAT?
IT'S A YOKAI LEGEND ABOUT THE KUSAKA SHRINE!!
AS THE STORY GOES, HE SAW A STRANGE LIGHT AROUND THE LANTERN THAT HE THOUGHT WAS A YOKAI, AND WENT TO SLAY IT, BUT IT WAS ACTUALLY A GUARD TRYING TO LIGHT THE LANTERN.
WHAT DO YOU THINK? IT'S A STRANGE LANTERN, ISN'T IT?
Let's go check it out.
OH ...

TABLE OF CONTENTS

NURA: RISE OF THE YOKAI CLAN

NATSUMI TORII

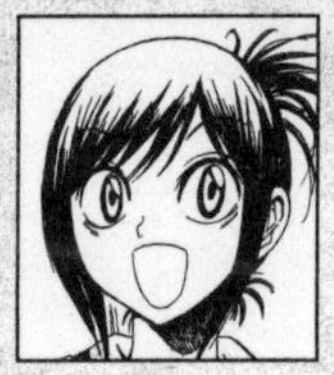

A member of the Kiyojuji Paranormal Patrol, but like Maki, she has no particular interest in yokai. At one point, a yokai curse put her on the brink of death.

SAORI MAKI

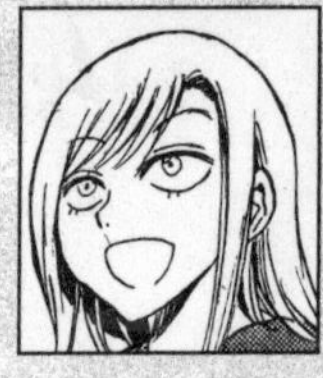

Although she participates in the Kiyojuji Paranormal Patrol, she has no particular interest in yokai. She has a well-proportioned body for a middle school girl.

HAGOROMO-GITSUNE

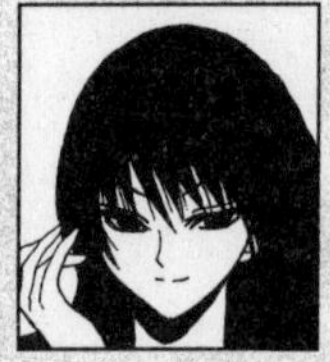

A great Kyoto yokai who has a fateful connection to Nurarihyon and the Keikain family. He possesses humans and forces them to do evil things. She was revived after 400 years.

RYUJI KEIKAIN

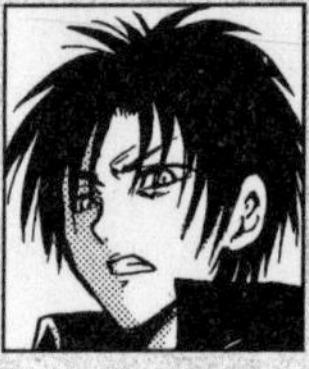

Yura's brother is a Keikain family onmyoji. Cool-headed, he views yokai as absolute evil. He controls a water shikigami and uses his smooth tongue to confuse enemies.

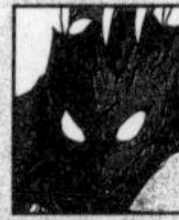

AMEZO

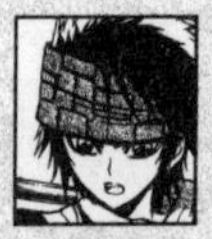

ITAKU

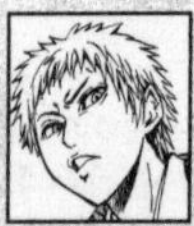

ZEN

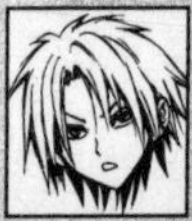

KUBINASHI

STORY SO FAR

At a glance, Rikuo Nura appears to be just another average, normal seventh grader at Ukiyoe Middle School. But he's actually the grandson of the *yokai* Overlord Nurarihyon. Right now he's an underboss of the Nura clan, the most powerful yokai family in Tokyo. But soon, he's expected to give up his human life and be the Overlord of the Nura clan.

While training to master new techniques to use against the yokai Hagoromo-Gitsune, Rikuo is attacked in the village of Tono by Kyoto yokai on a mission to recruit soldiers from the Tono family. Rikuo is able to defeat the attackers using his new skills and a move of his own creation.

Having broken five of the eight seals of Hidemoto, the revived Hagoromo-Gitsune, long thought dead, continues the invasion of Kyoto. The Keikain clan prepares to battle Hagoromo-Gitsune at the third seal, at Rokukinji Temple. Rikuo, along with the rest of the Nura clan and the Tono clan, race to Kyoto to help.

CHARACTERS

NURARIHYON

Rikuo's grandfather and the Lord of Pandemonium. He intends to pass leadership of the Nura clan—leaders of the yokai world—to Rikuo. He's mischievous and likes to dine and ditch.

RIKUO NURA

Though he appears to be a human boy, he's actually the grandson of Nurarihyon, a yokai. His grandfather's blood makes him one-quarter yokai, and he transforms into a yokai at times.

KIYOTSUGU

Rikuo's classmate. He has adored yokai ever since Rikuo saved him in his yokai form, leading him to form the Kiyojuji Paranormal Patrol.

KANA IENAGA

Rikuo's classmate and a childhood friend. Even though she hates scary things, she's a member of the Kiyojuji Paranormal Patrol for some reason.

YUKI-ONNA

A yokai of the Nura clan who is in charge of looking after Rikuo. She disguises herself as a human and attends the same school as Rikuo to protect him from danger. When in human form, she goes by the name Tsurara Oikawa.

YURA KEIKAIN

Rikuo's classmate and a descendant of the Keikain family of onmyoji. She transferred into Ukiyoe Middle School to do field training in yokai exorcism. She has the power to control her shikigami and uses them to destroy yokai.

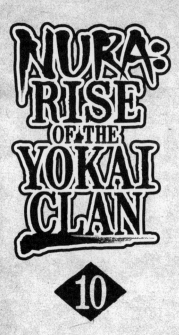

NURA: RISE OF THE YOKAI CLAN

10

KYOTO IN DARKNESS

STORY AND ART BY
HIROSHI SHIIBASHI

NURA: RISE OF THE YOKAI CLAN
VOLUME 10
SHONEN JUMP Manga Edition

Story and Art by HIROSHI SHIIBASHI

Translation – Cindy Yamauchi
Adaptation – Mark Giambruno
Touch-up Art and Lettering – Vanessa Satone
Graphics and Cover Design – Fawn Lau
Editor – Joel Enos

NURARIHYON NO MAGO © 2008 by Hiroshi Shiibashi. All rights reserved. First published in Japan in 2008 by SHUEISHA Inc., Tokyo. English translation rights arranged by SHUEISHA Inc.

The rights of the author(s) of the work(s) in this publication to be so identified have been asserted in accordance with the Copyright, Designs and Patents Act 1988. A CIP catalogue record for this book is available from the British Library.

Printed in the U.S.A.

Published by VIZ Media, LLC
P.O. Box 77010
San Francisco, CA 94107

10 9 8 7 6 5 4 3 2 1
First printing, August 2012

www.viz.com   www.shonenjump.com

We've reached the tenth graphic novel in the series!! In the actual magazine, the 100th episode is about to be published. It is due to your support that we have been able to reach these milestones! Being a newcomer, the lineup of Night Parade of a Hundred Demons covers made my heart race, but to see them steadily increase I am very happy. I thought about changing the design once I'd reached the tenth volume, but now I may try to see just how far I can push this. (BTW, did you notice that the covers actually combine to form a larger image?)

—HIROSHI SHIIBASHI,
2010

HIROSHI SHIIBASHI debuted in BUSINESS JUMP magazine with *Aratama*. NURA: RISE OF THE YOKAI CLAN is his breakout hit. He was an assistant to manga artist Hirohiko Araki, the creator of *Jojo's Bizarre Adventure*. *Steel Ball Run* by Araki is one of his favorite manga.